The Philadelphia Inquirer

Bicentennial Journals

The Founding City

The Philadelphia Inquirer

Bicentennial Journals

The Founding City

Editor, David R. Boldt
Art Director, David Milne
Senior Editor, Willard S. Randall
Associate Editor, Leslie West

The Philadelphia Inquirer
PHILADELPHIA, PENNSYLVANIA

Chilton Book Company
RADNOR, PENNSYLVANIA

Published by the Philadelphia Inquirer, Philadelphia, Pennsylvania
and the Chilton Book Company, Radnor, Pennsylvania

1 2 3 4 5 6 7 8 9 0   5 4 3 2 1 0 9 8 7 6

ISBN 0-8019-6565-9
Library of Congress Catalog Card Number: 76-16711

Manufactured in the United States of America

Contents

Introduction

During the pleasantly warm first four days of July in 1776, the Continental Congress, convened in Philadelphia, took the required steps for founding the "States of America" as an independent nation.

On July 1 and 2, during proceedings punctuated by violent thunderstorms, the delegates finally took the long-delayed vote on the resolution made by Richard Henry Lee of Virginia, stating that the colonies "were, and of right ought to be, free and independent."

The next two days were taken up mainly with wrangling over paragraphs, phrases, and punctuation in a Declaration written by young Thomas Jefferson, also of Virginia, that explained exactly why it was that the political bonds which had connected the colonies with England had to be dissolved.

These were days of great excitement and drama, though sometimes our modern understanding of them is marred by misunderstanding and confusion.

For instance, the Declaration of Independence was not a declaration of war. By July of 1776, the war had been going on for more than a year, ever since the opening shots had been fired by the minutemen and redcoats at Lexington and Concord in April 1775. The Battle of Bunker Hill had been fought; the British had evacuated Boston; George Washington had been appointed commander-in-chief, and on July 4, 1776, he was martialing his forces in New York to meet an anticipated British attack. And on July 4 the sails of the British armada, constituting the greatest armed force ever assembled, arrived off Staten Island. A newspaper editor trying to put together a front page for the next morning would have been hard put to decide whether the banner headline should read: "INDEPENDENCE DECLARED" or "BRITISH ARMADA ARRIVES."

For another thing, the delegates did not actually *sign* the Declaration of Independence on July 4. It took until early August to get the document reproduced on parchment for the formal signing. The only people who signed on July 4 were John Hancock, the president of the Congress, and Charles Thomson, secretary of the Congress, who attested to Hancock's signature.

Interestingly, by the time of the formal signing, some of the delegates who had actually taken the treasonous

step of voting for independence had been replaced in the Congress, and missed out on the chance to achieve immortality as a "Signer."

Another intriguing circumstance is the fact that there was some confusion at the time as to whether July 2 or July 4 would be remembered as the national birthday. John Adams, for one, assumed incorrectly that July 2, the day on which the Lee Resolution was approved, would be the big day. Ebulliently, he had written to his wife, Abigail, after the vote, "The Second Day of July will be the most memorable Epocha in the history of America. I am apt to believe that it will be celebrated by succeeding generations as a Day of Deliverance by solemn acts of devotion to God Almighty. It ought to be solemnized with pomp and parade, with shows, games, sports, guns, bells, bonfires and illuminations, from one end of the continent to the other, from this time forward, forevermore."

The nation, however, decided to celebrate the explanation of independence rather than the act itself, and so Adams was two days off.

The drama of the event centered on the efforts to make the vote unanimous, a goal that was not actually achieved. New York had to abstain on the final vote on the Declaration of Independence because its delegates were still awaiting fresh instructions from a newly convened state convention. So all that could be said initially was that the Declaration was adopted without dissent, 12-0.

This was a large improvement over the preliminary vote that had been taken July 1, which had shown only nine colonies in favor (New Hampshire, Massachusetts, Rhode Island, Connecticut, Virginia, Maryland, New Jersey, North Carolina, and Georgia), two opposed (Pennsylvania and South Carolina), and two (Delaware and New York) abstaining.

South Carolina changed its mind later, and the switch of Delaware into the pro-independence column provided one of the great moments of the crucial four days. Initially, the Delaware delegation was deadlocked, 1-1. Its third member, Caesar Rodney, had returned to his farm near Dover because of his wife's illness. He himself was suffering from a painful and ugly facial cancer. Another delegate to the Congress remembered Rodney in this way: "He is tall, thin, slender as a reed, pale, his face is not bigger than a large apple, yet there is sense and fire, spirit, wit, and humor in his countenance."

And he was for independence. Now that the crucial moment had arrived, the pro-independence member of the Delaware delegation, Thomas McKean, dispatched a messenger, who found Rodney plowing in his fields.

The next morning, as sheets of rain splattered against the closed windows of the State House where the Congress was meeting (now Independence Hall), there was clatter of hooves, and few moments later the gaunt horseman entered, his clothes muddy and dripping from the night's ride through the rainstorm. A green kerchief was pressed against the cancerous sore on his face. Quietly he inquired whether he had arrived in time for the vote.

He had.

The change in the Pennsylvania delegation reflected an inner drama that took place in the heart and mind of John Dickinson, one of the Pennsylvania delegates. For months Dickinson had been the leading spokesman for reconciliation, and, failing that, for judicious delay. He and Adams had been chosen to represent the opposing sides in the arguments in a special reprise that was staged for the newly arrived New Jersey delegation on July 1. Dickinson had been eloquent, if unavailing, in what would be his final plea to the Congress — that declaring independence at that point would be like tearing one's house down in winter without having another one ready.

But Dickinson and another Pennsylvania delegate ostentatiously stayed away from the proceedings on the 4th, and the remaining Pennsylvania delegates, led by Benjamin Franklin, cast that state's vote for independence.

The following day Dickinson enlisted in the Pennsylvania militia to fight for the independence he had so long, and with brilliance, opposed. (The full story of "Dickinson's Dilemma") is covered later in this book.)

The four days in July put sufficient pressures on the protagonists to allow some intriguing personal insights. This was perhaps particularly true in regard to Thomas Jefferson, who made extensive records of the period, noting, among other things, the temperature at various times each day, and every expenditure he made.

Jefferson's records add an interesting bit of evidence to John Adams' belief that July 2 was the crucial day. That was the only day for which Jefferson made no entries. On the other hand, we know that the experience of watching the Congress edit his declaration was an acutely painful experience. To the end of his days he regarded the changes as mutilations, and he sent copies of his original version, together with copies of the version that Congress finally approved, to friends, asking whether they did not concur that the original was better. But he did his sulking quietly, never rising to defend his phrasings and sentiments. That task was left to John Adams, who had also been a member of the committee formed to draft the Declaration, and who had insisted that Jefferson be the draftsman.

But at least insofar as his records were concerned, things appeared to have returned to normal by July 4. He recorded that the temperature as of 6 a.m. at 68 degrees. (By 9 it had risen to a little over 72; it would reach a high of 76 degrees at 1 p.m.)

Presumably, if he followed his usual procedure, he had arisen a few moments before taking the temperature reading, and plunged his feet into a tub of ice water that would have been brought for him by one of the two Negro slaves he had brought with him to Philadelphia. (A doctor had told him it would prevent his migraine headaches.)

Later he would be shaved by a barber named Byrne who came each morning at about seven to Jefferson's lodgings on the second floor of the small new red-brick house that bricklayer Jacob Graff had built for his family at Seventh and Market Streets. Jefferson had chosen the house because it was on the outskirts of the city, and he felt that it might be cooler than locations nearer to the State House. But he never did learn to spell his landlord's name right, consistently instructing correspondents to send his mail in care of "Graaf."

After being shaved, Jefferson went to City Tavern at

Second and Walnut, where he habitually ate breakfast and dinner. And at some occasion on the 4th of July, Jefferson paid three pounds, 15 shillings for a thermometer to a merchant named Sparhawk, from whom he had bought a set of spurs a few days earlier, and, at another shop, paid one pound and seven shillings for seven pairs of women's gloves.

This last purchase was probably a sign that his thoughts were turning forward toward his return to his home on the hill at Monticello, and to his pregnant wife, Martha. They may have been worried thoughts. Martha's pregnancies were always perilous for her.

But before he could return, Jefferson would have to suffer in silence through this day of argument over the Declaration. Franklin had attempted to console Jefferson with an anecdote about a hatter named John Thompson, who had designed a sign for his store and made the mistake of showing it to some friends.

Originally the sign said: "John Thompson, hatter, makes and sells hats for ready money." But the first friend told him to omit "hatter" as superfluous; the second suggested that "makes" was unnecessary since potential customers wouldn't much care who made the hats, as long as they were good ones; still another contended that "ready money" could be deleted since no one would expect Thompson to give credit.

By now only "John Thompson sells hats" and the picture of a hat. But then another busybody happened along with the thought that "sells" wasn't needed since no one would expect young Thompson to give them away, and, for that matter, the picture of a hat obviated the need for the word "hats." What was left was a sign that had just Thompson's name and the picture of a hat. The point of Franklin's story was that even though all sense of character and spirit had been removed from the sign, nonetheless the store prospered, and John Thompson, hatter, made and sold hats for ready money.

The editing did not, however, change the document profoundly. Some of Jefferson's friends who were given the opportunity to peruse both the original and the final versions would have had to tell Jefferson, if they were brutally honest men, that the final version was better, or, at the least, that the changes had made little difference.

At the beginning, as an example, Jefferson had proposed that the Declaration start: "When in the course of human events it becomes necessary for a people to advance from . . . subordination . . . ." When the meddling editors among the delegates were through it read: "When in the course of human events it becomes necessary for one people to dissolve the political bands which have connected them with another . . . ."

The delegates did take out Jefferson's contention, in a long paragraph near the end, that King George III was responsible for the continuation of the institution of slavery in America. The speciousness of this argument was quickly shown as the delegations from South Carolina and Georgia, offended by Jefferson's passionate attack on slavery, demanded removal of the paragraph.

Delegates of Scottish descent objected to Jefferson's inclusion of "Scotch" soldiers as "foreign mercenaries" in the Declaration's complaint about the King's decision to send foreign troops to fight against the Americans. And they also cut out most of an arresting passage Jefferson had included speaking about the heart-wrenching emotion that would be involved as families and friends would be split apart by the coming war.

●

Still and all, if the truth be told, the central fact about the Declaration of Independence is that it seems so dated to us today. Unlike the Constitution, it was clearly a document that was designed for a specific moment, to excite the patriotic passions of a nascent nation.

And it accomplished its mission. A large crowd gathered to hear it read in Philadelphia on July 8, and all the bells of the city rang out a salute. The following day the Declaration was read to Washington's troops in New York, who were so excited that, assisted by some local hoodlums, they tore down a large equestrian statue of King George III. After the crowd in Boston heard the Declaration, they ran right up to the State House, tore down the King's coat of arms, and burned it in the street. Shortly after copies of the Declaration reached East Windsor, Conn., a newborn child was named "Independence."

But many of the complaints about the King seem unfamiliar to us, and some of them seem needlessly exaggerated and trumped up. For example, the Declaration complains that the King "has made Judges dependent on his will alone for the tenure of their offices, and the amount and payment of their salaries." Actually, the situation had been quite the reverse. The King and his ministers were unable to get American judges and courts to enforce many English laws, particularly those dealing with smuggling. John Hancock, the Boston merchant who was sitting as the president of the Congress, was but one of many successful and respected men in Massachusetts who had literally dozens of smuggling indictments outstanding against them at the start of the Revolution.

One resonant and exciting (if somewhat cryptic) phrase does come echoing out of the document today with perhaps as much force as it had in 1776. That is Jefferson's evocation of the American Dream and Ideal, that all men are entitled to an equal right to "life, liberty, and the pursuit of happiness."

And throughout the document are shards and pieces that show the beginnings of a new set of definitions for a new kind of nation. It is infused with the feeling that infused America —that somehow, by luck and design, they had in their hands the opportunity to create something both new and beautiful; that, in fact, much of the creation had already been accomplished.

But to understand the full meaning and portent of these bits and pieces it is necessary to go back and consider as a whole the events and people that animated the American nation in 1776, and the way in which the aspirations of a continent became focused in those warm early summer days in Philadelphia, the Founding City.

It is to that purpose that this book is dedicated.

Acknowledgments

The editors wish to express especial thanks to
Charles G. Dorman, curator at Independence
National Historical Park, who has worked with us as a
consultant; and to Marilyn Kochman, whose expertise
in locating pictorial material we relied on.

Edwin Wolf 2d, librarian of the Library Company of
Philadelphia, was generous with both his expertise and
his counsel. James P. Mooney, director of the Historical
Society of Pennsylvania, was another source of
important and valuable advice. The picture credits
throughout the book pay recurrent tribute to the
assistance that was afforded to us in that regard by the
Library Company and the Historical Society, as well as
by the Free Library of Philadelphia and the
Philadelphia Museum of Art.

The article "Haym Salomon: The Patriotic Money
Manipulator" was excerpted from *The History of the
Jews of Philadelphia* by Edwin Wolf 2d and Maxwell
Whiteman, with the permission of the publisher, the
Jewish Publication Society of America.

William H. Matthaeus of the *Inquirer's* library staff
assisted us greatly in research and authentication.

And a final, profound word of affectionate thanks
must be extended to Fereshteh Boldt and Johanna
Milne.

The Philadelphia Inquirer

Bicentennial Journals

The Founding City

Philadelphia Life, 1776

Philadelphia Life—1776

"The poetry of history," someone has written, "lies in the quasi-miraculous fact that once, on this earth, once, on this familiar spot of ground, walked other men and women, as actual as we are today, thinking their own thoughts, swayed by their own passions —but now all gone, one generation vanishing after another, gone as utterly as we ourselves shall shortly be gone, like ghosts at cockcrow."

And that is the principle on which this first chapter has been based. The goal has been to portray what life was like not for a signer of the Declaration of Independence, but, instead, for a member of the crowd that cheered for it.

Meet the Joneses of Old Philadelphia

With a sunrise to sunset workday and an unceasing succession of household duties, the typical family wasn't worried about what to do with its leisure time

By Kathy Nagurny

In the pre-dawn darkness of this October morning, the Philadelphia of 1775, quiet and asleep, seems at first to live up to the most romantic of possible illusions.

The small, squarish brick homes that line the streets and back alleys of the already densely populated area of the city along the Delaware are quaint and attractive. The patterns of red brick and black glazed headers are simple, but the over-all impression is of a sort of earthy homey-ness, that to our modern eye evokes the traditional virtues of sturdiness and craftsmanship.

The effect is also one of domestic tranquility. The city is quiet, the houses and streets are only dimly apparent from the flickering oil street lamps and a lantern at the watch house, together with the morning twilight. The only sounds are the restless rustling of horses in their stables, the occasional barking of a dog, and — when the night watchman strides down one of the few paved streets — the echoing of a man's footsteps.

Even the city's accustomed odors are in abeyance. The air is crisp—almost cold—and a breeze has been blowing in from the forests and farms of New Jersey, cleaning the dusty, fetid aromas of manure and sewage that had become ripe indeed during the past summer. The cooling weather has also had an ameliorating effect on the flies and mosquitoes which all summer had swarmed in and around the homes of Philadelphians, exiting and entering at will through the unscreened windows.

The city's immense population of rats and mice, however, is still very much present, and as the watchman strides along he sometimes catches the skittering shadows of fleeing rodents at the fringe of his lamplight, hearing their scurrying sounds and frightened squeaks.

Occasionally, too, he comes across one pig, or perhaps several, rooting through a pile of garbage in the gutter, or asleep in one of the large puddles that collect in the dirt roads during each rain, some of which are big enough to remain, albeit with diminishing circumference, until the next shower, as sort of miniature ponds.

As the sky lightened over New Jersey, a few early risers begin walking their cows to the communal grazing areas, and the roosters, of which there seemed to be several in every block, undertake their task of heralding the morning. The only other sign of the day's imminent activities are the wagons already rolling along the outlying highways, headed into the city with farm produce for market day.

There was as yet no stirring of any sort inside the small house on an alley off Third Street where John Jones, his wife, Sarah, and their two children, Samuel, 12, and Elizabeth, 8, lived. Both Jones and his wife were native Philadelphians, born of English parents who had arrived in the city a few decades earlier and still lived nearby. Jones had completed his apprenticeship as a pewterer, winning the traditional beaver hat as part of his "freedom clothes" on becoming a journeyman, and now worked as an assistant at a shop a short distance away on Second Street.

Neither of the Joneses was a Quaker. Although Quakers had founded Philadelphia as a city, and long dominated the city's political and commercial affairs, they were now a minority. The leading Quaker families, whose immense power had made them a sort of ruling oligarchy, were now gradually yielding place to a disparate amalgam of families.

The Joneses were Anglicans and worshipped regularly, if not necessarily with great fervor, at Christ Church on Second between Market and Arch Streets.

The Joneses formed neither a particularly large, nor an especially small, household. Families in the city were generally smaller than those in the country, though babies died at an appalling rate

No one wrote much about the common man in Philadelphia in 1775 and 1776. He apparently didn't have the time or inclination to write much himself, and people who did have time to write didn't find him very interesting. His clothes and household goods, being, by definition, rather ordinary, weren't preserved by museums and historical societies.

The accompanying article on a day in the life of Philadelphia Family Jones represents an attempt to fit together bits and pieces from a wide variety of sources, including books, documents, historians, archaeologists, and others. But it is not serious historical scholarship. When the sources disagreed, for instance, we made arbitrary choices between them.

Our intent was to come up with a reasonable approximation of what life was like not for one of the framers of the Declaration of Independence, but for someone who was just a member of the crowd that cheered the Declaration.

Free Library of Philadelphia

Artist's view of "a colonial good morning."

Library Co. of Philadelphia

Christ Church, where the Joneses might have worshipped.

A Colonial craftsman fashions a pitcher.

Free Library of Philadelphia

THE FOUNDING CITY

in both areas. Two of the Jones children had died in infancy.

John and Sarah were asleep in what was, during the day, the kitchen and dining room. They slept on a straw mattress which rested on a network of ropes strung through the wooden frame of the bed. During the day the frame, which was fastened to the wall on hinges, was hooked up against the wall and covered with homespun curtains. At night its foot was rested on two heavy logs.

The two children slept on smaller, but basically similar beds in the family's front room.

Despite the embers that still glowed in the fireplace, the rooms were cold. The night air had seeped in through the walls, the gaps around the windows and door, and even up through the floor from the damp, unfloored cellar. To keep warm, the family members slept with much of their clothing on.

It was not, however, as cold as it would be on nights during the winter. On the coldest evenings of December, January, and February, all of the family would sleep in the kitchen, but even in that room, any water left in a pottery jar or basin would have a coating of ice on it by morning. A major budgeting concern in the winter was to be sure there was enough money to buy wood for the fire.

Jones rented the house, and the rent was steep. Housing was much in demand in the city, and even a small back-alley house like this one cost about $300 a year, or about one-quarter of Jones' pay. The house was brick, with the door and other trim painted cream, like almost every other house in the area.

The uniformity didn't bother the Joneses and their neighbors, although visitors to the city often remarked on how boring and undifferentiated the domestic architecture of the city was.

The house was about 17 feet wide and 25 feet deep. Its main floor was divided into two rooms, and there were two small bedrooms upstairs. Many Philadelphians used their front room as their shop, though the Joneses did not.

Almost all activities centered around the kitchen — cooking, eating, yarn-spinning, butter-churning, drinking, courting, and, on frosty nights, sleeping which was what was going on there at the moment.

Elizabeth was the first one up, running quickly across the cold floor to give her brother a poke. She waited until his eyes opened, then ran into the kitchen and jumped onto her parents' bed. Discipline of children was stringent — even harsh by the standards of a later century — but family life was marked by a sense of warmth and closeness. The Puritanical mode, widely thought of as typical of colonial America, was mainly a New England phenomenon. Little girls, then as now, probably were able to infringe upon the decorum of the household at certain times and in certain ways without incurring the switchings that were the general answer to misbehavior.

John Jones ruled his household, and both law and custom accorded him great latitude of action in enforcing his rule — though there were restrictions. In some cities, there were regulations stipulating that a husband could not hit his wife with a stick thicker than a man's finger, and in no event was he allowed to kill or permanently incapacitate her. (In New England, wife-beating was entirely prohibited.)

Occasionally, unhappy wives ran away from husbands. In that event the husband would advertise in the newspaper, with the advertisement often appearing next to the advertisements for fugitive slaves.

Compared to women in Europe, however, American women were well ahead in terms of status. Women in Philadelphia and its environs ran taverns and retail stores, operated ferries, managed farmlands, practiced obstetrics as midwives, and were coming to dominate the colonies' teacher corps as schoolmarms.

Women had come a long way in other respects. In America, unlike England, they drank spirits freely. The custom of an early-morning eye-opener of rum or other spirituous beverage was surprisingly prevalent, and was practiced by both men and women. It did tend to take the chill off the morning.

Women also smoked pipes, and were accustomed to both hearing and using profane language.

Samuel Jones' first job was to fill the family water bucket, which was used for washing, at a nearby communal pump. There was no toothbrushing, however, for the Joneses. Toothbrushes were used only by the very well-to-do. The more ordinary citizenry rubbed their teeth with a chalked rag, or picked them with a sassafras root.

Actually, there was little washing of any sort. Taking a bath was virtually unheard of for the lower classes. About the only time a Philadelphian got wet all over was when he went swimming in the summer.

The water from the wells was often contaminated from the outhouses, which were set up behind the homes. In addition, Philadelphia water, then as now, didn't taste good.

Tea was also popular, though under a cloud politically, and coffee was just coming into vogue. When they didn't have tea, or chose not to use it, colonial wives brewed home-grown substitutes, including the leaves of strawberry, ribwort, and currant plants.

Such ersatz concoctions were known as "liberty tea."

By boiling the water for tea, the colonial housewife unwittingly, but effectively, rendered the water safe.

Mrs. Jones was up herself by now. She added wood to the fire and began preparing a porridge made of milk, with bread boiled in it. As a special treat, she was also preparing some "pop-robins," which were buns soaked in a flour and egg batter and dropped into boiling milk.

Many of the meals were built around milk as the main source of protein — milk and hasty pudding, milk and stewed pumpkin, milk and baked apples, milk and berries. Milk was also made into butter and cheeses, often by the housewife herself.

The milk came, of course, from the milkman. He was a farmer from out in what is now Kensington who brought his cows into the city at daybreak, stopping at each house along his route to fill the housewife's jar or pitcher straight from the teat. As each cow went dry, she went to the rear of the line.

Neither Mrs. Jones nor the other housewives baked their own bread. Making bread in a colonial oven, with its hard-to-figure temperatures, was a difficult process, and working around the live coals of the fireplace in a long skirt posed real dangers. Bakeries were common all over the city, and generally the ladies of the house would buy bread there each afternoon for the following day.

As they sat down to breakfast, the Joneses' attire presented a more or less typical picture of what not particularly well-dressed people were wearing in Philadelphia. There was no such thing as children's styles, and the two young Joneses wore costumes that were almost duplicates of what their parents were wearing.

John and his son, Samuel, wore buckskin britches which had once been a bright yellow, but were now a dingy tan. They also put on checked shirts and red flannel jackets. When John left for work, he would also don a heavy leather apron.

He and his son wore shoes of coarse, heavy leather with a buckle on top of the arch. There was no such thing as a "left shoe" and a "right shoe" — both were the same. Richer families in Philadelphia wore shoes made of calfskin. Boots made of buckskin were also becoming popular in the city at the time.

The two male Joneses wore their hair brushed back and tied at the back of the head with a ribbon.

Affluent merchants wheeled and dealt in the Old London Coffee House.

Wigs had been widely used in the city until a few decades before. The decline of wigs coincided with the arrival in the city of the remnants of Braddock's force who, fresh from their defeat at the hands of the French and the Indians, showed up without wigs.

The wigless style supposedly caught on with the rest of the military, and then with the civilian populace, which had never been as pro-wig as, for example, Londoners were. The defeat may have seemed to indicate that European styles

of warfare — and attire — were not necessarily sensible in the American environment.

Although class distinctions were not absolute, as they were in England, it was easy enough to distinguish an artisan like Jones from a gentleman of affluence, who would be wearing a ruffled shirt and a broadcloth coat (silk in summer), the skirts and lapels of which were stiffened with wire or stiff buckram. A gentleman's coat and vest might be adorned with silver buttons, sometimes engraved with his initials. Buttons were often made of pewter or shells, as well. (Ordinary buttons were wooden, sometimes cloth-covered.)

Mrs. Jones and daughter Elizabeth wore simple frocks which were distinguishable from those of richer women only by the lack of lace, silk, and embroidery trimmings. Mrs. Jones' dress was protected by a long white apron. The skirts of the dress reached to the floor and covered one or more petticoats, which were held up by a new invention recently perfected by a Massachusetts woman — suspenders.

More fashionable women sometimes wore a series of hoops which extended the skirt outward as much as two feet from where it would normally have fallen on its own.

The hoops made the negotiation of

narrow doorways hazardous, and forced a woman in full hoop regalia to push her way through such places sidewise, "crab-like . . . pointing her obtruding flanks end foremost," according to a contemporary account.

Fancy dresses, or gowns, often had no fronts. They were designed to display the petticoat, or finely quilted silk worn with patterned silk slippers.

Most often, women's shoes were black leather with high heels, worn over white silk or thread stockings. In wintertime women often wore wooden clogs.

Women generally kept their hair covered, and Mrs. Jones was not an exception. She wore a "muskmelon" bonnet, so called because the parallel line effect created by the whalebone stiffeners inside the bonnet made it seem, to the irreverent, that the woman was wearing a cantaloupe, or muskmelon, on her head. The color was usually white or black.

The family's clothes were kept in a huge walnut chest of drawers which stood against one wall of the front room; this rather recent acquisition was the source of much family pride.

The flame grain walnut chest, with its shiny brass handles, was a spectacular addition to the otherwise plain, white plastered room.

The only other furniture in the front

THE FOUNDING CITY

room were two stiff, straight ladder-back armchairs next to the window and an old rectangular table that had been Mrs. Jones' mother's, and which stood between the chairs.

There was no carpet on the floor. The Joneses had one neighbor who had acquired a small piece of English carpet, which they spread on the floor of the front room. That family enforced a special rule that no food should be eaten in that room, and whenever the Joneses visited, they were careful to walk around it on the wooden floor.

The table at which the Joneses were now sitting down to breakfast was the other major piece of furniture in the house. It was an old gate-legged, drop-leaf table that John had bought at an auction for about $7. The round legs had been chiseled on a lathe to create curved forms that gave the table a certain sense of style, even though it was clearly the style of an earlier time. Even in 1775, the table was old-fashioned.

Because Jones was a pewterer, the family had several pewter basins. Many of their neighbors dined out of wooden trenchers.

The family didn't seat itself until the blessing was said, and, in general, the children didn't speak unless they were spoken to, a rule that became more rigid when relatives or other adults were present. The main breaches of good manners that parents guarded against were eating bread without breaking it, and throwing bones under the table.

The Joneses passed a red earthenware jug, which contained the milk, around the table, and ate quickly. When breakfast was completed, the basins and plates were scraped and rinsed, then placed back on the shelves.

John Jones left for the shop. He worked a long day. It was hot and dangerous work, melting the complex alloy of tin, antimony, copper and other metals and pouring the molten metals into molds. (Much of the metal came from scrap pieces of pewter.) He would return home for lunch, then not be home again until evening. The work didn't go, perhaps, at an assembly-line pace, and there would be time for a visit to the tavern at the end of the day, but it was a rigorous workday.

Two factors, though, helped to make it bearable. One was the satisfaction of seeing the product created, from the melting of the old pewter items to the sale of the new ones to the customer.

The second was an optimism about what the future would hold. There was every reason to believe that he would shortly have his own shop, with his own assistant or apprentice.

There was clearly a growing market in Philadelphia for such products. Plates and tankards of pewter were the object of prideful possession in the homes of Philadelphia's mushrooming middle class.

If his skills were as great as he himself felt them to be, with a reasonable amount of luck in attracting influential customers there was virtually no limit as to what he might expect. Other pewterers were among the more affluent citizens of Philadelphia, with their own well-furnished homes and other accoutrements of success.

Jones had reasonable hopes that his son could go even further than that. Samuel already was attending one of the many private secondary schools in the city that taught promising youngsters on a semi-scholarship basis, and at which the children of working-class parents sat on the same benches with the children of the city's elite. Philadelphia led the colonies in recognizing the need to provide basic education to as large a number of students as possible.

Most of the schools were church-sponsored. The Quaker, or Friends', schools were perhaps the best known, but the Presbyterians, Anglicans, and Lutherans also had schools, among others. Many students from adjacent colonies came to the schools in Philadelphia to prepare for entrance into a European university, or one of the growing number of American colleges.

Jones could easily see his son becoming a rich merchant, a lawyer, or . . . well, anything.

The scale of even some of the major business enterprises didn't seem more than a rung or two above the pewter shop he foresaw for himself in the near future. A major merchant of the 18th century had an establishment that was hardly more than a large store. The merchant and a partner, together with a full-time clerk and an apprentice or servant to help with errands, could carry on the business by themselves.

Philadelphia, even more than London, was a city of small shopkeepers. The entrepreneurial spirit was abroad in the city. At times Jones could not help reflecting that had his own parents remained in London, he would not have been able to hold such hopes for himself, or his son.

Jones' own apprenticeship had included little book learning, but he could read well enough to follow written instructions, and do sufficient arithmetic to keep customer accounts in order.

His daughter, Elizabeth, was still too young for school, her parents felt, but her mother in particular hoped that in a year or so they would be able to afford to send her to one of the so-called "dame schools," at which a woman teacher endeavored to teach the fine points of needlework and home economics, along with some reading and other academic subjects, including, perhaps, a genteel smattering of French. Elizabeth's mother had always wished she could have done so herself.

But on this particular day Elizabeth was accompanying her mother to the market.

As they prepared to leave, Elizabeth's mother noticed that her daughter's cough seemed to have disappeared. It hadn't seemed serious, but illness was a frightening and mysterious enemy.

Doctors were there, to be sure, for those who could afford them. They even

Market day became such a large affair that this new market building was built on Second Street, to augment the buildings on High (Market) Street.

made house calls. Dr. John Morgan, who had arrived in 1765 after completing his medical training at the University of Edinburgh in Scotland was sometimes credited with having invented the practice.

Most Philadelphians relied on home remedies of various sorts to keep themselves out of the doctor's clutches, and to avoid the doctor's bills. John Winthrop reported in his correspondence that ulcers responded wondrously to a self-mixed potion containing an ounce of red seeds called "crab eyes," together with four ounces of wine vinegar. The application of tobacco to cuts also had a beneficial effect in his experience, Winthrop reported.

If sickness persisted one repaired to the apothecary. Medications, then as now, were subject to the fad syndrome. Mithridate, which was imported direct from London, was the Vitamin E of the late 1700s. Philadelphians were told — and apparently believed — that it could cure the plague, madness, leprosy, cancer, gout, and dysentery. It was also a sure antidote for most poisons.

When an illness went away, as Elizabeth's cough apparently had, it was looked upon as an act of Providence.

The town bells had already rung out the announcement that the market was open, and sales could begin. Selling was prohibited before the bells sounded at around 6 a.m. in the summer, and 7 a.m. in the winter.

Selling was also prohibited except in the designated market places, the principal one being on High (now Market) Street. The farmers set up their wares in a series of connected sheds.

Market day was always something of a show, as markets always have been around the world in all times. The fairs that were held in conjunction with the market in the spring and fall for three days at a time heightened and compounded the normal level of excitement and crowding, which was high enough. Jokesters sometimes tried to clear a path for themselves by holding frogs with which they would attempt to frighten the shopping women.

Mrs. Jones looked over the array of fruits and vegetables which, during the summer, had included cauliflower, eggplant, rhubarb, sweet corn, peas, beans, okra, and even artichokes, but which now, in the autumn, was sparse. There was just the last of the corn, some dried apples, pumpkins, potatoes, carrots, beets, and other root vegetables.

There were never any tomatoes for sale to eat in the market. Tomatoes, which were then called love apples, among other names, were believed to be poisonous.

Other items were available, including preserves, pickles, apple butter, as well as candied nuts and fruits. Several stalls offered smoked meat from the fall butchering. The meat was sold by the barrel, with a barrel being equal to about 31 pounds. Lamb, pork, ham, and chickens were offered for sale by farmers. Hunters brought in geese and ducks; delicacies like crabs, oysters, swans, eel, smelt, and trout were available at times, as were such grains as oats, barley, wheat flour, and rye flour. Cloth, clothing, and wool were on sale as well.

Mrs. Jones bought some vegetables, dried apples, which were a sweet treat of sorts for the children, and a chicken, which she would use in the stew she was making that day. On the way back the mother and daughter stopped at the bakery to pick up the day's bread — rye, as usual — and they admired some of the cakes that other housewives had brought in on that day to be baked.

All told, Mrs. Jones spent about half of the family's money on food and other necessities. The goal of the family was to save about one-quarter of their income toward the shop they intended to open, and so far no emergency had come along to strip them of their savings. She reflected for a moment on her good luck.

Back at home, the unending round of household duties continued. When the cleaning, washing, and regular sewing were done, Mrs. Jones might elect to spin thread for clothes, although she could buy thread and cloth in the shops, and it was an enormously time-consuming process. To spin enough thread for a single wool petticoat, one person would have to work constantly from breakfast to bedtime for four days. The thread could then be taken to a weaver to be made into cloth.

With no end of things to do at home, a husband who worked six days a week, and church services on Sunday that featured two-hour sermons, the question of what to do with one's leisure time was not one of the major dilemmas facing the household. But that doesn't mean there weren't lots of amusements available.

On the holidays that came up about 20 times a year, Philadelphians, including the Joneses, would gather along the Schuylkill for boating, swimming, and dancing parties. "Country fairs" were well attended, and one didn't have to go far to get out to the country. One of the most popular ones was held in the suburban area around Front and South Streets.

Horse-racing was popular, and, for men, there were games like wrestling, bowling, quoits, and shuffleboard. As Quaker influence waned, bull-baiting and cockfights became regular events.

Women had sewing circles, and sometimes enjoyed occasions that were essentially borrowed from the countryside, like quilting parties.

Children rolled hoops, spun tops, rode hobby horses, and pitched pennies, which was known as "skying a copper," and involved guessing whether the coin would land heads or tails. They also played many games that are still familiar today, like tag and hide-and-go-seek.

Taverns were, of course, another source of amusement and pleasure. Some of these drinking places, which had a sort of quasi-public status as neighborhood and civic gathering places, offered special attractions to patrons, such as the opportunity to gaze at "The Great Hog's Portrait," a depiction of a very large American-bred pig that supposedly weighed in at 900 pounds.

Other bars offered puppet shows, or the chance to examine such items as a 17-foot model of the city of Jerusalem, done by two Germantown men, and the wax figures of Biblical characters while the patrons quaffed. Several tippling houses offered bowling greens.

But mostly the entertainment was talk, and the opportunity to catch up on the news. Very few Philadelphians could afford subscriptions to the weekly newspapers, of which the city had several, but the papers were passed around a lot, and some probably found their way to the taverns, even workingmen's places.

A variety of beverages were available, including beer, rum, whiskey, various wines, and "Cyder Royall," which was cider fermented with applejack. An enterprising cleric tabulated 45 different kinds of drinks being offered for sale in various taverns he had visited during the course of his travels through the colonies.

Beer brewing and pricing were actually regulated by the city's judges in Philadelphia, as a result of complaints about quality in the 1720s, including allegations that large quantities of sediment, dirt and filth were turning up in customers' tankards.

The taverns had, of course, already spawned legends of drinking prowess. One of these concerned a Thomas Apty, who had walked into the Red Lion Inn on Elbow Lane several decades earlier, and bet a half crown that he could drink a gallon of cyder royall within the ensuing hour and half. He did so, and then died on the spot.

Or so the story went.

The sunset was now reddening the sky above the countryside to the west of the city. (The built-up area of the city actually only extended as far as Seventh Street.) The Jones family was gathered again around its table, and the chicken stew was dished out onto the plates, and the blessing said.

Outside, the city's activities were slowing. Boys of other families were returning home after having brought the family's livestock back to barns located on the outskirts of the city. The flames in the street lamps were being lighted.

Inside their small alley home, the Jones family sat quietly bathed in the warm light from the flames of the fireplace and the table's candles, presenting a tableau that was utterly ordinary to them, and yet which would seem somehow richly evocative, a simpler, more wholesome, and warmer era to Philadelphians who saw it in their minds' eye two centuries later. ★ ★ ★

The kitchen of Jerg Muller, a Lebanon County miller, evokes the rural Pennsylvania way of life.

Rhineland Refuge in the Countryside

After William Penn had lined up his Quaker countrymen to become the craftsmen, merchants, and speculators in his new colony, there still remained the problem of getting farmers over there to till the soil and grow the food.

His solution to this problem leads one to believe that Penn's blood may run today in the veins of Pocono resort development land dealers. Penn went to the Rhineland of Germany in 1671, a decade before he himself actually came to America, and conducted what were, in effect, sales meetings.

His presentations even included spiffy brochures (spiffy for the times, anyway) informing his prospects on such matters as do-it-yourself plans for their forest hideaways in the woodlands of his Holy Experiment. "This may seem a mean way of building," one conceded, in an early example of truth-in-advertising, "but 'tis sufficient and safest for the ordinary beginner."

Penn's listeners, of course, were seeking more than a refuge from the *sturm und drang* of hectic urban living, which is the basic sales appeal of land salesmen today.

Penn was offering these Protestant German farmers an escape from ravaging bands of soldiers, vindictive religious persecution, and ever-spreading plagues of pestilence, all of which were part of the Thirty Years War era in the Rhineland.

Many of these landsmen came.

First they traveled down the Rhine to Rotterdam, and from there they went to England, where they boarded slow, evil-smelling sailing ships bound for Pennsylvania. The first Germans who came with

The Pennsylvania Dutch constructed a culture from patchwork pieces of ravaged Europe that became a "Celebration of Life." It all happened because William Penn had the right message. He was selling freedom.

Francis Daniel Pastorius settled in Germantown, and, to a large extent, assimilated into the basically English ways of Philadelphia.

But later arrivals moved farther out into the country, where they joined some other Germans who had come down into the interior valleys of the Susquehanna and other rivers from the Schoharie region of New York state.

Here they settled down behind a language barrier and developed their own folk culture.

They were not, in the beginning, a homogeneous group. Clarence Kulp, an expert on Pennsylvania folklife, points out that there was, in fact, a broad diversity of communities and traditions.

These included Mennonites from The Netherlands, Mennonites from Switzerland, Lutherans from Prussia and Saxony, German Reformed from North Germany, Moravians from Moravia and Bohemia (now Czechoslovakia), Schwenkfelders from Silesia (now part of Poland), Huguenots from the Alsace, Dunkers from Westphalia, Catholics from Bavaria and Austria.

The dialects and traditions of these groups continued as separate strains within the overall patterns that came to be called "Pennsylvania Dutch," an appellation that sprang from the corruption of the word *Deutsch,* or "German," by English-speaking Pennsylvanians.

But at the same time a great sense of togetherness, which they termed *gemeinschaft,* also united them. No precisely correct English translation of the word exists. What it meant was that when a German had to build, butcher, harvest, or any other major work, his neighbors would gather together with him and make a frolic of the project.

Making apple butter would become an apple butter party, with the job of stirring of the apple butter in its big copper bucket becoming ancillary to the dancing and drinking.

And the Germans did their drinking with the same profound sense of hefty enjoyment that characterized other aspects of their lives. One Delaware County farmer wrote, "Nothing could be done without drink. At house and barn raisings a cedar branch, fastened at the top of the building, announced that good cheer would (be available) . . . in liberal quantity."

And enjoyment of spiritous beverages went beyond simple refreshment after hard labor, and included the non-German farmers as well. The Reverend Robert A. Brown, a minister in the Philadelphia area countryside, recalled that "the storekeeper kept liquor free for his customers on the counter. The guest in respectable homes was treated to it universally. The pastor was expected to drink it as a pledge of hospitality on entering a dwelling, and again to drink it at his departure . . . it is a wonder that religion survived."

The culture of the Pennsylvania Dutch, of course, went beyond their linguistic commonalities and happy gatherings. They developed a distinctive artistic tradition that experienced its principal flowering in the 18th century, in the era of the American Revolution.

The decorative designs and colors that characterized Pennsylvania Dutch art permeated their environment. Pennsylvania Dutch master potters decorated pie plates with birds and tulips; itinerant artists "fraktur" painted hearts and pomegranates on items ranging from house blessings and birth certificates to dower chests and wardrobes.

Smiths fashioned buds and leafy vines on hardware, farmers whittled birds and carved butter prints. The weaver used the same vocabulary of design on coverlets, and housewives appliqued the designs onto quilts.

This magnificent artistic celebration of life lasted about a century. In the 1800s the colors became duller, the designs became simpler, and the decorations were stamped or stenciled. Other labor-saving short-cuts were also introduced, and the apprenticeship system, which had enforced standards of quality, died out.

By the time of the Revolution, the countryside around Philadelphia was well beyond the pioneering stage and large numbers of Scots-Irish had joined the Germans. In many instances, the first rough log houses, with their characteristic three-room, first-floor design — the *kiche* (kitchen), *stube* (great room), and *kammer* (sleeping room) — had given way to more substantial brick and stone farm houses.

But most of the Pennsylvania Dutch farm houses built in the 18th century still had a small window in the kammer

called the soul window, which was opened when there was a death in the family so that the soul could escape to heaven.

The farm buildings other than the house were often more impressive. Dr. Benjamin Rush, the Philadelphia physician, observed of the Pennsylvania farmers that they "always provide large and suitable accommodations for their horses and cattle before they lay out much money in building a home for themselves."

They built their huge "Swiss Bank" barns against the side of a hill, so that the second floor would be at ground level on the uphill side to allow wagons to be driven in. The barns faced south to allow sunlight to fall into the barnyard, and the patterned brick endwalls often had openings for ventilation.

The colorful painted "hex" signs that adorned the barns were not to scare away "evil spirits," as is widely believed, but rather were a sign to the traveler that "German Is Spoken Here."

•

Peter Kalm, a traveler who wrote extensively of his experiences in the Philadelphia area during the 1750s, said of the experience of sleeping on a farm, "When I was obliged to lie at night in the huts and beds . . . I was so plagued by the immense quantity of fleas that I imagined that I had been put in a burning fire. They drove me from the bed, and I was very happy to sleep on the benches underneath the roof of the hut.

"Dogs and men lie promiscuously in the huts," he continued. "A stranger can hardly lie down and shut his eyes before he is in danger of either being squeezed to death or stifled by a dozen or more dogs, which lie around him and upon him in order to have a good resting place."

Sometimes, bedsteads were made of sassafras wood, the strong scent of which was said to be a deterrent to bedbugs, but Kalm says that the smell apparently lost its effect after a while.

Kalm may have just had bad luck, though. Some homes were meticulously clean, and had bedsteads and other furnishings that were as impressive as those in a comparable city home. In many households the members of the family pulled feather-filled covers over themselves that were warm, clean, and reasonably bug-free.

Meals were hearty. The family rose at dawn, or earlier, and had already put in several hours of work before coming in for breakfast at about 6:30 or 7.

Breakfast was prepared mostly in the frying pan, and it consisted of fried sausage, scrapple, ham, and potatoes, together with pie. Potatoes and pie were served at every meal.

Dinner at noon would be one of the famous Pennsylvania Dutch one-pot meals, perhaps ham, *schnitz* (apples), and *knepp* (dumplings) in a stew. Or it might be chicken pot pie with potatoes, or pork, sauerkraut, and dumplings.

Supper, served just before the sun set, would feature a thick, hearty soup with lots of vegetables, meat and noodles, along with cheese, cold meat, bread, and pie again.

A typical school lunch would include two big pieces of pie—one a fruit pie, and the other a custard pie—an apple, and a sugar sandwich, which consisted of two thick slices of home-baked bread spread with home-churned butter and sprinkled with sugar.

Bathing was a very sometime thing for most people on farms —except the Swedes. They built bath houses that were log structures roughly 14 feet square, without windows, and with a large fireplace. Large stones were heated to a high temperature and then plunged into kettles of water, creating a cloud of hot vapor.

Around the walls were narrow planks on which the bathers reclined, unclothed. They perspired freely in the steamy heat, and the body's circulation was further stimulated by lashing oneself with birch switches. After becoming well heated, the bathers would come directly outside, even in winter, when they would roll in the snow.

An account from the 1600s, which probably still applied in the next century, noted that "men and women used the bath without any concealment of dress, or, most surprisingly, even being influenced by an emotion of attachment . . . A strange scene would meet the eye of a visitor who happened to look into such a bath house when it was filled with bathers, from the new-born child carried there by its mother, to the old man of 80."

One of the reasons that the Germans became and continued to be the dominant group in the area is that they stayed in place, while others moved on. Some historians have attributed this to the fact that when they arrived the Germans had selected sites in the valleys, where the tallest trees grew for their farms, knowing that this was the richest soil, even when such locations were a good distance from the nearest road.

Other nationalities, notably the Scots-Irish, were attracted to the natural meadowlands, and areas where the forest growth was sparse — and the soil

Photos by Russell T. Salmon

The rural ways of colonial Pennsylvania are recreated at the Colonial Pennsylvania Plantation, at Ridley Creek State Park in Edgmont. Students participating in the research project, directed by Dr. Jay Anderson, dress in colonial dress and carry out the same tasks that a farm family accomplished on the farm in 1776.

No wonder the greatest boon to the farmer was rest. "Rest for the weary" was the supplicative sentiment of many a hymn intoned on the Sabbath in the countryside

less fertile. As they used up the soil, they moved on. The German farmers also used crop rotation to return nutrients to the soil.

Moreover, the Germans didn't fear the hard work that went with clearing the forested land, and in the continuing business of farming. Their diligence became the pattern for all farmers in the region.

"Everyone who is able to do anything is as busy as nailers on the farm," an elderly Delaware County farmer told an early 19th century historian. The farmer continued, "I know many men who are worth thousands of pounds who will mow, make hay, reap, and draw hay and grain into their barns as hirelings. And those that are able, if they do not work, are looked upon with a kind of contempt. Here in the country they are slighted and are not company for anyone."

No wonder the greatest boon to the farmer was rest. "Rest for the weary" was the supplicative sentiment of many a hymn intoned on the Sabbath in the Philadelphia countryside.

But the diligence and hard work was moderated by an easy-going attitude. The farmer's work depended on the seasons, and on the weather, but he had no deadlines. The attitude was reflected in characteristic German sayings as the one which translates, "So I don't come today. I come tomorrow."

Until the year 1800 the fields were tilled by plows not greatly advanced from the crooked stick of Biblical times. Great improvement in plows resulted from a dissertation by Thomas Jefferson in 1798 that explained how to make the most efficient shape for a plow.

In the 1700s the farmer also had to rely mainly on wooden hand tools and pitchforks. The metal rakes and hoes and spades that might be made by a local blacksmith were heavy and clumsy.

Planting was frequently the job of the women and children in the family. "One for the black bird, one for the crow, one for the cutworm, and one to grow" was the rhyme repeated while planting corn.

Women did a surprising amount of heavy work. Dr. Rush of Philadelphia was intrigued to note that "the wives and daughters frequently forsake for awhile their dairy duties and spinning wheels and join their husbands and brothers" in the fields.

Margaret Dwight, a visitor from Massachusetts, was shocked by what she saw in Pennsylvania at the turn of the century. "Women in New England," she noted, with a certain amount of Massachusetts chauvinism, "are employed only in and about the house ... in the proper business of (their) sex. I do not know that I was ever more struck with strangeness of any sight than with the appearance and business of these females."

The average farmer had about three horses, four cows, seven sheep, and six children, according to 18th century tax records. And the average farm was about 135 acres.

Much of that land was in grain, and the major job of the harvest was cutting it down. For that task, a scythe or a cradle, which was a scythe with additional blades, was used. A farmer with mighty biceps, and an unbreakable back, might cut four acres in a day.

Close mowing required a stone-free meadow, because a collision with even a small, egg-sized stone could be disastrous for the blade. One of the young boys would often walk ahead of the scytheman, checking for rocks.

Wheat, oats, and barley were generally threshed under the feet of horses. Wheat, rye, and peas were flailed.

A flail consisted of a long handle to which a somewhat heavier and shorter stick was attached by a thong. The cut grain would be spread on the barn floor and two flailsmen would strike alternately at the kernel-bearing ends of the stalks. The grain would be turned periodically and the process continued until all of the kernels had been beaten out.

When the process was finished, the chaff and grain were shaken out, and the straw, still straight and unbroken, was bound up to be used in weaving baskets.

Grain flailed most easily on cold winter days. It was regarded as pleasant employment for rough weather, a good way to keep warm.

On the farm, the man of the house had to be his own blacksmith, carpenter, cabinetmaker, and shoemaker. It's perhaps not surprising that, with their blend of skills and diligence, the farmers of Pennsylvania were able to establish several industries.

Blacksmiths and wheelwrights combined their talents to develop the famous Conestoga wagons, characteristically painted red and blue, which with their white "sails" were to become the ships of the prairies when America moved west. Already they were being used to bring grain to Philadelphia for shipment abroad.

The Kentucky rifle is so called because Daniel Boone became famous when he carried one of the long-barreled Pennsylvania rifle into the Kentucky wilderness, where he shot a bear, among other things, with it.

One of the students at the Colonial plantation boils lard to make soap.

Participants in the Colonial Plantation program sit down to dinner in the style of 1776.

Supper, served just before sunset, would feature a thick, hearty soup with lots of vegetables, meat, and noodles, along with cheese, cold meat, bread, and pie—again

These weapons reached their highest development in the hands of Pennsylvania gunsmiths. The long stocks of curly maple were decorated with shiny brass inlays and patch boxes. Six companies of Pennsylvania riflemen carried these weapons in the Revolution.

The farmer traveled somewhat more than might be expected. He walked, and went by horseback. When he needed a place to stop for an evening, he knocked on a door and offered to help with some work in exchange for a night's lodging.

From Montgomery County he would bring his harvest into Philadelphia, often bringing his wife and kids along, braving the highwaymen and the muddy roads.

They would spend the night in one of the taverns along the Skippack Pike, or in Chestnut Hill, before taking his wagon load of vegetables, butter, eggs, chickens, and other items in to the market the following day.

In the city he could buy a gun, a pocket watch, some imported calicoes, dye stuff, or perhaps some imported English china. Sometimes he would fill his empty wagon with oysters, which would be brought back home for an oyster supper at the church.

If he brought some cash back, he could spend that at the startlingly well stocked country general stores. They carried shoes, buckles, window glass, paint colors, among other items, and the store-keeper was willing to buy some items, like applejack.

The generous spirit and desire to give an extra measure was perhaps the central characteristic of the Pennsylvania Dutch lifestyle. This was reflected in the heft of their furniture, the thickness of the boards they used, the fullness of form in baskets and jars.

It was by remembering this fact that researchers were able to solve what had been a particularly baffling mystery concerning the Henry Antes house in Frederick Township, Montgomery County. The problem was that the measurements of the old farmhouse were screwy; they didn't conform to any known standard of measurement.

Finally, someone noticed that all of the measurements, when expressed in inches, were divisible by 13. The answer was immediately apparent.

Henry Antes had built his house on the basis of a 13-inch foot. — *DRB*

City Style, Country Ways

" . . . Asking a Philadelphia gentleman to step out of his English drawing room and walk into the house of a Pennsylvania farmer was to ask him to step out of modern times and leap precipitously back into the Middle Ages . . . "

By Lita Solis-Cohen

Life in Pennsylvania was as varied in colonial times as it is now, and generalizations are just as perilous. But few would contradict the assertion that in Philadelphia, the English taste prevailed.

Even Benjamin Franklin, when abroad to promote the American cause, wrote home to his wife, Deborah, urging her to "follow the latest London fashions." The best work of Philadelphia craftsmen was based on English pattern books by Swan, Gibbs, Chippendale, and others.

Yet it is possible to distinguish American-made furniture from English. Most experts would agree that American designs tend to have more of a vertical emphasis and seem more open. Historian Allen Gowans has suggested that the furniture itself projects the vigor and confidence of a people that feels itself to be on the brink of great accomplishment.

"The architecture and furnishings," Gowans has written, "sprang from the same disciplined self-confidence, the same assurance in absolute rules of life and art, that motivated the great classical eras of the past."

Be that as it may, the fact is that to ask a Philadelphian to step from an essentially English drawing room and enter the house of a Pennsylvania farmer was asking him to undergo an aesthetic shock, to step from what seemed to him to be modern times and leap precipitously back into the Middle Ages.

The Germans, French Huguenots, and Swiss who settled the counties beyond Philadelphia kept alive the remembered old world traditions of the Rhinish villages from which their ancestors had fled after the Thirty Years War. They passed on their vernacular styles through apprenticeships and courses of instructions as involved as any the city craftsmen had gone through.

Their painted chests, stretcher tables, plank chairs, and benches look like those in paintings done by Flemish master Pieter Breughel 200 years before. The rooms have low doors, small windows, exposed beams, thick stone walls, covered with whitewashed plaster—all traditions of the peasant builder.

The flowers, birds, and hearts painted on birth certificates, dower chests, boxes and dishes have been called the last flowering of the medieval art of illumination. These depictions brightened everyday life for the Pennsylvania farmer, just as the miniature paintings touched with gold had illuminated medieval psalters.

The illustrations which follow, all of which show items that are in the collections of the Philadelphia Museum of Art, show the two extremes of the spectrum of lifestyles. There was, of course, every shade in between. There were Germans in the city, and Englishmen in the country. And everywhere they exchanged aspects of their respective heritages with one another.

It is perhaps interesting to note that John Elliott, an importer of the latest Chippendale-style looking glasses from London, thought the tastes of his customers of English and German descent, sufficiently similar that he had his labels printed in both languages.

1.

2.

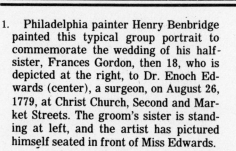

5.

3.

4.

6.

1. Philadelphia painter Henry Benbridge painted this typical group portrait to commemorate the wedding of his half-sister, Frances Gordon, then 18, who is depicted at the right, to Dr. Enoch Edwards (center), a surgeon, on August 26, 1779, at Christ Church, Second and Market Streets. The groom's sister is standing at left, and the artist has pictured himself seated in front of Miss Edwards.

2. A Pennsylvania Dutch potter made this plate to commemorate the wedding of a fellow potter in 1793, a few years after the Edwards-Gordon nuptials. He drew the image of his friend joining hands in marriage with the bride with the "scratch," or *sgraffito,* method. The tribute may be somewhat simpler in form that Benbridge's, but the potter was able to add an inscription to his work, which translates to read: "All beautiful maidens hath God created; they are for the potter, but not the priest."

3. By the 18th century Europeans had, of course, long since pressed on to India, Columbus' destination; not only that, but they had brought back with them a novel idea for a form of hot weather refreshment called "punch," in which various combinations of spiritous beverages were mixed with fruit juices. The idea was seized upon with enthusiasm in America.

As the framers of the Declaration of Independence pursued their work in Philadelphia, they may at times have paused for a refreshing glass of such a concoction, which was probably ladled from a large bowl like this Chinese porcelain one.

4. One cannot be quite as certain as to the type of delicious items that might once have been contained in this jar fashioned by a potter from the red clay of Bucks County in 1787.

He mixed clay with water until it reached the consistency of thick cream to make a substance called "slip," with which he added the decorative tulips and birds.

He achieved the varying tones by using both light and dark-colored slip, which he also used to put the date on with. Green accents were added by brushing copper sulfate here and there under the lead glaze.

5. This Chippendale-style looking glass was probably made in London, and brought to Philadelphia for the express purpose of reflecting a room in which candlelight would glint off polished mahogany furniture and the silks of elegantly attired gentlemen and ladies.

The mirror itself, with its gleaming mahogany and silvered glass frame, would have added a glittering embellishment to the scene.

6. A Lancaster County craftsman may have seen a Chippendale mirror frame on a visit to the home of a city cousin in Philadelphia, but he was strictly on his own when he embellished his two-foot high walnut frame with a design of hearts, tulips, and pinwheels similar to those designs that are found on Pennsylvania Dutch documents and pottery.

7.

8.

9.

10.

11.

12.

7. Instead of buying imported English chintz, loyal Philadelphians patronized John Hewson, who had come here at Benjamin Franklin's suggestion to set up a textile printworks.

With the wooden blocks on which the designs were cut, he printed this cotton coverlet, which measures 32 inches square, using red, green, brown, and blue dyes.

During the Revolution, the British offered a reward for his capture, but he survived to win a gold medal from the Manufacturing Society in 1789 for the best calico printing in Pennsylvania.

8. In contrast to the delicate butterflies, birds, and flowers on the Hewson coverlet, traditional bright red-and-green pinwheels whirl around the central red and green tulip motif appliqued to an orange printed cotton on this country quilt.

This version was probably warmer and more durable. It is quilted to an underlayer and a layer of fill. A running stitch follows a marked-out pattern.

9. Coffee was becoming a popular drink

as the split with England came near, and Philadelphia silversmith Philip Syng Jr. made this coffee pot "in the new French taste," as the expression went, for Joseph and Grace Galloway about 1760. On the bottom he stamped his mark, "PS-PS-PS," and scratched the weight of the item, 39 ounces, 1 pennyweight, and 12 grains.

Galloway was a long-time political ally and close friend of Benjamin Franklin, but the two were soon to part over the issue of independence. Galloway became the most assertive and articulate of America's Loyalists, and in October of 1778 he left Philadelphia for London, never to return. He took the coffee pot with him. It came back when the Philadelphia Museum of Art acquired it in 1966.

10. This particular coffeepot was made in Bucks County about 1840. That doesn't mean that it took until then for coffee-drinking to spread from the city into the rural areas; folks in Bucks County had, in fact, been drinking coffee out of pots

very much like this one for quite some time before 1840.

Indeed, what this pot illustrates is the way in which 18th century forms lived on in the work of 19th century country craftsmen.

The pot was cut in sections from a pattern, decorated with raised dots, shaped, and soldered together. Again, the designs are traditional — a tulip, six-pointed stars, and overlapping circles.

11. This wainscot arm chair is too stiff and straight to be comfortable during long periods of sitting, which probably didn't bother the Pennsylvania farmer who owned it much because he had precious little time for sitting.

Made of walnut, and standing a little less than four feet high, it is built in a traditional form that was already a hundred years out of date. The sturdy proportions and the generous use of wood reflect the owner's needs and values.

12. By the time of the Revolution, Philadelphia furniture makers were producing such pieces as this elaborately

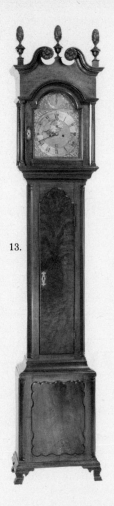

13.

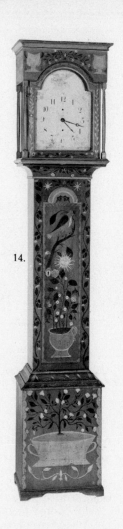

14.

15.

16.

Photos courtesy of the Philadelphia Museum of Art

carved easy chair, fashioned from mahogany and covered with French brocaded taffeta.

One uncle cautioned his nephew by letter, on hearing that the young man intended to ship furniture back from London, that Philadelphia craftsmen could produce "household goods . . . well made from English patterns"—and at lower prices.

The favorite patterns were Thomas Chippendale's, the London furniture-maker whose stylistic ideas were in such vogue that his name has been applied to the entire period's furniture and interior architecture.

13. Clocks driven by pendulums were enclosed in tall cases like this nine-foot walnut one, which was made in Philadelphia around 1760. Again, it is done in what was called Chippendale style, carved with scrolls, rosettes, and, at the very top, flame-and-urn finials.

The clocks themselves gradually metamorphosed into tremendously complex mechanisms called orreries that not only told the time, the month, and the year,

but also showed the current position of all of the planets in the solar system.

Wealthy men would commission scientist clock-makers like Philadelphia's David Rittenhouse to make ever more complex versions, so that they could put themselves one step ahead of their neighbors in terms of their awareness of what was afoot in the universe.

14. The country clock, made in Mahantongo Township, Schuylkill County, about 1810, is painted pine, and stands a somewhat more modest 7'7". It is bright orange, and decorated with depictions of flowers, a bird, and vines.

The country craftsman came up with an intriguing ploy aimed at dealing with a constant problem posed by such clocks: how to keep the kids from opening them and playing with the pendulum.

This clock has a green rattlesnake painted inside its door. As a result, parents could tell their children, in all truthfulness, "Don't touch. There's a rattler inside."

15. Quaker merchant Levi Hollingsworth

ordered this mahogany-and-walnut high chest of drawers for his Philadelphia home sometime around 1775. An 18th century Philadelphia gentleman kept his sometimes rather considerable wardrobe in chests like this one, which stood about eight feet high.

Normally, the chest was accompanied by a matching dressing table in the shape of the lower half. Hollingsworth's order, in fact, was for two chests and two dressing tables.

The fine proportions, well-figured wood, and crisp carving show the mastery of Philadelphia cabinetmakers — and the elegance of the time.

16. Out in Hereford Township, Berks County, Martin Eisenhauer kept his clothes in this wardrobe, which he called a *schrank*. His name and the date the piece was built — 1794 — are painted under the cornice of this seven-foot-high piece of painted pine furniture. Blue paint was sponged onto the raised door panels, which are also embellished with connected hearts painted ivory.

Boom Town Grows Along the Delaware

Philadelphia in 1776 was "the busiest square mile on the American continent," and one of the greatest cities in the world. If it smelled bad, the odor was at least in part the smell of success.

By Willard S. Randall

The fact that Philadelphia was 75 miles upriver from the open sea didn't prevent the city from becoming, by 1776, the leading seaport in North America. Philadelphia, in fact, had been from its beginning a funnel that collected and concentrated the essentials of colonial life, then poured them into the mainstream of American commercial life.

Along its crowded mile-long waterfront were 22 wharves off of which moved food, timber and marine supplies from the middle colonies to ports on both sides of the Atlantic. They received, in exchange, manufactured goods, clothing and finery from Europe, and sugar and rum from the islands of the Caribbean.

On most ice-free days between 1750 and 1775, upwards of 100 merchant ships and many more shallops, barges and boats crowded the port, waited to load and unload, and shuttled between Philadelphia and smaller ports up and down the river.

On any given day in these boom years, there were easily 1,000 sailors bending their backs to their work aboard ship or their elbows in 165 inns and ta-

This view of Philadelphia from the New Jersey shore was made in 1754. The highest spire, in the center, is Christ Church, at 2nd and Market Sts. Independence Hall is the highest spire to the left of the church. The docks end approximately at Vine Street. Modern Philadelphia is shown below.

verns within easy walk of the water-front.

But as one moved away from the wharves, Philadelphia, like London, was a city of shops and shopkeepers.

Any immigrant could, with enough skill, hard work and thrift, parlay his passage to Philadelphia into a front-parlor shop, then to a store.

If his health held, he could be well on his way to becoming a merchant prince with a warehouse near the water, a townhouse a short walk away and a county seat a few hours by carriage beyond the

city limits.

The dream of such success, virtually impossible in Europe, made Philadelphia the busiest square mile on the vast American continent by the time of the Revolution. Crowded into one square mile — from Vine Street on the north boundary to Lombard on the south, from the Delaware River west to the edge of town at Seventh Street, were an estimated 35,000 Philadelphians.

It was one of the largest cities in the British Empire (after London and Edinburgh) and the largest in America, so

crowded that any back-alley house brought high rent. And there were other still familiar urban complaints. Philadelphia by 1776 was noisy and dirty; its waters were polluted and, in certain neighborhoods the streets unsafe after dark.

Things hadn't, however, been that way in the very beginning.

The first settlers on the river came to Delaware Bay to set up whaling tryworks at Cape May in 1633 (the oil of one large whale brought $4,000 in gold). Five years later the Swedes landed at Tinicum Island, just south of the forks of the Dela-

ware and Schuylkill Rivers, to farm and trade for furs with the Indians. Though forced to recognize Dutch sovereignty to the area by a Dutch fleet from New Amsterdam, the Swedes nevertheless stayed on, welcoming the first Quaker settlers in the 1670s.

These Quaker religious refugees from England bypassed Philadelphia at first, founding towns at Salem on the Jersey shore in 1675 and at Burlington, the river's first major port, in 1677. Only when their leader, William Penn, arrived in 1682 did he have the good sense to develop Philadelphia. He landed at a swampy but protected cove known as the Dock at the foot of what is now Pine Street, where he saw that ships up to 500 tons could berth.

Penn didn't interfere with the Swedes settled at Southwark, mapping out his city between the Delaware and the Schuylkill in a rectangle above Southwark, with streets running north-south and east-west. He named only two of them, the main cross arteries of Broad Street and High Street, which became known early as Market Street, because that's where the market was held.

The first sign that the early Quakers had perceived the city's great commercial potential came in 1683, when Penn chartered the Free Society of Traders in the section later called Society Hill. Most of the trade was in real estate as the town lots were sold and resold. But gradually the Quakers branched out into trade with the Indians, with the German farmers who flocked from the Rhine, and with farmers and loggers from New Jersey who quickly stripped the tall oak, cedar, and pine forests to ship back to the hungry ship yards of England. The commercial houses and the houses of merchants, craftsmen in the marine supply business,

and artisans crept steadily north until, by 1723, when 17-year-old Benjamin Franklin arrived on the ferry from Burlington, the wharves had reached well above Market Street.

Farming, however, was still the region's mainstay for half a century. In 1709, the first covered markethouse had been built on Market Street between Second and Third Streets. The brick structure, erected by Samuel Powel, followed the old English custom of having the courthouse upstairs and stalls and a shambles for farmers on both sides of the street level.

So fast did the commerce grow that this market was overcrowded inside ten years. In 1720, a block-long covered Jersey Market was built between Front and Second Streets. A third covered market was built between Third and Fourth Streets in 1759. Still later, markets were built on Second Street between Pine and Lombard, on Callowhill Street in the Northern Liberties section of the city, and a fish market on Dock Street.

More, however, was pouring into Philadelphia than food and ships. People were coming as well. The combination of religious tolerance and easy access over the best roads of the day to cheap lands in the west made Philadelphia the chief port of entry by 1760.

But not all immigrants wished to pass through Philadelphia to the frontier. Workers and their families settled south of the city limits in such numbers that in 1762 Southwark could boast 603 houses and official status as a district. The Northern Liberties, growing even faster, were given equal footing in 1771, when there were 553 houses there.

Settlement also followed the Ridge road out of the city to Germantown, a

unique community with German-speaking families, schools, newspapers, shops and some of the finest country homes for rich Philadelphia merchants seeking to escape the summer heat. By 1776, tradesmen and wealthy merchants had moved as far north as Camp Hill, where merchant George Emlen maintained a splendid country house with a 15-mile-long view of Philadelphia.

For the majority of Philadelphians, however, the houses were small and crowded, usually one and one-half stories, with shops in the largest room, the front parlor.

Many of these shops were connected with the maritime industry. A study of 275 homes in the Middle Ward between Arch and Walnut Streets and Front and Seventh Streets shows 47 shopkeepers and artisans in trades related to shipping, including coopers, carpenters, cordwainers, merchants, a boatbuilder and a ropemaker.

If they failed to work long and hard enough, there was the grim prospect of the almshouse and the debtor's prison. But if they remained thrifty and hardworking, they could move up in business and society: there were no real class barriers in the city in the 18th century.

While neighborhoods developed early with special ethnic flavors such as Germantown and Southwark, the rest of the city was an amalgam of all sorts of people and trades. Living and working together in the Middle Ward, for instance, were hatters, tailors, common laborers, bakers, brewers, hucksters, tinkers, potters, butchers, a goatkeeper, druggists, tobacconists, a plumber and staymakers, stockingmakers and silversmiths.

Generally prosperous, Philadelphia nonetheless had few public improvements before the Revolution.

Paving of all the streets did not begin until Joseph Wharton, a rich merchant, was thrown and badly injured when his horse slipped in deep mud in the unpaved road near his Second Street home. Private subscriptions resulted, and Second Street was the first paved street in the city, its cobbles running past many of the city's finest houses. Before the Revolution, much of Market Street would also be paved and provided with footwalks.

The paving projects, however, were geared more to commerce — to help keep the farmers' and traders' wagons moving in and out of the city — than to aesthetics or safety.

And by this time, filling local supply and demand had been shouldered into second place by the more lucrative foreign trade. The influx of British troops,

The Old London Coffee House at Front and Market streets became a center for commercial dealings.

Free Library of Philadelphia

THE FOUNDING CITY

money and supplies also helped to make Philadelphia a major port during the last French and Indian War in the early 1760s.

Then there was the matter of the West Indies trade, an economic situation that was to have pronounced political effects in the coming years.

For more than a century, there had been a freewheeling, if illegal, trade with the West Indies for rum, sugar, molasses, and slaves. England had passed Navigation Acts requiring payment of customs duties as early as 1660, but colonial merchants and royal officials winked at them, and England actually lost money trying to collect the duties.

The high cost of the last war with France and the new prosperity in America, however, led Parliament in 1764 to clamp down and collect the duties, backing up its laws for the first time with the now unemployed Royal Navy.

At first, the West Indies trade was with English colonies such as Barbados, Jamaica, Antigua and St. Christopher's. Philadelphia merchants paid cash to farmers for their flour, bread and meat and then shipped them to the Caribbean plantation islands for sale.

Their ships, at first working on sheer speculation, came back loaded with rum and sugar. But while the profits could run as high as 500 percent, more often they were low or nonexistent. The sensible Philadelphians decided, instead, that a conservative five percent markup on all orders made better sense.

By the late 1760s, the Philadelphia merchants held the upper hand: Barbados planters were sending rum to be sold on consignment and were ordering long lists of Philadelphia-made goods.

The English crackdown on customs tax violators in 1765 led, first, to a brief but deep depression along the Philadelphia waterfront. Crowds of unemployed sailors, laborers and artisans roamed the waterfront, ready to mob customs collectors, often tarring and feathering them, until few men were willing to take the job.

But American ingenuity devised an answer to the problem: smuggling.

Everyone knew about it and, even though the Quaker meeting forbade the practice, as one leading Quaker merchant drily put it, he and his colleagues "occasionally evaded the Navigation Act," shipping casks of tobacco with such labels as "bread" and bribing all but the most recalcitrant royal officials.

Smuggling became one of the key issues in the growing argument with England. Irate Benjamin Franklin wrote in 1770: "The English never hesitated to

The docks at the foot of Arch Street bustled with activity.

Free Library of Philadelphia

avoid payment of duties when they could, even though they had made their own laws, as the Americans had not.

"When I hear them exclaiming against every little infringement on the acts of trade or obstruction given by a petty mob to an officer of our customs, calling for vengeance against the whole people as rebels and traitors, I cannot help thinking that there are still those in the world who can see a mote in their brother's eye while they do not discern a beam in their own."

Smuggling was, by then, a mite more than a mote. At one time in the late 1760's, British agents counted 120 American ships in the French molasses smuggling port of Monte Christo on the north coast of Santo Domingo, where Philadelphia merchant John Reynall admitted "it is very profitable and many from here have made great voyages."

Yet the bulk of the smuggling came through New Jersey overland to Philadelphia, with wagon trains rumbling through the Pine Barrens day and night under heavily-armed escorts. The chief

smuggling ports were Cape May, Little Egg Harbor, Chestnut Neck, Toms River and Greenwich. Teamsters and guards stopped along the way at taverns that sprang up, and soon towns such as Lower Bank, Pleasant Mills and Blue Anchor blossomed around the illicit $4 million-a-year trade.

When customs officers dared intervene, they were harshly treated. One example was James Hatton, at various times the unsuccessful collector of the ports of Greenwich and Cape May. When Hatton complained that the ships were unloaded and the wagons hauled right under his window in Cape May, the royal governor, William Franklin, brushed him aside as a troublemaker and nuisance.

Hatton and two aides once tried to seize a smuggler's ship unloading claret off Cape May, only to be beaten and robbed by the smugglers.

Hatton persisted, sending his son to Philadelphia to enlist the aide of John Swift, the Quaker City's collector of customs. Together they found the smuggled goods and a wild reception. Young Hatton was chased by a mob, hid in a house, was dragged out, tarred and feathered, beaten with sticks as he was dragged with a rope around his neck through the streets, put in the pillory, and, for good measure, thrown into the river.

sure, thrown into the river.

Again, Governor Franklin thought better than to punish anyone, instead chastising Hatton for not getting along with his neighbors.

The end of the French and Indian Wars also meant the reopening of the rich trade with the Indians beyond the Appalachians. Four months after Major Henry Bouquet's victorious expedition to quell the Indians, the Philadelphia merchant house of Baynton & Wharton sent the first train of 83 pack horses west, laden with brandy, guns, gunpowder, English-made hatchets, blankets, and knives.

The farmers of the Conococheague Valley, between Shippensburg and Mercersburg, were furious at what they saw as an arms deal with their enemies, the Indians. The farmers intercepted the train, dispersing the escort of Black Watch guards with heavy gunfire. After they burned the trade goods, the farmers besieged Fort Loudoun and its Black Watch garrison, forcing its surrender.

Local magistrates refused to arrest the raiders, who were known as James Smith and his Black Boys.

When the trade was resumed, the Black Boys struck again, with 18 men slipping into Fort Bedford and forcing its garrison to surrender.

Not all of the commercial activities of Philadelphia involved violence and/or illegalities, however, The city's ever-mushrooming middle class of prosperous artisans, craftsmen, and merchants could by now afford more than the bare necessities of life. They began to acquire rather cultivated affinities for imported British goods. This trend was enchanced by laws passed in England that forbade the colonists to make a growing list of manufactured goods, from hats to iron.

The center of this English import trade was the London Coffee House, on the southwest corner of Front and Market Streets. Here, every day at noon, the merchants met to place orders, insure their cargoes, bid on goods arriving from England, read the newspapers and dicker with the captains for space on empty ships.

Outside the coffee house, shipments were auctioned off and slaves were sold as Quaker merchants sipped lemonade and their less strait-laced counterparts drank liquor.

The rewards of sharp trading made the merchant's life the envy of most visitors. Merchant John Cadwalader's profits enabled him to build a handsome house between Spruce and Delancey Streets with formal gardens one block deep.

While the Quakers officially frowned on such luxury, some of them were counted among the 84 Philadelphians who could afford to ride the short distance to work in carriages. The carriages also were useful to take them to the "vapours" of their cool country seats, mostly painted jonquil yellow with green

shutters, along the Schuylkill.

The high style of living of many Philadelphia merchants by 1776 accounted for the large number of fine craftsmen who had come from England and Ireland to produce their wares, many of them superior to the goods available from England.

Most of the leading merchants, the Powels, Pembertons, Willings, Mifflins, Norrises, Callenders and Allens, preferred the ornate silver services of Joseph Richardson. The merchant elite also vied for the honor of having a David Rittenhouse tall case clock chiming in their drawing rooms. They filled their walls with prints of paintings by Swarthmore-born Benjamin West, Historical Painter to the King, and displayed their finery in formal portraits by local artist Charles Willson Peale.

But the highest mark of success in Philadelphia's merchant circles was to have enough money to avoid working at all.

Samuel Powel, Philadelphia's "Great Builder," had retained 90 of his solid brick houses for rent. By the time his grandson of the same name graduated from college, he could look forward to a life of total leisure. He could afford to serve as Philadelphia's mayor for two terms, during which he entertained lavishly at his large townhouse on South Third Street, and at his vast country estate in the fox-hunting country of Gloucester County, New Jersey.

Third-generation merchant aristocrats, beginning with Francis Rawle in 1748, began the tradition of the "Grand Tour" of Europe as the finishing touch of their educations before settling down to the drudgery of Philadelphia business and society.

The generation of great prosperity would be brought to an abrupt and unanticipated end, however, by the onset of revolution. Significantly, the first effective American weapon was economic boycott in the form of associations for non-importation and non-exportation that crippled London merchants.

This device, made possible by flourishing illegal trade and manufacturing that continued to supply vital needs, hurt Philadelphia's merchants in the long run. The irony was that fully 21 of the 39 leading Pennsylvania revolutionaries were Philadelphia merchants, such as Robert Morris, Thomas Willing, the Whartons and John Cadwalader. Before the Revolution was over, they would all suffer severely from the economic dislocations — and inflation.

When a young French immigrant named Stephen Girard arrived in Philadelphia in June 1776 from Santo Dom-

Shipbuilding became a major Philadelphia industry.

THE FOUNDING CITY

ingo, he found most American ships idled by the British blockade. Soon, Girard would write home to France of the runaway inflation: by October 1779, the price of pork was $6.80 a pound.

Coffee was $14 a pound wholesale, tea $40 a pound, lard was $7 per pound, sugar sold for $40 a pound — many times the pre-war prices.

The havoc of Revolution led, ultimately, to the arrest and imprisonment of many of the leading Quaker merchants and the flight with the British army of many more leading Philadelphia merchants.

And while some substantial fortunes were built on war profiteering by such notables as Robert Morris, some of these same merchants, including Morris, would eventually end up, as a result of speculation of their own making, serving long terms in the debtor's wing of the Walnut Street Jail.

At war's end, only the hardworking artisans and skilled craftsmen who had

Robert Morris and Stephen Girard: Philadelphia moneymen . . .

remained at their trades or returned after service in the army would recover quickly, as if in answer to Ben Franklin's

Benjamin West and Charles Willson Peale: Painted the city's elite . . .

maxim in *Poor Richard's Almanac.*

"Keep thy shop, and thy shop will keep thee." ★ ★ ★

Glimpses of Philadelphia Life 1776

Traffic was murder, the mosquitoes fierce; in many ways it was a time much like our own —with some exceptions.

By Richard S. Dunham

Trying to recapture a complete sense of what daily life was like in a city of a different time isn't simple. Then, as now, life was characterized by the hundreds of events of every single day, by chance occurrences, by the weather, by the habits of the people. The following are, in more or less random fashion, some glimpses of some of the things that gave life in Philadelphia its flavor and texture on the eve of the Revolution:

The flies, mosquitoes and other insects were a legend in the early days of the Republic. "You cannot conceive," wrote Captain John Hein-

ricks to friends in England, "of the superabundant swarms of flies."

Flies played a part in the historic events that took place in Philadelphia. Thomas Jefferson tended to attribute the speed with which the delegates finally approved the Declaration of Independence to the torture they were enduring on that day from the bites of horseflies, which would bite through their silk hose.

Elizabeth Drinker commented in her diary, with somewhat greater delicacy: "The flies are so numerous . . . that if I sit reading or writing for an hour, I find it necessary to wash my face and hands; the reason is obvious . . ."

●

About the only defense colonists had against insects was a pesticide called "Webster's Liquor," which

was concocted by John Webster, an upholsterer by trade. The contents of the "bug wash," as it was described, are not known, but they presumably had some effect. In any event, "Webster's Liquor" made Webster a rich man.

"Dirt" Was Hardly the Word

The streets in Philadelphia then were, of course, dirt, but that alone fails to adequately describe the condition of some of them.

Thomas Powel recorded that in some byways, the "stumps or roots of some of the original pine trees" were still jutting up, a constant threat to the unwary pedestrian. Henri Bouquet, a French visitor, wrote rather ungenerously to his Philadelphia host, "I never saw anything but dirt and dust in and about your city."

Philadelphia mayor Thomas Lawrence complained publicly about "the heaping of great piles of dirt and filth near the gutters, so that the same is raised two or three feet above them, thereby stopping the water courses and, in consequence thereof, occasioning an intolerable stench at this season, whereby distempers will in all probability be occasioned."

•

Traffic on the streets was regarded as hazardous. Wagons were often upset, and there were many reports of erratic or reckless driving in the city. Often vehicles veered onto the footpaths to avoid wandering livestock. In 1780, Gouverneur Morris was thrown from his wagon when the horse ran away. His leg was injured so badly that amputation was necessary.

A Philadelphia woman wrote of one near-tragic collision: "A young fellow with a mad colt galloped against our mare with such force as occasioned my falling out (of the carriage) ... Having the child asleep in my arms, and endeavoring to save it, I fell with all my weight on my right foot, and hurt it so

Shipwright

Cork Cutter

much that I was unable to set it to the ground for upwards of three weeks. The child, through mercy, escaped unhurt."

She added that this was no isolated occurrence. "I have lately met with so many frights that I cannot

bear to think of riding with any satisfaction," she wrote.

•

Noise was regarded as a problem even in the 18th century. In 1774, the Pennsylvania Assembly passed an ordinance that outlawed the firing of guns and other "excessive noise-making" during the Christmas season. A fine of $2.50 was assessed to every noisy house.

Marital Fidelity Here Stupefies French

On matters of sex and morals, Americans tended to be more strait-laced than was the European custom at the time. The Frenchman Rochambeau reported with some amazement that "American women once they have entered matrimony give themselves to it." Talleyrand, the famed French ecclesiastic, statesman, and philanderer, found that even French wives, accustomed to freer ways in their homeland, adapted to American mores once they arrived. He wrote that a Madame de la Tour du Pin, an aristocratic Frenchwoman then in America, was actually sleeping with her husband every night.

"It is essential," he reported, probably with a certain sadness, "to have a good reputation in this country."

By Order of His EXCELLENCY
ŚIR **WILLIAM HOWE,** K. B.
General and *Commander in Chief,* &c. &c. &c.

PROCLAMATION.

WHEREAS the Cart Ways of the several paved Streets, Lanes, and Alleys within the City of PHILADELPHIA and its Suburbs, contrary to former Usage, are much incommoded with Mud, Dirt, and other Filth, to the great Annoyance and Inconvenience of the Inhabitants, as well as endangering the Health of His MAJESTY's Subjects: For Remedy whereof, I DO, by Virtue of the Order aforesaid, and in Concurrence with the Magistrates of the Police, hereby enjoin and require, all and every of the Inhabitants and Occupiers of the Houses and Lots, and every Porter, Sexton, and other Keepers of Churches, Meeting-Houses, Academies, Schools, Public Buildings and Burying Grounds, within the said City and Suburbs; to rake

Library Co. of Philadelphia

British General Howe attempted to clean up the city's "mud, dirt, and other filth" by proclamation during the British occupation.

THE FOUNDING CITY

Brick Maker

Pavior

Which is not to say that there wasn't some playing around in those days; and, in upper-crust society at least, a definite double standard was adhered to.

Gouverneur Morris, whose unfortunate accident resulting in the loss of his leg has been described previously, was a legendary ladies' man.

John Jay, who was a delegate to the Second Continental Congress with Morris, wrote to a friend back in New York that "Gouverneur is daily employed in making oblations to Venus." Historian Joseph J. Kelley Jr. comments that Morris' "subsequent career bore out the confident statement that he was still a better man with one leg than most with two."

It can be argued, though, that the fashions of the time were a deterrent to intimate relations. Sarah Eve, a Philadelphian, recorded in her journal that kissing "decomposes the economy of one's handkerchief, it disorders one's high roll (coiffure), and it ruffles the serenity of one's countenance. Women hate to be kissed, especially as it is accompanied with such inconveniences."

•

Meeting young ladies was fairly easy, though. An atmosphere of neighborliness and friendly warmth

suffused Philadelphia in the 18th century, at least according to the reminiscences of Philadelphians who grew up during the period. John Warder wrote many years later that it was customary in

warmer weather, as evening approached, for families to dress up a little, then go out on their front porches. Neighbors would stroll by to talk.

It was an excellent opportunity, Warder recalled, to meet and become friendly with members of the fair sex, and Warder did so with great enthusiasm.

The arrangement did have its disadvantages, though, since one had to undertake these romantic overtures with virtually the entire community looking on. The entire arrangement, Warder noted, also made possible the rapid spread of gossip, and he confesses that he was often the target of it.

•

Things were somewhat more relaxed, in terms of boy-girl relationships, out on the farms around the city. Young couples were allowed to lie in bed together with no greater protection against immoral activities than fear of the Lord. The practice was known as "bundling."

Johann David Schoepf outlined

Hair styles for men . .

Library Co. of Philadelphia

. . . and women around 1800.

The Friends' Alms House was part of the city's welfare program.

The First Presbyterian Church stood opposite the market.

the way the practice worked in Pennsylvania in 1783: "It is the custom for young men to pay visits to their mistresses, and the young woman's name is in no ways impaired . . .

"The parents are present and these meetings happen when the pair is enamoured and merely wish to know each other better. The swain and the maiden spend the evening undisturbed by the hearth or, it may be, go to bed together without scruple; in the latter case

with the condition that they not take off their clothes.

"And if the anxious mother has any doubt of the strict virtue of her daughter, she takes the precaution of placing both the daughter's feet in one large stocking, and in the morning looks to see if the guardian is still properly fixed. But the inquiry is (usually) . . . superfluous. . ."

The practice, according to a history prepared by the Pennsylvania Historical Commission, was de-

prived of its "innocence" when many young men returned to Pennsylvania after the French and Indian Wars. In the army camps, the account explains, "they had acquired loose habits." By 1800, bundling was in "general disrepute at the bar of public opinion."

Bigamy was not unheard of in the countryside. Mary Dicks left her husband, John, in 1764 after a year of marriage to live with William Ford. In the next sixteen years she had by him six children before leaving him to marry William Pearce, allegedly "knowing full well" that both of her previous husbands were alive and well, according to accounts. In 1781, Pearce was lost at sea, so Mary went to live with William Walter Humphries.

Domestic Slaves

Despite the opposition to slavery of most Quakers and German farmers, there were 11,000 slaves in Pennsylvania in 1751. At the time of the Revolution, New Jersey had the second largest number of slaves among the colonies. (To be sure, the states of the Deep South that later became the principal slaveholding areas were thinly settled wildernesses at this point.)

Most of the slaves in Pennsylvania were probably domestic servants rather than field hands, but that didn't diminish the degradations of servitude. They were sold, in Philadelphia, usually by newspaper ads, "like so many bullocks," according to one account. Their masters could send them to the city's jail for whippings.

Thomas Seabright wrote of seeing "Negro slaves driven over the National Road arranged in couples and fastened to a long, thick rope or cable, like horses. This was a common sight in the early history of the road, and evoked no expression of surprise or censure."

•

At the same time, though, there were a large number of freed slaves in Philadelphia, some of whom owned businesses and became leaders of the commercial community. Among the most famous of these was James Forten, a sailmaker.

Racially mixed marriages were not unheard of in Philadelphia. In particular, Frenchmen fleeing to Philadelphia from the insurrection in the West Indies brought their black wives or mistresses with them.

Pennsylvania became the first state to abolish slavery. Its abolition act, passed by the Pennsylvania General Assembly on March 1, 1780, called for the gradual abolition of slavery by 1827.

Fiscal Policies

A popular method of raising funds was a public lottery. Lotteries were officially sanctioned to finance schools, churches, courthouses, turnpikes, bridges, wharves, street paving, and for general operating expenses.

•

Inflation was of intense concern to housewives as the Revolution began. In 1774, enraged housewives called protest meetings over a two-cent increase in the price of flour. This was a hefty increase indeed, considering that before the hike flour sold for about 1¼ cents a pound.

•

Unemployment was a troubling problem for the city in 1770. To help solve it, the city built a textile factory that employed 100 spinners and weavers.

Attention Toothless Men!

The big medical story of the late 1700s was tooth transplants. A Philadelphia dentist of the 1780s reported that over the previous six months he had "put 123 teeth that were formerly in the heads of others" into his patients' mouths. He offered, by newspaper advertisement, to pay "two guineas" for every tooth offered him by "persons disposed to sell their front teeth."

The Philadelphia Itch

Philadelphians didn't bathe regularly in the 18th century, and as a result tended to suffer (often acutely) from scabies, ringworm, miscellaneous other itches, lice, and, of course, B.O. When they did bathe, it was regarded as a grand experience.

After Elizabeth Drinker, in 1799, had a shower installed in her back yard, she recorded her first experience with it in some detail: "I bore it better than I had expected," she wrote, "not having been wet all over once in my life."

A French visitor to Philadelphia complained of contracting an itch while he was in Philadelphia, and at great pains attempted to retrace his steps to figure out what lower-class person he had been in contact with who could have communicated the disorder to him. He assumed that only the lower orders bore such afflictions.

Finally, he concluded that he must have contracted it as a result of clasping the hand of the housekeeper of Stephen Girard, an eccentric Philadelphia plutocrat. But a Philadelphia woman to whom he related his theory disabused him of

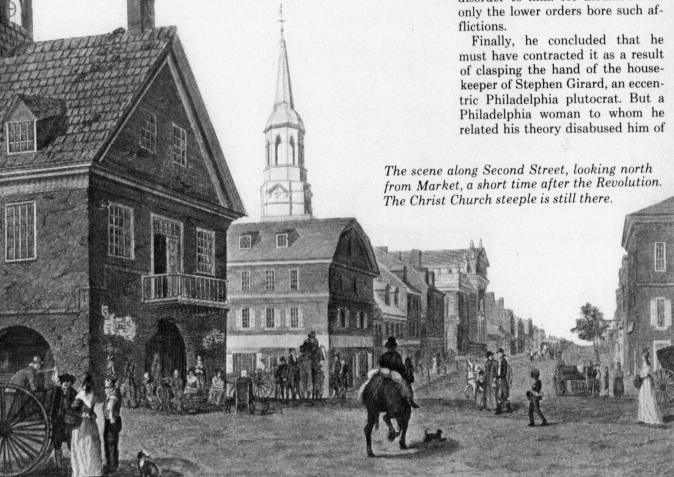

The scene along Second Street, looking north from Market, a short time after the Revolution. The Christ Church steeple is still there.

There were Dilworths in the Philadelphia schools even back in 1773.

his notion that only the serving class suffered from the itch. "Everybody had it in Philadelphia," she told him candidly, and he duly recorded the information in his papers.

"... A Remarkable Rumbling ..."

A number of strong earthquakes rocked old Philadelphia during the 1700s. One in 1727 "shook china off the shelves"; and in December of 1838 one occurred at night, "accompanied by a remarkable rumbling," one Philadelphian recorded. "People waked in their beds, the doors flew open, bricks fell from the chimneys. The consternation was serious, but, happily, no great damage ensued."

Other earthquakes of varying force, occurred in 1755, 1763 (two), and 1772. One of the two 1763 quakes occurred on a Sunday morning, during church services, which were adjourned, according to an account, "without a benediction."

Low Life Along the High Road

Ordinary people rarely traveled, in large part because means of transportation were slow and full of hazards. Roads were dusty in dry weather, mudholes in wet, circuitous, and ill-marked.

It literally was faster and easier in 1776 to go from Philadelphia to London by boat than to go from Philadelphia to Charleston, S. C.

For Indians in 1776 Philadelphia was a nice place to visit, but they didn't want to live there.

The difficulties of travel were among the reasons why Georgia didn't bother to send delegates to the First Continental Congress in 1774.

Only the very rich could afford the luxury of a carriage.

Just the same, roads in Pennsylvania were among the best in the colonies. The "Great Philadelphia Wagon Road," which ran west from Philadelphia to Lancaster and York, then on into Virginia and the Carolinas, was the "most important and heavily thronged highway in all America," according to historian Carl Bridenbaugh.

The covered wagon, known as the Conestoga wagon because of its use in trade between Philadelphia and the area along the Conestoga Creek near Harrisburg, had long since made its appearance as the major hauling vehicle by the time of the Revolution. It has been estimated that there were 20,000 wagons in Pennsylvania in 1765.

•

Public coaches traveled along the Great Wagon Road, but passengers often complained because of the cramped space and bumpy roads. Ten riders fit on the coaches, but they were cramped onto three small wooden benches. Often, a passenger sat next to the driver. There was no

overhead space for luggage, so the riders were forced to stow their things between their legs. The seats had no back, and curtains blocked all view of the countryside.

Thomas Twining, a Philadelphian, registered the following complaint: "It would be unreasonable to expect perfection in the arrangements of a new country, but ... the three passengers on the back seat were obliged to crawl across all of the other benches to get to their places ... There were no backs on the benches to support and relieve during a rough and fatiguing journey over a rough and ill-made road."

•

A woman traveler wrote a more caustic account of a trip to Lancaster: "In our journey we found the roads so bad that we walked part of the way ... (at one point) we climbed three fences to get clear of the mud ...

"We left Lancaster ... and in good spirits, but, alas, a sad accident ... for W. was driving care-

lessly and happily engaged with the lady he had the pleasure of driving with, and not mindful enough of his charge, drove against a large stump which stood in the way, by which the chair was overturned and the lady thrown out to a considerable distance, but happily received no hurt."

The same woman traveler wrote of her stay in a roadside inn:

"This evening our landlady, a dirty old Dutch woman, refused changing very dirty sheets for clean ones ... (After we insisted) we found to our mortification (that) she had taken the same sheeets, sprinkled them and then ironed them and hung them by the fire, and placed them again on the bed ... we necessitated to use our cloaks, etc., and this night slept without sheets."

•

Taverns offered overnight accommodations to travelers, though few would rate as first-class by today's standards. For starters, there was

virtually no such thing as a private room. One could go to sleep alone in the evening, and wake up to find two or more persons had joined him as bedfellows during the night.

John Adams, after spending a night in one such establishment, wrote that taverns are "places where the time, the money, the health, and the modesty of most that are young and many that are old, are wasted; ... (where) diseases, vicious habits, bastards, and legislators are frequently begotten ..."

A Scalping In Tulpehocken

Nearly 3,000 Indians lived in what is now the Philadelphia area when William Penn stepped ashore, but by 1776 there were virtually none. The last chief, Isaac Still, was known as "The Christian Indian," and had lived on the Logan estate, Stenton, and educated his son at the private Union School in Germantown. But in 1775, Still appar-

A grand jury was commissioned to investigate the drinking situation, and it discovered, among other things, that one out of every ten houses in the city was licensed to sell spiritous beverages

Free Library of Philadelphia

Colonial Philadelphia featured two taverns named "Indian Queen." This one was on Fourth Street.

ently decided that he had had enough of the white man. So he gathered together the few remaining members of his tribe and set off for the banks of the Wabash.

Indian-settler relations had been somewhat strained. In 1755, a six-year-old girl had been scalped in Tulpehocken, and an angry group of citizens offered a $700 reward to anyone who would murder two Delaware chiefs. The Indians tended to regard this as peculiar, since neither of the chiefs had had any connection with the scalping.

Pennsylvania Gov. Robert H. Morris declared war on the Indians in April of 1756. (The timing was interesting because he made the declaration immediately after receiving a letter from an anti-proprietary Quaker group called "The Friendly Association for Regaining and Preserving Peace With the Indians" urging him *not* to declare war on the Indians.

A Colonel Armstrong took his troops into an Indian village, massacred the inhabitants, and declared a victory. Philadelphia, at municipal expense, struck a medal to commemorate the occasion.

Labor Strife

America's first strike occurred in Philadelphia in 1782. The city's printers walked off the job demanding that their pay be increased to six dollars a week. They got it.

Crime and Violence

Philadelphians regarded their city as safe. Andrew Burnaby wrote to a friend that "upon dark nights, it (the city) is well lighted and watched by a patrol." The lighting consisted of flickering oil lamps, and the patrol consisted chiefly of Carlisle, the constable.

Not that everything was absolutely peaceful. Vandalism was occasionally a problem. Young hoodlums apparently enjoyed cutting off rain spouts, as well as stealing bells and door knockers. The stealing of door knockers became such a problem that a door-knocker-maker named Daniel King developed a new type, which he advertised in newspapers as follows:

"I have invented a brass knocker, the construction of which is peculiarly singular, and which will stand proof against the united attacks of those nocturnal sons of violence in their abominable and detestable executions."

Gang warfare between the rowdy "uptown" and "downtown" boys broke out on some occasions, with sticks, stones and firsts being the principal weapons. An occasional window would be broken.

These two carved figures were on display in taverns.

THE FOUNDING CITY

Brawling was also a frequent feature of tavern life, and the collection of taverns at the Delaware River end of Race Street was known as "Helltown," because of the many disturbances of the peace that occurred there.

One Philadelphian later recalled that inside the "Jolly Irishman," located at the northeast corner of Race and Water Streets, was "one continued scene and sound of daily riot and nightly brawl."

Initially, Philadelphia tavern licenses were restricted to widows and aging men judged to be of "good moral character." Eventually, though, it was realized that there were lots of thirsty Philadelphians and not enough widows and aging old men around. Licensing strictures were relaxed.

This proliferation of taverns (or "tippling houses," as they were sometimes called) dismayed the moralists of the period, who straightforwardly regarded alcohol as the tool of the devil.

A grand jury was commissioned not long before the Revolution to examine the situation, and it discovered, among other things, that "almost every tenth house in the city" was licensed to sell spiritous beverages.

•

Tavern names were often copied. Philadelphia had two taverns called the "Indian Queen," and two called the "Kouli Khan." At Fourth and Chestnut Streets, a man named Sober operated his Cross Keys Tavern, while only a block away Israel Israel had *his* Cross Keys.

Brokerage in Droppage

Joseph Dix, watchmaker, carried on a successful sideline related to the basic facts of life in early Philadelphia.

The facts were these—that nearly all of the pots, pans, and dishes were made of pottery, that the pottery tended to smash when dropped on the stone floors of the houses, that people tended to drop it, and that it was relatively expensive to replace.

His sideline was china repair and he declared in advertise-

Free Library of Philadelphia

The Old Tun Tavern was another popular meeting place.

ments that china brought to his shop at Front and Lombard would be "riveted" in a "very secure and neat manner." His specialty was providing replacement handles and spouts for all sizes of teapots.

How Race Street Got Its Name

Horse races were held on Race Street during the early days of the city, before it became a busy thoroughfare. (Later the race meets moved to Center Square — where City Hall now stands — and to tracks in Germantown and Bustleton.) Racing was one of the city's most popular spectator sports, along with bull-baiting and cock-fighting.

Horse racing was banned, however, by the Continental Congress at the beginning of the Revolution as part of Congress' efforts to curtial "extravagance and dissipation."

•

Theater was a popular pas-

Horse-racing was popular until Congress banned it it as part of putting the nation on a war footing.

time until it, like horse racing, was proscribed by Congress. The first theater company in the colonies opened in Philadelphia in 1749, presenting Shakespeare's *Richard III* and Congreve's *Love for Love*.

And by the Revolution there were two theaters, the Southwark and the New Theater. Tickets in the orchestra ran a fairly hefty 75 cents, but gallery seats were available for much less, usually 35 cents.

The "gallery gods," as the lower-priced seat-holders were known, were severe and wrathful critics. If they did not like a performance, they would fling tomatoes, pears, and loud remarks at the actors. When they really panned a show, rotten fruit and beer would rain down on the stage. During one particularly unpopular performance, the orchestra was forced to flee.

There were sometimes differ-ences in judgment between the gallery denizens and more sedate theatergoers. A newspaper critic excoriated "some ruffian in the gallery, who so frequently inter-rupted the performance, and in the most interesting scenes."

Keeping Dry Was for Sissies

The big fad in 1771 was the

Letter-press Printer

Ladies Dress-maker

. . . regarded as effeminate.

umbrella, and Philadelphia was the first place it arrived. Initially, it was used mainly as a sun-shade, but its potential for protecting its bearer from the rain was quickly recognized. Women bought them in great numbers, though use of the umbrella by men was slow in catching on. Many men regarded use of an umbrella as effeminate.

Frowsting at the Catamount

At the end of the Revolution, the Congress considered a proposal to make Greek the national language. The switch, it was argued, would not only help the new nation make a clean break with England, but also might infuse America with some of the genius of Athenian democracy.

The proposal failed and with it went the last remaining hopes

Brass Worker

that the English language could be saved from the outrages that would ultimately be inflicted on it in the United States. Already, Americans were exhibiting a gift for slang and improvisation of the mother tongue, as this Philadelphia newspaper social note indicates:

"By the Great Horn Spoon, the number of folk frowsting at a sponging at the Catamount Tavern fourbled and fivebled on a nippy evening in late October 1781. They lifted blackjack tankards and toss pots of ale, perry quince, cider, and flip to toast General George Washington's de-

Glass Blower

feat of Cornwallis at Yorktown . . ."

For those wishing a translation, "By the Great Horn Spoon," was a common phrase of the time, appropriate to almost all occasions. "Frowsting" meant lounging; and "sponging" was a drinking bout. "Fourbled" and "fivebled" meant fourfold and fivefold. "Blackjack tankards" were beer or ale cups made of wax coated leather, and "toss pots" were large cups. "Perry quince" was a popular spirituous beverage made of fermented pear juice, and "flip" was a hot drink made of sweetened rum mixed with beer or ale. ★ ★ ★

Songs such as this were heard in taverns as defiant Americans vented their spleens.

Behind the Gehrets' home (the modern 'wing' is on the left) is their kitchen garden, in which nothing grows that wasn't grown in the 18th century — and that includes the roses.

A Family's Journey into the Past

The Gehrets of Montgomery County find that adopting the life style of the 1700s is instructive — and fun. It also enhances their appreciation of self-cleaning ovens.

Photos by J. G. Domke

By Lita Solis-Cohen

Ten years ago, Philip and Ellen Gehret bought an old stucco farmhouse in Montgomery County, and went to work. Down came the wall which made the entranceway dark and cramped; in went new wiring, intercoms, and baseboard heating units; on went fresh new plaster and paint.

It all turned out to be a big mistake. Or almost all.

Over the past ten years the Gehrets have been diligently at work stripping off the plaster inside, and the stucco outside, and taking out much of the wiring, and putting the old walls back. In short, they have changed the house not just back to the way it was when they bought it, but back to what it was in 1754, when it was first built.

Moreover, they have re-created for themselves portions of the kind of life that was lived inside that house during the 1700s, when it was the home of Conrad Grubb, farmer and weaver. The Gehrets have even reinstalled an 18th-century loom in the upstairs room where they had found the marks made by the original weaving

Ellen Gehret gathers vegetables for the evening meal.

Ellen Gehret and Melanie compare kittens at the door.

gear in the old floorboards.

Each member of the family has — and wears on frequent occasions —the clothing of the period; they do cooking and baking in the huge walk-in fireplace that was discovered behind some plaster; and they have re-built the domed beehive baking oven on the original foundations.

It all happened because Ellen went on a house tour of historic homes sponsored by the Goschenhoppen Historians, a group devoted to preserving — and re-cre-ating — the history of the area around the Gehrets' house, which was called Goschenhoppen by the Penn-sylvania Dutch settlers.

Ellen Gehret mentioned during the tour that one of the doors in her house had a "thumb latch" like the one in the house being visited. The guide immediately asked if she would give him a tour of her house.

That began a sequence of discoveries, starting with a determination, from land records, of the true age of the house. Then the Gehrets found an old will that

itemized all of the 18th-century furnishings, and set out to find similar items at antique shops and auctions. It took them a whole summer to track down the proper red tiles to put on the roof of the bake oven.

Largely for fun, they read up on the costumes, food, and manners of the 18th century, and then tried them out. Each year the Gehrets put on their costumes and participate in the annual Goschenhoppen Folk Fes-tival, where old-time crafts and cookery are featured. The Gehrets call their colonial activities "living his-tory."

They don't try to live in the colonial era all the time. In fact, the Gehrets and their four children — Jef-frey, 15; Melanie, 13; Rodney, 12; and Beeky, 10 — keep themselves firmly anchored in the 20th century. Phil Gehret operates a successful sod business, the children attend local public schools, and the family indulges in such non-colonial pastimes as sailing vacations on Che-sapeake Bay.

Indeed, "new" sections of the house (built circa

Frying sausage over the open fire.

1810) have been kept in remodeled condition. That includes the very modern kitchen, and the tiled bathroom, which is preferred to the restored "two-holer" behind the house. Another glaring concession to modernism is clearly visible close by the authentic 18th-century "bottom" barn that the Gehrets moved to their farm board-by-board and rebuilt. The anomaly is a neatly fenced, floodlit, decidedly un-quaint tennis court.

What the Gehrets have done is to mix large amounts of 18th-century living into their 20th-century lives. One day a week, on the average, Ellen Gehret and her friend, Nancy Roan, get together to prepare a colonial meal for their families in black iron pots over the open fireplace.

On a fall evening, it might consist of fried homemade sausages, along with cabbages and potatoes from the Gehrets' "kitchen garden" (where nothing is grown, flowers or vegetables, that wasn't actually grown in Pennsylvania gardens in the 1700s).

Preserved beans and cherries, apple butter, sugar candy, dried apple (*schnitz* in the Pennsylvania Dutch dialect), together with homemade bread and berry pies, might also be served.

On the 130 acres around the farmhouse and barn, Phil Gehret raises beef cattle, pigs, and lambs. In the fall, more than a dozen neighbors will come over to assist with the butchering, which is again carried out according to colonial practice, except, of course, that much of the meat ends up in non-colonial-style freezers. Butchering becomes a three-day fall feast, with each family bringing its contributions for the mealtime groaning boards.

The men do the slaughtering, while the women trim and wrap the roasts. The women also make sausage and scrapple. The children cut up the fat, and render it for lard. The lard is used in pie crusts and for soap. (Ellen grates the soap up for her automatic washer, and says it works just fine.)

Part of the enjoyment of these experiences is dressing up in costume. Clothing and textiles are Ellen's areas of special expertise. She has written a book on the subject and lectures frequently.

Her costume consists of a white cap, a short white gown over a long petticoat, with a blue and white checked apron and kerchief. (Her research has shown that buttons were not in general use by women in rural areas of Pennsylvania until the 1820s.)

Phil wears a long, full-sleeved shirt, with a knotted kerchief around his neck, together with a vest and breeches of homespun linen. The clothes are made of homespun and woven materials, some of which he has

THE FOUNDING CITY

The Gehrets feel that some of the nicer aspects of 18th century life have disappeared. 'They had a sense of family,' says Ellen.

made on their loom. (Women didn't do weaving in the 1700s and the Gehrets have preserved that distinction. Phil does all the weaving.)

Getting authentic-appearing shoes is more difficult. Phil's shoes are black Kinney loafers to which buckles have been attached to give a colonial effect.

The question naturally arises: why do the Gehrets and their friends do it?

"Well, we don't water-ski, and you've got to be hooked on something," says Nancy Roan.

"Why do people like Beethoven?" asks Ellen.

There's more to it than that, though. The Gehrets clearly would like to borrow some aspects of 18th century life that they feel have disappeared or deteriorated over the past two centuries.

"They had a sense of family" and shared participation, says Ellen of her colonial forbears.

The Gehrets try to recapture some of this in their weekly suppers and fall gatherings. "No one could survive alone in the old days. We get together with friends for all kinds of projects. Living history is our social life."

The Gehrets say that they also gain enjoyment from watching the way in which aspects of colonial life being renewed today are the latest in solutions to the problems of modern society. "The food we have is all home grown," says Ellen. "You pay a pretty price for organically grown produce at health food stores."

She is particularly amused to see supermarkets stocking dried apples, under various trade names, as the latest solution to the problem of how to get low-calorie sweet snacks. "No matter what you call them, it's just *schnitz,*" she says.

One thing is clear: the Gehrets do this mainly for themselves, and not with any sense that they are performing, or making a presentation to other people. "We used to have Girl Scouts and school groups come here,

Neighbors come over to help with tasks like flailing grain, and, in the fall, butchering.

Melanie's bedroom furniture includes a real feather bed.

but not any longer," says Ellen Gehret. "I tended to feel as if I was living in a museum, which is not what we're trying to do."

The Gehret children do invite classmates to come over and visit, and they enjoy sleeping on straw mattresses and the meals that often include colonial specialties cooked over the open fire.

"It's fun," says Melanie.

Colonial life, the Gehrets and their friends say, has other appeals. "There are countless pleasures for all of the senses," says Nancy Roan. "The smells from cooking over a wood fire, the sounds of the barnyard . . . the warm colors of the redware pie plates and the crocks,

the smooth texture of old pewter, the ripple (of the grain) in old wood, the rough feel of coarse homespun and straw baskets are some of the nicest. Knowing that all of these things were made by hand from materials that come from the earth gives us a good feeling."

But the Gehrets don't regard colonial life with uncritical adoration. "Hoisting a cast iron pot when it's full is a lot of work," Ellen says. "Doing that kind of work," she continues, "makes me respect my self-cleaning oven and self-defrosting refrigerator. And don't that I don't appreciate plumbing, the car, and modern medicine. Using deodorant is a lot better than tucking a sprig of basil under your bonnet." ★★★

Franklin and His Friends

Franklin and His Friends

The title of this chapter takes a certain amount of liberty with the facts. Truth to tell, we aren't sure Franklin really liked all of the people we have included; in fact, there may be a couple that he never even met, though all were contemporaries of his in Philadelphia.

But our intentions were honorable that the people of Philadelphia in 1776 were just that — people. To an amazing extent, they knew one another, were friends (and enemies), and, just like now, they had their successes and failures, good days and bad, ups and downs.

For Better or Worse, Franklin Made Us What We Are

A far more complicated Franklin is hidden behind the usual picture of a crank with a kite who wrote a lot of quaint little sayings. In many ways he was a 20th century American accidentally born in the 18th.

By Willard S. Randall

In the late 1820s, a poor boy from County Tyrone, Ireland, wandered into a used book shop in Belfast and purchased a small volume for a few pennies. The boy was Thomas Mellon, who was to become the founder of the Mellon banking dynasty in Pittsburgh, and the financier behind Andrew Carnegie, John D. Rockefeller and assorted other millionaires. The book he bought, read, and made his Bible was the autobiography of a man who had become, within the few decades since his death in 1790, the most obscure and forgotten of the American founding fathers: Benjamin Franklin.

From the autobiography emerged a picture of Franklin as a penny-pinching, hard-driving, self-disciplined young businessman who became the model for robber barons and laborers in the America of the late 19th and early 20th centuries. Mellon's discovery was repeated by millions of others. The slogans of Franklin's "Poor Richard," such as "A penny saved is a penny earned" and "Early to bed and early to rise makes a man healthy, wealthy, and wise," became ingrained in the American psyche.

But behind this somewhat artificial picture that Franklin had constructed of himself for posterity there remained a deeper, more important, and much more fascinating Franklin, whose true dimensions remain elusive even today.

This was the Franklin whose direct influence on the foreign affairs of America was felt for more than a century. Indeed, even today, as America enters its third century, after it has become the longest-lived republic in the history of the world, it is partly because of Franklin that we are the most emulated and loved, the most hated and reviled, and the most misunderstood nation on earth.

It wouldn't be until the 1930s that historians began to look piercingly behind the simplistic view Franklin liked to convey of himself, especially in the pages of his brief, incomplete autobiography.

They found that, in the complex years not covered by the autobiography, Franklin had become a world-renowned scientist, statesman, and man of letters. They also learned that many of his more important contributions were made anonymously, in anterooms and caucuses, in clandestine meetings with spies and emissaries, in unrecorded meetings of committees and corporations, in private conversations with world leaders.

What has emerged in recent years is a picture of Franklin as an apostle of modern times, a man so far ahead of his 18th-century contemporaries that few Americans appreciated or understood him during his lifetime or afterwards.

Moreover, by the time Americans became aware that Franklin was anything more than a crank with a kite and key in his hand or the author of a quaint little

book of sayings, thousands of his more important letters, papers and documents were scattered or lost.

His birthplace and subsequent residences had been torn down while other revolutionary leaders' homes were restored into historic shrines. Far from being preserved, Franklin's papers, the evidence of his greatness, had been plundered by Hessians, left to moulder in a stable, given away as souvenirs, and even used by a London tailor as patterns for clothing.

One reason for his early obscurity was that he was too old to become a candidate for President. He was a generation older than George Washington and John Adams, two generations older than Thomas Jefferson, James Monroe and James Madison, and was, throughout his political career, more interested in diplomacy than elective office. He spent most of his life outside the country he helped to create.

Except for minister plenipotentiary, the highest rank he ever held was the equivalent to governor of Pennsylvania, which he achieved for a few years shortly before his death. He was, in fact, the only great leader of the Revolution who did *not* become President; his papers were never made a part of the National Archives, and there are no monuments dedicated to him by the federal government.

Philadelphia, his adopted city, did, somewhat belatedly, honor his memory with a scientific institute founded in 1824 bearing his name, and, one hundred years later, with the Benjamin Franklin bridge across the Delaware River.

Fortunately, one of the institutions Franklin helped found more than two centuries ago set out to gather and preserve every scrap of his artifacts it could find. The American Philosophical Society has acquired more than 13,000 of his letters, plus numerous portraits, prints, furnishings and personal possessions of Franklin and his family.

Still, it must be said that if Benjamin Franklin's true importance has only recently come to be understood, part of the fault lies with Franklin himself. Among his futuristic inventions was personal public relations. Many of the tales he told on himself were half-truths aimed at projecting the image he wished to portray. Many axioms he gave the world to follow he himself ignored. He was a man full of contradictions, a man who dealt harshly with his own family while soliciting the friendship of casual strangers, a man who colored facts to sharpen the points of his stories.

Not that the facts needed embellishment; everything about Franklin was, from his boyhood, extraordinary,

While the birthplaces of other founding fathers were being converted into national shrines, Franklin's family home in Boston was torn down. Many of his papers were lost, and for a time, he was nearly forgotten.

and, considering his unpropitious start in life, virtually everything he achieved was amazing.

One of 17 children of a Boston soap and candle-maker, Benjamin Franklin was born January 17, 1706, and seemed destined, as the tenth child, for the clergy. His father, Josiah, a staunch Puritan, wanted to offer Benjamin as a tithe to the church, so he sent him at age eight to study at Boston Latin School. This was Ben Franklin's only formal education. He failed arithmetic, excelled in reading and writing, was exposed to music and dancing —and was taken out of school by the age of ten to go to work in his father's candle-making shop.

Benjamin wanted to go to sea, but an older brother, Josiah, had been lost at sea and his father would not hear of it.

Benjamin foiled this plan by running away and hiding on a privateering ship.

When he returned, his father had abandoned the idea of both clergyman and candle-maker, and had decided to sign Benjamin to a nine-year apprenticeship under another older brother, James, a London-trained printer.

At age 12, Benjamin began to learn the printer's trade that would make him rich by age 40. In his brother's shop, he also came in contact with the best young minds in Boston, most of them rebels against the austere, autocratic religious establishment that ruled almost every aspect of the colony's life, who came in to transact business, or just talk.

An ambitious, arrogant young student of writing, Benjamin quickly learned his trade and mastered the art of satire, the form of writing he preferred from first to last. He used it in his "Silence Dogood" letters, written at age 15, and stealthily on Sundays when other Boston boys were in church. These letters, which he slipped under the door of his brother's shop before it opened Mondays, were masterful parodies of the London writings he had studied from books sneaked out of bookstores, before they were put on sale, by apprentice friends.

The letters, 14 of them, created a stir in Boston, making his brother's paper, the *New England Courant,* even more controversial, and Benjamin cockier than ever, especially after he finally revealed that it was he who had written the saucy critiques of the Puritan way of life.

Another result was that the already strained relationship between Benjamin and his printer brother became even more strained. Benjamin began thinking of ways to break his indenture and leave his discipline-minded brother, and the opportunity came soon enough.

James Franklin was jailed for accusing the legislature of conniving in the thriving piracy along the New England coast, and served a month, during which time 16-year-old Benjamin ran the paper.

On his release, James took up the editorial cudgels again. In January 1723, in an early test of freedom of the press in America, he was ordered to cease printing "any pamphlet or paper of the like nature, except it first be supervised by the secretary of the province."

James and his friends decided to dodge the issue by putting out the paper in Benjamin's name. James returned the lad's indentures of apprenticeship, "whereby I became free," Benjamin wrote years later. Actually, new and secret papers were made out, but Benjamin knew his brother dared not produce them—and used this fact to illegally break his apprentice's bond.

With the help of a young friend who enlisted the sympathy of a ship's captain by telling the captain that Benjamin had gotten a girl pregnant and was trying to run away, the 17-year-old sold some books and slipped aboard ship, sailing for New York. Unable to find work there, he walked most of the way to Philadelphia, arriving in the rain with an empty stomach.

Already independent, a rebel, an opportunist, a journeyman printer and a fair writer, young Franklin had little trouble talking his way into a job in Philadelphia, where he prospered. Inside seven months, the tall, strong, brash young man had saved enough to buy a new suit and return to Boston to try to make peace with his family — and borrow the money to sail to England to buy his own printing equipment on credit.

His family turned him down. His father said anyone who gave credit to a mere boy was a fool. His brother learned to like him even less for showing up with hard money jingling in his pocket and buying drinks for envious apprentices.

But Franklin had to go back to Philadelphia without any financial assistance having been proffered. Once he got back, though, an alternative seemed to open: Pennsylvania's royal governor William Keith promised to send letters of introduction and credit to influential people in London on Franklin's behalf. After receiving this promise—and, incidentally, giving his own pledge of matrimony to Deborah Read, his landlady's daughter— Franklin sailed for London in 1724.

When he arrived he discovered that the unreliable governor had failed to send along the letters. It was his first lesson in dealing with British officials. But Franklin took jobs in two of London's largest and best printing houses, and accomplished several things. He made good money, became an expert at his trade, loaned much of his savings to friends who squandered it, consorted with a variety of women and men of low station and high. He even managed to meet the secretary of the Royal Society by offering to show him "curiosities from the northern parts of America." He managed to sell one of them, an asbestos purse, to the society for the handsome sum of one guinea.

After two years in London, he returned, first taking a job with a merchant, becoming, in his own words, "expert in selling." When the merchant died, the nervy young man asked for his old job back from printer Samuel Keimer — and got it. Franklin left Keimer again and went into a partnership with a young friend. The partnership split up, and at age 22, Franklin was the sole owner of a successful printing business, and publisher of the *Pennsylvania Gazette.*

Franklin improved every business venture he put his hand to. When he became postmaster of Philadelphia, in part to get free mailing privileges for his newspaper, it produced only 150 pounds a year. By the time the British fired him from the post four decades later, Franklin was making 1,500 pounds a year, and turning an additional 3,000 pounds profit over to the Crown.

Established in business, he decided to settle down, being, by his own account, tired of "that hard-to-be-governed passion of youth (that) hurried me frequently into intrigues with low women that fell in my way which were attended with some expense and great inconvenience, besides a continual risk to my health by a distemper which of all things I dreaded, though by great good luck I escaped it."

(One of the "inconveniences" was an illegitimate son, William. The identity of the child's mother was Franklin's most carefully-guarded secret. His paternity was acknowledged by Franklin when the child was brought to live above the print shop late in 1730.)

On September 1, 1730, according to Franklin, he "took to wife" Deborah Read. This wasn't as straightforward a proceeding as it might sound because Deborah's mother had talked her into marrying John Rogers, a potter, during Benjamin's absence in London. Rogers, who was rumored to have been a bigamist, left town a short while later, leaving behind Deborah and a large number of angry creditors.

Formal marriage was out of the question so long as Rogers' death could not be proven, and, in any event, Franklin would have had to assume Rogers' debts to make the contract binding. So the couple lived as common-law for all of their 44 years together.

The arrangement and the business thrived. Franklin made himself known throughout the city in many ways. He set up a reading group, called first the "Leathern Apron Club" and then the Junto, whose members debated literature and science; he bought books for the subscription library that was the forerunner of the city's first public library. He also made himself humbly conspicuous, pushing a wheelbarrow filled with newspapers for sale through the street, a task usually performed by an apprentice.

His specialized skills as a printer enabled him to take on a large press run of Pennsylvania currency with such dispatch and skill that he was named to the sinecure of clerk to the Pennsylvania Assembly. All of the province's printing and advertising flowed to the little shop hard by the Jersey Market on High Street, where Franklin supervised the printing while Deborah sold crown soap made by the Franklins of Boston, printing and writing materials, legal forms, books, quills, ink parchment, sealing wax, spectacles, and soon, a new Franklin production, *Poor Richard's Almanac.*

Franklin had, for that time, the rare gift of the gambler's instinct combined with shrewdness in business that led to his lifelong ability to parlay one asset or accomplishment into the next.

One early manifestation of this instinct was his introduction of an almanac on an already-crowded market in 1732. Besides the Bible, almanacs, with their combination of weather forecasts and folksy sayings, were one book found in almost every colonial home. Most almanacs, though, were poorly printed and poorly written. Franklin combined his printing and writing talents to produce a sensation that soon was selling 10,000 copies a year and did more than anything else to make Poor Richard's creator a rich man.

The secret of its success wasn't originality. The title was a more or less straightforward steal from "Poor Robin," a personality created by Benjamin's brother James. What Franklin did was take the thoughts of others, and polish them into homilies, parodies, aphorisms, and epigrams that usually had a practical point, sometimes took a risque slant, and always possessed a memorable quality.

Here's a sampling:

"He that lies down with dogs shall rise up with fleas."

"To lengthen thy life, lessen thy meals."

"Marry your son when you will, but your daughter when you can."

"He that falls in love with himself will have no rivals."

"It is easier to suppress the first desire than to satisfy all that follow it."

"Work as if you were to live 100 years, pray as if you were to die tomorrow."

If any expressions of the pioneer American virtues could have been more timely, it is hard to imagine. Europeans with little money were flocking through Philadelphia to settle the lands to the west, and Poor Richard's homespun philosophy went with them.

He was also perpetually pursuing plans for self-improvement, a drive for "moral perfection" as he put it.

The scheme, well publicized (by him) in later life, included keeping a list of items of his personal conduct needing improvement and then grading himself weekly. The 13 headings, together with a latter-day evaluation of how he did, included:

"Temperance. Eat not to dullness, Drink not to elevation."

Franklin evolved from a vegetarian in his teens into a trencherman who preferred old Madeira and good champagne (he kept five kinds in his French wine cellar), but he was never seen drunk. He never took snuff or smoked tobacco.

"Silence. Speak not but what may benefit others or yourself. Avoid trifling conversation."

Garrulous when among friends, Franklin kept silent in public, except to ask or answer questions. He often gave the appearance of being asleep.

"Order. Let all of your things have their places. Let each part of your business have its time."

Franklin's inevitable failure. He was too busy most of his life to organize his time and papers. His records as minister

to France were such a mess that he made John Adams nearly apoplectic with rage. Fortunately, Franklin had a superb memory that compensated somewhat for this failing.

"Resolution. Resolve to perform what you ought. Perform without fail what you resolve."

As a young man, he paid more heed to this item than as an elder statesman who had learned the advantages of necessary changes of position and direction.

In three categories — frugality, industry and justice — Franklin would rate himself higher than others would. Under "cleanliness," he would earn high marks from the French secret police, who investigated him at one point and marveled at the cleanliness of his linen underthings.

But in two areas of self-perfection, Franklin failed badly. Under "Sincerity . . . use no hurtful deceit," he'd have to admit that in this regard his love of the written hoax and the spoken evasion had won out, especially in his masterfully deceptive diplomacy.

When it came to "Justice. Wrong none, by doing injuries or omitting the benefits that are your duty," he was, for starters, grossly unfair in words and deeds to his brother James, whom he libeled regularly and often throughout his life.

He was also unyielding and inflexible to his son William. When he disapproved of William's choice of a wife, he sailed home to America a short time before the wedding and was cold and formal to the bride, neglecting her, even when she was dying during the Revolution.

Under the heading "chastity," Franklin was most vulnerable to attack. His common-law relationship with Deborah and his illegitimate son made him the target of political mudslinging.

After taking Deborah "to wife," however, there's no convincing evidence that he ever philandered, other than a remarkable sketch made by Charles Willson Peale in London in 1767 through the cracked door of the 61-year-old Franklin's apartment, showing a couple in amorous encounter. The features of both lovers are indistinct, however, and it may or may not have been Franklin and his landlady's daughter, pretty Polly Stevenson, who was with Franklin much of her life and was with him at his death.

Franklin also tried to order the lives of his family, again with mixed success.

His wife, Deborah, who endured a great deal from him and apparently loved him greatly, needed little prodding. In the early years together, she made all his clothes in addition to keeping his house and his shop. Yet, by his lights, she strayed occasionally, as Franklin later at-

tested, particularly in regard to frugality.

"My breakfast was for a long time bread and milk (no tea) and I ate it out of a twopenny earthen porringer with a pewter spoon. But mark how luxury will enter families, and make a progress, in spite of principles.

"Being called one morning to breakfast, I found it in a china bowl with a spoon of silver. They had been bought for me without my knowledge by my wife and had cost her the enormous sum of three and twenty shillings, for which she had no other excuse or apology to make but that she thought *her* husband deserv'd a silver spoon and china bowl as well as any of his neighbors."

•

Deborah bore Franklin a son, Francis Folger, and a daughter, Sally. Frankie was Benjamin's favorite. The child's death at four of smallpox was one of the great blows of Franklin's life.

Years earlier, Benjamin and his brother James had attacked the first inoculations in Boston in James' newspaper as an unwise experiment. When an epidemic swept Philadelphia in November 1736, Franklin hesitated until the boy could recover from a fever. In the meantime, the child died. As would inevitably have been the case, he must have held himself to blame for the child's death. Worse still, there was some basis for the self-indictment.

To save others his grief, Franklin editorialized in favor of inoculation in his *Gazette,* but nearly half a century later, he still broke down and cried when he talked of his little Frankie.

Benjamin Franklin's first excursion into local prominence came when he successfully organized militia to counter French privateering raids up the Delaware River in 1747.

For years the city had trembled with fear periodically, exposed as it was to enemy attacks because the controlling Quaker pacifists refused to violate their religious scruples by appropriating funds for defense. When Franklin organized a volunteer militia association, more than 1,000 men immediately flocked to his standard.

Secretly, the Quakers were pleased: their business and properties, not to mention their lives, were protected at no financial or moral cost to them. The ruling Penn family, however, was annoyed, mainly since they saw Franklin as a potential threat.

In the late 1740s, Franklin stayed out of local politics, drawing from both the Proprietary Party loyal to the Penns and the Anti-Proprietary Party for contributions to the numerous public charities

Franklin stove: Conserving energy . . .

Franklin chair-step ladder: For libraries . . .

Franklin's personal tankard: A rare extravagance . . .

he espoused, including the founding of Pennsylvania Hospital and the Academy of Philadelphia.

But more and more after 1750, the prosperous middle-aged printer-post-master-philanthropist, by now obviously one of the leading figures in the colony, was drawn into the melee of Philadelphia and Pennsylvania politics. In 1751, he became an assemblyman.

As French and Indian invasion again threatened in 1754, Franklin became the military leader of the province. After bloody Indian raids in Northumberland County at present-day Easton and Bethlehem, he supervised construction of forts along the frontier and, although he wore common buckskin and slept in cold cabins with the other citizen-soldiers, he heard himself gratefully called "General Franklin" by the German immigrants.

Pennsylvania couldn't adequately defend itself, however, so long as the Quakers blocked the appropriation of funds for arms, and so long as the Penns refused to allow their huge land holdings to be taxed equitably.

The first impediment was removed when many Quakers abandoned provincial politics rather than renounce their religious beliefs in the face of angry outcries over the slaughter in the frontier settlements. The second obstacle — money from the Penns — would prove greater.

In 1757, the Assembly voted to send Franklin to London to prevail personally on the Penns; that failing, he was to lobby before Parliament and the court to convert the province into a crown colony and bring it under royal protection.

The esteem given a colonial agent in London in that era was even less than

that accorded a Harrisburg lobbyist today, especially when the Penns were forewarned and had organized their powerful friends against him.

Yet Franklin had a new form of influence. Since April 1756, Franklin had been a member of the prestigious Royal Society, a tribute to his pioneering experiments in electricity, which had been going on, at the time he was elected, for more than a decade.

He had begun them at age 42, when he had sold a half-interest in his business enterprises for a modest fortune, and decided to devote himself, and his time, to things that interested him. Steadily, he drifted into the still-primitive domain of science.

When Franklin's Junto had, a few years earlier, turned its attention to scientific reading and discussion, the idea of leather-aproned artisans dabbling in science was considered something of a scientific curiosity in itself. To egg them on, an English Quaker merchant named Peter Collinson, who closely followed events in Philadelphia and was book-buying agent for the Library Company, sent the library the present of a large glass tube, over three feet long and thick as a man's wrist, with instructions for making sparks.

Collinson's gift of glass served to further focus Franklin's interest.

"I never was before engaged in any study that so totally engrossed my attention and my time as this has lately done," Franklin wrote Collinson March 28, 1747. "I have during some months past had little leisure for any thing else."

Franklin, the one-time mathematics dunce, spent five years of tedious and repetitive trial and error, working with the crudest of tools: glass tubes, tubes of resin, a gun barrel and a cork, iron shot, wax and glass plates. He reported each step to Collinson, who published Franklin's results in a series of five articles in the proceedings of the Royal Society.

Franklin was the first to grasp the principle that electricity flows in a current like a fluid, never destroyed, "the fire only circulating." He coined the terms "positive," "negative," "plus," "minus," "armature," "battery," "brush," "charge," "condense," "conductor," as he went along. His theories and statements on electricity made in those first supercharged months of experimentation still stand, with few changes, more than two centuries later.

Interestingly, Franklin himself did not initially appreciate what he had done. After three years, Franklin halted his experiments temporarily, disappointed, he wrote Collinson, "that we have hitherto been able to discover nothing in the way of use to mankind."

By this time, fortunately, he'd sent off to England his theories on thunderstorms and electricity. "The electric current is attracted by points," he wrote Collinson July 29, 1750. "We do not know whether this property is in lightning. But since (it) agrees in all particulars wherein we can already compare them, is it not probable they agree likewise in this? Let the experiment be made."

Franklin was well aware of the dangers electricity posed. Six of his friends had been knocked senseless during one electrical experiment in his house; he himself had been knocked out twice and badly bruised by electrical charges; and, in an attempt to make use of electricity's lethal potential, he had even used the current to kill and cook a turkey for a picnic.

It wasn't until a muggy June day in 1752 that Franklin finally got around to testing his own hypothesis in a thunderstorm in an open field (now called Franklin Square) used to graze sheep near his house.

With his tall, 22-year-old son William, Franklin put on a loose coat and took an odd-looking kite made of a large thin silk kerchief with a 16-inch wire atop it. At the other end, an insulating tail of silk ribbon was connected to the twine leader by a small housekey. They hurried through the pelting rain to a shepherd's shed at the edge of the common.

While Benjamin stood inside the shed, William raced across the field to get the cumbersome kite aloft.

The first pass was a flop; no bolt of lightning darted down the wire, and the kite collapsed.

Again, William streaked across the field. The kite soared, whirled. Thunder roared. This time, the puzzled Franklin didn't tap the key with his knuckle — but watched amazed as the silken strands on the ribbon stood out separately, straight. Carefully, Franklin touched the key. Electric current coursed through his arm.

Luckily, the electricity had come from the dense clouds; it was not lightning as such. Had lightning danced down the wire, Franklin and his son would have been incinerated. As it was, Franklin had proved his point, and when the loose-knit fraternity of fellow scientists learned of his feat first from the Royal Society's journal, he became world-famous.

Not only was living with Franklin risky in those days, it was also kind of crazy. At times he was the archetypal mad scientist, cramming his house with odd-looking paraphernalia and wiring it with lightning rods and wires running down hallways and walls, wires that were connected to bells that made a thunderstorm worse by ringing, ringing, ringing whenever current passed down the wires through the house.

By the time Franklin left for England, he'd made other, more immediately

'. . . Of all the things England has,' Franklin wrote, 'I envy it most its people . . . .'

useful inventions — bifocals, a copying machine, the Franklin stove, the first catheter. He made them all public, along with his lightning rods, and never patented them. He was not interested in monetary profit from his scientific inventions. His new pre-eminence was bringing him dividends of another sort, the correspondence and, later, the friendship of the leaders of government and letters of his time, most of them amateur dabblers in science themselves.

Franklin was able to make even more effective use of his new intellectual credentials, and the entree it gave him in England, where his reputation as a scientist and philosopher and preceded him, and made him a sensation during his first visit as Pennsylvania's agent from 1757 to 1762. He received one honor after another: a reception at Cambridge University with "particular regard shown by

AN ADDRESS
To THE PUBLIC,
FROM THE
Pennsylvania Society for promoting the Abolition of Slavery, and the Relief of Free Negroes, unlawfully held in Bondage.

Signed by order of the Society,
B. FRANKLIN, *President.*

Philadelphia, 9th of *November*, 1789.

Franklin served as president of the Pennsylvania Society for Promoting the Abolition of Slavery, despite the fact that he owned two slaves himself. They functioned as his manservants, and he had taken them to France with him. The conflict between his roles as slave-owner and abolitionist appeared not to bother him.

the chancellor and vice-chancellor," a triumphal trip through Scotland and Ireland. Edinburgh made him a burgher and guild brother of the city; St. Andrews University made him a doctor of laws. He also received an honorary degree from Oxford.

Franklin remained in England for five years, parlaying his scientific fame into political influence and collecting accolades.

And, if no great triumph had been achieved, the years had not been uneventful. For one thing, William Franklin had followed his father's errant example and fathered a bastard son of his own, William Temple Franklin. Notwithstanding this indiscretion, William, now 32, had also won appointment as the royal governor of New Jersey.

However, Franklin and his son had the aforementioned falling-out over William's decision to marry a West Indian woman. The elder Franklin had unceremoniously sailed for home, boycotting the nuptials.

The full reasons why Franklin came home are not crystal clear. He had, apparently, toyed with the idea of settling permanently in England, but had discarded the notion. He told a friend, William Strahan, that he couldn't stay because his wife couldn't make the voyage, and he wrote to her, "I gave . . . two reasons why I could not think of removing hither. One my affection to Pennsylvania, and long-established friendships and other connections there; the other (being) your invincible aversion to crossing the seas." It was not, at all events, to be an auspicious homecoming.

During Franklin's absence, his constituents had routinely returned him each year to his seat in the Pennsylvania Assembly. But on returning, he found growing opposition to himself and to his anti-Penn feud. Quaker leaders, usually divided, joined forces to unseat him, dredging up his by then nearly-forgotten insult against the Germans (whom Franklin had called "the Palatine Boors") to turn out the German settlers against him. Franklin was drubbed by 1,000 votes.

It seemed Pennsylvania was determined to drive out its most honored citizen. To Strahan in London, Franklin wrote: "No friend can wish me more in England than I do myself. But before I go, everything I am concern'd in must be settled here as to make another return to America unnecessary."

Then he continued wistfully, "Of all the enviable things England has, I envy it most its people. Why should that petty island — which compar'd to America is like a stepping stone in a brook, scarce enough of it above water to keep one's shoes dry — why, I say, should that little island enjoy in almost every neighborhood more sensible, virtuous and elegant minds than we can collect in ranging 100 leagues or our vast forests?"

Franklin had lived well in London, hiring a coach and giving lavish dinners for his friends, and he had witnessed the zenith of British imperial conquest, the victory over France and the resplendent coronation of young George III. There was little to compare to this in provincial Philadelphia; yet he tried to console himself by ordering construction of a handsome, three-story house with courtyard and arches set back from Market Street just beyond Third.

He wasn't to stay in Philadelphia long enough to see it finished, however. Soon after his trouncing in the Assembly, his party, still in control, sent him back to London as colonial agent. This time, they had openly voted for a change to royal government. Governor John Penn wrote to relatives in London that Franklin and his aide, Galloway, had been like two sorcerers, manipulating members in secret caucuses to accomplish this.

Again, Deborah stayed behind. In the last 18 years of her life, she was with her husband only this once.

Franklin returned to an England preoccupied with more important matters than Pennsylvania's form of government. The long war with France had mired England in debt. The new government was insisting that America, which, after all, had been freed by British arms from the French menace, pay its fair share of the debt.

In February 1764, a few weeks before Franklin landed, George Grenville proposed a Stamp Act in the House of Commons. The measure touched off a year of riots in America — and struck a match to the long fuse of revolution.

Because he'd recommended two of the three American stamp tax commissioners and several collectors, Franklin was suspected at home of advocating the unpopular measure in the first place, and, in fact, initially he did think it was a good idea. For nine days, his family and friends had to barricade themselves inside the house on Race Street with guns until the mob's ardor cooled.

Ultimately, though, Franklin got the message that Americans didn't like the Stamp Act, shifted his ground, and, more than anyone else, could claim credit for the Stamp Act's repeal.

Franklin first met with Prime Minister Grenville to protest the tax and suggest alternate schemes for raising revenue.

Then he gathered information from his American correspondents and took it to Lord Dartmouth, president of the Board of Trade who, in effect, controlled the commerce and government of all the American colonies.

Dartmouth ignored him, but meanwhile, back in America, delegates from nine colonies were gathering in New York for an unauthorized and extralegal Stamp Act Congress. The delegates, among other things, resolved that "no taxes have ever been or can be constitutionally imposed but by their respective legislatures." They also voted to break off trade with England.

America had actually called a British law unconstitutional. Both sides were now in an exceptionally ugly mood, and real trouble was in the offing, when a sudden change opened the way for reconciliation.

In January 1766, Grenville's regime fell and a more liberal government came to Whitehall. Gathering around ailing William Pitt, liberals challenged the anti-American policy then in force, and called for an end to the stamp duty. A great debate began.

"The Americans are the sons, not the bastards of England," Pitt reminded Parliament.

That was January 14, 1766. Three weeks later, as protests flowed in from British merchants and manufacturers that thousands of workers faced unemployment if American trade continued to decline, Benjamin Franklin was called to the bar to testify on behalf of America before the House of Commons.

Night and day for three weeks he'd been lobbying intensively, buttonholing and visiting dozens of pro-Pitt members. He hired a man to hand out cartoons at the entrance of Commons, wrote a series of articles for his friend Strahan's *London Chronicle*. Now, as the unofficial ambassador of America, he'd been called to answer questions carefully planted among Pitt's friends.

Now his testimony could make it all pay off. For four exhausting hours, Franklin coolly and impassively stood the grilling of friends and foes, fielding some 170 questions. During those hours, he gave England's rulers a rare view of the mind of America, a mental picture that would linger for decades. It can be argued that had Parliament paid even closer attention, and kept the memory fresher, England might have kept her American colonies.

At the bottom line of Franklin's performance was the key to the quarrel, expressed succinctly in one of the questions: "Is there a power on earth that can force (the Americans) to erase the resolutions (of the Stamp Act Congress)?"

"No power, how great soever," Franklin replied, "can force men to change their opinions."

When Franklin had arrived back in England in 1764, he'd presented Pennsylvania's petition for royal rule to the Privy Council, where consideration of it was postponed indefinitely.

Instead of accepting this defeat, however, Franklin dug in for a long fight, making himself a part of the political landscape of London it was increasingly impossible to overlook.

In the meantime, though, he sought to use his status as the most celebrated American in England to the private advantage of himself and his friends.

With his son William, the Whartons of Philadelphia, Sir William Johnson (the Indian commissioner for the northern colonies) and many of the leading figures in English politics, he formed a grandiose venture called the Grand Ohio Company to seek a royal charter for a vast new western province covering present-day Indiana and Illinois.

The bold scheme nearly succeeded, but the continuing seditious activity in New England turned English leaders sour on anything that might benefit Americans by the early 1770s. When Bostonians polluted their harbor with 10,000 pounds' worth of East India tea, Franklin had to set aside his personal speculations.

He also undertook a step that quickly ended his career as a British official. The city of Boston has been a tinderbox since 1768, when two regiments of tough British regulars were unloaded on Long Wharf, but few Bostonians knew that two Americans were responsible for the good fortune of having the troops visited upon their city.

In his function as postmaster for the colonies, Franklin had apparently become aware of correspondence from Massachusetts Governor Thomas Hutchinson and Hutchinson's brother-in-law, Andrew Oliver, the Massachusetts chief justice, to a certain former British official.

The letters indicated that Hutchinson and Oliver had urged the British to send in troops, and to take a hard line to punish the Boston patriots. In his role as agent to Massachusetts, Franklin saw fit to forward the purloined letters to Sam Adams and other radical Bostonians for their private delectation. Only Sam Adams couldn't keep a secret, as Franklin probably well knew, and soon all America and England knew of the correspondence.

At first, Franklin kept his involvement secret. But then the son of the man who had been the addressee accused one of William Franklin's friends of having purloined the letters. The two fought one indecisive duel, and had scheduled a rematch when Franklin finally decided to step forward. He admitted his misdeed in the *London Advertiser*.

Immediately his enemies seized this chance to have him hauled before the Privy Council; in effect, Franklin was placed under arrest.

In the darkest scene of his life, Franklin appeared at the Cockpit, the grand hall where the Privy Council of the House of Lords met at a long table, before a packed gallery, on January 29, 1774. He was treated to a merciless four-hour lambasting by British Solicitor General Alexander Wedderburn.

As part of an uninterrupted series of mocking, slashing rhetorical questions, Wedderburn declared that "no gentleman's letters would now be safe" from the postmaster general.

"Franklin will henceforth esteem it a libel to be called a man of letters," Wedderburn chided.

Throughout the sarcastic tirade, Franklin stood stoically silent, but there was no concealing his deep humiliation. When the hearing was over, he left without uttering a word in his defense. The next day, as expected, he received a letter firing him from the post office.

Franklin refused to follow the advice of family and friends to come home. He refused to give up his personal crusade for American causes, although he was savagely and variously attacked in the British press as "this old snake," "the grand incendiary," "this living emblem of iniquity in grey hairs," "Old Traitor," "Old Doubleface." Even his once-popular flat was now dubbed "Judas's office in Craven Street."

"My situation here is thought by many to be a little hazardous," he wrote home with considerable understatement, "for that, if by some accident, the troops and people of (New England) should come to blows, I should probably be taken up (arrested); the ministerial people affecting everywhere to represent me as the cause of all the misunderstandings . . ."

In this crisis, Franklin suffered another blow: the news that his wife, despairing of ever seeing him again, had suffered a stroke and, on December 19, 1774, died.

Finally, Franklin decided to sail for home. He arrived in Philadelphia on May 5, 1775, this time to a tumultuous welcome. In a few days, he was elected to the Second Continental Congress as a special delegate from Pennsylvania.

With him he'd brought his handsome grandson, Temple as he was called, the 16-year-old offspring of William, who now formally acknowledged him. The three Franklin men met in Philadelphia and began one of the most painful dialogues any family ever endured.

Meeting at the Trevose farm of Joseph Galloway, Benjamin and William argued over drinks of port late into a night and again the next day over Benjamin's decision to rebel against arbitrary English power and William's determination to remain loyal to his oath of office to the King.

Something about the debate was unnatural — the old, wise man arguing for rebellion, the younger man for order, stability, reconciliation. But their points of view were as irreconcilable as those of England and America. After one more attempt to win his son over, Benjamin plunged back into the work of Congress.

Franklin was the first American to understand that most of the important work of government is done in small committee meetings, not in the public eye in open debate, and he managed to serve on no fewer than 10 key committees.

In addition to chairing the post office committee and becoming postmaster general, he supervised construction of defenses and obtained munitions for Philadelphia and for American forces as far away as Charleston and Cambridge. He remodeled Pennsylvania's cumber-

This painting of Franklin's kite experiment is wrong on several counts: Franklin was standing inside his shed, his son William (left) was 22 and taller than his father, and no lightning actually flashed, among other things.

THE FOUNDING CITY

A 19th century magazine illustrator's idea of what the scene looked like when Benjamin Franklin was presented to the French court in 1778 to begin negotiations.

some revolutionary government into a close-knit, autocratic Committee of Safety, a mode that was quickly emulated by other states and later adopted in the French Revolution by the Jacobins.

"My time," the 69-year-old congressman wrote his close friend, chemist Joseph Priestley in England, "was never more fully employed. In the morning at six I am at the Committee of Safety . . . which holds till near nine, when I am at the Congress, and that sits till after four in the afternoon." His congressional activities continued into the night.

In the full sessions of the Congress, Franklin rarely spoke, sitting with eyes closed most of the time as John Adams rasped, John Dickinson orated, and Richard Henry Lee droned.

It soon became apparent to Congress that America couldn't withstand the inevitable British onslaught without foreign aid.

As news reached Philadelphia that England was hiring Hessian mercenaries and assembling a mighty armada. Franklin became America's first emissary and a sort of secretary of state all at the same time. He was, initially, a wandering trouble-shooter, going first to Canada, where he found that the time was now too late to effect an alliance.

•

On July 4, 1776, as Franklin led the

Pennsylvania delegation in voting for independence from England, the British invasion forced sailed into New York harbor; its admiral, Lord Howe, was authorized to offer the hand of peace on England's terms and, failing that, the fist of punishment.

Franklin and Howe knew and respected each other. They'd talked of reconciliation in London during chess matches in Howe's sister's house. Now they parlayed again on Staten Island.

One of Franklin's fellow emissaries, John Adams, would later complain about a lot of habits of Franklin's, but one from that trip which he and Franklin made together to Staten Island stood out in his memory years later. At a tavern in Perth Amboy en route to the peace talks, they could find only a single room in a crowded tavern.

An advocate of fresh air at night, Franklin opened the window. Adams, like most people of that age, believed night air bore disease and slammed it shut. Franklin objected that he would suffocate. He launched into a long dissertation on his theory of fresh air baths (neglecting to mention, probably, that he'd once caught pneumonia adapting the practice to his first London winter).

But before Franklin could finish, Adams gave in, opened the window and fell asleep.

The next day, Admiral Richard Howe,

General Sir William Howe's brother, offered the Americans the olive branch — on the condition that the Americans recant their declaration of independence. The British admiral also refused to recognize Congress. Concluding that further talks were pointless, the American emissaries returned to Philadelphia. The British prepared to invade.

Now a new phase began.

As early as December 1775, Congress had appointed Franklin to a supersecret committee with "the sole purpose of correspondence with our friends in Great Britain, Ireland and other parts of the world." Most of them were Franklin's contacts and old friends. Now Franklin took a fateful step: twice he had fought France, and he'd grown up, like most Americans, fearing and hating the French; yet now he felt that America had to turn to them for help against the British.

At Franklin's urging, Congress took the next step, dispatching Connecticut merchant Silas Deane to France to attempt to buy arms. Meanwhile, Franklin dashed off letters to old friends there, asking them to feel out the mood of the French government.

Finally, a long letter came back indicating that Franklin would be received sympathetically if he came to France. As the British unleashed their New York offensive, Congress unanimously, and secretly, voted to send Franklin at once as minister to France.

He was not, interestingly, entirely pleased by the honor, or the idea. "A virgin state should preserve the virgin character, not go about suitoring for alliances, but wait with decent dignity for the application of others," he wrote.

Moreover, at 70, he was 25 years beyond the normal lifespan of his time and the possibility of dying in an alien land saddened him.

When the vote in Congress was taken, however, he turned resignedly to young Dr. Benjamin Rush and said, "I am old and good for nothing; but, as the storekeepers say of their remnants of cloth, 'I am but a fag end, and you may have me for what you please.'"

Saying what he was sure were last goodbyes to his daughter Sally, Franklin took his grandson, Temple, whose father already had been packed off to a Connecticut prison as a Loyalist, and his grandson, six-year-old Benjamin Franklin Bache, aboard the sloop *Reprisal*, which then set sail for France.

Twice outrunning British cruisers (Franklin most assuredly would have been hanged for treason had he been intercepted), the fast little ship made the rough winter passage in six weeks, putting into Nantes December 3, 1776, where Franklin was treated to a hero's welcome.

Aboard ship, Franklin had suffered one of his recurring outbreaks of what was probably acute psoriasis, making it impossible for him to wear his customary wig. Instead, he donned a fur hat he'd bought in Canada. The sight he presented with a fur hat, wispy gray hair, spectacles and plain brown suit charmed the French. It was to be their lasting image of the American, and Franklin would remain for years their symbol of the new republican man. "Everything in him announces the simplicity and innocence of primitive morals," exuded one French philosopher on the scene.

Medallions were cast with his likeness and sold by the thousands, portraits were painted, pamphlets rushed to press. More importantly, Franklin and Deane met French officials, who began the flow of arms and cash to America.

On December 28, 1776, two days after George Washington's surprise victory at Trenton (but weeks before the French knew about it), Franklin met for the first time with Vergennes, the French foreign minister. Franklin extended the lure of a commercial treaty, avoiding asking outright for a military alliance.

Eight days later, he wrote to ask officially for much more — eight fully equipped and manned ships-of-the-line. Knowing such a grant would draw

France into the war, he added that by "the united force of France, Spain (France's ally) and America, she (England) will lose all her possessions in the West Indies, much the greatest part of that commerce which has rendered her so opulent, and be reduced to that state of weakness and humiliation which she has, by her perfidy, her insolence and her cruelty, so justly merited."

For France, it was a tempting — and dangerous — prospect. Since the humiliating Treaty of Paris in 1763 that had authenticated England's victory in the Seven Years' War, France had been smarting.

The treaty had stripped her of almost all her foreign possessions, and she had gone deeply into debt as a result. But Vergennes, the French minister, knew it would be another year before France's fleet would be rebuilt to the extent he could risk renewed war with England.

Before such a fateful step, he also needed evidence America would still be able to help stem the British invasion.

It would be another year, therefore, until France, electrified by news of the stunning defeat of the British at Saratoga by Americans armed with French weapons, and with much of its fleet restored, gave Franklin a promise of significant French military aid.

Franklin helped things along by waging his own war of nerves on the French, opening a correspondence with his British connections that he made to appear like serious peace negotiations. On January 6, 1778, this maneuver led to a two-hour talk with British master spy Paul Wentworth, a meeting that did not escape the notice of the French.

On February 5, 1778, Franklin was summoned to the French foreign office at the palace of Versailles to sign the formal alliance. Edward Bancroft, a member of Deane's staff (who, interestingly enough, later turned out to be a British spy), observed that Franklin was dressed in an old suit of Manchester velvet he dimly recalled seeing somewhere years before.

Then Bancroft realized that it was the same suit Franklin had worn during his humiliation by the Privy Council at the Cockpit. When Deane asked Franklin why he was wearing such an out-of-style outfit, Franklin smiled and said, "To give it a little revenge."

It would take three years of delays and fighting before joint Franco-American forces scored a decisive victory at Yorktown that, coinciding with French naval victories in the Caribbean and collapse of the pro-war British cabinet, made England eager for peace. The negotiations, which took almost two more years, were to prove Dr. Franklin's greatest diplomatic achievement.

Franklin's chance decision to wear his fur hat of Canadian marten on arriving in France created an image of Americans that lasted for years.

Three days after receiving reports of Yorktown, British diplomat Thomas Pownall made the first British overture to end "this curs'd war."

England offered America a ten-year truce while she continued fighting France. Franklin angrily replied he could never think "of deserting a noble and generous friend for the sake of a truce with an unjust and cruel enemy."

Months elapsed. A new British envoy, an ugly one-eyed Scottish merchant with no previous diplomatic experience named Richard Oswald, appeared at Franklin's door in Passy. The two old businessmen hit it off instantly.

Franklin opened the bidding by pointing out the enormous damage wrought by the British in America. Then he offered more than peace. He offered the prospect of reconciliation, a renewal of trade — if England would throw in all of Canada as a token of renewed faith. In exchange, he held out the possibility of reimbursing dispossessed Loyalists for losses at the hands of the rebels. The British decided that this wasn't all that good a deal.

More months passed, during which Britain still had not formally recognized American independence. Finally, a new British mission was sent to treat with "France and her allies." But the negotiator was none other than the son of Grenville, the hated English minister who had started the trouble with the Stamp Act 20 years earlier. Franklin wrote the British foreign office to send back Oswald and he would negotiate.

The British complied.

When Oswald came, Franklin abruptly changed ground, withdrawing his offer to compensate the Loyalists. His son William, who had led the Loyalist forces in raids after his release from two years in a rebel prison, had recently arrived in London to press the Loyalist claims for compensation. There were whispers that the Franklins had deliberately taken opposing sides so that, no matter the outcome, the Franklins couldn't lose.

While the idea is just the sort of thing that Franklin's mind might have conceived of, this was not, in fact, the case, and Franklin wanted to take action that would quickly disabuse everyone of the notion.

Then Franklin made his astonishing demands: full and immediate independence, withdrawal of all troops, a western boundary along the Mississippi and a north border along the Great Lakes and above Maine, fishing rights on the Grand Banks. Boldly, Franklin was bidding for twice the lands that the 13 colonies had occupied at the outset of the war.

The final round of negotiations, occurring after a time-out for another change of government in London, lasted six days and nights. The British were adamant about Loyalist compensation (England was thronging with 30,000 vociferous refugees) and equally insistent that the Americans be barred from the prized fishing grounds off Newfoundland.

Bitterly, Franklin refused to give in on the Loyalists. The most he would allow was a *recommendation* that Congress reimburse their losses. (He knew, of course, that Congress years ago had turned treatment of the Loyalists over to the individual states, so that such a recommendation was worthless.)

John Adams had joined Franklin by now, and he skillfully led the British to give New England fishermen the "liberty" to fish off Newfoundland instead of the "right" they had earlier claimed.

The shading of these two words appeased the British negotiators, anxious above all for an end to the fighting that once again had bankrupted England. Without protest, they signed away the rights to all the land between Canada and the Gulf of Mexico, between the Atlantic and the Mississippi.

Franklin had won one-fifth of the continent, the rich land from the Appalachians to the Mississippi so long coveted by frontiersmen, without ever seriously arguing the point.

Back in Philadelphia, Dr. Franklin was quickly elected president of Pennsylvania, an office he filled three years until the pain of gout and bladder stones forced him to dose himself with too much opium to enable him to carry on his duties of office.

Curiously, Franklin also allowed himself to be elected president of the Pennsylvania Abolition Society, an office he held while owning a slave: for 30 years, he'd kept slaves. The anomaly, like many others in his life, seemed not to disturb him in the least.

Carried to sessions of the constitutional convention during the blistering summer of 1787 in a sedan chair borne by prisoners from the Walnut Street Jail, Franklin as usual left the brunt of the debating to others until the very end.

On the last day, he rose painfully, adjusted his bifocals and read from a paper in his hand:

"Mr. President," he said, turning to George Washington, "I confess that there are several parts of this constitution which I do not at present approve. But I am not sure I shall never approve them . . . for having lived long, I have experienced many instances of being obliged by better information . . . to change opinions even on important subjects . . .

"But though many private persons think almost as highly of their own infallibility, few express it so naturally as a certain French lady who, in a dispute with her sister, said, 'I don't know how it happens, sister, but I meet with nobody but myself that's always in the right.' In these sentiments, sir, I agree to this constitution, with all its faults, if they are such."

On Saturday evening, April 17, 1790, Benjamin Franklin died at 84, after two years of intense suffering. With death, as with most things, Franklin held few illusions. Years before, already old, he'd written to an old friend:

"Let us sit till the evening of life is spent; the last hours were always the most joyous. When we can stay no longer, 'tis time enough then to bid each other good night, separate, and go quietly to bed." ★ ★ ★

An artist's conception of Franklin's return from Paris in 1786, which was far more triumphal than his first return in 1762.

Franklin and His Friends

James Forten:
'Free Man of Color' Sails With America

Some moments were bitter. At one point Forten angrily suggested that Philadelphia change its name from 'City of Brotherly Love' to 'Mob City.'

By Franklin S. Roberts

War is a game to young boys. Nine-year-old James Forten and his playmates played at war and marbles, while the real war, in which British lobsterbacks were sweeping through New Jersey in the fall of 1776, was raging to the north. Their street games would be interrupted by dusty riders arriving in the city with pleas for more gunpowder for the retreating Americans, by promoters coming to the city to seek government contracts, and by farmers seeking redress for confiscated mules. But then they would return to mock soldiering, or, when James had his preference, a daring fantasy attack on His Majesty's ships-of-the-line.

Forten's earliest memories were stories of adventures at sea. Home from his work as a sailmaker in Robert Bridges' sail loft, Thomas Forten had fueled his son's imagination with talk of vessels from England, spice ships from the Indies — and the pirates who stalked them. Questions would pour from the boy — questions about sea monsters, exotic countries, and shipwrecks.

Comfortable around the open fire, Thomas Forten repeated to his son the stories that the ship captains told the sailmakers, embroidering here and there, and wondering when the boy would recognize the stranger-than-fiction drama of his own heritage. Young James Forten's great-grandfather had been a slave who had been captured in Africa, chained and stuffed in a dark hold with a terrified mass of black humanity, and then sold into bondage, probably somewhere in the Middle Colonies.

Forten's grandfather, the second generation of American Fortens, worked for wages "after slave hours" to buy his freedom. Then he redoubled his efforts to buy his wife's freedom.

James' father, Thomas Forten, was then born a free man. He was also a proud and diligent worker, one of the best sailmakers in Bridges' loft. Bridges was a fair man, more concerned with the quality of an employe's work than his color. He paid all forty of his workers equal wages; ten of them were black.

Forten's family history, though, paled beside the accomplishments that he himself would attain. James Forten would amass a small fortune in the sail business, become a civic leader in Philadelphia, and become intimately involved in the twisting and tortured history of blacks in America during the first half of the 19th century.

He himself would win the admiration, respect, and friendship of blacks and whites in Philadelphia. His funeral would involve one of the longest processions Philadelphia had ever seen. Black and white, almost 5,000 strong, the people of the city he helped to build would come to pay their last respects to James Forten.

Forten's childhood was touched by tragedy when his father died as a result of injuries suffered from a fall into the Delaware. This happened just the year before the Revolution broke out, when James was 8, and it curtailed his studies at Anthony Benezet's free school for blacks.

To support his widowed mother and his brothers and sisters, James ran errands for a grocer, and served as a helper to a chimney sweep.

By 1781, when Forten was 14, he had become a sturdy, man-sized boy, almost six feet tall, and his mother found herself unable to curb any longer his desire to go to war. He signed on as a powder boy aboard the *Royal Louis*, an American privateer commanded by Stephen Decatur Sr. Many blacks served as sailors during the Revolution; Forten, for instance, was one of 20 blacks serving on the *Royal Louis*.

Forten's introduction to naval warfare

was as dramatic —and triumphant — as any of his childhood fantasies might have led him to believe. The *Royal Louis* captured the British brig *Active* after a fierce fight. Then a fat brigantine, the *Phoenix,* loaded with rum, coffee, pimento, and tobacco, fell victim to the privateer.

The *Royal Louis'* second voyage in 1781, however, showed that there was another face to war. The *Royal Louis* spotted the British man-o'-war *Amphyon,* and Decatur decided to gamble — to stand and battle the larger British warship. No sooner was the decision made, however, than the odds turned hopelessly against the *Royal Louis.* Two more British men-o'-war appeared on the horizon. Belatedly, the *Royal Louis'* crew crowded on canvas and tried to make a run for it. But the winds favored the British. The American ship surrendered, and the blacks in the crew faced the terrifying prospect of being taken to the West Indies and sold as slaves.

But Forten encountered a bit of luck. On board the *Amphyon* was a cabin boy named William, who was also the son of the captain of the warship, Sir John Beasy. After a bit of sizing each other up, the two teenagers became friends, and, thanks in part to his son's pleas, Captain Beasy agreed to treat the black Americans as regular prisoners of war.

The change in status was only a marginal improvement, however. All of the prisoners were brought to the prison ship *Jersey,* where more Americans died than in any single battle.

Forten survived seven months in the dark, disease-ridden hold of the *Jersey* before being released in a prisoner exchange a short while before the end of hostilities.

Now 17, he still retained his itch for the sea and adventure. Earning passage to Liverpool as an able-bodied seaman, he remained in that city for a while, working as a stevedore. For a time he considered making England his home, but the squalor of the old English cities, along with the constant exposure to the trafficking in slaves, determined him to return to America, where he took a job with his father's one-time employer, Robert Bridges.

Within two years, Forten had worked his way from apprentice to foreman of the large shop. The 22-year-old Forten was clearly stamped as a leader. At about this time, early in 1793, Forten met another remarkable man, Captain Paul Cuffe, commander of the schooner *Mary* out of Westport, Conn. Cuffe was part Negro and part Pequot Indian and he had his own dream of a new life for American blacks, which he confided to Forten. Cuffe's plan would ultimately

force Forten into one of the most difficult dilemmas of his life.

But all of that lay in the future.

His own career was, however, advancing steadily. The aging Bridges relied increasingly on his able young foreman. One day in 1798 Bridges called Forten to his office, and made him an offer that, in 18th century America, was unheard of. Bridges offered to sell his business to the young black man.

Forten accepted, and as the century turned, he was the 32-year-old owner of a large, profitable sailmaking business. And while it would continue as a highly successful enterprise, Forten showed right from the beginning that he intended to put principles above profit by turning down a sizable order from a West Indies-based slave ship. He also announced publicly that he would not accept orders from ships dealing in human cargo.

Forten also began to take an active interest in efforts outside his business that were related to blacks in America. His name appeared on a petition protesting the nation's Fugitive Slave Act, which encouraged the use of bounty hunters to track down slaves who had escaped to the North, and which sometimes resulted in free Negroes being abducted and sold back into slavery. (As a result of an act passed in 1780, virtually all of the slaves in Pennsylvania had been freed by this time.) Forten also helped many slaves to buy their freedom.

A new threat to Pennsylvania's blacks developed when the legislature in 1813 proposed a registration law to control Negro entry into the Commonwealth; it also imposed registration fees and special taxes on Negroes for the support of the poor, and even gave the state the authority to sell, for a term of years, the services of Negroes convicted of crimes — the reintroduction of slavery.

Outraged by the proposals, Forten published *A Series of Letters By A Man of Color,* which outlined arguments that helped defeat the registration bill.

Forten was involved in much more than simply black causes. He gave large sums of cash to help the American sailors idled by the embargo on foreign trade that was imposed in 1807. When the city was threatened during the War of 1812, he helped to organize work gangs to prepare the city's defenses.

On several occasions he recklessly dove into the Delaware to save drowning persons, possibly seeing in the rescues a chance to atone in part for having been unable, as a small boy, to save his own father. He received a public award for his lifesaving exploits from the Philadelphia Humane Society.

At about this time Forten's old friend, Cuffe, came to ask Forten's aid on a plan to transport American Negroes to Africa, and establish a colony that would, under Cuffe's plan, become prosperous through trade with America.

Forten was troubled by the idea. His family had lived in Pennsylvania for generations. He believed that, despite the burden of racial prejudice, America still offered the black man immense opportunities, and his own life had shown what could be achieved. But finally he yielded to Cuffe's appeals, and agreed to become the Philadelphia head of the "London African Institution," which had already founded a colony of former British Negroes in Sierra Leone.

Almost immediately a bizarre chain of events was set in motion. Within a year an intense group of white men met in Washington to discuss America's "free people of color." Many of those who met were sincere in their concerns. They believed they saw a way to atone for the sins of slavery by recompensing American blacks with a stake to a new life on their native continent; others, though, simply wanted to protect the institution of slavery by getting rid of dissident free blacks.

Together they formed the American Colonization Society on Jan. 1, 1817. Judge Bushrod Washington, a nephew of George Washington, became president of the new society. Henry Clay, Andrew Jackson, Francis Scott Key, and Richard Rush (the son of Dr. Benjamin Rush of Philadelphia) all served as officers.

Forten was appalled. Here was a white cabal, including widely known slave owners, acting to decide the destiny of black Americans. He saw an attempt to twist Cuffe's dream of creating a new alternative for American blacks into a drive to deport them. Most damning of all was the fact that the new society said nothing about freeing slaves — only of dealing with blacks who were already free.

An atmosphere of panic spread through Philadelphia's black community. Three thousand blacks met at the tiny Bethel Church to oppose the "measure to exile us from the land of our nativity."

Forten was asked to serve as chairman, and as he wielded the gavel, resolutions were passed spurning the Colonization Society's implied allegation that blacks were "a dangerous and useless part of the community," and further informing the society that the free blacks of Philadelphia "will never separate ourselves voluntarily from the (fate of the) slave population in this country."

Judge Washington and his associates nonetheless persisted, proceeding with plans to acquire territory in Africa, lobbying (unsuccessfully) for federal funds, and preparing plans to form an Auxiliary Colonization Society in Philadelphia. The ultimate irony came when Forten was offered a high post in the new African government.

He declined the offer.

Late in that troubled year of 1817, Cuffe died. His death was the first in a series of disasters that befell his colonization effort. Among other things, the offers of choice land that the African chiefs had promised fell through.

The Colonization Society, meanwhile, settled for a site 50 miles south of Sierra Leone where the land was less fertile, the weather somewhat less favorable, and the natives more hostile. The settlers there, as in Sierra Leone, suffered from disease and from the attacks of native Africans. Some deserted the colony. But most persevered, and, bolstered by a continuing flow of new arrivals from America, proclaimed the Republic of Liberia in 1847.

Thus ended, for the most part, one of the strangest and most difficult to interpret episodes in American history. The colonization effort never achieved the dreams that Cuffe had for it, the hopes that the American Colonization Society promulgated, or the fears that Forten came to hold.

Forten's civic activities widened in the later years of his life. He was called on to help adjudicate the problems that arose when Philadelphia's blacks were attacked for the "crime" of trying to establish their own fire company.

Emulating Benezet's school that he had attended as a boy, Forten began holding classes in his home, which were later moved to St. Thomas Church. (It was not until 1822, four years after the concept of public school education was established in Pennsylvania, that Negroes were allowed to attend them.) Forten also created an early version of the Head Start program called the Infant School for Colored Children.

In September 1830, with Forten in the lead, free Negroes from seven states gathered at the Reverend Richard Allen's Mother Bethel Church in Philadelphia, an historic first for America's free blacks. Forten's agenda for Pennsylvania included the problem of unemployment and declining wages that blacks here were suffering because of competition with the inflowing waves of Irish and German immigrants.

It was also at about the time of this conclave that a thin, balding, and bespectacled 26-year-old white Yankee added his fiery voice to the drama. William Lloyd Garrison announced that he was starting a new abolitionist paper, *The Liberator,* which would demand equal rights for all black Americans, not just plead for them.

Garrison wrote to Forten asking help, and Forten sent back money for 27 subscriptions, the first of many contributions he would make, marking the beginning of a deep friendship between the two men. Forten would describe his meeting with Garrison on the occasion of the First Annual Negro Convention, held in Philadelphia in 1831, as "a green spot in the desert of life."

Forten, now 65, and young Garrison collaborated on plans to establish a college for blacks in New Haven, Conn., but the plan foundered in the tide of antiblack feeling that swept over the nation after a slave rebellion led by Nat Turner broke out, also in 1831.

In Pennsylvania, a bill was introduced in the legislature "to protect the citizens of this Commonwealth against evils arising from the emigration of free blacks into this Commonwealth."

Again it was Forten who demanded reason and justice. He wrote:

"Unfounded is the charge that this population fills the alms houses with paupers, and increases, in an undue proportion, the public burdens. We appeal to the facts and documents which give abundant refutation to an error so injurious to our character."

Armed with evidence from the public record, Forten showed that black Pennsylvanians paid more in property taxes than the state spent on the Negro poor. He also pointed out that blacks had taken steps on their own to provide help to blacks in sickness or need, including the establishment of over 50 mutual aid societies.

He argued that blacks were not unemployed by choice, but, quite to the contrary, were desperately trying to acquire working skills, despite the difficulty of "getting places for our sons as apprentices to learn the mechanical trades, owing to the prejudices with which we have to contend."

For the moment, the legislature chose not to add to the repression of blacks.

On a muggy August day in 1832 an amusement park argument over horses on a merry-go-round triggered an outbreak of racial violence in Philadelphia. Young whites from the city's outskirts marched into the park and began fighting with blacks. The merry-go-round and several buildings were destroyed.

The following day a white mob formed near Pennsylvania Hospital, and started moving through the nearby black neighborhoods, beating Negroes and destroying property. Two divisions of city police, led by Mayor John Swift, finally put the hoodlums to flight.

The city became an armed camp. Three hundred special constables were sworn in; the City Troop and the Washington Grays, two local militia units, distributed arms as everyone awaited the next round of violence.

The wait was brief. Irish laborers in the Schuylkill coal yards attacked black workers nearby. A Negro church and several houses were burned to the ground, and order was not restored until troops and artillery occupied the riot areas.

In the aftermath Philadelphia blacks were bitter. They felt that all of white society, even the Quakers, had deserted them. Forten found his faith in his city — and his nation — shaken, but not destroyed. He clung to the belief that men like Garrison would ultimately dominate American thinking, and gave financial help to Garrison's paper throughout the 1830s.

But his faith was due for another profound shock when, in 1838, a proposed version of the Pennsylvania Constitution declared that black men were to be deprived of their vote in Pennsylvania. Only free white men were to be permitted to vote.

With the assistance of his son-in-law, Robert Purvis, the aging Forten wrote *The Appeal of 40,000 Citizens.* It declared:

"This is not the first time that northern statesmen have bowed to the dark spirit of slavery, but it is the first time that they have bowed so low!

"Is Pennsylvania, which abolished slavery in 1780, and enfranchised (all of) her taxpaying citizens in 1790, now, in 1838, to get upon her knees and repent of her humanity, to gratify those who disgrace the very name of American liberty, by holding our brethren as goods and chattels?"

It was indeed. In October of 1838 the new constitution was ratified, with the article on suffrage unamended. Blacks would not vote again in Pennsylvania until the Fifteenth Amendment to the U. S. Constitution was passed in 1870, following the end of the Civil War.

This humiliation of Pennsylvania's blacks didn't mollify the city's street mobs. Negro and abolitionist meetings were attacked. Forten could bear it no longer. "Philadelphia should no longer be known as the City of Brotherly Love," he wrote, "but Mob City. No other northern city treats us so badly."

It is probable that Forten was able to derive some satisfaction from his own personal life, even as the social and political situation for blacks disintegrated around him.

Certainly he could take pleasure in his accomplished children. James Jr. earned a reputation as an outstanding orator, debater and singer. Robert Bridges Forten became a gifted mathematician, whose skillfully constructed telescope was displayed at the Franklin Institute. All of his daughters were educated and musical; they painted and wrote poetry.

He had also accumulated a small fortune. A will he made out in 1835 showed assets of more than $300,000, though much of that would be depleted by his continued philanthropy in the final years of his life.

And he could take credit for having helped thousands of slaves to escape via the network of escape routes known as the "underground railway." Forten and Purvis, his son-in-law, organized the Vigilant Committee of Philadelphia to finance and guide escaped slaves northward.

Early in 1842 Forten's strength gave out, and a man who had never really suffered major illness took to his bed. He died on Feb. 24. The *North American*

Daily Advertiser, in a typical obituary, lamented the "Death of An Excellent Man."

William Lloyd Garrison wrote of Forten: "He was a man of rare qualities, and worthy to be held in veneration to the end of time. He was remarkable for his virtues, his self-respect ... an example like his is of inestimable value, especially in the mighty struggle now taking place between liberty and slavery . . . reason and prejudice." ★ ★ ★

Peggy Shippen:
The Case of the Lovely Traitoress

Everything that made Benedict Arnold unpopular with the Patriots in Philadelphia delighted Peggy — especially his decision to turn traitor.

By John Holland

The catastrophe struck unexpectedly on a Monday morning in late September.

Peggy Shippen Arnold, formerly of Philadelphia, was upstairs in the handsome mansion secluded in a wooded grove not far from the Hudson that served as quarters for her husband, Benedict Arnold, commandant of the American forces at West Point. Mrs. Arnold, a woman of uncommon beauty, was nervously preparing herself for the imminent arrival of General George Washington, who was coming to West Point on an inspection trip. Alexander Hamilton and other members of Washington's and Arnold's staffs were downstairs finishing breakfast.

Suddenly Benedict Arnold burst into the room, and disclosed the disaster. John Andre, a British officer in civilian clothes, had been captured behind American lines. A search had disclosed that Andre was carrying the plans to West Point. The troops who had captured him had sent messengers with the news to Arnold and to Washington. The messenger sent to Arnold had reached him. It would only be a matter of hours — perhaps minutes — before the message sent to Washington reached the commander-in-chief.

While the troops who captured Andre had not figured out that Arnold had provided the plans, Washington could be expected to deduce this in short order. There was no choice. He must run for his life. His wife, however, could remain. She would not be suspected.

Just at this moment an aide came to the room to announce the imminent and most impropitious arrival of George Washington. Arnold rushed downstairs, past the staff officers still sitting at the breakfast table, and out the back door. He ordered a horse saddled, and galloped away, eventually gaining refuge aboard the Brit-

Peggy Shippen and her son. Her beauty had dazzled the British officers who had sought her company during the British occupation of Philadelphia. "We were all in love with her," wrote a British captain.

Franklin and His Friends

ish warship *Vulture,* which was anchored farther down the Hudson.

Washington eventually rode off, puzzled at Arnold's behavior, but as yet without a clue as to what was going on. Perhaps Arnold, a brilliant but temperamental commander, had misunderstood and intended to meet him at the fort itself. He left Hamilton behind with other members of the two staffs.

Peggy Arnold had remained in her room until Washington rode off. Then she summoned one of her husband's aides, who found her in hysterics. She shrieked and moaned, accusing the American soldiers of ordering the death of her baby. She was, in any event, a very high-strung person, and it has also been suggested that she understood full well the unsettling effect that a good strong show of hysterics could have on people — especially men.

The 23-year-old Hamilton, for one, was deeply moved by Peggy's behavior, which he described in a letter to his fiancee:

"One moment she raved, another she melted into tears. Sometimes she pressed her infant to her bosom and lamented its fate, occasioned by the imprudence of its father, in a manner that would have pierced insensibility itself. All the sweetness of beauty, all the loveliness of innocence, all the tenderness of a wife, and all the fondness of a mother showed themselves in her appearance and conduct."

Somewhat incredibly, even after the messenger reached Washington, and Arnold's part in the plot was deduced, no one suspected that Peggy could have had a part in it. "We have every reason to believe she was entirely unacquainted with the plan," Hamilton continued in his letter. Peggy's first knowledge of it, he believed, had come when Arnold "went to tell her (that morning) that he must banish himself from his country and from her forever."

Arnold's aides were subject to grueling questioning about the plot, of which they knew nothing. Peggy, who knew everything, was comforted and sent home to her father's big home at Fourth and Locust Streets in Philadelphia under escort. Peggy Arnold was the beneficiary of the male attitude of the times. Washington and his aides simply couldn't conceive of a woman becoming a party to a treasonous conspiracy. Such a thought would have been ungentlemanly.

Arnold himself clearly understood this. From the *Vulture* he wrote to Washington asking no favor for himself ("I have too often experienced the ingratitude of my country to attempt it," he wrote); but he did ask Washington to protect his wife "from every insult and injury that a mistaken vengeance of my country may expose her to. It ought to fall only on me; ... she is as good and innocent as an angel, and is incapable of doing wrong ..."

What is more incredible still is that this chivalrous fiction should have continued into our own time. Harry Stanton Tillotson, a devout biographer of the colonial beauty, asserted in 1932:

"Duplicity and intrigue are so foreign to the character of Peggy Arnold, as we are able to analyze it from her letters and from contemporary accounts of her personality, that we are justified in believing that she was completely innocent of any part in the plot that — had it succeeded — might have wrecked the patriot cause."

The fact of the matter, however, was that Peggy Shippen Arnold was a schemer and a traitor, from the tips of her daintily manicured toes to the top of her beautifully coiffed blonde hair. About all that historians grapple about over her story today is whether it was her idea or Arnold's to turn traitor initially. The weight of circumstantial evidence suggests that it was hers.

In 1941 the full story of Benedict Arnold's treason — and Peggy's role as a co-conspirator — was told for the first time with the publication of Carl Van Doren's *Secret History of the American Revolution,* which used one of the richest historical finds in two centuries — the covert Arnold-Andre messages dating from the moment Arnold began working for the British.

The correspondence, discovered among papers at the University of Michigan, provides conclusive evidence not only that Peggy was Arnold's willing partner by the time Arnold escaped on that September morning in 1780, but also that Peggy knew of her husband's treachery from the time it began a short time after their April 1779 marriage.

"The bride was in the plot from the first," declares James Thomas Flexner in *The Traitor and the Spy,* an even more recent and exhaustive study of the conspiracy.

The woman who was to play such a leading part in the most famous treason of the Revolution was born June 11, 1760, to Edward and Margaret Shippen. A prominent Quaker and the grandson of the city's first mayor, Edward Shippen had won considerable success practicing law.

Peggy was the youngest of the three Shippen daughters, and the family favorite. She bore her mother's name — Margaret — but, like her mother, she was known as Peggy. From an early age she was known to be subject to fainting spells and occasional hysteria. She probably received training in music, dancing, and drawing. In later life she would recall her education as "the most useful and best ... that America at that time afforded." She also became proficient at needlework.

Her father's home on Fourth Street was a gathering place for jurists, merchants, men of science, and other fashionable elements of Philadelphia society. When Peggy was 14 her father entertained a Virginia planter, George Washington, who was attending the First Continental Congress as a delegate. The young woman's world was filled with color, excitement, and romance.

Peggy was 17 when General Sir William Howe and his British and Hessian troops occupied Philadelphia in the fall of 1777. In a city of divided loyalties, the occupying force found a surprisingly warm reception not only from avowed Loyalists, of which there were many, but also from those who, like Peggy's father, strove to maintain an appearance of neutrality.

While Washington and his band of rebels took up their wretched quarters in Valley Forge, Philadelphia was transformed into an extravagant social playground filled with endless dances, theatrical events and parties.

It was hard to say who were more enchanted — the British officers or their American belles.

"General Howe has not taken Philadelphia; Philadelphia has taken General Howe," Benjamin Franklin observed when he heard of the goings-on.

Peggy swept into a fairytale winter. She moved from one officer's arm to another, and charmed them all. A Lord Rawdon said she was the most handsome woman he had seen in America. A captain recalled, "We were all in love with her."

It was during the occupation that Peggy first met John Andre, Howe's popular and talented aide. Among other things, Andre drew her picture. The sketch still survives. It reveals a pretty girl with soft features, but says little about the young woman's character. Andre was preoccupied with Peggy's elaborate costume.

It's not known whether Peggy meant as much — or more — to Andre than another Peggy in Philadelphia, Peggy Chew, to whom he also paid court. Evidence of any romance, if it existed, would probably have been destroyed later — by the Arnolds or the Shippen family — to obliterate the trail to the West Point conspiracy and to preserve the myth of Peggy's innocence.

But it has been recorded that to the end of her life Peggy Shippen kept a lock of John Andre's hair.

Peggy's ultimate triumph that remarkable season should have occurred at the Meschianza, the Revolution's most lavish entertainment, thrown by the British officers on May 18, 1778, to honor Howe on the eve of his departure to England. The architects of the war in London believed that Howe had been spending too much time entertaining Americans in Philadelphia, and not enough attacking them at Valley Forge. He was to be replaced by General Sir Henry Clinton. Howe's officers were signaling their wholehearted approval of their commander — and his policies.

Along with her two sisters and 11 other Philadelphia beauties, Peggy was invited to dress as a Turkish maiden and watch while 14 British officers in equally fantastic costumes jousted as medieval knights. But his

American soldiers, confronting Andre, searched him and discovered the plans to the fortifications at West Point.

Benedict Arnold made good his escape, riding down the banks of Hudson to a point where he was picked up by sailors from the British warship Vulture.

daughters' partying with the British officers was already providing enough scandal to Edward Shippen's sober Quaker friends. At the last minute, he told his three daughters that they couldn't go to the extravaganza.

They were crushed.

But Peggy had an even worse disappointment in store. A month later, under their new commander, the British troops evacuated Philadelphia to consolidate their forces in the British stronghold, New York.

Unkempt rebel soldiers replaced polished British officers in the streets of the city. An atmosphere of austerity supplanted the heady glamour. It all seemed most unfortunate.

Then Peggy, now 18, met Benedict Arnold, the new military governor of Philadelphia.

It's difficult today to picture Arnold the dark and handsome general seen by Philadelphians when he arrived in the city that summer. His subsequent actions have served to obliterate him from our histories, to make him almost an "unperson." Few Americans, for instance, know that Arnold was as much an architect of the successful surprise attack on Fort Ticonderoga as Ethan Allen, who is somewhat better remembered.

In the first winter of the war, Arnold had led an epic march through the wilderness of what is now Maine to attack Quebec. The effort failed, principally because the French Canadians, contrary to what the Americans had expected, did not rise up in rebellion when the opportunity was offered by the American attack. Nonetheless, by a daring attack during a snowstorm late in December, Arnold breached the city's defenses, and narrowly missed victory when he was wounded, leaving his men without decisive direction at the crucial moment. In the privacy of their professional journals, military historians concede even now that Arnold's generalship in the campaign was daring, resourceful — even brilliant.

At Saratoga, it was Arnold's leadership of a key echelon of American forces, at complete disregard of his own personal safety, that preserved the epochal American victory. Arnold was wounded again, in the leg.

So great was the importance of Arnold's efforts that a much later generation would feel constrained to honor them in some way, despite the treason that would classify Arnold as the most evil of American villains, a true Iago. They erected a statue of Arnold's wounded leg.

But Arnold was already souring over the failure of the Congress to award him the promotions he believed he deserved, and of the people to accord him the accolades he desired. Arnold also loved display, fast horses, well-tailored uniforms — and beautiful women.

To get them he was willing to be more than a little careless with public moneys, and lost few, if any, opportunities to enrich himself in questionable, perhaps even illegal, commercial deals.

What outraged the rebels about Arnold delighted Peggy, who had learned to love exciting men and expensive surroundings.

For his part, on spotting Peggy among the girls who flocked around him, Arnold decided he must have her.

The assault of the 37-year-old widower on the girl's heart was as studied as a military campaign. First of all, he stuck to tactics he had tested in the past. A few months earlier Arnold had drafted a marriage proposal to another woman, a Boston beauty. Though she rebuffed the overture, Arnold was convinced that his passionate letters could not be improved upon. So he simply rewrote them — slightly — and addressed Peggy on Sept. 25:

"Twenty times have I taken my pen to write to you," he began. Arnold also had tried writing to the Boston girl 20 times. He continued: " ... as often has my trembling hand refused to obey the dictates of my heart ... Dear Peggy, suffer that heavenly bosom (which cannot know itself the cause of pain without a sympathetic pang) to expand with a sensation more soft, more tender than friendship ..."

When Peggy seemed troubled by his crutches — he was still recovering from his leg wound — Arnold threw them away and began hopping about with a cane.

Contact with Peggy had other effects. Philadelphians began to note Arnold's leniency to Tories and some speculated that Arnold was a Tory himself at heart. Depending upon their loyalties, the writers either blamed or credited Peggy for Arnold's behavior.

Meanwhile, the Pennsylvania Supreme Executive Council drew up a formal complaint containing eight charges that Arnold was profiteering from the war, treating Tories with warmth, and snubbing patriots.

The charges in fact were an accurate reflection of Arnold's lifestyle, but Arnold was outraged at what he saw as further ingratitude for his unstinting military service. His anger was fueled by sympathetic support from Peggy and her British-loving friends.

The accusations of corruption were published in newspapers in February 1779, but Arnold would not have a chance to clear himself before a military tribunal in Morristown, N. J., until nearly a year later. By then Arnold would be guilty of far more serious crimes.

Romantically, things went better. Benedict Arnold, standing with the support of a soldier, married Peggy Shippen in a quiet evening ceremony in Philadelphia on April 8, 1779. Within a month, the Arnolds offered their services to the British.

It must have been Peggy who suggested that they contact John Andre, her friend on Sir Henry Clinton's staff in New York. Arnold had never met Andre. To carry their offer to Andre, the Arnolds chose Joseph Stansbury, a Philadelphia crockery dealer and a British sympathizer. The Arnolds first wanted assurances their work would be well-paid. If that was forthcoming, Benedict were willing to join the ranks of the British Army immediately in a dramatic and open change of loyalties.

Or he would cooperate in any other plan devised by Sir Henry Clinton.

Stansbury secretly journeyed to New York with the message, and widened the plot to include Jonathan Odell, an Episcopalian minister and former British officer who was active in the British secret service.

Andre was understandably ecstatic when he received the message. But he decided, and Clinton agreed, that Arnold would be more useful in the guise of a rebel. Replying to "Monk" — Arnold's code name — on May 10, 1779, Andre instructed Arnold to forward military and diplomatic intelligence. Andre also assured Arnold that his services would be rewarded, especially if his information gave the British means to strike a decisive blow against the rebels.

Their secret communications, Andre decided, would take the form of invisible writing — decipherable by holding the paper up to firelight or by treating it with acid — between the lines of innocuous letters. As a further precaution, the invisible messages would be in code — numbers keyed to words in agreed-upon books.

Arnold's first message to the British could appear in letters written to Andre from Peggy Arnold and her close friend, Peggy Chew. Andre suggested the plan in this way:

"The Lady (Peggy Arnold) might write to me at the same time with one of her intimates (Peggy Chew). She will guess who I mean, the latter remaining ignorant of interlining & sending the letter. I will write myself to the friend to give occasion for a reply.

"This will come by a flag of truce, exchanged officer & every messenger remaining ignorant of what they are charg'd with. The letters may talk of Meschianza & other nonsense."

The Arnolds decided not to involve Peggy's friend, but Benedict replied that Andre's response otherwise was satisfactory. And he supplied the first intelligence: Washington and the army would move to the Hudson River as soon as they obtained forage . . . Congress would not order a defense of Charleston in case of a British attack . . . the French fleet had conditional orders to return to the Continent . . . Congress wasn't doing anything to stop inflation.

He also added a postscript: "Madam Ar(nold) presents you her particular Compliments."

The correspondence would continue for more than a year — until that fateful day in September.

Arnold's resentment of the way he was being treated by the rebels was flamed red hot in January 1780, when he was found guilty of two of the eight charges brought against him by the Pennsylvania council. His punishment was a reprimand from Gen. Washington.

In the fall Arnold had his chance to strike a decisive blow against the churlish American politicians, and for his new employers. At his own urging, and with Washington's backing, he was appointed commander of West Point, the crucial American strongpoint on the Hudson.

Communications with Andre, however, were becoming hopelessly tangled. Some of the messages flowed between West Point and New York; others between New York and Peggy in Philadelphia and between Peggy and West Point. In one letter to Peggy, Benedict adopted the tone of a fervent patriot in discussing military maneuvers. This time, the Arnolds' code name was "Moore."

In passing the letter to Andre, Odell scribbled, "You will observe that the above extracts are from Letters written to Mrs. Moore, but with a view of communicating information to you — this remark explains the reason of a Stile which would appear extraordinary in letters directly addressed to Mr. Anderson *(Andre's code name)*. I wish it were possible to open a shorter road of correspondence."

Steps were then taken that shortened the various lines of communication for the crucial task of turning over the plans of the West Point fortifications. First Peggy joined Benedict at West Point, bringing along their five-month-old son, Edward. She arrived on Sept. 15, 1781, after enduring a five-day stagecoach trip from Philadelphia.

It was further decided that Andre would come personally. Andre undertook the dangerous trip behind American lines wearing, of course, civilian clothes, which made him, by definition, a spy. He met with Arnold on Sept. 22 and received the plans.

It was by sheer mischance that on the following day he was detained by a wandering detachment of Americans, who, for some reason, decided to search him, despite the safe conduct pass from Arnold that Andre was carrying.

While Arnold escaped, Andre did not. The brilliant young man — who had so delighted Philadelphia society a few seasons earlier with his artistry, his talents as an impresario, his manners and his charm — was hanged.

As stated earlier, Peggy Shippen was sent back to Philadelphia to, among other things, regain her composure. There is a report that during this trip that she confessed her complicity in the treason to a close friend.

The story is hearsay, published after all the principals were dead. Peggy, according to Aaron Burr's biographer, told Theodosia Prevost in Paramus, N. J., that she was "heartedly tired of the theatricals she was exhibiting" and confessed that "she was disgusted with the American cause and those who had the management of public affairs, and that through unceasing perseverance she had ultimately brought the general (Arnold) into an arrangement to surrender West Point."

Theodosia Prevost was later Aaron Burr's second wife. She reportedly told the story to Burr, who supposedly repeated it to his biographer, who published it after Burr's death.

The Shippen family responded with another story: Burr, they claimed, invented Peggy's so-called confession out of spite, to retaliate for Peggy's refusal to receive Burr's advances. Other defenders rallied to Peggy's memory. Burr, at all events, had something of a reputation as a traitor himself.

The story is still suspect, but Carl Van Doren observes, "Now that unmistakable evidence has come to light, there is reason enouth to suppose that (Peggy) may have felt such relief at Paramus as to tell Theodo-

If Andre had been captured in uniform, he probably would have been exchanged by Americans for an American officer. But because he was captured in civilian clothes, he was hung as a spy.

sia Prevost what she told Burr and what he — who also had known Peggy from childhood, and better than Washington — kept secret till it could do no harm to living persons."

Peggy's reception in Philadelphia was cool. One reason was that during a search of Arnold's papers a letter from Andre to Peggy had turned up in which Andre had offered to buy Peggy some goods from the New York stores.

While this was the only evidence then indicating that a relationship between Peggy and Andre had continued after the British departure, there was a tendency on the part of some to believe that the letter to Peggy represented more than a nice gesture by an old friend. Many Philadelphians remembered Peggy's behavior during the British occupation, and the *Pennsylvania Packet*, for one, was ready to believe that Peggy was involved in the conspiracy.

"We should have despised and banished from social intercourse every character, whether male or female, which could be so lost to virtue, decency, and humanity as to revel with the murderers and plunderers of their countrymen," the newspaper editorialized.

Edward Burd, Peggy's cousin and brother-in-law,

reported in a letter at this time that "the popular clamor is high." Convinced of Peggy's innocence, Burd worried that her "peace of mind seems to me entirely destroyed." Peggy kept to her room and stayed almost continually in bed, but the public fever did not abate.

On Oct. 27, 1780 — less than a month after Peggy's arrival in Philadelphia — Pennsylvania's Supreme Executive Council banished her from the state for the duration of the war. Peggy rejoined Benedict in New York, where she gave birth to her second son, James Robertson. When news of Cornwallis' surrender at Yorktown came to New York in October 1781, the Arnolds sailed for England.

It would be nice to report that Benedict and Peggy died broken and repentant a short while later. This does not, however, appear to have been the case. The family lived in England with its share of happinesses and disappointments, but with no sign that Destiny was seeking to punish their infamous treason. Neither showed any particular remorse.

Benedict pursued a somewhat checkered and profligate, but immensely colorful, career consisting mainly of a series of trade ventures that took him to Canada and the West Indies. (Among other things, he fathered an illegitimate child while in Canada.)

One touch of affecting irony was injected into his adventuring on one island during a war. When he was imprisoned he gave his name as Anderson — Andre's code name during their wartime correspondence.

The incarceration was short. After a brief period Arnold made good a reckless escape plan.

The family lived fairly comfortably, if somewhat beyond their means. They received an annual pension of about 1,200 pounds, roughly the equivalent in today's dollars of between $18,000 and $24,000. They also received a lump sum payment of 6,000 pounds — equal to something between $90,000 and $120,000 — as compensation for the property they had lost.

Arnold, however, never achieved the wealth or position that he and Peggy craved, and constantly sought. His efforts to obtain a commission in the British Army were rebuffed, and his inquiries about other government positions were similarly unavailing.

One mean-tempered official, replying to one of his entreaties, noted that while Arnold's efforts had been impressive, and had entailed considerable risk, the fact of the matter was that the British had still lost the war. Arnold's fortunes, he intimated, would have been better if the outcome had been otherwise.

Peggy had three more sons and two more daughters between 1783 and 1794, though one boy and one girl died in infancy. She visited Philadelphia once, about a decade after her exile began, but it was clear that the wounds had not healed. Her reception was chilly, and she never returned. There's no indication that she was particularly distraught about this.

Benedict Arnold died in London in 1801, at 60, and did leave considerable debts. "I have been under the necessity of parting with my furniture, wine, and many other comforts provided for me by the indulgent hand of affection," his widow wrote in one letter.

But the debts were not insurmountable, and finally Peggy could report proudly in a letter to her son that "I have not even a teaspoon, a towel, or a bottle of wine that I have not paid for."

She died four years after her husband, on August 24, 1804. She was 44.

It cannot even be said that the sins of the parents were visited on the children. Benedict and Peggy's children, almost universally, fared well. One son, James Robertson Arnold, became a lieutenant general in the British army. A grandson, Theodore Stephenson, served the British as a major general in World War I.

★ ★ ★

Benjamin Rush: The Doctor Was In Everything

By Wilmer S. Roberts

Of the two busy Benjamins who helped found this nation and give it direction, Benjamin Rush is, by far, the least well-known.

It could be argued that the situation should be the other way around. Benjamin Franklin, after all, was mainly a front man. He took William Smith's idea and turned it into the University of Pennsylvania. Thomas Bond came to him with a dream for the Pennsylvania Hospital and Franklin steam-rollered it into a reality. As the celebrated elder statesman, Dr. Franklin signed the Declaration of Independence, then spent the Revolutionary War years overseas polishing his reputation as Mr. America.

Benjamin Rush, on the other hand, was a most eminent busybody behind the scenes. He stuck his nose into every political, scientific and cultural pot within carriage distance. His influence with the big-name patriots was tremendous. As a sensitive, creative humanitarian no founding father was his equal.

Without Rush, *Common Sense*, the fiery call for immediate independence from Great Britain, would have never become the raging best-seller of '76, and its author, Thomas Paine, would have remained comparatively unknown.

John Adams called Rush a "main prop of my life." And Thomas Jefferson found no man "more benevolent, more learned, of finer genius, or more honest."

Rush was also, at times, cocksure, caustic, unfair and dead wrong. And because he tried to cashier George Washington as commander-in-chief during a critical moment, he never quite made it back on the heroes' dais. He remained

'I called upon Mr. Paine and suggested to him the propriety of preparing our citizens for a perpetual separation from Great Britain . . .'

Free Library of Philadelphia

throughout his career, though, America's pre-eminent man of medicine.

When Benjamin Rush wrote his autobiography, he had mellowed sufficiently to dispense with some of his more embarrassing recollections, but he did include brief, matured personal impressions of several colleagues in the Continental Congress and other worthies of his times.

He took shots at a wide variety of targets — George Washington, King George III, the army's medical brass, the city of Philadelphia, and the Pennsylvania Assembly — together with a host of other subjects including slavery, tea, liquor, tobacco, air pollution, tooth decay, dress, schools, prisons, and the prevailing morals.

But when he'd finished with everyone else he offered, with epitaph-like succinctness, an uncharacteristically modest self-appraisal: "Benjamin Rush — He aimed well."

He did, in fact, aim well, and often.

In September 1760, the College at Princeton, N.J., unleashed the 15-year-old Rush, clutching his diploma. He then completed five and a half years of grueling apprenticeship to Dr

John Redman, a medical luminary of Philadelphia, a period of training that would have seemed sufficient to most prospective medicos. But eager beaver Rush set sail for Scotland to earn a bona-fide medical degree from Edinburgh, probably the most prestigious medical school in Europe. There he developed the know-how, contacts, and credentials for a rapid climb up colonial academic and professional ladders.

And at Edinburgh, by coincidence of time and place, he would be given the opportunity to unveil himself as a master of the art of persuasion, in his own style, which was rarely gentle.

Affairs at Princeton were at a crucial stage. The college urgently needed a new president and battle lines were drawn between two factions: the Old Side Presbyterians, who wanted to take over the College, and the New Light Presbyterians, who refused to relinquish control, and who turned to their native Scotland for a strongman. They had a candidate, the Reverend Dr. John Witherspoon of Paisley, a town that happened to be just a few miles from Edinburgh.

The Princetonians had already written the strongest possible appeal to Witherspoon. "The young daughter of the Church of Scotland, helpless and exposed in this foreign land," they implored, "cries to her tender and powerful parent for relief."

The successful, settled minister had, however, refused to accept the overseas assignment. A distinguished emissary, Richard Stockton, made the long, arduous sea journey from the colonies in vain.

It was only then that young Rush, bubbling with the youthful exhilaration of a tall challenge, came into the picture, and he quickly discovered what the trouble was. Mrs. Witherspoon was deathly afraid of the sea voyage to America, and terror-stricken about the perils of life in what she perceived as the American wilderness at Princeton.

At first she was too fear-filled to even discuss the matter with Rush. But after several rebuffs, he finally gained an audience with the reluctant lady and, by means and arguments that have gone unrecorded by historians, mollified her fears.

On August 22, 1767, a letter left Scotland bearing the remarkable news of the medical student's successful negotiations. John Witherspoon, destined to become a signer of the Declaration of Independence and one of the most influential forces in American political, educational and religious life, came to the new world, courtesy of a 21-year-old who wouldn't take no for an answer.

In a High (now Market) Street book shop in 1775, Rush was introduced to

THE FOUNDING CITY

a fellow book-browser named Thomas Paine. He learned that his new acquaintance had suffered financial reverses in England and escaped to America to open "a school for the instruction of young ladies in several branches of knowledge which, at the time, were seldom taught in the female schools."

"We conversed a few minutes," recalled Rush. "Soon afterwards I read a short essay with which I was much pleased ... against the slavery of the Africans in our country, and which I was informed was written by Mr. Paine. This excited my desire to be better acquainted with him ... He told me the essay to which I alluded was the first thing he had ever published in his life. When the subject of American independence began to be agitated in conversation, I observed the public mind to be loaded with an immense mass of prejudice and error relative to it. Something appeared to be wanting, to remove them beyond the ordinary short and cold addresses of newspaper publications."

Rush was a fast man with a quill himself; his words gushed out into the public prints under such pen names as XYZ, Hamden, G.S., A Manufacturer, Ludlow and Nestor. But Rush had gotten into a little trouble with a recent anti-slavery publication from his pen that shook up the local slaveholders and resulted in depression in his medical practice as patients dissatisfied with Rush's politics took their maladies elsewhere.

But now Paine had appeared as the perfect pawn to take on this next potentially explosive polemical task, which Rush believed had to be undertaken by someone. First of all, Paine had the talent. He "possessed a wonderful talent of writing to the tempers and feelings of the public."

And from a practical standpoint, he faced none of the pressures and perils Rush had to confront. Paine was a new boy in town, traveling light, with a minimum of social and financial responsibility.

"At this time," Rush confessed, "I called upon Mr. Paine and suggested to him the propriety of preparing our citizens for a perpetual separation of our country from Great Britain by means of a work of such length as would obviate all the objections to it. He seized the idea with avidity and immediately began his famous pamphlet in favor of that measure. He read the sheets to me at my house as he composed them ..."

Rush and his protege didn't always agree. Rush complained that one passage "was struck out which I conceived to be one of the most striking in it. It was the

Not all of Rush's contemporaries saw him as 'the greatest physician this country has produced.' William Cobbet said he was a quack who had slaughtered thousands.

following: 'A greater absurdity cannot be conceived of, than three millions of people running to their sea coast every time a ship arrives from London, to know what portion of liberty they should enjoy.' "

Finally, only a title was needed. "Mr. Paine proposed to call it *Plain Truth.* I objected to it and suggested the title of *Common Sense.* This was instantly adopted, and nothing remained but to find a printer who had boldness enough to publish it."

Rush accomplished this too. The author and printer were brought together by Rush and *Common Sense* burst from

the press "with an effect which has rarely been produced by the types and paper in any age or country."

One reader, George Washington, who had made no public statement advocating independence, checked his mail from home and decided it was time to jump off the fence. "I find *Common Sense* is working a powerful change in the minds of men."

As a physician, Rush was a towering figure — and also a figure of controversy.

Nathan G. Goodman, the distinguished biographer, has written that Rush was "undoubtedly the most conspicuous character in the medical profes-

Dr. Rush presumably wrote Medical Inquiries and Observations Upon The Diseases of the Mind *in this house, where he lived most of his life. The book earned him the title "Father of American Psychiatry."*

Franklin and His Friends

Dolley Madison:
'A Fine, Portly, Buxom Dame'

By Joan Springer Papa

She is perhaps best remembered as Dolley Madison, the First Lady and grande dame of Washington society, dressed in pale velvet, plumed turban, and pearls, a woman of warmth, charm, poise, and elegance.

But before she was Dolley Madison of Washington she was Dolley Todd of Philadelphia, and it was here, in her mother's house at Fourth and Walnut Streets, that the widowed Dolley confided to a friend, "Aaron Burr says that the great little Madison has asked to be brought to see me tonight."

James Madison was 17 years her senior, and somewhat smaller. (He would be the smallest of the American Presidents at 5'6", and barely 100 pounds.) Author Washington Irving described him as a "withered little apple-john."

But he had won acclaim as "the father of the Constitution" and was now a member of the House of Representatives. He would later serve as secretary of state to his neighbor in Virginia, Thomas Jefferson, and, finally, become President himself.

And Dolley, whom Irving described as "a fine, portly, buxom dame," was going with him. Three months after their meeting they were married.

Dolley Todd Madison was actually born Dorothea Payne in 1768 in Guilford County, N.C. ("Dolley" became

her nickname.) The family moved to Philadelphia in 1783 so that the children could get a better education, and so that her father could begin a starch-making business. An account of

---

sion in 18th century America, raising his profession to a higher level than it had ever achieved before." S. Weir Mitchell, a famous physician of the late 1800s, called Rush "the greatest physician this country has produced." Historians in this century have added further accolades.

Not all of Rush's contemporaries saw him that way. His use of blood-letting as a remedy for a great variety of maladies provoked the wrath of many of his colleagues as well as two particularly vitriolic critics. John Fenno, editor of the *Gazette of the United States,* called Rush a lunatic. William Cobbett, under the pen name of "Peter Porcupine," labeled him a quack who slaughtered thousands of citizens. Rush, infuriated, sued Cobbett for libel. The jury, after a sensational trial, returned a verdict in favor of Rush. Ultimately, of course, many of his theories and practices, including bloodletting, would be discredited. The medicine of the 18th century was unquestionably primitive—though improving.

Philadelphia commanded the world's respect as the medical center of the United States. No one man was more responsible for this status than Rush. After earning his M.D. in Edinburgh, he returned to the College of Philadelphia (later the University of Pennsylvania) to

begin a marathon series of lectures that might qualify for the *Guinness Book of Records.* In 40 years some 3,000 students listened attentively to a "voice like a flute" and spread his medical gospel throughout the land.

•

Few facets of medical practice escaped his attention.

Rush was interested in veterinary medicine and pediatrics. He could lay claim to being the first to contribute to the study of aviation physiology. At his request, the French balloonist Blanchard filed a medical report for Rush after completing the first balloon flight in America here. Rush was the first American physician to link cancer with tobacco.

Rush's book, *Medical Inquiries and Observations Upon The Diseases of the Mind,* earned him the title "Father of American Psychiatry." His enlightened concern, while unsophisticated in many ways, came in an era when the insane were cruelly treated as wild animals.

There was virtually no important place in the city, or aspect of its history, in which he had not been involved. In 1774 he inoculated poor Philadelphians against smallpox in the State House (later Independence Hall) as a physician

of the Society for Inoculating the Poor Gratis.

His selfless efforts to aid the sick during the yellow fever epidemics of the 1790s were legendary, and the books he wrote about the epidemics became an important part of the medical literature of the time.

Benjamin Rush was, perhaps, too much of an individualist to be a good soldier. But he tried. In December of 1776, he joined the Philadelphia militia as a volunteer physician, and almost immediately he stepped out of bounds by criticizing George Washington. He passed along the latest underground gossip in which the commander-in-chief was appraised, in the words of Patrick Henry, as "only fit to command a regiment," or according to General Mifflin, as "fit only to be the head clerk of a London Counting House."

In spite of this, Rush was appointed Physician-General of the Middle Department of the Continental Army in April 1777. But the sad-sack Medical Department of the Army gave Rush a legitimate cause for aggravation. The first man to head the department, Dr. Benjamin Church, was found to be a traitor and promptly exiled, to be lost at sea.

Unlucky Dr. John Morgan, his successor, was removed by Congress in Jan-

her as a young girl says that "her fair skin (had been) . . . scrupulously protected from the southern sun; her eyes were blue, and her hair was black . . . ."

She met her first husband, John Todd Jr., a Philadelphia lawyer, and they were married on Jan. 7, 1790, the first year of Washington's presidency.

During the summer of 1793, yellow fever struck Philadelphia. In September alone nearly 1,500 people died. Panic swept the city. In great fear Todd moved his small family, which now included a boy of 1½ and a small baby, out of the city to Grays Ferry, but returned to the city himself each day to care for the property and estates of his clients. He was stricken suddenly one day, and barely made it to his home to die in Dolley's arms. The bereaved widow moved in with her mother, and eight months later Madison came to call.

Dolley began her domination of Washington society when her husband became secretary of state in 1801. (President Jefferson was a widower.) The domination continued, with only occasional interruptions, for almost half a century.

It's hard to define what made her such a successful hostess. She was not, apparently, a woman of great beauty. A British diplomat would remark undiplomatically that she was "fat and forty but not fair."

What she did have was an inherent friendliness, a remarkable memory of persons and their interests, and an unfailing tact. She was, according to one account, "brilliant in the things she did not say and do." Representative Jonathan Roberts of Pennsylvania wrote of her: "By her deportment in her house, you cannot discover who is her husband's friends and foes."

She had her faults. Cards were a favorite pastime, her tobacco-stained fingers betrayed a weakness for snuff, and she was "said to rouge," but her friends excused her faults on the grounds that "if she added all the faults to all the graces," she would be too much beloved.

One contemporary summed up her extraordinary qualities this way: "'Tis not her form, 'tis not her face, it is the woman altogether."

And she was also a woman of courage. On October 24, 1814, she was awakened in the White House by the roar of British cannon, as the British began their successful assault on Washington durimg the War of 1812.

Alone in the White House — her husband was away at a meeting — she watched the proceedings through a spyglass, supervised the removal of Gilbert Stuart's portrait of Washington, and wrote to her sister: "Mr. Madison comes not. May God protect him! Two messengers covered with dust come to bid me fly; but I wait."

Finally, after getting a message from her husband to leave, she calmly scooped up what silver and state papers she could, and arranged for food to be served to the American troops. She left just as the British were about to seize the White House, and it was the redcoats who ate the meal. ★ ★ ★

---

uary 1777, after being accused of inefficiency, wrong-doing and other assorted crimes of neglect.

Rush's boss, Dr. William Shippen — an aristocrat with close congressional ties — was also, in Rush's estimate, a malpractitioner.

Distressed by the horrible medical conditions in the hospitals and fields, Dr. Rush addressed letters to Washington and others placing the responsibility for the filth and neglect in Shippen's lap and, for good measure, accused him of embezzling hospital supplies. Thoroughly disgusted at his *persona non grata* status, Rush finally resigned his commission, terminating a less-than-glorious career in military medicine.

During this turbulent period, though, one significant constructive contribution was produced. The *Pennsylvania Packet* of April 22, 1777, carried Rush's *Directions for Preserving the Health of Soldiers. Recommended to the Consideration of the OFFICERS in the ARMY of the UNITED AMERICAN STATES.*

"FATAL experience," it began, "has taught the people of America the truth of a proposition long since established in Europe, that a greater proportion of men perish with sickness in all armies than fall by the sword."

Rush's *Directions* included advice on dress, diet and cleanliness. He suggested a hairstyle that would become famous as the "G. I. haircut," and by recommending flannel shirts instead of linen he unknowingly recommended a mosquito-proof garment, and may have cut the incidence of mosquito-borne yellow fever and malaria in the army.

This document, extraordinarily perceptive for its time, has held up remarkably well over the years. Its merit was recognized to the extent that it was published as a pamphlet in 1778. It was reprinted more than once during the Civil War, and as recently as 1908 in *The Military Surgeon.*

Rush was a man with many faults. Some, like Washington, tried to understand and forgive him. Others were less charitable. Throughout the years one woman did put up with all his shortcomings, bore 13 children and ran a tight household.

Rush's wife, Julia, was the daughter of Richard Stockton, an early Rush friend, Princetonian, and co-signer of the Declaration.

The Rev. Dr. Witherspoon himself married the couple on January 11, 1776.

According to Rush, Julia had only one fault—she put too much wood on the fire. On their tenth wedding anniversary, he presented her with a little handmade booklet. In this revealing, unpublished manuscript, he analyzed himself, and, with tongue in cheek, listed his faults "as kept by me, Julia Rush":

"1. He is too passionate.

"2. He is too impatient in health, & too peevish in sickness.

"3. He neglects to converse with, or to improve his wife.

"4. He suffers Carlisle College to swallow up all his thoughts & cares & affections & conversation.

"5. He cares nothing about the manners, morals, or education of his children.

"6. He suffers his servants to do as they please.

"7. He spends most of his evenings from home in political clubs.

"8. He suffers every body to cheat him that he deals with.

"9. He gives to colleges, churches & schools more than he can afford.

"10. He neglects to wait upon strangers that are recommended to him.

"11. He neglects to visit with me, or to conduct me home when I go abroad.

"12. He neglects to collect his debts, except when he is pressed by necessity, or the want of market money.

"13. He involves himself by buying too much land.

"14. He sets up late at night, & lies abed too long in the morning." ★ ★ ★

Robert Morris: Nation's Financier Goes Bankrupt

By Gary Sanborn

Robert Morris walked slowly, almost deliberately, around the prison yard.

It was late November 1798; it would not be long before the weather precluded taking his daily exercise. He dropped a pebble from his hand as he completed each round of the yard, his means of insuring he had walked 50 laps daily. He had put on some weight in prison, appearing somewhat heavier than usual, though he had always been a large man, standing nearly six feet tall. His loose gray hair fell to his shoulders.

As he walked, Morris, now 63, probably contemplated the irony of his situation. Here he was, at an age at which, he had had reasonable cause to expect, he should be contemplating a gradual retirement that would feature the increasing enjoyment of a rather vast fortune.

Morris had been one of the most spectacularly successful and widely admired men in America. He was a signer of the Declaration of Independence. During the Revolution he had been called upon to manage the finances of the entire American government — and had done so, often writing his own personal notes because his credit was infinitely better regarded than the revolutionary government's.

His efforts had been effective. The management he gave the country sharply reduced the cost of the war, and yet provided the army with the provisions, supplies and pay that its soldiers required at crucial points during the conflict.

Yet in the years after the Revolution he had been unable to manage his own finances. Morris indulged wildly in land speculation, at one point owning six million acres in several different states. He was anticipating, correctly, that a tremendous wave of expansion would hit the United States following the war. Unfortunately, the wave did not break quite fast enough to prevent Morris from going bankrupt.

And here he was, like hundreds of other common debtors, locked in the Walnut Street prison, which was located between Walnut and Prune (now Locust) Streets. Just like a common debtor, he was unable to get out to work for or raise money to pay his debts. Also, he was forced to pay rent on his small cell, which contrasted sharply with life at his estate

Morris knew that a wave of economic expansion would sweep the country after the Revolution — but it didn't break soon enough to save him.

on the Schuylkill, "The Hills," where he had grown lemon trees, orange trees, and pineapple plants in hothouses, and entertained expensively.

But Morris was not an ordinary debtor. For starters, he owed an estimated $3 million. No ordinary man could possibly have avoided jail long enough to accumulate so much debt.

And the visitors who came to see him were somewhat different from those the other prisoners received. Former President George Washington himself had been by to see him earlier in the year.

And he could derive some satisfaction, perhaps, from the sentiment of another of his visitors, who wrote, "I visited that great man in his Prune St. debtor's apartment and saw him in his ugly, whitewashed vault. In Rome or Greece, a thousand statues would have honored his mighty services ... in America, republican America, not a single voice was raised in Congress or elsewhere in aid of him or his family...."

It was, however, a difficult dilemma for Morris's friends, including Washington. Morris's troubles were not directly connected with his services for his coun-

Rebecca Franks:
'Witty, Clever Tory Belle'

By June Avery Snyder

Rebecca Franks was the pretty and clever Tory belle of Philadelphia.

She wasn't, like Peggy Shippen, a scheming traitor. She was just simply, openly, and straightforwardly pro-British. And while she was undoubtedly somewhat more outspoken when she was with the British — as she was during the British occupation and after her exile to England — she remained irreverent even in rebel company.

On the occasion of Martha Washington's rather formal reception for the French minister shortly after the British had left, Rebecca tied a French cockade to her dog's neck, and then bribed a servant to let the pet in to run amok at some suitably solemn moment.

She was quick. On one occasion, apparently a party, a group of the guests were drawn to the window, where they saw a woman in the streets with bare feet and ragged skirts, but with her hair done in the exaggerated style of Tory belles.

"The lady is equipped in the English fashion," chortled a colonel in

Washington's Continental Army.

"Not altogether, Colonel Stewart," replied Miss Franks, "for though the style of her head is British, her shoes and stockings are in genuine Continental fashion."

Unquestionably, though, she was happier in British company. She was the youngest child of David Franks, a wealthy Jewish merchant who was also His Majesty's agent for Pennsylvania, and his wife, Margaret, a Quaker. During the occupation a virtual procession of handsome British officers came to visit her at either the family's large town house or at Woodford, the family mansion in what is now Fairmount Park. General Sir William Howe called on her several times himself.

Exhibiting a naive, if charming, understanding of the political realities of the moment, Rebecca, 19, wrote to Nancy Paca in Maryland, whose husband was a signer of the Declaration of Independence: "Oh, how I wish Mr. P. would let you come in for a week or two — tell him I'll answer for your being let to return. I know you are as fond of a gay life as myself — you'd have the opportunity for raking in as much as you choose either at plays, balls, concerts, or assemblies. I've had but three evenings alone since we mov'd to town. I begin to be almost tired."

Within a short while after the departure of the British —Woodford went into mourning for the occasion, according to legend — the Franks followed the redcoats to New York. Rebecca married Lieutenant Colonel Henry Johnson of His Majesty's 17th Regiment of Foot, and went with him to Bath, England, where she lived until 1823.

But she retained a certain affinity for Philadelphia. During her period of residence in New York, she wrote to her sister, "Few New York ladies know how to entertain company unless they introduce the card tables." ★ ★ ★

---

try. He had brought them on himself.

Moreover, there was a lot of popular sentiment against Morris. Several times during the war Morris had been accused of profiteering.

Some of the trouble was occasioned by the fact that, as historian Henry Steele Commager has put it, "the distinction which now, in principle at least, obtains between public and private interests was at best dimly perceived in the era of the Revolution."

So it was that Morris had indeed profited from the war. His firm of Willing & Morris secured several contracts for obtaining arms and gunpowder at a time when Morris was chairman of the Secret Committee of Commerce charged with obtaining war materiel.

Morris also owned a fleet of priva-teers which reportedly earned him as much as $1 million while he was Agent of Marine, a position comparable to Secretary of the Navy today. (Privateers were privately owned warships licensed to sack shipping, and allowed to keep a portion of the proceeds from their plunder.)

Yet a committee of Congress which investigated Morris—at Morris's request —reported that he had "acted with fidelity and integrity and an honorable zeal for the happiness of his country." With regard to the contracts made with Willing & Morris, it said, "The purchases made by them for the public account were done on the best terms."

And the value of Morris's service was unquestionably immense. Alexander Hamilton, who, as Washington's secretary of the treasury, had gotten the

young nation's economy moving forward, said of Morris's financial management abilities:

"I believe that no man in this country but himself could have kept the money machine a-going during the period he (was) . . . in office."

Morris came to Philadelphia as a boy in 1747, shortly after his arrival in America from Liverpool. When his father, also Robert Morris, died in a freak accident in 1750, it was arranged for the younger Morris to become an apprentice in the mercantile firm of Charles Willing.

Morris didn't waste any time demonstrating his profit-making ability. The young apprentice caused a minor stir in the city when he bought all the flour he could get his hands on after he learned the price of flour had risen in foreign markets. Charles Willing, who had been away on a trip to Europe, praised Morris's business instincts rather than condemning him for depriving Philadelphians of flour.

It was this ability of Morris, to see an opportunity and seize it, which led him to become one of the country's leading merchants. Following Charles Willing's death in 1757, his son Thomas formed the partnership with Morris which was later to come under question for its dealings with Congress. Although Willing had been the principal in most of the firm's early business, it wasn't long before Morris became the dominant force in the firm.

By the time of his marriage in 1769 to Mary White, Morris was already a successful businessman with a penchant for the good life. He became known as a man who enjoyed good wine and good conversation.

On the eve of the Revolution in 1775, Morris was no doubt living quite comfortably as evidenced in a letter to an acquaintance: "It is known that besides our capital in trade we possess valuable landed estates (and) that we are totally free from encumbrances."

The success of the firm of Willing & Morris in its triangular trade with Britain, Europe, and the West Indies made Morris one of the most prominent businessmen in the city prior to the war. Six years later, having expanded his interests greatly, Morris had been "elevated to a position where he was acknowledged as the most prominent merchant in America," according to Clarence Ver Steeg, his most recent biographer.

It was no wonder then that Congress turned to the nation's premier businessman when the nation's financial affairs were in need of redemption.

Actually, Morris's dedication to the Patriot cause was not always as apparent as it was during his service to the new nation. Morris had been a reluctant signer of the Declaration of Independence. He and other Pennsylvania delegates to Congress failed to sign the document when it was approved unanimously on July 4, 1776.

Morris was not convinced that independence was the only means of achieving liberty.

"If they can offer peace on admissible terms, I believe the great majority of America would still be for accepting it," he wrote to President of the Congress Joseph Reed on July 20, 1776.

But Morris signed the document in August, and few can doubt that there were many more dedicated patriots than Morris became.

Morris remained in Philadelphia during the winter of 1776-77 when the other members of Congress fled to Baltimore as the British swept south.

Washington, preparing to launch his surprise Christmas counterattack at Trenton, sent a request to Morris at this time for $50,000, noting that the troops were likely to mutiny unless they were paid. Morris, ever confident that he could raise the money, replied to Washington, "I mean to borrow silver and promise payment in gold, and then will collect the gold in the best manner I can."

Washington got the money. After the crucial American successes, Morris wrote to Washington offering any further assistance that might be necessary. "It gives me great pleasure," wrote Morris, "that you have engaged the troops to continue; and if further occasional supplies of money are necessary, you may depend on my exertions, either in a public or private capacity."

When Congress sought to place the muddled monetary affairs of the country in the hands of one capable man in 1781, Morris seemed the natural choice.

The revolutionary government was mired in financial difficulties. In March 1780, Congress had declared the nation bankrupt. Continental paper money was worthless. Foreign loans were harder to come by than before. The army was having difficulty purchasing supplies with the worthless paper money sent to it by the Board of Treasury.

Morris had outlined the situation in a letter to the president of Congress decrying the depreciation of paper money:

"It is very mortifying to me when I am obliged to tell you disagreeable things; but I am compelled to inform Congress that the Continental currency keeps losing credit. Many people refuse openly to receive it ... Some effectual remedy should be speedily applied to this evil or the game will be up," wrote Morris.

Hamilton wrote at the time, " 'Tis by introducing order in our finances, by restoring public credit, not by winning battles, that we are finally to gain our objective."

The war debt was growing annually and the lack of any significant taxing power provided no means of funding it. Taxation was left to the states. Any attempts by Congress to raise taxes were looked upon with suspicion by the individual colonies, jealous of their own prerogatives.

Congress elected Morris unanimously to the position of superintendent of finance at an annual salary of $6,000 on Feb. 20, 1781. He was authorized to "oversee and direct the disbursement of public money, to investigate the state of the public debt, and to report a new plan of administration."

Morris did not immediately accept the appointment. In March, he wrote to the president of Congress and told him that after 20 years of business he was ready for some relaxation. He officially accepted the appointment in May, however, writing as follows: "Putting myself out of the question, the sole motive is the public good; and this motive I confess comes home to my feelings," he wrote.

Even Morris, a perpetual optimist, was sobered by what he faced. He wrote to Benjamin Franklin: "Imagine the situation of a man who is to direct the finances of a country almost without revenue ... an army ready to disband or mutiny; a government whose sole authority consists in the power of framing recommendations."

And there was a clear understanding, in some quarters at least, of what he was up against. Washington wrote a correspondent in June 1781, "I have great expectations from the appointment of Mr. Morris, but they are not unreasonable ones; for I do not suppose that by art magick, he can do more than recover us, by degrees, from the labyrinth into which our finance is plunged."

Not long after he took office, Morris was asked to finance Washington's Yorktown campaign. There was a feeling that the great victory the American army needed, and which had eluded it for years, might be at hand. But the army needed everything — food, equipment, and clothing.

Morris was forced to issue notes of his own, as the nation's credit was void. These were paper notes, usually accepted as cash, which were guaranteed by Morris personally. He also advanced $12,000 of his own money for army supplies. He was able to get another $20,000 from the French just in time for the troops on their way to Yorktown, the loan again being backed by Morris personally.

His shrewd reform of the management system of the government enabled him, though, to do the impossible: to get more for considerably less.

The annual cost of the war during the year before Morris took over had reached an annual high of nearly $20 million. Under Morris's measures of economy, the costs were reduced to about $5 million a year.

Morris saved the nation considerable amounts in the method of obtaining supplies for the army.

Prior to his administration, the states were requested to provide the army with specific supplies for which suppliers were given certificates of indebtedness. The whole system was open to corruption and resulted in a wide fluctuation of prices.

Owners of supplies were often handed certificates valued far more than market prices warranted.

Morris was able to set up a system of sealed competitive bidding for supplies which assured more equitable pricing for items the army needed.

But not even the eventual surrender of Cornwallis at Yorktown, and the winding down of the war that occurred following that victory, did much to solve the nation's fiscal problems. Morris still had to cope with the whopping debts that had been run up, and the nagging embarrassment of the back pay owed the soldiers.

The financier took on the problem of deflated currency. He accepted paper money for payment of taxes and prevented its reissue in order to reduce the amount of worthless currency in circulation. Morris then urged Congress to establish a national bank to serve as a repository for the paper money coming in.

Morris saw three advantages of the national bank: it could absorb the worthless paper, replacing it with bank notes; it could unite the states in a financial sense; and it could loan the states large sums of money to conduct the war.

Congress listened and the Bank of North America was established in 1782. The institution loaned the nation more than $1.2 million during Morris's administration. Thomas Willing, Morris's former business partner, was elected president of the bank, which was located on Chestnut Street near Third.

Meanwhile, Morris was busy making plans to collect revenue from the states. This was perhaps his most difficult task. Congress had power under the new Articles of Confederation only to request taxes from the states. Morris often criticized this lack of power. "While it (the Articles of Confederation) confers upon Congress the privilege of asking every-thing, it has secured to each state the prerogative of granting nothing," Morris wrote.

The states as a whole were assessed $8 million, proportioned according to population and payable on a quarterly basis. Morris urged the states to pay in hard cash. The response was minimal. For instance, Pennsylvania was assessed $1.1 million payable in quarterly sums beginning in April 1782. By the end of 1782, only a little more than $107,000 had been paid.

Of the required $8 million, only $125,000 had come in by September 1782. When the first quarterly payments were due, only New Jersey contributed anything. Three states — North Carolina, Delaware, and Georgia — had contributed nothing monetarily by August 1783.

At one point, Morris had written the governors of the states, "In matters of public credit, long delay is equivalent to direct refusal."

When the peace treaty was signed in 1783, little progress had been made toward eradicating the national debt or paying the army their back pay. On the other hand, Morris had revived the nation's credit long enough to conduct the war, had maintained supplies to the army, and had successfully reduced the nation's expenditures drastically.

"Our financier has hitherto conducted himself with great ability, has acquired an entirely personal confidence, revived in some measure the public credit, and is fast conciliating the support of the moneyed men," wrote Hamilton in 1782.

The financier remained in office until Nov. 1, 1784, although he had resigned in March of the previous year, and Morris by no means ended his public life when he left office. He was a member of the Pennsylvania convention to adopt the new constitution and was one of the state's first two senators. He served six years in that capacity but little is known of his activity.

His debt troubles apparently began to plague him while he was still serving as a senator. As early as 1790, he wrote to his wife, "The bitterest moments of my present life are those in which I contemplate you as the partner of misfortunes of which I am not only the victim, but in some degree perhaps culpable in not having guarded better against them."

It is, perhaps, also to his credit that later, when all his money was tied up in land, with no further loans available, and as the full extent of the disaster he had wrought was becoming clear to him, Morris retained his unquenchable optimism.

"Hard, very hard is our fate," he wrote to his agent in Washington in 1795, "to be starving in the midst of plenty, for here we have abundant property. Money (loans) cannot be obtained for any part of it at present, but it will come by and by."

Historian William Graham Sumner wrote of Morris's land speculation, "He piled one form of credit upon another, and it is plain that he soon became entirely lost, so that he did not know the amount or forms of his liabilities."

Within a few years he was in debtor's prison, where he served three years, six months, and ten days, slightly longer than he had served as the country's financier. He was released in 1801, and died five years later, at the age of 71.

His life — both the good parts and the bad — might have been summed up in a sentence he had once written to Franklin: "The wonder, then, is that we have done so much, that we have borne so much, and, the candid world will add, that we have dared so much." ★ ★ ★

Haym Salomon: The Patriotic Money Manipulator

By Edwin Wolf 2nd and Maxwell Whiteman

Of all the Jews who sought asylum in Philadelphia during the Revolution, the most distinguished was the man who had little to say in all of the many languages at his command. His genius in discounting foreign notes and converting them into a spendable cash helped the worried government out of one of its many difficulties. If Haym Salomon had not escaped British rule in New York City, his life would have been as worthless as Continental currency. He arrived in Philadelphia in 1778 penniless; yet shortly thereafter, with diligence and devotion, he helped chart the course of the country's finances.

Salomon was born in Lezno, Poland, in 1740, of poor parents. Poland during the 18th century gasped for freedom, but continued to heave between the Prussian west and Russian east. The Jews desired to live as freely as Poland herself wished to be, but the Poles gave little thought of the aspirations of their Jewish fellow-sufferers. A weak, disintegrating country, which persecuted its Jews, fought bravely but hopelessly for its own freedom, and finally was swallowed up by its more powerful neighbors.

It was not alone the oppressiveness and uneasiness of the times which dispersed many of the Jews of Lezno. In 1767 the city was partly devoured by a fire which destroyed many of the wooden shacks of the Jewish section, forcing the homeless to flee to other nearby towns or distant lands.

The fogginess of myth which has obscured the course of Salomon's life before he came to America hides as well the facts of his career after his arrival. It is known that he brought with him a knowledge of several European languages, acquired in the various countries in which he had traveled, and enough experience in European commerce to be able to solve the mysteries of foreign exchange. The exact date of his arrival in New York is not known, but it would seem to have been some time around 1775.

Neither is it known how he first earned a living. If he followed the pattern set by other immigrants from Europe, he would have worked as a clerk or assistant for one or another of the Jewish merchants of the city. In the summer of 1776 he is described in a document as "a distiller," and that may well have been his old country trade, for Lezno had earned a local distinction for brewing and distilling.

Before he could develop this venture, the fast-moving events of the war drew him into its vortex. For a short time in 1776 he was a sutler to the American troops at Lake George, where he went with a recommendation that he had "hitherto sustained the character of being warmly attached to America."

Shortly after the British occupation of New York in the autumn of that year, he was arrested as a spy by General Robertson, and confined in the dread military prison, the Provost. Soon after, as Salomon later explained to Congress, he was released "by the interposition of Lieut. General Heister who wanted him on account of his knowledge in French, Polish, Russian, Italian &ca. Languages," and he was turned over to the Hessian commander to act as purveyor of commissary supplies. In this position he worked quietly, performing his tasks for the British, while at the same time he helped French and American prisoners with money and with plans for their escape to the American lines.

He was moreover, permitted to continue his business, now apparently a very profitable trade in ships' provisions. Advertisements in the first half of the next year show Salomon located at various addresses on old Broad Street between the Post Office and the City Hall in New York, offering "ships bread and rice" and other supplies for "Captains of Ships and others."

During his peculiar and dangerous respite he married 15-year-old Rachel Franks on July 6, 1777. Ezekiel, his first son, was born on July 28, 1778, and even this added responsibility did not prevent Salomon from

'. . . Morris needed a broker with two assets: an understanding of European finance, and unimpeachable credit . . .'

working as best he could for the American cause. While interpreting for the Hessians, he tried to propagandize them into desertion. But before his son was two weeks old, the British got wind of his actions and issued orders for his arrest.

In some undetermined manner Salomon made his escape, and, leaving his family and all his material possessions behind him, he successfully crept through the British lines, crossed New Jersey, and reached Philadelphia and safety two weeks later.

Nothing that can be substantiated has survived to give us a picture of Salomon's life in Philadelphia from his arrival in the late summer of 1778 until late in 1780. With foreign money in the form of bills and drafts coming into Philadelphia as a result of the loans negotiated by Franklin and others in Europe, there was opportunity for a broker who knew foreign exchange. It also seems logical that Salomon, with his European financial background, should have chosen this field in which to support himself, and by 1781 he had established himself firmly. Meanwhile, again in some unknown fashion, he had managed to get his wife and son to Philadelphia, and the Salomons kept increasing their family year by year.

His first advertisement in the Philadelphia press on February 28, 1781, modestly noted there were "A few Bills of Exchange on France, St. Eustatia & Amsterdam, to be sold by Haym Salomon, Broker." Unlike some of the other refugee New Yorkers who were able to secure offices, counting-houses, or modest shops, Salomon was at first without benefit of his own place of business. He stated in his notice that he would "attend every day at the coffee-house between the hours of twelve and two, where he may be met with, and any kind of business in the brokerage will be undertaken by him."

A month later, when he had added English bills to his list, he announced that in addition to his midday attendance at the Coffee-House he could be "met with at Jacob Mier's in Front street, next door to Stephen Shewell's, facing Pewter-platter-alley, in the forenoon and afternoon."

Salomon's newspaper advertisements trace his transition from a humble and obscure businessman to the authorized broker to the Office of Finance. In July 1781, he offered "Bills on Holland, France, Spain, England, St. Croix, &c.," stated that he would sell "on commission, loan-office certificates, and all other kinds of merchandise," and gave evidence of his rise up the mercantile scale by referring to "his office in Front-street, between Market and Arch streets." Yet, the bustling Front Street Coffee-House remained the center of his activity, for there, amid the hubbub, smoke and ale, bills of exchange and merchandise were bought and sold by the merchants who used that tavern as their bourse.

On May 10, 1781, Robert Morris was appointed the first superintendent of the Office of Finance, a pre-constitution secretary of the treasury. He found the country's credit low, its need for funds great, and its financial affairs in a muddle. He proceeded with imagination and administrative skill to arrange the money matters of the government so that the needs of the army and the new government could be met. And one of his main problems was to turn the foreign bills of exchange, which the United States was receiving in the form of loans, into usable cash without losing so much in discount that the loans failed in their purpose.

Morris needed a broker with two assets: an understanding of European finance and an unimpeachable credit. Haym Salomon had both. He had found a secure niche in commercial Philadelphia, and the Philadelphia merchants had learned to respect him. When Robert Morris "agreed with" Salomon to assist him, he already found that he was working officially for the French army, converting its government bills into hard cash, which in turn was used to buy supplies for its troops. Morris's diary entries are key sources of information for Salomon's relationship with the Office of Finance. The first of more than a hundred of the references to Salomon there, on June 8, 1781, reads:

"I agreed with Mr. Haym Solomon the broker, who has been employed by the officers of his most Chris'n Majesty to make sale of their army and navy bills to assist me."

Why the French, now America's chief ally, chose Salomon to handle their affairs is not known. Previous investigators have been misled into writing that Salomon actually negotiated the French loans. The fact is that he was employed as a trusted agent of the French government for the most logical of reasons: he understood their language, and he understood the complications of Franco-American finance.

Morris's choice of Salomon was also logical. He would have as his agent the man who was at the same time the agent for the government with whom the Americans were most financially involved.

The fall of 1781 was a decisive one in American history. With much effort supplies had been obtained for the final campaign in Virginia. The French fleet sailed south, and the French troops joined the Americans already there. On October 19, 1781, Cornwallis surrendered to Washington at Yorktown. The fighting war was over, but the financial battles continued. A more subtle enemy — inflation — plagued the former colonists, and maintained a hidden war when British guns had been silenced. Continental currency, English counterfeits, Pennsylvania paper bills and the like from each of the new states circulated at unequal values and with no gold or silver to back them.

In the face of speculators, who worked in quiet but consistent opposition to the vital interest of the United States, Haym Salomon undertook the task of selling on the Philadelphia market bills of exchange and government notes for the highest price obtainable. Morris and Salomon had agreed that his commission would not exceed one-half of one percent, which was Salomon's total profit on each transaction; and this was at a time when other Philadelphia brokers were charging from two to five percent.

Small as his commission was, Salomon must have made up for it by volume, for his advertisements which began appearing with increasing frequency told of an enlarged business. In the *Pennsylvania Packet,* which came out three times a week, Salomon's advertisements appeared 19 times from January to July.

The week of July 12, 1782, Robert Morris observed

in his diary that "This broker has been useful to the public interest and requests leave to publish himself as a broker to the office to which I have consented as I do not see that any disadvantage can possibly arise to the public service but the reverse and he expects individual benefits therefrom."

Consequently, a week later, Salomon announced himself with a new title, and described what had become, by then, manifold activities:

Haym Salomon
Broker of the Office of Finance, to the consul general of France, and to the treasury of the French Army, at his office in Front Street, between Market and Arch Streets, buys and sells on commission.

Bank stock, bills of exchange on France, Spain, Holland and other parts of Europe, the West Indies, and inland bills, at the usual commission. He buys and sells loan office certificates, continental and state money, of this or any other state, paymaster and quartermaster generals' notes; these and every other kind of paper transactions (bills of exchange excepted) he will charge his employers no more than one-half percent for his commission.

He procures money on loan for short time and gets notes and bills discounted.

Gentlemen and others, residing in this state or any of the united states, by sending their orders to this office, may depend on having their business transacted with as much fidelity and expedition as if they were themselves present.

He receives tobacco, sugars, tea, and every other sort of goods to sell on commission, for which purpose he has provided proper stores.

He flatters himself, his assiduity, punctuality, and extensive connections in his business, as a broker, is well established in various parts of Europe, and in the united states in particular.

All persons who shall please to favor him with their business may depend upon his utmost exertion for their interest, and part of the money advanced, if required.

In August 1782, Morris delivered to Salomon a wagon receipt for 20 dry hides sent from South Carolina, and asked him to sell them to the best advantage of the United States, and also requested that he do the same with a "few Casks of Pott Ash or Pearl Ashes," which were government property. In the same sultry month, James Madison wrote his fellow delegate to Congress, Edmund Randolph:

"I cannot in any way make you more sensible of the importance of your kind attention to pecuniary remittances for me than by informing you that I have for some time past been a pensioner on the favor of Haym Salomon, a Jew broker."

This was a side of his business which brought Salomon thanks, but no money. Yet he understood the difficulties of Madison and others who were serving their country at great sacrifice to themselves, and made personal loans to them.

The pattern repeated itself, and other names appear in his ledger — General St. Clair, Baron von Steuben, his fellow Pole Kosciusko, General Mifflin, Edmund Randolph, Colonel Mercer, James Wilson, and James Ross. Madison had to return to the well, and again to Randolph he wrote:

"The kindness of our little friend in Front Street near the coffee-house is a fund which will preserve me from extremities, but I never resort to it without great mortification, as he obstinately rejects all recompense. The price of money is so usurious that he thinks it ought to be extorted from none but those who aim at profitable speculations. To a necessitious delegate he gratuitously a supply spares out of his private stock."

It is noteworthy that the "Jew broker" had become "our little friend." But chances are that neither Salomon nor Madison noticed the change; both were occupied with more serious matters.

Salomon's activity now embraced all the usual phases of brokerage. His services, if not the best in America's largest city, were apparently the most reliable; his endorsement on a note made it "undeniable." When the sudden exhaustion of American funds drawn on French loans left many bills of exchange worthless, Salomon announced that all such bills bearing his endorsement would be guaranteed. Even then the signature of Haym Salomon was worth a good deal of money.

Like other brokers, he expanded his interests into the field of real estate, and the valuable square "bounded by Chestnut, Walnut, Seventh and Eighth Streets" was but one of the many city and country properties which were placed with him for sale. As far as existing evidence shows, none of this was owned by Salomon. He did have some property in the northern part of the city, but its location is not now known. In spite of the fact that his purse was open to Jewish charities, the general welfare, and individual patriots, his name was entered on the delinquent tax list for this property in 1784. Paradoxically, in this year, the last of his life, the volume of his businesses moved steadily forward.

Merchants and brokers who had achieved success moved their families as quickly as possible from the bustle of Front Street commerce to homes more in keeping with their financial standing. Salomon, more unassuming, lived in the same building where he conducted his business. The family lived above and behind the office, and their quarters, if not spacious, were appointed with a suggestion of newly acquired luxury. Mahogany furniture and silverplate helped fill the two rooms used for the living space of a family, now grown to five persons. A horse and chaise met the needs of comfort and transportation. This was not fancy living for one to whom great wealth has been ascribed. Compared to lesser known Jews, who had neither five years' residence in Philadelphia nor Salomon's financial ability, he had not acquired much in worldly goods.

When he died in January 1785, he left assets which barely covered his debts consisting of notes which he

This monument in Chicago pays tribute to the importance of Haym Salomon (left) and Robert Morris (right) in financing George Washington's army.

had guaranteed; the executors of his estate were hard put to provide sufficient money from his tangled affairs to enable his widow and children to live in even the most modest fashion. The *Independent Gazetteer,* which only the week before had carried his advertisements in English, Dutch and French, printed the following obituary:

"Thursday last, expired, after a lingering illness, Mr. Haym Salomon, an eminent broker of this city; he was a native of Poland, and of the Hebrew nation. He was remarkable for his skill and integrity in his profession, and for his generous and humane deportment. His remains were yesterday deposited in the burial ground of the synagogue, in this city." ★ ★ ★

Franklin and His Friends

Charles Thomson: Philadelphia's Own Sam Adams

As a man of independent means, he was free to pursue whatever interested him. He found revolution fascinating.

By Willard S. Randall

From the time Charles Thomson was ten, he had to find his own irregular path through life. And, of all the revolutionary leaders, he was no doubt the most naturally successful opportunist, and perhaps the best manipulator in the new nation. He was, at least, Philadelphia's answer to Sam Adams.

After his mother died in his native County Derry, Ireland, Thomson and five brothers and sisters were brought to America by his father, who died on shipboard within sight of Cape May. A "bound boy" for a while, young Thomson soon managed to escape his blacksmith guardian and attract the attention of a wealthy woman in New Castle, Del., who gave him a good home and a classical education.

Catching the eye of a kindred spirit, Thomson allowed himself to be persuaded by Benjamin Franklin to teach Latin and Greek at Franklin's new Academy of Philadelphia. The two became trusted friends, and Thomson soon occupied a townhouse next door to Franklin's house on Market Street above Third.

Eventually he lost his teaching job as the result of a factional battle for control of the school and became a merchant, beginning in 1760. Boosted by a series of propitious ventures, commercial and marital, his affairs continued on an upward spiral.

Thomson, like many other Philadelphia merchants, invested in the thriving, if illegal, iron works at Batsto, deep in the New Jersey pine barrens. (The works was set up in somewhat clandestine fashion to make bar and pig iron, because the British had forbidden the colonists to engage in such activities so that they would have to buy British products.)

And, in 1774, on the eve of the convening of the First Continental Congress, Thomson, a widower, married Hannah Harrison. The new Mrs. Thomson brought a dowry of 5,000 pounds, together with a fine country house called Harriton, in what would eventually become Bryn Mawr. Socially, she was extremely well connected. Her brother-in-law, for instance, was John Dickinson, author of the incendiary *Letters From A Pennsylvania Farmer*.

It was fortunate for Thomson that he was now a man of independent means, for he had, over this period from 1760 to 1774, become so deeply involved in politics that he had little time to manage his business affairs.

From very early on he had become one of the leaders of the radical merchants, mechanics, and laborers who formed Philadelphia's unofficial cell of the Sons of Liberty, and who busied themselves, beginning around 1763, with the task of protesting every new British policy.

Thomson was able to assemble some 800 stalwarts at a moment's notice, and no one dared to oppose his will in Philadelphia without some real concern about the possible consequences.

When Franklin returned to England in 1764 to see the Stamp Act passed, he wrote Thomson along the lines that the Act was unfortunate, but not cataclysmic. "The sun of liberty is set," Franklin conceded, but suggested that it was time for Americans to "light the lamps of industry and economy."

Thomson saw things somewhat differently. "Be assured," he replied to Franklin, "we shall light torches of a different sort."

Thomson did, though, look out for his old friend and neighbor Franklin, whose family and home became the target of anti-Stamp Act mobs (other than those controlled by Thomson). He organized the artisans who defended Franklin's home.

A decade later, in the summer of 1774, Thomson's maneuvering helped to bring the First Continental Congress to Philadelphia, where it was less than welcomed by a majority of the inhabitants.

The sequence of events began when Paul Revere, the regular messenger between the radical groups in Boston and points south, including Philadelphia, arrived at the London Coffee House in Philadelphia with the news that the port of Boston had been closed down in retaliation for for the Boston Tea Party. Thomson immediately went to work, and worked around the clock to arrange a spontaneous mass meeting.

Later Thomson would write a somewhat peculiar account, in the third person, of his own display of revolutionary zeal at the meeting:

"He (meaning, of course, Thomson himself) pressed for an immediate declaration in favor of Boston and (of) making common cause with her. But being overcome with the heat of the room and fatigue, for he had scarce slept an hour for two nights past, he fainted and was carried out into an adjoining room."

He had also, before taking his dive, issued a stirring call to the Pennsylvania Assembly to convene a congress of all the colonies in Philadelphia. After his performance the more moderate persons present, including Dickinson, found it fruitless to try to restrain the revolutionary spirit of the gathering.

The Pennsylvania governor, a Penn appointee, attempted to thwart Thomson's plan by exercising his right to refuse to call the assembly into session. Thomson promptly outflanked this move by calling another mass meeting at which 8,000 Philadelphians gave support, by voice vote, to the resolutions to set up a revolutionary Committee of Correspondence, to send food and money to Boston, and to convene a general congress in Philadelphia.

The maneuvering continued as the delegates arrived. Thomson participated in the plan to switch the site of the meeting from the State House, where it could be more easily influenced by the conservatives who dominated Pennsylvania politics, to Carpenters Hall, which, it was believed, would be a more conducive setting for the radicals.

Franklin's friend and colleague, Joseph Galloway, became an exiled Loyalist. In 1774, though, he was still the major force in Pennsylvania politics, and he was able to pull the right strings to keep Thomson off the Pennsylvania delegation.

But Thomson, John and Samuel Adams of Massachusetts, and other radicals at the Congress successfully conspired to have Thomson elected secretary of the Congress.

Galloway wasn't prepared for this. "To my surprise," he wrote to William Franklin, governor of New Jersey, "Charles Thomson was unanimously elected (secretary of Congress . . . the move was) privately settled by an interest made out-of-doors," which was the phrase of the time for a back-room deal.

Persons who have not had a long association with legislatures and parliaments find it difficult to understand how positions like "secretary to the Congress" can be influential. But the truth of the matter is that in such bodies power flows to such persons. They prepare the schedules and records, they see all of the documents, they are frequently in a position to see the exalted members in some of their lower moments and, most basic of all, they are the only ones *who know what is going on.*

Thomson seemed to understand this almost innately, and became one of the most important figures in the Congress. There is no indication that he used his power for his own financial gain like some early Bobby Baker; his uses (and abuses) of power were aimed principally at his political goal — the smooth and rapid progression of the Congress toward a declaration of independence.

One of the things along the way that Thomson probably had a hand in was getting rid of Galloway. Shortly after Galloway nearly won the Congress over with his conciliatory "Plan of Union," he received a box containing a hangman's noose and a torn-up insurance policy.

Eventually Galloway's plan was rejected, and Thomson added insult to the humiliation by having Galloway move to have all reference to the plan expunged from the minutes. After these events, and a few more instances in which Thomson and others outmaneuvered him, Galloway resigned from the Congress.

Even congressmen who shared Thomson's politics were put off by the high-handed liberties he took with the journals of the proceedings, which he was charged with keeping. John Adams, who was the one who gave him the sobriquet "Sam Adams of Philadelphia," commented at one point on the "extraordinary liberties taken by the secretary to suppress, by omitting on the journals, the many motions that were . . . disagreeable . . . These motions ought to have been inserted verbatim on the journals with the names of the people who made them."

Among Thomson's peculiar methods of minute-taking, Adams observed, was the fact that "when he couldn't write 'Resolved unan(imously)' in the records (because there had been opposition), he simply stopped with the word 'Resolved,' and if a motion was tabled or defeated, he didn't record it all."

Thomson actually kept two sets of records. One was his own personal working notebooks, in which he noted down pretty much everything that everybody did, and the other was the official journals, which contained the expurgated version of events that Adams was complaining about.

Thomson also distinguished himself as the first U.S. congressional aide to clash physically with members of the Congress. He did so on two occasions. The first time was during a debate with Henry Laurens over whether to censure Benedict Arnold for misdeeds as military governor of Pennsylvania. The second incident was a duel of canes with a Pennsylvania congressman. The duel ended only after both men's faces were laid open with deep cuts.

The elected delegates suffered him for 15 years, because he was essential. But when the government switched to its new form under the Constitution, an opportunity was seen to get rid of him — and it was taken.

He was not invited to join the government of President Washington in 1789. In fact, he wasn't even invited to the inauguration, although he had invited himself to Mount Vernon, and accompanied Washington to New York, where the inauguration took place.

But Thomson got in the last shot.

Subsequently he declined to write a history of the congresses he had served despite the importunings of John Jay, Benjamin Rush and others. One of the reasons they thought he might write one was that Thomson had been gathering vast numbers of state documents and private papers from members, *saying* that he was going to use them to write a history.

But now he wrote Rush, saying, "No, I ought not (write it). . . Let the world admire the supposed wisdom and valor of our great men. Perhaps they may adopt the qualities that have been ascribed to them, and thus good may be done. I shall not undeceive future generations." ★ ★ ★

Benjamin Lay:
'. . . a Hell-Raising Dwarf. . .'

By Wilmer S. Roberts

He disturbed a snow white society with his uncompromising, incessant — and occasionally bizarre —demands that slavery be abolished.

"There is some passages in my book," Benjamin Lay wrote with uncharacteristic modesty in a preface to his anti-slavery book, "that are not so well placed as could be wished; some errors may have escaped the Press, the Printer being much incumbered with other Concerns; thou are lovingly intreated to excuse, amend, or censure it as thee please, but remember that it was written by one that was a poor common Sailor, and an illiterate Man."

Benjamin Lay "signed" his author's note in big, bold type, a gesture that was far more characteristic of his unashamed belligerency. The book was anything but reticent. Its pugnacious stance was set forth in its rather lengthy title, which began: *ALL SLAVE KEEPERS That keep the Innocent in Bondage, APOSTATES Pretending to lay Claim to the Pure & Holy Christian Religion . . . .*

And Lay did more than write books. The hunchbacked little man carried out a series of dramatic — some might say bizarre — happenings to focus attention on the evils of slavery. At one point he kidnaped a child from a Quaker family so that the family could get a chance to experience what it's like to have one's family torn apart, an experience common in slavery.

Lay was not, to be sure, alone in his anti-slavery position. Isolated voices among the Quakers and other groups had spoken out against slavery and the slave trade almost literally from the time the colony had been founded. These voices included those of Francis Daniel Pastorius, George Southeby, John Woolman, and Anthony Benezet.

In 1775, the Society for the Relief of Free Negroes Unlawfully Held In Bondage was founded by Philadelphia Quakers, and the following year, 1776, was appropriately observed by the Philadelphia Yearly Meeting of Friends, which declared that members must free their slaves or be banned.

And on March 1, 1780, the Pennsylvania legislature passed a law that, in effect, abolished slavery. Its principal provision decreed that all persons born into slavery after that date would be freed on reaching age 28, or on the death of the slave's master. An additional law, passed in 1788, set a fine of 1,000 pounds for anyone participating in the slave trade.

To be sure, slavery had never been widespread in Pennsylvania. The Quaker influence had militated against it. The family-sized farms established by the German settlers didn't require slave labor. The census of 1790 reported only about 3,800 slaves in Pennsylvania, out of a total population of around half a million, not counting Indians.

Nonetheless, the abolition of slavery in Pennsylvania was a signal achievement, however gradual the process may have seemed to Lay and the other militants of the time. Pennsylvania was the first state to do it. (Vermont had eliminated slavery in the Constitution it had passed in 1777, but Vermont was not yet officially a state.) And Pennsylvania did it with style. The law passed in 1780, while the Revolutionary War was still in progress, with a ringing preamble:

"We conceive that it is our duty, and we rejoice that it is in our power, to extend a portion of that freedom to others, which hath been extended to us, and a release from that thralldom, to which we ourselves were tyrannically doomed, and from which we have now every prospect of being delivered."

The printer "much incumbered by other Concerns" who brought out Lay's book in 1737 was Benjamin Franklin. Many years later Franklin would credit none other than Benjamin Lay, the hell-raising dwarf in a snow-white society, with having started the anti-slavery movement in Pennsylvania.

Another history, based on recollections of 18th century Philadelphia, depicts Lay as "the first public disclaimer against slavery."

There are other candidates for the honor of having been "first," but certainly Lay was the most conspicuous, uncompromising advocate of his times.

Benjamin Lay was born to a Quaker family in England in 1677. As a youth he went to sea. He subsequently returned home to marry an Essex woman of appropriately dwarfish stature. (Lay was apparently about four feet high.) His argumentative nature stirred up trouble and the English Quakers expelled him from membership, an occurrence which expedited his decision to emigrate to Barbados, where he engaged in business, and was appalled by the deplorable living conditions of the large black population there. He was also appalled at his lack of success in convincing the whites there of the injustice of their ways, so he set out for Pennsylvania, where he was confident that a more enlightened audience awaited him.

He arrived in Philadelphia in 1732 and took up residence in a cave somewhere near Abington, which was furnished with, among other things, his library of nearly 200 volumes. "His dress was always the same," according to one Philadelphian's account. It consisted of "light-colored, plain clothes, a white hat, and half boots . . . His milk-white beard . . . hung upon his breast."

He found that the Quakers were loosening the ties of black slavery, but only cautiously. Lay, burning with impatience, was infuriated by their reluctance to sever the bonds that tied slave to master completely and immediately.

The most fervent and imaginative demonstrators of recent times would have been impressed by his flair for dramatic protest. One freezing winter Sunday he lay down in the snow in front of the Friends Meeting House so that the worshippers would be immediately confronted, upon their depar-

Lay is depicted standing in front of his cave holding a book by English Quaker Thomas Tryon, entitled The Way To Health, Long Life, and Happiness . . .

ture, by Lay's bared leg protruding from the snow. To all who paused to inquire as to what he was up to, he delivered a tongue-lashing, more or less in these words: Ah, you pretend compassion for me, but you do not feel for the poor slaves in your fields who go all winter half-clad.

On another occasion, he attempted to emulate Christ's feat of fasting for forty days. Only the conscientious care

of friends saved him from starving himself to death.

A somewhat less dangerous suicidal drama was enacted when Lay, before an amazed congregation, seemed to thrust a sword into his body, shouting as red berry juice gushed out from the ersatz wound, "Thus shall God shed the blood of those who enslaved their fellow creatures."

While the crusade to abolish slavery

consumed most of Lay's energies, he also found time to condemn the use of liquors, tobacco and tea. In fact, when tea was first introduced in Pennsylvania he held a little "tea party" of his own. From the balcony of a public building he flung a shower of tea, along with, for good measure, the Lay family china.

He advocated less harsh treatment of prisoners, and militated against the

Franklin and His Friends

RUN away from the subscriber in SOUTHAMPTON county, Negro fellow named TOM, about 20 years old something cross eyed in his looks, is a short well set fellow, and had on when he went away a Negro cotton jacket and an osnabrug shirt and breeches He was lately taken up by some person near Williamsburg, but made his escape. He is a sensible crafty fellow, and has been used to the water being raised near *Smithfield*, and may probably attempt to make his escape in some vessel or other. Masters of ships are therefore cautioned not to employ him, as they will for so doing be prosecuted to the rigour of the law. Whoever will secure the said fellow so as I may get him again, or bring him to me, shall be reasonably satisfied for their trouble, besides what the law allows.

HENRY THOMAS.

TEN DOLLARS REWARD.

RUN AWAY on Friday the 26th of August 1774, from the subscriber, living in Middle-patent, North-Castle, Westchester county, and province of New-York, A NEGRO MAN, Named WILL, about 27 years of age, about five feet six inches high, somewhat of a yellow complexion, a spry lively fellow, very talkative; had on when he went away, a butter-nut coloured coat, felt hat, tow cloth trowsers; he has part of his right ear cut off, and a mark on the backside of his right hand.

Whosoever takes up said Negro and brings him to his master, or secures him in gaol, so that his master may have him again, shall have the above reward and all reasonable charges, paid by JAMES BANKS.

N. B. Masters of vessels are hereby warned not to carry off the above Negro.

Advertisements offering rewards for runaway slaves were common in colonial newspapers, including those in Philadelphia — although the 1780 manumission act effectively abolished slavery in Pennsylvania.

use of animals for food and clothing.

But slavery, and the often ambivalent attitude of Quaker leaders toward it, were his principal concerns. He never let up, calling them "very religious seemingly . . ." but being, in his estimate, "the choicest treasure" of the Devil. He chastised the "proud, lazy daughters," who, "rather than rise from the seats, call the poor slave from her drudgery to come wait upon them."

Lay died in 1759, at the remarkably advanced age of 82. The engraved portrait of him pictured here was probably printed shortly after his death, and was reprinted many times, even into the 19th century. Both Franklin and George Washington owned copies, and Benjamin Rush noted that the picture was on view in many Philadelphia houses.

The legend under it reads, in part, ". . . he observed extreme temperance in eating and drinking. His fondness for a particularity in dress and customs at times subjected him to the ridicule of the ignorant, but his friends who were intimate with him thought him an honest, religious man." ★ ★ ★

The Rights of Americans

Philadelphia Museum of Art

Rights of Americans

One theory about the American Revolution is that we fought it to preserve our rights as Englishmen. Unfortunately this doesn't hold up under close examination. As one historian has noted, Americans at the time of the Revolution had slightly more rights than Englishmen anywhere else in the world, including most especially Englishmen in England.

Our editors could print things they would have been drawn and quartered for in England. We had no established church; religion was, in Jefferson's phrase, a matter "between a man and his Maker." Our belief in such matters as the right to trial by jury and the right of the citizen to be secure in his home was already ingrained.

We fought not for the rights of Englishmen — but for the rights of Americans.

Heaven, Hell, and William Penn —Religion 1776

By Larry Eichel

In 1698, on the northwest corner of Second and Chestnut Streets in the 16-year-old city of Philadelphia, there stood a crude wooden storehouse called Fort Barbados. It is, of course, long gone, succeeded today by a Greek restaurant, a French restaurant and an Italian restaurant.

But if it were still standing, it would be a fitting monument to the city's central contributions to colonial America: the concepts — and more especially the practice — of religious toleration and religious freedom.

In that warehouse, amid sacks of West Indian sugar waiting to be converted into rum, two congregations, one Baptist and one Presbyterian, shared the same make-shift sanctuary. The Baptists used it one Sunday, the Presbyterians used it the next. They even shared the same minister, an ecumenical spirit named John Watts.

When they set up this remarkable arrangement, the Baptists told the Presbyterians: "We do freely confess and promise for ourselves that we can and do own and allow of your approved ministers." They expected their fellow tenants to do the same "so each side may own, embrace and accept of each other as fellow brethren and ministers of Christ . . . for peace."

The marriage of congregations lasted for three years and ended amicably. The Presbyterians moved up Second to Market and built a more permanent place of their own. A few years later the Baptists moved to a new building at Second and Arch.

By 1776, each religion had moved on yet again to even more elaborate places of their own. But the Baptists and Presbyterians, along with at least 10 other groups including Catholics and Jews, were sharing a city in peace, which was rather remarkable in itself for the world at that time. In fact, there were 409 houses of worship in the Pennsylvania colony, including the churches of the Anglicans (Church of England), the German Reformed, the Lutherans, the Quakers, the Moravians, the Mennonites, the Dutch Reformed, and the Dunkers, as well as 27 Baptist and 68 Presbyterian churches.

Pennsylvania had become, in the words of Anglican minister Thomas Barton, a "swarm of sectaries" professing a

The Free Library of Philadelphia

Christ Church at Second and Market Streets was one of the city's principal Anglican (Episcopal) churches in 1776. It still is today.

The Rights of Americans

81

The Rev. Richard Allen, founder of Mother Bethel Church, with the first pulpit and communion jug used at services.

Ex-Slave Leads Blacks To God

By Gilbert Ware

Richard Allen spent a portion of his childhood on an estate in Germantown where the visitors included the most distinguished men of the day. In time, for example, George Washington, Benjamin Franklin, John Adams, and Dr. Benjamin Rush all came to visit.

Just how much Allen may have mixed with these distinguished visitors is not entirely clear. Allen was a slave. Both he and the estate were the property of Benjamin Chew, who, at various times, was the colony's attorney general and chief justice.

At all events, Allen didn't stay there long. While he was still young, Chew sold him, his parents, and three other children to a farmer named Stockley, who lived near Dover. Stockley later sold Allen's

mother and several of his brothers and sisters, but kept Richard at the farm, where he became increasingly interested in religion.

In 1777, in the second year of the Revolution, Richard Allen, then 17, converted to Methodism, a new strain of Protestantism that followed the teachings of Englishman John Wesley, and which stressed personal religious experience, rather than the formal membership in an institution that characterized the Church of England at the time.

Allen subsequently converted Stockley, his owner, to Methodism. Stockley, probably because of both conscience and cash flow problems, made Allen and his brother an offer they could not refuse: freedom for a hefty sum of money.

Allen now became an itinerant preacher, spending the next half dozen years traveling through Maryland, Delaware, New Jersey, and Pennsylvania preaching to gatherings of blacks and whites. Then, at

variety of "raving notions and fanaticisms." He did not approve, but that did not matter much. There was then, and is now, nothing in the notion of religious freedom about having to like the other fellow's belief.

•

In fact, by 1776, a lot of Pennsylvanians had become rather proud of their "swarm" of religious sects. Local Quakers, with more than a touch of self-righteousness, delighted in confronting the dignitaries from other states — in town for the Continental Congress — and demanding to know why religious freedom was only an idea, not a fact of life, in the rest of America.

Outside of Pennsylvania, the idea of religious freedom was not the law of the

land, even though most of the colonies had started as havens for the victims of religious persecutions. Baptists were being whipped, beaten and arrested in Massachusetts and Virginia. Catholics were getting harassed almost everywhere.

Thomas Jefferson wrote a statement of religious freedom into the Virginia Bill of Rights, but it wasn't included in the Declaration of Independence. That was supposed to be a consensus document, and freedom of religion was not part of the consensus.

Not yet.

Thirteen years later, the newly-independent states would demand the assurance of religious freedom as their price for ratifying the constitution. That assurance would be, not insignificantly, part of the First Amendment.

In its early commitment to religious freedom, Pennsylvania was the exception that would prove the rule. At least in this respect, Philadelphia was more than just a convenient meeting place for patriots from Massachusetts to Georgia.

The idea of religious freedom had been central to William Penn's "Holy Experiment" from the founding of the colony in 1682. Penn was, of course, a Quaker, and the Quakers believed that God revealed his will to each individual through an Inner Light. Man had to be free to follow the Light. Government had to stay out of it.

But in Pennsylvania, religious diversity was not to be merely tolerated as it had been in Europe between religious wars; it was to be actively encouraged. Penn, eager to find the settlers needed to

age 26, he came to Philadelphia, where his sermons attracted many blacks to St. George Methodist Episcopal Church. While there he discussed the idea of establishing a black church, but it was an idea whose time had not come — yet.

An incident that occurred the following year, in November 1787 at St. George, brought the need for a black church into sharper focus. Allen accompanied two other blacks, Absalom Jones and William White, to services at the church on an occasion when another minister was preaching.

The pews on the main floor where they usually sat were filled, and a sexton directed the trio to the gallery, where they arrived just as the elder said, "Let us pray." They knelt to pray.

"You must get up," a trustee shouted at them. "You must not kneel here."

Inadvertently the three blacks had taken places in the central pews that were reserved for whites, rather than the pews along the walls that were for blacks. The trustee's command startled Allen as well as Jones, to whom it was directed. "Wait until prayer is over," Allen told the trustee, as the trustee began to haul Jones up.

"No, you must get up now, or I will call for aid and force you away," the trustee said, according to accounts of the incident, and a second trustee came to help the first, despite Jones' repeated plea, "Wait until prayer is over and I will trouble you no more."

The prayer ended, and the episode concluded with Allen and other blacks, whose labor and money had helped provide the church's new gallery and furnishings, walking out of the church, resolved to establish their own.

The first step was the creation of the Free African Society, which W. E. B. DuBois described in his book, *The Philadelphia Negro: A Social Study*, as a "curious sort of ethical and beneficial brotherhood" that was significant as "the first wavering step of a people toward organized social life." The society was influenced by Quakerism.

During the yellow fever epidemic of 1793, Jones and Allen volunteered the services of the members of the Society to nurse the sick, bury the dead, and furnish information to Dr. Benjamin Rush, the city's pre-eminent man of medicine. It isn't entirely clear why they did this. Allen and Rush were close friends, though, and there was a belief during the early part of the outbreak — later proved false —that blacks were immune to the fever. Most of the early victims cared for by the Society's black members were white. Probably Allen also saw it as the Society's Christian duty to do something to help in this time of overwhelming tragedy.

Although Rush, Philadelphia Mayor Matthew Clarkson, and some other whites praised the Society for its selfless work, the response of other Philadelphians wasn't entirely one of gratitude. Some accused

the Society of theft and extortion. The Society was even blamed for Dr. Rush's controversial treatment, bleeding and purging, which probably was detrimental to many fever victims.

Allen and Jones replied to the charges with heat, contending that the lesson of the episode was that blacks had "more humanity" than whites, and pointing out that the Society's efforts during the epidemic had hurt the Society financially. They pointed to cases like that of a black named Sampson who had nursed whites without charge, but who could find no whites willing to help his family when fever struck him down.

The controversy made both Allen and Jones more determined to establish churches for blacks. The Society ended its six-year experiment with Quakerism and spawned two churches. The first was Jones' First African (Protestant Episcopal) Church of St. Thomas, and then Allen established his African Methodist Episcopal Church, which was popularly called Bethel, in keeping with the prayer at dedication offered by the Methodist elder, John Dickens: "That it might be a Bethel to the gathering in of souls."

Today the church, called Mother Bethel, is still at 419 S. Sixth St., the site that Allen purchased for it. Allen also purchased the blacksmith shop that comprised the first church structure, and moved it to the site with his own team of horses. He then hired the carpenters that converted it into a house of worship.

A long and bitter struggle ensued as white Methodists tried — unsuccessfully — to get control over Mother Bethel. Allen used the church as a base to establish the African Methodist Episcopal Church (A.M.E.), of which he became the first bishop, serving from its inception in 1816 until his death on March 26, 1831. The church also opened schools in Philadelphia for black children and adults, and provided a haven for runaway slaves, among other activities aimed at helping blacks in both Philadelphia and the growing nation as a whole.

Mother Bethel was also Allen's base of operations for resisting the American Colonization Society, which advocated the removal of blacks to Africa, for establishing missionaries in Haiti, the West Indies, and Canada, and for battling to have slavery abolished. "He who knows how bitter the cup is of which the slave has to drink," Allen wrote, ". . . ought . . . to feel for those who yet remain in bondage."

But beyond these activities, Allen was an American patriot. As a slave, he had hauled salt for Washington's army during the Revolution. During the War of 1812 he had joined together with Jones and another prominent black Philadelphian, James Forten, in recruiting 2,500 blacks who prepared the city's defenses at Gray's Ferry.

"This land," he wrote, "which we have watered with our tears and blood is now our mother country...." ★★★

make his colony a success, journeyed through the Palatine region in western Germany, urging members of persecuted sects — people who called themselves Mennonites, Dunkers and Schwenkfelders — to come to the New World to pursue their faiths in peace.

Penn's Frame of Government — the founding charter — stated the principle clearly enough:

"That all persons living in this province who confess and admit the one almighty and eternal God to be the creator, upholder and ruler of the world . . . shall in no way be molested or prejudiced for their religious persuasion or practice in matters of faith and worship, nor shall they be compelled at any time to frequent or maintain any religious worship, place or minister whatever, but shall

freely and fully enjoy his or her Christian liberty without any interruption or reflection."

Rhode Island had been founded on similar principles 45 years earlier. But in the 1670s the tiny New England colony had been decimated by an Indian war, and it was not a power in inter-colonial affairs. The task of protecting the practice of religious freedom fell almost entirely to Pennsylvania.

By 1776, the noble idea had undergone some stress in Philadelphia, mainly due to the presence of small groups of Catholics and Jews, neither of whom William Penn had given much thought to when he wrote his fine-sounding words. America had been a Protestant nation in 1682; it was still a Protestant nation in 1776. When Americans talked of religious free-

dom, they were sure that it extended to all Protestants (or at least most Protestants). A lot of them weren't sure it extended any further.

A lot of them were sure it didn't.

Had either the Catholics or Jews flaunted their presence, or demanded immediate correction of the small indignities they suffered, there might well have been trouble, even in the City of Brotherly Love. As it was, each group realized that discretion was required to gain toleration, when one is greatly outnumbered.

Protestants — even unusual sects like the Dunkers, who wore long tunics and hoods, who didn't shave, and who kept men and women apart except for the sacrament of the love feast — never had any problem in Philadelphia. The Dunkers

Not everyone was pleased with religious tolerance. One minister complained that Pennsylvania was "a swarm of sects" and "ridiculous freaks" professing "raving notions and fanaticisms." But freedom endured.

(also known as Tunkers, Tumblers, Dumplers and Dunkards) settled happily and without incident in Germantown, just like the Mennonites and a variety of other German sects, most of whom our friend Rev. Barton dismissed as "ridiculous freaks."

Like the Baptists and Presbyterians, the Anglicans and Quakers built their initial houses of worship in the heart of the city, near the waterfront. By 1695, the Anglicans had a building on Second, north of Market, where the stately white steeple of Christ Church would stand in 1776, and stands now.

The Quakers had abandoned their first meeting house, built in the wilderness around what is now City Hall, and were also on Second, just south of Market. The Methodists were on North Fourth in a simple, red brick church that a German Reformed group started but abandoned after it couldn't get a loan from the Anglicans to finish the job.

City records suggest that Catholics and Jews began trickling in shortly after 1700. But they had the good sense to keep it to themselves for a while.

In 1729, the Catholics, who would number only 403 as late as 1757, came out of the closet. They bought a small tract for a church off Willings Alley, south of Walnut between Third and Fourth. But they still kept it as quiet as possible. They conveniently forgot to record the deed of purchase.

With similar discretion, they built a modest, red-brick church. According to legend, it was young Benjamin Franklin himself who suggested that they set it back from the street where it could be reached only through a narrow archway.

They named it St. Joseph's. A lot of people didn't even know it was there — which was the whole idea.

By 1742, a second priest had come to Philadelphia, prompting an Anglican minister to moan that the city had become a "nursery of Jesuits." The place would soon be overrun with "papists," he predicted. If this were allowed, a flood of Moslems could not be far behind, he further warned.

Still, the Catholics were left to themselves, except that they were barred from holding public office, until the French and Indian Wars started in 1756. Anti-French sentiment became anti-Catholic sentiment here, and many Catholics were

arrested, but that, too, passed.

The Catholics achieved tolerance with the coming of the Revolution and full civil rights, including the right to hold office. But they did not escape the disdain of some members of the Protestant hegemony which led the nation into revolt.

Listen to John Adams, supposed man of reason and goodwill, describing a service at St. Mary's: "(It was) . . . awful and affecting; the poor wretches finger their beads, chant Latin, not a word of which they understood; their Pater Nostrums and Ave Marias; their holy water; their crossing themselves perpetually; their bowing and kneeling, and genuflecting before the altar . . . Here is everything which can lay hold of the eye, ear and imagination, everything which can charm and bewitch the simple and ignorant. I wonder how Luther broke the spell."

The Catholics were aware, of course, that this kind of prejudice existed, but apparently they preferred to look on the more positive side of things. Some years before the Revolution the Reverend Henry Neale, a priest at St. Joseph's, wrote to a friend that "we have at present all liberty imaginable in the exercise of our business, and are not only esteemed, but reverenced, as I may say, by the better sort of people."

The Jews were initially even more discreet. Many solved their religious dilemmas by joining the Anglican church. Jews lived and died in Philadelphia before any Jewish religious services were held. There was a Jewish cemetery — Mikveh Israel on Spruce west of Eighth — long before there was a Jewish house of worship.

When the Jews did finally gather a *minyan* (10 adult men) for worship, the site was a private home on narrow Sterling Alley, north of Cherry Street. The year was about 1745. The holy books, the Torah, appeared in 1761. Eight years later came the first Jewish wedding. There were also minor, scattered expressions of anti-Semitism.

A temporary synagogue was built on Cherry Alley in 1771, and by the start of the revolution, the Jewish community, 300 strong, was thriving. It was, in fact, the third biggest in the country. Jews could not vote or hold political office, but they felt in 1776 that the time was not yet ripe to argue about it. There was no public outcry when the new state constitution restricted public offices to believers in Christ. (That was progress. At least the Catholics were now included.)

Only after the Revolution would Jews get full political rights in the Bill of Rights and a new state Constitution.

The First Presbyterian Church on High (Market) Street was located directly across from the market stalls.

Philadelphia's First Catholics Kept Out of Sight

This bell summoned parishioners to mass at Old St. Joseph's. There were few other outward signs of the religious observances conducted there.

The chapel was small, only 18 feet long and 28 feet wide, and it looked like an ordinary house. The walkway leading up to it from the alley was narrow and almost invisible from the street. The entrance was simple and hidden, hardly giving the impression of a house of worship.

This was Old St. Joseph's Church, Philadelphia's first Catholic church, as it looked to the 11 persons who celebrated the first mass there, Father Joseph Greaton presiding. While the exact date of the mass is uncertain, most historians agree on Feb. 22, 1732. If so, it was apparently a propitious day for a beginning in America. It was the day George Washington was born.

The church at Fourth Street and Willings Alley, south of Walnut Street, was unobtrusive because the people who built it wanted it that way. The few Catholics in Philadelphia, while welcome in principle under Penn's charter, did not care to press the goodwill of their Protestant neighbors just yet.

The modest structure, decorated on the inside with a few paintings of saints, lasted only 25 years before the demands of the expanding Catholic community forced a new one to be built in its place. That second building lasted for 80 years until it was replaced by the Old St. Joseph's Church that stands there today.

On that site, mass has been offered—legally—for nearly 244 years. It is a span unmatched in any English-speaking country.

The plaque in the church archway tells the story:

"When in 1733, St. Joseph's Roman Catholic Church was founded and dedicated to the Guardian of the Holy Family, it was the only place in the entire English-speaking world where public celebration of the Holy Sacrament of the Mass was permitted by law."

Catholics had actually been in the colony of Pennsylvania almost from the beginning. One, John Tatham, came from England in 1685, three years after the colony's founding. Others came from Maryland, which had been established to offer refuge to Catholics, but where Catholics were being persecuted by 1700.

Mass was celebrated in Philadelphia as early as 1708 in the home of Lionel Brittin, at the northeast corner of Trotter's Alley and Strawberry Street, near Second and Market. Every other Christian denomination in the city had a church.

But the Catholics refrained from building a church for a rather fundamental reason—they were not exactly sure where Philadelphia was. In the early 1700s, because of conflicting land claims, it was not so obvious. Maryland had a claim on the city, and in Maryland it was clearly illegal to build a Catholic church. Only after that claim was disposed of could St. Joseph's be built.

The opening of the church, even though it was modest and unobtrusive, created quite a stir. The lieutenant governor of Pennsylvania called his council together on July 25, 1734, to consider whether "that religion was contrary to the laws of England." It may have been, but it was not contrary to American traditions, and six days later the council decided that the Catholics could have their church. The decision was the first real test to see whether religious liberty in principle would become religious liberty in fact.

The population of this first congregation remained small for 20 years. In 1755, 450 Acadians (of Henry Wadsworth Longfellow/Evangeline fame) arrived from Canada, literally doubling the city's Catholic population within two days. Two years later St. Joseph's was torn down and a new, larger chapel was built in its place. The new chapel created a new problem. It took up most of the designated burying ground. So the parish bought a plot across Fourth Street for a cemetery.

By 1763, the burial ground had a chuch on it too, a bigger, more ornate one called St. Mary's. It quickly became the "Sunday church" for Philadelphia Catholics. St. Joseph's was relegated to the role of everyday church.

In the years after independence, St. Joseph's continued its role as the less important of the city's churches. But there was some factional infighting to liven things up. The Jesuits, who had founded the church, lost control of it in 1799 to the Augustinians, and won it back in 1833. In 1844, a few years after the final rebuilding, St. Joseph's became a simple parish church.

It is that now, a simple parish church — and a national shrine celebrating religious freedom. —L.E.

In its tolerance, Pennsylvania, while out ahead, had never been alone. Almost from the beginning, religious freedom had been more or less accepted in New Jersey, Delaware, and New York. Outside these so-called "Middle Colonies," though, religious freedom had been just an idea for most of the colonial period.

Most of New England had been settled by the Puritans, who left England to avoid religious persecution. But once they arrived, they didn't seem to worry much about persecuting people who didn't agree with them.

The Quakers were among their favorite victims. Quakers did annoying things like interrupting services and running through churches naked to protest how decadent the Puritans had become. The Puritans compared the Quakers to the plague — unfavorably. In the 1650s, Massachusetts decided the best way to deal with the annoyance was to banish Quakers altogether.

If a Quaker dared ignore his banishment and return, he faced the loss of one ear, then the other, then a good whipping, and then a hot iron on the tongue. If he came back for more, he went to the gallows. Four Quakers were hanged in Massachusetts before King Charles II of England said enough was enough, and ordered a stop to the practice.

Ironically, in the 1600s, it was the British, not the colonists, who assured at least a measure of freedom for religious dissenters in America, especially after Parliament passed the Act of Toleration in 1689.

To Parliament, tolerance made good business sense. "A free exercise of religion . . . is essential to enriching and improving a trading nation," the Lords of Trade in London wrote the Council of Virginia. "It should be ever held sacred in His Majesty's colonies."

By 1776, the more repressive customs had disappeared but the Puritan (Congregational) church was very much the "established" church in New England, meaning you paid taxes to support it whether you wanted it or not.

While New England was all Congregational, the South was almost all Anglican, which became the Episcopal Church after the Revolution. The Church of England was the established church in all the southern states, even Maryland, which had been founded originally as a haven for Catholics.

But these established churches were themselves changing. During the middle of the 18th century, there had been a great change in Protestant America, a movement called the Great Awakening. It was an evangelical movement, featur-

ing fiery sermons on damnation and redemption from men named Jonathan Edwards, George Whitefield, and Gilbert Tennent. Religion had become too cold, too traditional, too rational for these men and their followers. It had to become emotional and personal again.

The Awakening swept across the colonies, including Pennsylvania, New Jersey and Delaware, engulfing every Protestant denominations: the Anglicans, the Presbyterians and others. It was an attack on established churches, their dogma and ritual. It was a reemphasis on simple faith. And when the fires of Awakening died down in the 1750s, America was a place far more open to religious freedom than it had been 20 years before.

The Awakening changed America by encouraging religious diversity, by opening people's minds and making them question the religion of their birth. The Baptists gained new adherents in New England and the South; Presbyterians became more numerous all over; and Methodism arrived.

More importantly, the Awakening weakened the established churches even as it increased the importance of religion in American life. In some states, established churches would remain entrenched long after the Revolution (until 1833 in Massachusetts) but they would never again have the influence they once had.

The idea of religious freedom was free to spread in the years before independence. It would spread because there were thousands of Americans who cared desperately about their religious beliefs, who felt those beliefs were extremely important and extremely personal. For them, religion was often a one-to-one relationship between each person and God, far too serious to be interfered with by government, or to be entrusted to one established church.

Their most eloquent spokesman was a Baptist minister from Massachusetts named Isaac Backus.

"Nothing can be true religion but a voluntary obedience unto His revealed will, of which each rational soul has an equal right to judge for itself," he said. "Each person has an inalienable right to act in all religious affairs according to the full persuasion of his own mind, where others are not injured thereby."

No government could be strong enough to impose beliefs on people. No government should try.

And the idea of religious freedom would spread because there were thousands of Americans who did not care about religion at all. Some were simply uninterested, but many of these believed

in God, some in Christ as well. Their feeling, though, was that organized religion, even a newly reawakened one, was what they or their ancestors had come to America to avoid.

One historian has estimated that even after the Awakening, 96 percent of the residents of the colonies were not regular churchgoers, though that estimate seems high. In 1780, the states had a lot of churches, almost 3,000 of them for 3 million people. That figures out to one for every 1,000 people.

Regardless of their number, the unchurched were influential, for among them were men named Thomas Jefferson, Benjamin Franklin and Thomas Paine. They called themselves Deists. They believed in God and in the practice of virtue, both as a means of worship and to assure a reward after death. It was a calm, rational belief, a reaction against the fire and brimstone of the Great Awakening.

For them, organized religion was a waste. It was not that government could not impose religion. It was that religion was not worth imposing. Beyond the basics — God and virtue — it was all irrelevant.

Ironically, that line of thinking led the Deists to the same conclusion about religious freedom as the Awakened — that it was absolutely essential.

"When a religion is good," said Franklin, "I conceive that it will support itself; and when it cannot support itself and . . . is obliged to call for the help of the civil power, it is a sign, I apprehend, of its being a bad religion."

In *Common Sense* Paine agreed: "As to religion, I hold it to be the indispensable duty of governments to protect conscientious professors thereof, and I know no other business which government has to do therewith."

Jefferson held his conviction that there must and shall be a complete separation between church and state in America with more fire. He had grown up in a Virginia where the Episcopal Church was established, and was himself taught at one point by an Anglican cleric whose bigoted opinions helped to sour Jefferson on organized religion for life.

Time and again in his writings he repeated his conviction that religion was "a matter between every man and his Maker." As for his own religious principles, he once wrote a friend, "I am of a sect by myself, as far as I know."

On an occasion late in life he dodged another inquiry regarding his religion by saying, "Say nothing of my religion. It is known to my God and to myself alone. Its evidence before the world is to be

The Deists:

Thomas Jefferson, Thomas Paine, and Benjamin Franklin (above, left to right) all believed that man's relationship to God could be direct, and did not require an organized church to serve as an intermediary. "I am of a sect by myself, so far as I know," Jefferson wrote.

sought in my life; if that has been honest and dutiful to society, the religion which has regulated it cannot be a bad one."

Jefferson's conviction that there must be no connection between religion and government was so strong that the spirit he burned with as he wrote Virginia's Statute on Religious Freedom can still be felt in re-reading the words today.

" ... Almighty God hath created the mind free," he wrote, reiterating the sentiments William Penn had brought to America fully a century before. Jefferson continued, saying that " ... to compel a man to furnish money for the propagation of opinions that he disbelieves and abhors is sinful and tyrannical ... Even forcing him to support this or that teacher of his own religious persuasion is depriving him of ... liberty ... "

In 1776, moreover, the idea of freedom of religion, and its corollary, a distrust of the power of organized churches, were being pushed by a new factor: the fear that England would try to use the apparatus of the Anglican Church as a tool to impose the will of the Mother Country on the rebellious colonies.

The Protestantism that had developed in the colonies by 1776 was more than just anti-Catholic. Increasingly, it feared and disdained any religious hierarchy. The churches of Presbyterians, Congre-gationalists, Baptists, and Quakers—who far outnumbered the Anglicans—were run by members of the local laity, not by a hierarchy away at the main office.

Local autonomy of congregations was partly a matter of principle, partly a matter of history, and partly a matter of adjusting to the geographic realities of the New World. If a congregation was out in the middle of Pennsylvania, it could not wait for decrees from Philadelphia, New York, London or Berlin.

And decrees from the big city might seem irrelevant to frontier life anyway.

The Anglicans suffered from geography as well. Their church was a hierarchical one, but the hierarchy was 3,000 miles away. To be ordained, a would-be minister had to go to England since there were no bishops on this side of the Atlantic. This seemed a little silly to colonial Anglicans, especially as a disturbing number of their brightest young men died in transit of disease or shipwreck.

The American Anglicans wanted an act of Parliament to give them a bishop. That seemed reasonable to them.

But it did not seem reasonable to all those other colonial Protestants. Once there was a bishop of America, the non-Anglicans reasoned, there could easily be an established Anglican church of America, supported by taxes from everyone and tolerating no dissent from anyone.

The Congregationalists, who had the power in New England, saw little advantage in giving the power to some other group. And all the other sects, which thrived in the absence of a dominant faith, were violently opposed as well.

So the reasonable request, never fulfilled, ended up boosting the colonies' even greater appreciation of the religious freedom. It also increased anti-British feeling in the colonies at a time when other factors has already heated those feelings to the boiling point.

The Revolution itself would remove whatever lingering doubts Philadelphia or most of the rest of America had about religious freedom. While each faith would produce its share of patriots, the smaller religious minorities tended to produce more than their share. They would prove they had earned a place in the new nation.

It remained only for Thomas Jefferson and James Madison, in long and eloquent debates in the Virginia House of Burgesses from 1776 to 1786, to develop the rationale for justifying the religious diversity that had developed in colonial America over 150 years of history.

But even without the elegant arguments, those doubts would surely have dissipated anyway. The new nation was simply too diverse, the tradition of individuality in religion simply too strong.

★ ★ ★

Mikveh Israel's cemetery, established in 1740, represented the first Jewish religious institution in Philadelphia.

Patriot Jews Found *Mikveh Israel*

By Laura Lippstone

Nathan Levy needed a place to bury his child. Neither Christ Church nor the Strangers Burying Ground would do. Levy was a Jew, and in his grief he was determined that only a Jewish cemetery would do. But there wasn't one in Philadelphia.

Levy dealt with the problem by puchasing a plot of land on Spruce Street, between Eighth and Ninth Streets, out in what was then countryside, and establishing it as a communal cemetery. It is still there, now crowded among the buildings of center city.

In a real sense, Levy's action marked the beginning of formal Jewish religious life in Philadelphia. The city's Jewish population grew steadily during the 18th century, reaching about 100 by 1765, and then tripled by 1776 as Jews fled British-held cities, like New York, which had a large, established Jewish community, for Philadelphia, the Patriot capital, which did not.

Even before the war, men with such surnames as Levy, Gomez, Mordecai, Phillips, and Gratz had joined together to "promote our Holy Religion, and establish a proper Congregation in this city." They had founded Mikveh Israel, the city's first synagogue.

Bishop William White: Chaplain to the Revolution

The dean of Philadelphia's clergy smoked cigars, drank wine, read novels, played cards—and was a one-man ecumenical movement.

By Charles G. Dorman

The door of the big, three-and-a-half-story red brick home on Walnut Street where the Reverend Doctor William White resided was opened to all who knocked.

The openness of Mr. White, who became the presiding bishop of the American Protestant Episcopal Church, was so proverbial that it was celebrated in an old piece of Philadelphia doggerel that relates the tale of a rat which was caught and sent as a prank to the homes of various prominent Philadelphians.

When the rat eventually arrived at the bishop's door:

Bishop White, free from sin,
  Opened the door and took it in.

Apocryphal though the story is, it is evidence of Bishop White's well-earned reputation for good works

At first, they had rented a house on Cherry Alley, which later became Cherry Street. The congregation then purchased a site with an old bake house on it a short distance away on Sterling Alley, which connected Race and Cherry Streets between Third and Fourth Streets. Difficulties emerged when the Reformed German Protestants next door complained that a synagogue would "disturb" them in some way that was never made clear.

The Jews replied, first expressing surprise that the Germans would think that they would be disturbed, then offering to sell the site to the Germans for what it had cost the synagogue. The letters went unanswered.

An emergency fund-raising drive gathered enough money to buy a second site on the north side of Cherry, between Third Street and Sterling Alley. Congregation Mikveh Israel opened its doors on Sept. 13, 1782. Haym Salomon, who had worked closely with Robert Morris in handling the precarious finances of the Revolutionary government, and who was the largest contributor toward the building of the synagogue, was accorded the honor of opening the door as the congregation walked from its old quarters to the new synagogue. Opening prayers were offered for "George Washington, the General Assembly, and friends and allies of the nation."

The red brick building was small—30 feet by 36 feet. Wooden benches were placed along either side of the room, both facing the center, one side being for women, and the other for men. On the east wall was the ark (a closet containing the Torah), and facing it was a special seat for the *hazan*, or congregational leader. The congregation would not have an ordained rabbi for many years.

The new synagogue represented an amalgam of influences from other cities in the New World and from Europe. Contributions had been solicited from congregations in Newport, Savannah, Charleston, Lancaster, Surinam, St. Croix, St. Thomas, and Cap Francois.

The congregation's first *hazan* had fled from New York, where he had been the leader of Shearith Israel. The Philadelphia synagogue also became the repository during the war of the New York congregation's ritual property. Many of the members were from New York, and the departure of the New Yorkers for their own city after the war created a temporary crisis for Mikveh Israel.

Handicapped by the lack of people trained in Jewish law, the congregation would find itself forced to write to congregations in Europe for help in unraveling thorny questions involving the legalities of intermarriage with non-Jews and other matters.

The lack of Jewish women made the problem of intermarriage a continuing one in the early years of the synagogue. Usually the gentile woman would convert and take a Jewish name; "Sarah Abrahams" was one that was ritually given. But there was resistance in the community to such marriages, particularly matches involving a Jewish woman and a non-Jewish man.

Rebecca Gratz, a woman whose great beauty and acts of charity literally became legendary in her own time (the character "Rebecca" in Sir Walter Scott's *Ivanhoe* is said to have been based on her), never married. It has been suggested that this was because the love of her life was Samuel Ewing, a gentile. When he died she quietly entered the room where the coffin lay and placed three white roses together with a miniature of herself on his breast.

Other problems faced by the congregation's ruling body, or *adjunta*, involved the enforcement of Jewish law on a Jewish community that had grown unaccustomed to discipline. Edwin Wolf 2d and Maxwell Whiteman in their book, *The History of the Jews of Philadelphia*, tell of one episode in which a Philadelphia Jew, on a business trip to Baltimore, was reported to have been seen getting a shave on the Sabbath. The case was finally dropped because of lack of evidence, however.

But the most profound problem faced by the congregation was the mixing together within it of two different Jewish traditions, the Sephardic and the Ashkenazic. The rift resulted from different patterns of migration following the conquest of Judea by the Romans and the destruction of the Temple.

Sephardic Jews were those who relocated to Spain and Portugal on the Iberian peninsula, and they were the first to come to the New World. Shearith Israel in New York, as well as the synagogues in Newport and Charleston, was Sephardic.

The *Ashkenazim* came to American from Germany and elsewhere in Europe.

Although Mikveh Israel had been founded in the Sephardic tradition, an increasing number of its members were Ashkenazic. The two traditions had different prayer books, different hymns, different orders of service, and some other differing religious customs.

Finally, in 1802, some members of Mikveh Israel broke away to form the city's first Ashkenazic synagogue, Rodeph Shalom, a short distance away from Mikveh Israel.

Both continue to exist today. Mikveh Israel, the only Sephardic synagogue in Philadelphia, has moved four times, and is now located at Broad and York Streets. A Torah and some ritual bells have survived from the original synagogue.

Rodeph Shalom, now at Broad and Mount Vernon Streets, became a Reform synagogue after it moved to Broad Street in 1870, when Marcus Jastrow was rabbi. It later achieved wider fame under Rabbi Henry Berkowitz.

One more move is in the immediate offing for Mikveh Israel. Its present building is for sale, and it move to a chapel adjacent to the Museum of Jewish History on Independence Mall. ★ ★ ★

and saintliness among all levels of Philadelphia society. It would appear that he and his friend Benjamin Franklin shared Philadelphia in their public-spirited endeavors, with Franklin founding the city's literary and scientific institutions, and Bishop White the city's welfare agencies. (The bishop, to be sure, also received a strong helping hand from the Quakers, who had started it all to begin with.)

He founded, or was instrumental in founding, Episcopal Academy, Episcopal Hospital, Philadelphia School for the Deaf, the Society for the Alleviation of Misery in Public Prisons, and other institutions, organizations, and societies.

But this is Bishop White, the the venerable living legend with long white hair. The Reverend Mr. White was even more interesting when he was helping to make American history. He was a close friend of Washington and Lafayette, as well as of Franklin and other founding fathers. One of the first and most prominent American Anglicans to support the Patriot cause, he became chaplain to both the Continental Congress and, later, the U.S. Senate.

It was largely through his writings and labors that the American Anglican (Episcopal) Church was preserved, but he was also a one-man ecumenical movement. At public events during the early decades of the new nation, the bishop was usually the spokesman for the clergymen of all faiths in the city. In Fourth of July parades, Bishop White led the city's ministerial delegation with the rabbi of Mikveh Israel on one arm and the priest from Old St. Joseph's on the other.

The bishop was incapable, it was said, of looking askance at any religious belief so long as it glorified God and encouraged righteousness among its adherents.

The bishop was also a true product of his Anglo-American gentleman background and the tradition of

The bishop's saintly image has to be amended somewhat to take into account the time he and Ben Franklin spirited Betsy Shewell from her bedroom.

the cultured, fox-hunting English parson (provincial version, of course). He believed that life should be lived to the fullest, so long as The Commandments were observed. He smoked cigars, read novels, went to the theater, drank wine, and played cards.

While still a very young man, "Billy" White was part of a plan aimed at re-uniting the young Philadelphia artist, Benjamin West, then in London, with his fiancee, Elizabeth Shewell. Elizabeth, or Betsy, as she was called, was an engaging young lady of 18 who resided with her brother. (They were orphans.) Brother Shewell took a dim view of his sister marrying a poor artist in faraway London, and was standing as a bulwark in the path of True Love.

White and his co-conspirators—Francis Hopkinson and Benjamin Franklin — arranged on a dark night to raise a ladder to her bedroom window, by which she escaped from the house.

The trick to the operation was to get the young lady aboard a ship at the last possible moment so that no frenzied cross-country ride the next day by Brother Shewell could cut her off at the mouth of the Delaware. Someone in the escape-planning group — and this writer tends to credit the crafty B. Franklin, printer — knew that a London-bound ship would, on this particular evening, drop down the Delaware with the 2 a.m. tide, and then stop at Chester to take on a supply of fresh water.

So the party rode overland to Chester, and when the ship stopped there, it took on not only water, but Miss Shewell and West's entire family. By dawn, the boat was a safe distance away on its route to England. Benjamin and Betsy, again in storybook fashion, were married in London and lived happily ever after.

Colonel Thomas White of Maryland, a prosperous, land-owning lawyer, was the bishop's father. As the 18th century progressed, and Philadelphia's destiny as the wonder metropolis of British North America unfolded, Colonel White moved to this city and established his residence on Market between Second and Third Streets. The home was in the middle of everything. The market stalls, the wharves, and the courthouse were close by. Moreover, the house was almost in the shadow of Christ Church.

A short time after his arrival, Colonel White, a widower, was married to Elizabeth Hewlings Newman, a widow from Burlington, N.J. From this union came "Billy" White, born April 4, 1748, and, the next year, Mary White. Mary would later marry Robert Morris, the financier of the Revolution.

Perhaps the closeness to Christ Church, with its superb bell chimes, exerted some subtle influence on the growing boy. At any rate, from an early age he aspired to be an Anglican clergyman.

William White was graduated at age 17 from the Academy of Philadelphia, which later became the University of Pennsylvania. He studied literature and theology after his graduation, and then in October of 1770 he departed for England to be ordained by the Church of England as an Anglican clergyman.

He spent a year and a half in England visiting relatives, sightseeing, studying, and becoming enamored of the English countryside. He returned to Philadelphia in 1772 to accept a position as assistant minister at both Christ Church and St. Peter's, and the following year took in marriage Mary Harrison, daughter of a prosperous merchant and former mayor. The young couple set up housekeeping in a house on Front Street, between Pine and Lombard, and began to raise a family.

The Rev. Mr. White had always been careful to keep a clean dividing line between his politics and his religion, and so he must have been particularly troubled when the storm of revolutionary fervor began to blow up. While he considered himself a Philadelphian and an American, he had to weigh as well the fact that his religious vows included a pledge of loyalty to the sovereign of England.

Yet after a brief, but traumatic, inner struggle he

chose the Patriot cause. His decision becomes more remarkable when one realizes that he was the only Anglican clergyman in Pennsylvania to go immediately over to the American side when independence had been declared.

When the Rev. White appeared at the State House as Independence Hall was then known, to sign a pledge of allegiance to the new state of Pennsylvania, he was greeted outside the building by an acquaintance of Loyalist persuasion who was noting all "rebels" for future reference.

The man said nothing as Mr. White passed, but nonetheless managed an eloquent gesture of warning. He placed his hands around his neck like a hangman's noose, and then gave an impression of the death grimace of a hanged man.

White got the point, and after taking the oath, returned outside and remarked to the Loyalist: "I perceived, by your gesture, that you thought I was exposing my neck to great danger by the step I have taken. But I have not taken it without full deliberation. I know my danger, and that it is greater on account of my being a clergyman of the Church of England. But I trust in Providence. The cause is a just one, and I am persuaded that (it will) be protected."

Because of his unwavering patriotism, he was made, together with Reverend Duffield of Pine Street Presbyterian Church, chaplain of the Continental Congress. He was notified of the appointment while on his way from Philadelphia to Maryland to escape the British, who were advancing rapidly on Philadelphia. He immediately turned his horse's head west, toward York, Pa., where the Congress had retreated.

He continued in that post throughout the war, but when the fighting ended at Yorktown in 1781, he turned his attention completely to the wreckage of what had been the American Anglican Church. As indicated at the beginning of our story, it was largely his work that transformed the American Anglican Church into the American Protestant Episcopal Church. In 1786 he went to London to be consecrated as its bishop.

In the late spring of 1787, when the newly consecrated bishop arrived back in Philadelphia, he found that his new house near the corner of Third and Walnut Streets was ready for the family to move in. It was much larger than the house on Front Street, and Bishop White had bought new windows "in the latest London style," with much larger panes than was customary in America, for the front rooms of his house.

The new windows failed to impress the the local fire insurance association, though, which wrote an extra clause into the bishop's policy saying that while the association had no objection to the bishop's having these stylish new windows, if the house burned down he was only going to be reimbursed for normal, American-size windows.

The bishop also brought back some pieces of furniture, but most of the new pieces he needed he ordered from his old friend and Christ Church vestryman, Jonathan Gostelowe, one of several masterful cabinetmakers then in Philadelphia.

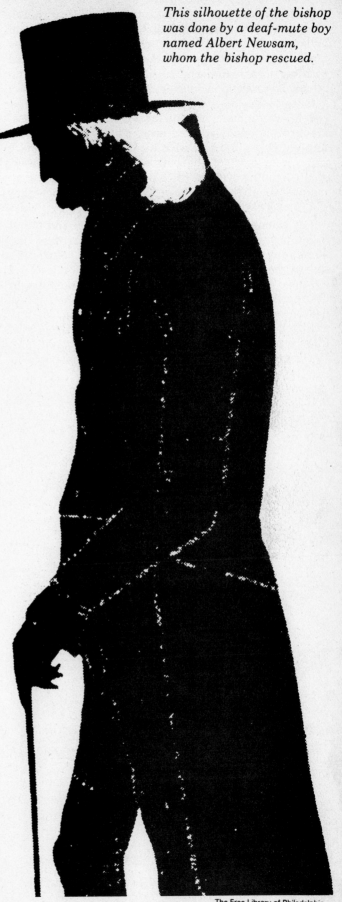

This silhouette of the bishop was done by a deaf-mute boy named Albert Newsam, whom the bishop rescued.

The Rights of Americans

Bishop White attended not only to his many church duties, but also to many self-assigned humanitarian and philanthropic ones. One day when he was passing by the City Hall, a boisterous area that was usually filled with vendors, mendicant musicians and veterans, and others, he came upon a particularly affecting scene.

A small boy, apparently in the charge of a large, rough-looking man, was cutting out silhouettes of passers-by who would stop to pose. The boy was marvelously quick and artful with his scissors and the black paper, and most of the patrons were greatly pleased, gladly handing over the price requested. But a few complained about the quality of the work, and when they did the big man would box the child's ears.

The bishop was outraged. He investigated and found that the man had taken the boy, who was deaf and dumb, out of an orphanage because of the youngster's skill at making silhouettes, which the man was now exploiting. Then he went into the building and brought the sheriff out. Before the day was out, Bishop White had become the child's guardian. The bishop, in turn, arranged for the boy to live with one of the Christ Church parishioners.

The episode marked the beginning of the bishop's interest in the deaf and mute, an interest that was to culminate in the establishment of an institution that eventually became the Philadelphia School for the Deaf.

Bishop White's efforts were rewarded by the loyal support of his congregation and his friends in Philadelphia. In the late 1790s, the bishop needed, for some reason, a short-term loan of $5,000. He sent a servant note expressing his need, and apparently offering his house as collateral, to one of his wealthiest parishioners, the lately-widowed wife of former Mayor Powel. She sent back a check for the amount requested, together with a letter in which she noted drily:

"Dear Sir, It will not be necessary for you to place your mansion as collateral for this loan, as you are in a non-hazardous profession."

The tragedy of Bishop White's life was that seven of his eight children died in young adulthood of various diseases, including yellow fever, tuberculosis, and cancer, after marrying and having children. As a result, all of the bishop's eleven grandchildren grew up under his care in the big house on Walnut Street.

Among these were several blossoming granddaughters, who, according to one much-smitten young ministerial student who came to visit, were "young, attractive, intelligent, and knew the contents of all the modern novels."

The bishop apparently brought them up with a practiced liberality. When the granddaughters requested to go walking of an evening with their beaux, their grandfather would characteristically say, "Yes, daughter dear. Just don't go into the woods beyond Ninth Street."

Bishop White, a true son of Philadelphia, lived 88 years, and died in his Walnut Street home on July 17, 1836. The house still stands today at 309 Walnut, and is a part of Independence National Historical Park. The scene inside is much the same today as it was in the days before his death, right down to the grandchildren's toys spread out on the floor of the front room.

One room, the bishop's study, is almost exactly the same as it was on the day he died, thanks to a gesture his granddaughters made in veneration of the old gentleman.

Soon after his funeral they commissioned John Sartain, a Philadelphia engraver and artist, to do a painting of the bishop's study, to provide, in effect, an almost photographic record of how the room looked on the day the bishop died. Incredibly, about 60 percent of the original objects had survived, and strikingly similar substitutes for most of the others were available.

Sartain's painting even included two half-smoked cigars the bishop had "parked" on a chair rail.

When the house, with the restored study, was officially opened to the public in October 1967, this writer personally undertook to add that detail to the restoration. Arriving an hour before the first guests—present-day parishioners of Christ Church—I furiously smoked halfway through two cigars. At the appointed hour, I was green, but the room was properly blue with the authentic haze of the bishop's cigars, which were placed on the chair rail—right where he left them. ★★★

Bishop White's house, at Third and Walnut, has been fully restored, down to the cigars on a chair rail.

The Colonial Press:
Guilty of Inciting to Revolt

By Mark Squires

In 1688, when Philadelphia printer William Bradford published Penn's Frame of Government, the constitution for the colony, without official permission, the deputy governor, John Blackwell, summoned him to his quarters. Despite the fact that he was the only printer within a hundred miles, Bradford would not admit he had printed the document. Neither would he deny it. He added that he would print anything he liked.

Bradford's bold assertion would have astounded his English counterparts, but from the very beginnings of English settlement in America, the press here took shape in peculiarly American fashion. When newspapers were established, they took and defended stands on any issue, whether the government liked it or not. They attacked the government, which the government did not like, and they did it all at a time when English newspapers were still the docile tools government, doing little more in terms of politics that reprint government announcements — when authorized to do so.

While many other aspects of American life represented adaptations of traditions and attitudes that were already established in Europe, it can be argued that

the American press grew up as an essentially American phenomenon, simply because there was no extensive European journalistic tradition to draw on.

When the first newspaper in Philadelphia, the *American Weekly Mercury,* went to press in 1719, it was the third to be established in the colonies — and only the fifteenth in the *world.* It's not surprising, then, that the press was the radical cutting edge during the events leading to revolution. Twenty-three American papers were committed to the Patriots; only two were Tory.

John Adams believed that "the Revolution was effected before the war commenced," that "the radical change in principles, opinions and sentiments of the people was the real American Revolution." If so, one can argue that the American press made the Revolution. Unquestionably its influence on America's "principles, opinions and sentiments" was profound.

The development of this influence — indeed the growth of the American press itself — is a remarkable success story. Despite Bradford's cheeky response in 1688, the very existence of a press was by no means assured.

Understandably, few colonists rushed into the printing business. The technol-

ogy of the time was rudimentary at best, and printing was a hard, tedious business. Things had barely changed since Johann Gutenberg had invented movable type three centuries before. In fact, printers in Mainz, Germany, had been able to print 600 copies an hour. Colonial printers were not going any faster.

It took four difficult pulls of the wooden, hand-operated, screw-pressure, flat-bed press to make one four-page newspaper. For the printers of larger papers, a weekly run in 1776 meant fifty back-breaking hours of work. And that didn't include the typesetting — picking up thousands of individual letters, placing them one by one in a composing stick, in which each line was assembled. Then the lines had to be arranged in galley forms.

But back pain may have been the least of the printer's problems. Most papers were printed with badly worn type, because getting a new set meant ordering from England. To combat chronic paper shortages, the printers frequently included in the paper's columns exhorations to women to save their rags for the few paper mills operating in the colonies. Some papers were printed on sheets that were mismatched in size, color, or quality.

American newspapers gave no sign that the principle of objectivity existed, and freedom of the press tended to extend only to Patriot papers.

THE

PENNSYLVANIA JOURNAL;

AND

WEEKLY ADVERTISER.

Thursday, *October* 31, 1765.   NUMB. 1195.

EXPIRING: In Hopes of a Resurrection to LIFE again.

The famous "tombstone" edition of the Pennsylvania Journal *reported—prematurely as it turned out—the death of American journalism because of the Stamp Act.*

In the winter and during bad weather it became difficult—if not impossible—to distribute the paper to the countryside. Ben Franklin filled his paper in bad weather with his own essays and fables, some of which were popularly believed in Europe. Other editors simply discontinued their papers for the winter. Cold weather also posed production problems. In poorly heated colonial print shops the paper sometimes froze when the ink was applied.

Adding to a printer's miseries were poor postal systems and the fact that many subscribers were perennial deadbeats.

Some Revolutionary editors complained that in the best of times a quarter of their subscribers failed to pay. With just such deadbeats in mind, Thomas Fleet, who became more famous for printing his mother-in-law's "Mother Goose" nursery rhymes than for his newspaper, bewailed the lack of "Justice and Common Honesty" in America.

And while colonists didn't wrap their garbage up in old newspapers — paper was too valuable for that — the papers were used in some unusual ways. Americans who couldn't afford glass windows, for instance, would apply a coating of grease to the newspapers, making them translucent, and use them for window panes.

That these tiny, precarious colonial newspapers — which could go under at any moment with a broken press, a bad winter, or too many deadbeats on its subscribers' list — could become effective "engines of opinion" in criticizing government seems remarkable in hindsight.

In the 17th and 18th century, freedom of the press was neither considered nor valued. Newspapers were still a new and relatively distrusted factor in the English-speaking world, and governments casually assumed the right of censorship.

The infamous British Star-Chamber Court, for example, convicted a printer in 1663 for having printed a tract which argued that a ruler should be held accountable to the people. Thirty days' hard labor? Hardly. He was drawn and quartered.

The colonies, fortunately, failed to import that kind of censorship, but the early governors and assemblies were hardly champions of press liberty. Governor William Berkeley of Virginia thanked God, in 1669, that his colony had no printing presses and no free schools. Even William Penn, who promised printer William Bradford Sr. a relatively free hand, reneged when Bradford began referring to the Proprietor derisively as "Lord Penn" in the almanac he printed in 1685.

Bradford, however, persisted in pub-

lishing documents without government permission, together with less controversial almanacs, proclamations, broadsides, and the like. (He did not publish a newspaper as such.) He was also arrested several more times.

But a comparison of what happened to Bradford and the fate of the hapless British printer mentioned above points up the important difference between press censorship in the mother country and in the colonies.

Bradford's most serious brush with the law began in 1692. In the heat of a battle George Keith was waging within the Quaker Meeting, Keith wrote a tract condemning his opponents, including a man named Jennings, who also happened to be a judge. The printer was summarily jailed.

In court, he put forward the argument that the eminent Philadelphia lawyer, Andrew Hamilton, would assert again 42 years later when he was defending a New York newspaperman, John Peter Zenger, against a charge of criminal libel and sedition. It was Bradford's contention that the jury, not the judges, should decide whether he was guilty of sedition. Under existing English law, juries in such cases were only to find whether the defendant did the printing and the judges decided whether the subject matter was seditious.

Bradford's case went to the jury with the traditional instructions and his conviction seemed certain, since there was no question that he had printed the "seditious" tract. But the jury, deliberating for two days, could not reach a verdict (whether Bradford's argument had anything to do with this will never be known) and Bradford was released.

Bradford's *avant garde* notion of freedom of the press in no way became government policy in America, and wasn't widely noticed. Benjamin Harris' Boston-based *Public Occurrences Both Foreign and Domestick* was permanently suppressed after its first issue appeared without permission in 1690.

Harris wrote in the issue that he was starting a paper "that something may be done toward curing the spirit of lying." He promised to correct mistakes, be accurate and expose rumor-mongers. That was apparently too much for the governor of Massachusetts, who declared the paper contained "reflections of a very high nature," apparently using "high" in its antique usage, meaning something that smelled badly.

In 1704, John Campbell began the *Boston News-Letter,* admitting without embarrassment that he awaited the governor's approval before printing. Though this was the first regularly issued paper in the colonies, Campbell never made much money from it, and never sold more than 300 copies per issue.

The source of its unpopularity is not hard to pin down. The paper was typical of the era: dull and cautious. A typical item: "On Thursday night last, Sampson Waters, a young man, went well to bed and was found dead next morning." Nothing more.

Campbell also stocked up foreign dispatches as they came off the ships, printing the oldest first. His four-page paper wasn't up to the task and Campbell eventually fell nine to thirteen months behind in the news.

Andrew Bradford's *Mercury*, Philadelphia's first newspaper, was a considerable improvement over Campbell's. But Bradford edited his paper much like every other editor would for the next few decades — hardly at all. Contributors, whose work was published unedited, and reprints accounted for all but local news items, which were given short shrift in those days.

The Bradfords became an early press dynasty in America. William Bradford — the one who had published Penn's Frame of Government without permission — finally left Philadelphia after a number of further quarrels, and went to New York, where he established a newspaper that, ironically enough, became the government mouthpiece in the Zenger case. William Bradford's son, Andrew, came back to Philadelphia and started the *Mercury,* and his son, William Bradford 2d, established the *Pennsylvania Journal.*

Bradford was no crusader; he avoided governmental criticism as much as possible. This was perhaps understandable. The first time he tried it, he avoided jail only by explaining to the legislature that he hadn't written the item, just printed it. (The writer had blandly called on the legislature to settle its budget crisis, and "restore us to our former happy times.")

Benjamin Franklin, writing for the *Mercury* under the pseudonym "Busy Body," was responsible for getting Bradford in hot water a second time. During an election, Busy Body made a comment that for some reason sounded libelously accusatory to the state legislators: "In Rome," he wrote, "none could pretend to courage, gallantry, and greatness of mind without being first of all possessed with a public spirit, and a love of their country . . . ."

Bradford, who was generally well regarded, was nonetheless able to avoid being prosecuted in connection with "Busy Body" Franklin's article.

Journalism — to Bradford and most other colonial printers — was simply a sideline. Besides taking on outside printing jobs, Bradford sold spices, tea, rum, patent medicines, books, quadrants, spectacles, mirrors, whalebone, and beaver hats.

Other printers who ventured into the newspaper field survived by putting out government proclamations, laws, license forms, manifests for shipowners, bills of lading, pamphlets for philosophers and preachers, ballads (especially when a juicy crime was committed) and almanacs. Until Ben Franklin founded his *Gazette,* no one even considered making even a major portion of his fortune in journalism.

It was actually Franklin's brother, James, who founded the first colonial newspaper really worth of the name — the *New England Courant* in 1721. The *Courant* was also the first paper deliberately founded to oppose governmental policies.

The result? James landed in jail and — eventually — he departed for Rhode Island. Seventeen-year-old Ben wound up running the paper, until he ran off to Philadelphia, via New York. The Bay Colony obviously wasn't quite ready for a paper published without permission.

By 1726, Franklin apparently thought that Philadelphia was ready. When Franklin returned to Philadelphia in 1726 from London, where he had gone to buy a press, he decided to start a paper. Unfortunately, he revealed his plans who betrayed him to Samuel Keimer, the printer who had been Franklin's first Philadelphia employer. Keimer then

Benjamin Franklin, whose printing shop is depicted, revolutionized newspapers by introducing well designed ads, and by making his writers express themselves clearly.

The Rights of Americans

Large initials, italics, and capital letters were all used to get the reader's attention. All nouns were capitalized, plus any words that struck the printer's fancy

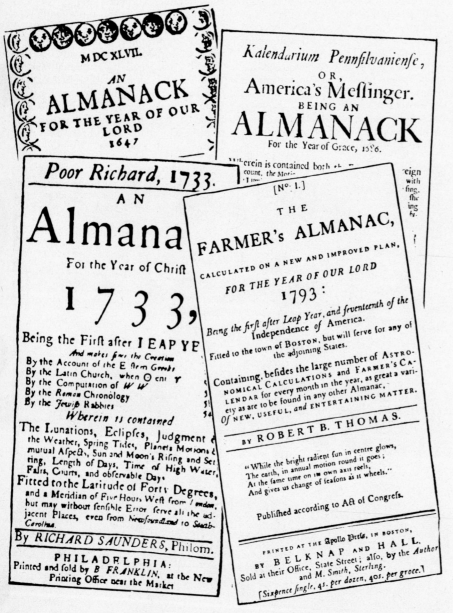

For most printers, newspapers were a sideline, almost a hobby; they made their big money on things like almanacs.

stole Franklin's idea (and potential subscribers) by putting out *The Universal Instructor in All Arts and Sciences; and Pennsylvania Gazette* in 1727.

Franklin retaliated by undertaking a campaign of ridicule against Keimer in Andrew Bradford's competing *Mercury*. Keimer, it seems, was an easy target for Franklin's biting wit. He had no nose for news and took to filling his pages with generous extracts from Chamber's *Dictionary of the Arts and Sciences* which had recently been published in London.

Apparently Keimer simply handed the book to one of his printers and told him to start with "A" and keep going alphabetically within space limitations. Eventually he printed the selection on "Abortion," and Franklin composed irate letters from two women ("Martha Careful" and "Celia Shortface"), which he sent to Bradford, who "thought fit to Publish" them.

"Martha Careful" expressed outrage:

"In behalf of my Self and many good modest Women in this City (who are almost out of continence) ... as a Warning to Samuel Keimer; That if he proceed further to Expose the Secrets of our Sex ... my Sister Molly and myself, with some others, are Resolved to run the Hazard of taking him by the Beard, at the next Place we meet him, and make an Example of him for his Immodesty ..."

(Franklin's use of the word "continence" was probably regarded as salaciously amusing by the *Mercury's* more literate readers. The word meant "self-restraint," but also had a sexual connotation, meaning that the women were declining to participate in relations of that sort.)

For almost a year Franklin used the *Mercury* to mock Keimer, but the unimaginative publisher was probably hurt more by his own lack of style and content; adding tales of English life and slices of Defoe's *Religious Courtship* to the dictionary excerpts did nothing to boost circulation. By 1728, Keimer's subscribers had declined from 250 to 90 and in 1729 the debt-ridden publisher sold out to Franklin, who shortened the paper's name to the *Pennsylvania Gazette*.

Other differences became apparent almost immediately. Franklin's first innovation was making the *Gazette* America's first semi-weekly, but that experiment failed almost at once, and the paper reverted to a weekly publishing schedule.

His stylistic innovations were more successful. He urged writers to use "the plainest word," so that even a "scrubbing girl might understand it." Journalism teachers are still urging the same thing today.

Franklin made better use of the paragraph as well, attempting to eliminate unbroken blocks of type, and he often added spicy editorial comments in passing. Without doubt, Franklin was the wittiest of colonial newspapermen.

He also had superior printing talent (he won a government job from Bradford by printing a proclamation Bradford had done in a more readable form) and a ruthless business mind.

To criticize the *Mercury*, for example, he once ghost-wrote a letter in his own paper complaining about the stale news in the *Gazette* in "Numb. 669." He then wrote an editorial reply, which politely noted that the letter should have gone to the *Mercury* since it was the only paper in town to have reached that number of issues — and, it was clearly indicated, the *Mercury* was the only paper open to the charge of printing stale news.

With this combination of skills, Franklin made the *Gazette* colonial America's most successful paper. When he sold out in 1766, he had made enough profit to enable him to retire quite comfortably.

What were the newspapers of Franklin's era like? Had you lived in 18th-century America, the paper you subscribed to —which you'd receive by mail or paperboy — would most likely have been called a "Gazette," since the law required official announcements to be printed in "the gazette." (Other popular titles included *Mercury, Journal, Post-Boy, Packet, Courant, Post.*) Its illustrations, typography, and layout would have seemed erratic at best.

Illustrations were, in fact, extremely rare. The first illustration in the colonial press was of England's new "United Kingdom" flag, printed in the *News-Letter* in 1708. The first editorial cartoon was Franklin's "Join or Die." (The cartoon was based on the folk belief that a grass snake would fragment when attacked, recombine and still live.) Generally, though, illustrations were limited to simple standing "cuts" — such as a ship sailing in front of the paper's departure column — because making woodcuts was simply too expensive and time-consuming for the harried colonial printers.

Colonial typography used large initials, italics, capitals and small capitals as attention-getters, rather than multi-column headlines. Until the 1760s all nouns were capitalized, plus any other word that struck the printer's fancy. Spelling was almost as erratic. Printer John Zenger wrote "Mundy," but allowed contributors to write "Monday."

Until the Revolutionary period, the major news was foreign news. Colonists hungered for news from "home," as they referred to England. Editors assumed everyone knew the local news anyway. Printer Thomas Fleet announced in 1775 that he wasn't going to print any news about Lexington because it had been "so variously discussed."

In an effort to survive, the struggling four-page papers early began the practice of giving over the back page to advertisements. This didn't always help a great deal because ads were treated rather cavalierly. The *Pennsylvania Chronicle* in 1770 noted, "Ads omitted in this issue will be inserted in the next."

The ads announced the sale of real estate mainly, but they also touted lotteries (for churches, libraries, roads and other projects), patent medicine, ship sailings, and so on. They were squeezed together like news stories; no display ads were used.

Then, as in so many other things, Ben Franklin stepped in. He spaced the ads out more attractively, used larger display type, wrote fine copy (for George Washington, among others), and generally convinced Philadelphia businessmen that advertising was a good investment.

He even wrote the copy.

"Super fine crown soap," Franklin wrote of his brothers' soap. "It cleans fine linens, muslins, laces, chinces, cambricks, etc., with ease and expedition." Fine washables, he noted, "often suffer more from the long and hard rubbing of the washing, through the ill quality of the soap, than the wearing," something that needn't occur with this washday miracle product.

Franklin also made good reading of "personal" ads like this one: "Taken out of Pew in the Church some months since, a Common Prayer Book, bound in red, gilt, and lettered D. F. on each cover. The Person who took it is desired to open it and read the eighth Commandment and afterwards return it into the same Pew again, upon which no further Notice will be taken."

The ads also betrayed some of the less attractive sides of colonial life. Even Franklin, who later became president of one of the early abolutionist societies, advertised the contracts of indentured servants and slaves. He even owned two slaves himself.

And as the Revolution began, grim single-line ads from fleeing Loyalists often appeared: "I intend to leave this colony immediately. Payment of all debts to me should be made at once," one read.

There were descriptions of army deserters: "LAZARUS CARMADY, American-born, about five feet seven inches high, has very sore eyes ... JAMES DRIGASS, a yellow looking scoundrel ... RICHARD SWIFT, American born, about five feet nine inches high ... he is a great coward."

Other ads were even more sensational. Since printers took no responsibility for what they printed, a husband could defame his wife in print (one angry woman took a counter-ad and accused her husband of "tyranny ... incredible abuses" and several attempts to murder her) and truth-in-advertising was virtually unknown.

A freak show advertised in 1756 a "21-foot-long snake with a four-year-old child and a live dog in its belly; has a horn on its tail seven inches long, and it ran as fast as a horse."

But despite their faults, newspapers continued to attract readers. By 1750, the papers had achieved an average circulation of 500-600. By 1775, circulations sometimes soared to 1,500, even while the number of papers proliferated. There were six papers in Philadelphia in 1776.

Certainly it was the excitement of the oncoming revolution that made newspaper reading an American habit. As one reader of the time put it: "At such a day as this, where is the man that is not anxious for himself and his connections, and from week to week is not uneasy until he received his newspaper?"

In addition to his other talents, Franklin was probably the premier political cartoonist of his time. His "Join, or Die," a woodcut depicting the colonies as part of a divided snake, was widely reprinted by other newspapers.

The Rights of Americans

The Editors: *Isaiah Thomas, a Massachusetts editor, pioneered the use of atrocity stories for propaganda; William Bradford was part of the first American journalistic dynasty; James Rivington was one of the very few Loyalist editors; John Dunlap printed the Declaration of Independence.*

It was also the pre-Revolutionary events which turned once dull and cautious printers into opinion-makers. Beginning with the enactment of the Stamp Act in 1765, the press became a major force in convincing the American populace to revolt.

The Stamp Act, which forced lawyers, merchants, newspaper publishers, advertisers, and colleges to pay a tax on the paper they used, was virulently opposed by almost all of the American press. For the newspapers it wasn't simply a matter of money. The editors viewed the Act as an attempt to stifle something that they had already come to view as a basic American right. "The liberty of the press" became their rallying cry.

The newspaper editor, in historian James Melvin Lee's words, "found he could violate the censorship now with impunity ... He became braver and more critical and enjoyed for a time the freedom which rapidly changed the character of the American press."

William Bradford Jr.'s *Pennsylvania Journal and Weekly Advertiser* published one of the most dramatic issues. His paper appeared with a heavy black outline in the shape of a tombstone. Bradford noted: "The liberty of the press has been justly esteemed as one of the main pillars of the liberty of the people."

Editor Henry Miller of Germantown's *Philadelphische Staatsbote* was even more hyperbolic. He informed readers ominously that the Stamp Act went into effect on the anniversary of the infamous Lisbon earthquake.

Such opinionated coverage, quite naturally, infuriated the Loyalists. One wrote angrily that lawyers like John Adams used the press the same way "preachers used the pulpit in times of Popery ... Nothing is too wicked for them." Franklin's son William, the governor of New Jersey, likewise decried the "many seditious inflammatory writings" emanating from Philadelphia and New York, which had set New Jersey's "populace afire."

When the Stamp Act was finally re-pealed, the American press recognized its own power for the first time. Some taxes against merchants were left intact; all were removed from newspapers. The British even pardoned all papers that had appeared without stamps on the ground that there was "no stamped paper to be had." (This was often true because the Sons of Liberty, a patriot group which included several editors, forced stamp agents to resign by threatening them with physical violence.)

The Patriots had no doubts about the influence and value of the press. Even lackluster, cautious papers were suddenly perceived as exciting, partisan defenders of freedom. A frequently heard toast in Patriot taverns was "To the press! Palladium of our liberties!"

The cheering over the repeal of the Stamp Act was barely over, however, when the British announced the Townshend Acts in 1767, which included a special incentive to anger editors: a tax on all paper, hurting the printer's newspaper, as well as his other business. It seemed even worse than the Stamp Act.

The newspapers, accordingly, went to war again. This time, a Briton visiting America wrote glumly, "Every suggestion that could tend to lessen the attachment to the mother country and to raise an odium against her have been repeatedly published. The people are familiarised to read seditions, if not treasonable, (news-) papers."

In this dispute, it was Philadelphian John Dickinson who helped solidify the almost unanimous anti-British newspaper front. His *Letters From A Pennsylvania Farmer*, which argued against the British right to raise money through taxation of Americans, was printed in 21 different colonial newspapers.

The British gave in again and the Townshend Acts were repealed. The colonies and the newspapers then settles back in temporary self-satisfaction until the British gave the East India Company a monopoly in the colonies.

To the astonishment of the British, tea — thanks to the newspapers — became regarded as little better than poisonous hemlock. Suddenly, tea was the cause of "spasms, hypochondrias, apoplexies of the serious kind, palsies, dropsies, rheumatisms, low nervous, miliary and petechial fever," according to politically motivated medical columnists.

An anonymous writer in Bradford's *Journal* claimed that because of tea "our race is dwindled, and become puny, weak and disordered." Dr. Benjamin Rush of Philadelphia confirmed for *Journal* readers that the "baneful (tea) chests" contained physical as well as political "slow poison."

Rush also warned of the dangers of monopoly, as in tea monopolies, and a *Chronicle* reader wondered whether the crown would continue to hand out monopolies until Americans became little more than "hewers of wood and drawers of water to them."

To this day, tea has never regained its pre-Revolution popularity in America.

The tea crisis exploded in 1773. Patriot mobs had little difficulty dissuading collectors of tea duties to resign, and ship captains bringing tea cargoes to go home in New York, Philadelphia, and Charleston — but in Boston the colonial authorities were determined not to give in. Just as determined were the most radical patriots in the most radical city in America.

On December 16, 1773, Samuel Adams, editor Benjamin Edes and others held the famous Tea Party. The party triggered a series of punitive acts quickly named the Intolerable Acts, one of which closed the port of Boston to trade.

The journalistic prose of American newspapers now took fire. The London *Press,* with some exaggeration, believed that "not a single newspaper in the colonies would admit so much as a paragraph in favor of the mother country."

This wasn't strictly true. John Mein, editor of the *Boston Chronicle* and a fiercely partisan Loyalist, did everything he could to counteract the flow of Patriot rhetoric. At one point he clubbed a Patriot editor, John Gill, on encountering him in the streets.

Mein's efforts, while perhaps commendably spirited, could not turn the tide. By April 1775, the newspaper war became a shooting war at Lexington and Concord. It was newspaper editor Isaiah Thomas who gave Paul Revere his famous lantern signal, and Thomas fought at Lexington the next day. On May 3, his *Massachusetts Spy,* which had moved to Worcester after Thomas was forced to leave Boston, carried the most dramatic story in the brief history of the American press. The headline set the tone: "Americans! Liberty or Death! Join or Die!"

The sensationalized story of the battles at Lexington and Concord reported that "British troops, unmolested and unprovoked, wantonly and in the most inhuman manner, fired upon and killed a number of our countrymen, then robbed, ransacked, and burnt their houses! Nor could the tears of defenseless women, some of whom were in the pangs of childbirth, the cries of helpless babes, nor the prayers of old age, confined to beds of sickness, appease their thirst for blood! — or divert them from their design of MURDER and ROBBERY!"

It was a pioneering effort in the phony atrocity story.

With passions running this high, "freedom of the press" became very relative indeed. Patriot publishers, by then, had virtually a free hand. Through the Stamp Act, Townshend Acts, Tea and Intolerable Act crises, not one Patriot editor had been imprisoned for seditious libel. It was the Tory editors who came under heavy fire as events in Philadelphia moved toward the Declaration of Independence.

Earlier, in 1774, the First Continental Congress, noting the patriotic fervor of the press, had given the papers the official duty of publicizing any violations of the various resolutions forbidding trade with England. "Congress had held out no punishments but infamy," a Patriot wrote happily.

The Philadelphia Committee of Observation and Inspection, which was supposed to notify newspaper editors of infractions, had, as its general rule of thumb, "No person has the right to the protection of a community or society he wishes to destroy." They did not believe in freedom of speech or press — for Tories.

Thus, when a letter-writer in the Loyalist *Philadelphia Ledger* claimed "9 of 10 would repair to the King's Standard if it were raised," the Philadelphia committee, including editor Bradford, forced the terrified writer to recant and swear to defend the constitutional rights of Americans with his life.

This same committee also complained constantly to its New York counterpart about ferocious Tory editor James Rivington of the *New York Gazeteer.* Rivington, the committee said, was "holding out to the world evidence of dissensions which do not exist."

In making its point further, the Philadelphia committee, led by Bradford, rounded up 50 Philadelphians who then subscribed to Rivington's Patriot rival, John Holt of the *New York Journal.* But even that wasn't enough for the fractious Philadelphians.

"In Philadelphia," a writer complained in Bradford's *Journal,* "he would have been called long ago to give up ... (the presentation) of so much falsehood." James Madison wrote to Bradford's son, saying he wished "most heartily we had Rivington and his ministerial gazettes for 24 hours in this place."

Rivington's Loyalist voice was silenced in the fall of 1775 when a mob of armed Patriots rode into New York, entered his shop, smashed his presses, and carried away his type. The group of armed men marched out of town to the tune "Yankee Doodle." The *Pennsylvania Journal* reported that "a vast concourse of people assembled . . . (and) on their leaving . . . gave them three hearty cheers . . . ."

When Rivington was finally forced to flee New York, Bradford couldn't resist a last dart: "We hope the non-exportation agreement to Great Britain will always except such traitors to the liberty of America." He was perfectly happy to see Rivington exported abroad.

Not even Benjamin Franklin was immune from the intolerance of the day. Franklin's partner on the *Gazette,* David sorship in Philadelphia's papers. Every Hall, warned him that somebody had started a rumor that Franklin had something to do with the Stamp Act and that it might be unsafe to return home from England for the moment. This came about while Franklin, writing under 42 known pseudonyms, and possibly more that haven't come to light, waged a one-man war in the British press against the Act. (In point of fact, though, Franklin had at one point thought a Stamp Act would be a fair way for the colonists to pay their share of the costs of the French and Indian Wars.)

There was a halt to the general intoler-

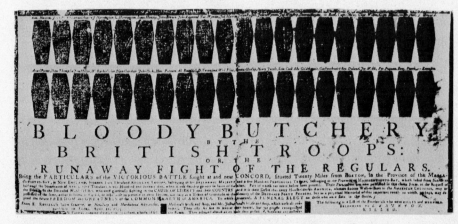

This colonial broadside showed two rows of coffins to sensationalize its account of the Battles of Lexington and Concord. (In point of fact, more British were killed than Americans.)

ance only when the Patriots gathered in Philadelphia in 1776 to debate independence at the Second Continental Congress. For a full six months, editors threw open their columns for hot, uncensored and historic argument.

Philadelphia, by then, was the publishing capital of the colonies, with seven weekly newspapers coming out on various days during the week, giving the city a close approximation of daily journalism.

In January of 1776, John Adams wrote that independence was still a Tory "scarecrow" used to frighten away Patriot support. It was a "hobgoblin of so frightful mien" as to throw the majority of delegates into "fits" if they looked it "in the face."

Six months later, every delegate — and everyone who read the newspapers — had looked the hobgoblin in the face.

It was the press which changed men's minds. During those six months, Americans argued freely and with no cen-editor — Hall of the *Post*, Miller of the German language *Straatsbote*, and even Tory James Humphreys of the *Ledger* — threw open his columns to the debaters.

The separationists made their stand clear: "He that is not with us is against us." They ridiculed the moderates, led by Dickinson, who believed peaceful reconciliation could be achieved. They predicted that a recent deal with the King of Prussia would lead to 20,000 Hessian soldiers in the colonies.

(They were right about the Hessians, but one newspaper essayist couldn't resist a little further embellishment: "The sceptered savage of Great Britain thirsteth for the blood of America. Hessians, distribution to the colonies. Towne's Brunswickers, Canadians, Indians, Negroes, Regulars, and Tories are invited to the carnage," he wrote.

Another writer pointed out in the *Journal* that Congress had already "made laws, erected courts, established magistrates, made money, levied war, and regulated commerce ... those who quail at the name of Independence support measures in the spirit of it."

To the moderates who feared the economic effects of separation, Thomas Paine retorted in the papers: "This unparalleled contention of nations is not to be settled like a school-boy's task of pounds, shillings, pence and fractions ... For the first and great question, that which involves every other in it, from which every other will flow, is happiness."

Finally, after debating the intentions of France, the practical chance for a military victory and other issues, the incessant discussion in the press, in John Adams' words, had "gradually and at last totally extinguished" the "rushlight of reconciliation."

On July 2 Congress voted nine to two for independence. Towne's *Post* managed a brief notice on the back page by nightfall: "Today the Continental Congress declared the united colonies free and independent states." The *Journal* and *Gazette* printed the news in a similarly terse fashion on July 3.

On Thursday, July 4, Congress speedily approved the full text of the Declaration by a 12-0 vote with New York abstaining.

Printer John Dunlap was hired to print copies of the Declaration for distribution to the other colonies. Towne's *Post* was the first to run the full text, however. It was printed on the front page on July 6 without comment. By August 2, every newspaper in the colonies had printed it.

And so the Revolution began. When the British came, the Patriot editors simply left town. When the British left, the Tory editors went with them.

Only three editors changed sides during the war. Benjamin Towne of the *Post* switched twice rather than move. As a Patriot, he had printed the text of the Declaration. He remained a Patriot until the British occupied Philadelphia. When the British evacuated, Towne underwent another change of heart, but he never quite got back into the Patriots' good graces. Dr. Benjamin Rush refused to contribute anything to Towne's paper until Towne admitted that "he had never pretended to be a man of good character" and was happy not to have been hung. Towne declined.

How much influence had the press really wielded?

New York Patriot editor John Holt wrote in a letter to Sam Adams: "It was by means of newspapers that we received and spread the notice of the tyrannical designs formed against America and kindled a spirit that has been sufficient to resist it and to repel the British."

The newspapers had been the main force linking the 13 colonies together. They "instigated, catalyzed, synthesized," to quote historian Arthur Schlesinger.

Newspaper editors, more than any other class, saw the colonies as one nation. They were often itinerant like Franklin, had wide family connections like Bradford and, through postage-free exchange copies (and what one Tory termed the "dirty habit of copying" one from another) knew what was happening everywhere.

And they printed it.

Wrote the secretary to British Admiral Lord Howe: "Next to the indecent harangues of the preachers, none has had a more extensive or stronger influence than the newspapers." A Patriot letter-writer put the papers ahead of the preachers. "More attention is paid by many to the newspaper than to sermons."

But the best evidence of the newspapers' growing power was the transformation of the press itself.

By 1800 over 500 newspapers had been started (though 50 percent failed within two years), and by 1820, 1,200 had been launched. The partisan Revolutionary papers had instilled in the public a respect for the press and a newspaper reading habit. By the end of the 18th century, the American press reported, and the American public read with satisfaction, that the King of England had called George Washington the greatest of all living men.

The Revolution had been won. ★ ★ ★

Printing was a slow, back-breaking process that hadn't changed since Gutenberg.

The courthouse was built in 1709 in the middle of Market Street, rising "almost majestically above the city's teeming produce markets. . . ."

The King's Crime: Obstructing Justice

By Mark Squires and Steve Twomey

The judges were seething. Here it was 1708 already and Philadelphia — bustling, booming, important Philadelphia — had no courthouse. "In the capital city of the government," the exasperated justices wrote, "the magistrates are obliged to hold court in an ale-house."

An ale-house, everyone agreed, was rather embarrassing. A fine place for saluting the King's health, but somehow not the right surroundings for murder trials, grand jury meetings, orphans' court, and all the other rituals of the ever-expanding colonial judicial system.

So, in a manner that would eventually become a Philadelphia political tradition, a deal was arranged between city and county officials. The county would build several needed bridges for city residents but would not tax them for it, while the city would build a courthouse and allow the county to use part of it for its courts.

The courthouse that resulted a year later, in 1709, certainly seemed worth the wait, not to mention the 616 pounds it cost to build. Rising almost majestically above the city's teeming produce markets in a striking array of high archways and windows, the rectangular brick building was unlike any other in the young town.

It occupied a place of honor: the center of High Street (now Market) just west of its intersection with Second Street. With its ornate cupola, which housed the town bell, the three-story structure towered above the pedestrian and wagon traffic that passed on either side, and above the homes and churches of the city.

From its east balcony, which overlooked the wooden stocks and pillory, governors gave inaugural addresses, ministers exhorted the faithful, and the curious soaked in a political panoply of meetings, encounters, and conspiracies.

One resident was so struck by the courthouse's beauty and importance that he was moved to write a poem which, inexplicably, another resident was moved to preserve, despite several tortured rhymes. Its final couplet read:

> *Here eastward stands the*
> *tracks to obloquy,*
> *And petty crimes, stocks,*
> *posts, a pillory.*

The issue was simple: Americans felt that their courts protected the "rights of Englishmen" better than English courts. And they were right.

The courthouse, miniscule by today's standards, was a significant step in the judicial history of Philadelphia and Pennsylvana. It showed how much the colonists believed in Law, and how far they had come in the practice of it.

Pennsylvania had been started a few decades before not only without a courthouse, but also without laws, courts, jails, judges and lawyers. What the Pennsylvanians did have right from the beginning, though, was the colonists' deep belief—an outgrowth of centuries of English common law tradition—in giving each man accused of a crime his day in court.

That belief became a major cause, three-quarters of a century later, for a Revolution to preserve and protect the integrity of the American judicial system.

By 1776, there was little doubt in the minds of colonial leaders — most of whom were lawyers — that among England's various wicked schemes was a plot to end trial by jury, install corrupt judges and stack the courts in favor of the Throne.

Their evidence was provisions in several acts of Parliament in the 1760s that expanded the power of royal courts and ended trial by jury for some offenses. The colonists also were worried about appointments to judgeships of several persons who looked suspiciously eager to please the King.

When it came time to catalogue the King's offenses in the Declaration of Independence, Jefferson duly noted George's attempt to deprive the colonists of their time-honored rights as Englishmen:

"He has obstructed the administration of justice by refusing his assent to laws for establishing judicial powers. He has made judges dependent upon his will along . . . (he has approved legislation) for depriving us in many cases of the benefits of trial by jury."

That England probably had no such plot did not matter. In history, reality often is not as important as illusion, and this was one of those cases. Oddly enough, the road that led to such an outburst of colonial anger over a perceived loss of judicial rights had an unexpected, and highly ironic, beginning, at least in Pennsylvania.

Unlike most of the people who came to his sylvan wilderness in America, William Penn didn't care much for courts. Nor did he think much of judges and lawyers. To him, courts indicated that

disharmony existed in the community. If he established a judicial system, he thought, it would be a sure sign that his City of Brotherly Love wasn't so brotherly. He preferred that men work out their differences one-to-one.

But disharmony did exist. Pennsylvania, like all the colonies, was being carved out of a wild, rough land. Men fought over property rights. They killed each other in fights. They drank to forget the trauma of the wilderness. They stole to eat. Too often one-to-one meetings ended in ale-house brawls, not justice. Laws were needed, and courts were needed to try violators of those laws.

Reluctantly, Penn began a judicial system. And once he had made the decision, there was little doubt or debate over what kind of system it would be: the English.

"All courts should be open," ordered the legal code of 1682. " . . . Justice should be neither sold, denied or delayed . . . All persons of all persuasions might freely appear in their own way and personally plead their cause . . . Fees should be modest and established by law that justice might be brought to the doors of all."

Grand juries would examine evidence and issue necessary indictments. A man who was arrested was entitled to bail, except in capital cases. Trial would be by jury, which was almost always composed of 12 men. A convicted man could appeal his case to the local Supreme Court and eventually all the way to the King himself.

In short order, county, orphans' and common pleas courts were established. Jurisdictions between courts also were defined. Early on, for example, the city council fined a Philadelphia court for hearing a Bucks County case.

The code even gave judges advice on the proper manner in which to conduct trials: "All pleadings, processes and recourses should be short, and in English, and in an ordinarily plain character that might be understood and justly speed administration."

Crimes also were outlined in the code, along with the proper punishments to be administered if convicted. While some of the crimes — murder, rape, arson — were obviously serious felonies then and now, there were quite a few criminal measures that, if enforced today, would threaten many Philadelphians' normal behavior, and probably would enrich city coffers sufficiently to wipe out any deficit.

The use of profanity, for example, brought a one-shilling fine and some time in the stocks. Card games, no matter how innocent, meant five days in jail and a five-shilling fine. Speaking ill of a city official meant 20 shillings or 10 days at hard labor.

Even the crimes that today might pass as serious often had rather extreme punishments. If convicted of bigamy, a man received life imprisonment. And if convicted of fornication, he often had to marry the object of his attention.

The publication of the code and its attendant punishments, coupled with the opening of the courts, gave the city a full-scale judicial system. But Penn's attitude continued to flavor the quality of justice administered here. In one opinion he issued as a high appeals judge, Penn told the parties to "shake hands and forgive one another," but then ordered "that the records of the court concerning the business be burnt" so no one would learn of it.

Despite Penn's reluctance, it seems clear that the criminal code was enforced to the letter, judging at least by surviving grand jury indictments. On July 28, 1702, the grand jury indicted Philip Eilbeck of Chester County for "making a pop" at Herman Debick and "uttering three curses to the terrifying of said Herman." (A "pop" was apparently the legal nomenclature for assault without battery.) On Sept. 3, the same grand jury indicted George Robinson for "uttering a grievous oath." Since that was the second such oath for George, he was fined 12 shillings.

One of the more curious indictments was handed down Dec. 2:

"We, ye Grand Jury of ye City of Philadelphia, present Sarah Stivee, wife of John Stivee, of this city, for being dressed in men's clothes, contrary to the nature of her sex, and in such disguises walked through the streets of this city and from house to house on or about the 26th of tenth month to the great disturbance of well-minded persons and encouraging of vice in this place."

Once convicted of a serious crime, of course, a felon had to go to jail.

The question of just what kind of jail Philadelphia ought to have troubled the city for decades. In February 1683, the city council ordered one William Clayton to build a seven-by-five-foot cage, but everyone quickly realized that would not do. The high sheriff then rented Patrick Robinson's house, equipped it with chains and declared that "with his attendance and that of his deputies, he had a sufficient gaol" and would take responsibility for escapes.

But that, too, proved inadequate. Two years later a four-room jail was built in the middle of High Street between Front and Second Streets.

The growing city's growing convict population quickly outstripped that facility. In 1702 an investigating grand jury declared the prison house and the prison-yard as it now stood in High Street as a common nuisance. Prisoners had no room to move about, facilities were woefully lacking and jailers had taken to oppressing prisoners to keep order.

So, once again, a new jail was built, this time at Third and High Streets, a block from the courthouse. It was actually two two-story buildings, one for criminal offenders and one for debtors, who came under an entirely separate branch of law.

Yet just as quickly conditions in the new jail deteriorated. There was only one blanket for every two men, it was said. There was no medical attention. Debtors, who had to remain in prison until they had repaid their debts, and who had to provide their own food while in jail, frequently died of starvation. In fact, in some ways the persons who fared the best were those who committed the most heinous crimes, for their sojourn in jail was mercifully short. They were quickly hung, often before large crowds.

Conditions at the Third and Market jail led in 1773 to authorization for another jail, this time at Sixth and Walnut Streets — the infamous Walnut Street Prison. During the Revolution, it was used by the British to house American prisoners under conditions that became notorious throughout the colonies.

•

While Philadelphia's judicial system may have been among the more advanced and renowned, it certainly was not unique. Throughout the colonies, court systems were slowly taking shape to deal with the turmoil and trauma of an increasingly complex, rapidly growing society.

By the 18th century, every colony had a supreme court, county courts, local courts and justices of the peace. Trials were being held, grand juries were issuing indictments, and, in some cases, legal history was being made. The trial of John Peter Zenger in 1735 firmly established for the first time in Anglo-Saxon legal history that truth could be used as a defense in libel cases.

Some colonies had moved ahead of Pennsylvania. New Hampshire, for example, had jury trials as early as 1641, and regular court sessions in Dover by 1649.

And each colony had its peculiar judicial traits. One Connecticut grand jury, for example, was called "to help oversee workmen in clearing the commons, to

William Penn, ironically, didn't like courts much. In one appellate decision he instructed the parties to "shake hands and forgive one another."

present indictments against idle persons, to present persons for selling drink, to take care the Sabbath was observed, and to see that Indian children learn to read."

A New Hampshire man, George Kenison, was convicted of perjury and given a choice of punishments: either pay a 10 pound fine or have his ears nailed to a pillory for an hour.

Some traits were fairly universal. The procedure used to draw and quarter was imported from England and was used for serious offenses. The felon was "to be led back to the place whence he came and from thence shall be drawn on a hurdle to the place for execution, and then shall be hanged by the neck, and then shall be cut down alive, and his entrails and privy members shall be cut from his body and shall be burned in his sight, and his head shall be cut off, and his body shall be divided into four parts and shall be disposed of at the King's pleasure."

It makes the act of signing the Declaration of Independence more profound when one realizes that every Signer realized that he had made himself liable, by that act, to this punishment, the standard description of which was widely known.

By the mid-18th century colonial justice had developed to such a high degree that the colonists had one of the most free and independent judiciaries in the world. The King and Privy Council retained ultimate control over cases, but few cases ever reached their jurisdiction, in large part simply because it took too long.

Then things started to go sour because the British began to assert those

powers that they had always had — but rarely used. When that happened, the American colonists quickly began to believe that the English common law tradition that they so revered was better protected in their own courts than in the new systems proposed by the King. Ultimately, they would fight to keep their own American courts and methods of justice.

The source of the difficulty was a heretofore harmless institution, the vice-admiralty court. For years these courts had existed without controversy in almost every colony to hear cases involving ships' cargo, trade and tariff laws, and wartime seizures of enemy vessels. Usually customs agents would seize suspected violators, and, if the ship's captain or owner was convicted, his ship or cargo would be auctioned. The resulting revenue went to the Crown.

Cases were tried without juries, but that fact hadn't, up to this point, bothered the colonials. Most Americans had little contact with admiralty courts, and, besides, most of the judges were native-born and reluctant to convict their brethren. Some even took bribes and one judge in the Bahamas, who was himself a participant in the illegal trade, routinely "took fees from Philadelphia merchants for releasing their vessels," historian Merrill Jansen notes.

Then, in 1764, the English prime minister, George Grenville, described by another historian as "a mediocre man of great obstinacy who made a fetish of efficiency," decided such flagrant, scandalous abuse of the British government's power and authority had to stop. The government, saddled with staggering debts from the French and Indian Wars, needed revenue. Because the wars had been fought largely to bail out the colonials, Grenville determined that they should pay for it. He also realized that he could not count on the local admiralty courts to produce sufficient numbers of convictions.

Something better was needed, so Parliament approved the Revenue Act of 1764, quickly dubbed the "Black Act" in America. The act's principal provisions dealt with changes in import duties, together with such matters as loading and unloading procedures. But one small part made a few adjustments in the admiralty courts. The changes horrified and enraged the American colonists.

An all-dominion vice-admiralty court was established in Halifax, Nova Scotia, and any customs agent was given the option of taking his case to the local admiralty court, where he took his chances with a local judge, or to the new, all-powerful court, where a judge appointed personally by the king sat.

That was irritating enough. But the act also stated that merchants would be considered guilty until proven innocent. They could not defend themselves until they had posted a bond to cover costs. They forfeited the bond even if found innocent.

Almost as odious to the colonists was the fact that British officials in America went about enforcing the new regulations using general warrants that authorized them to search any premises any time in search of unspecified contraband.

Such warrants had been used in England as part of the infamous Star Chamber proceedings in which the King would carry out vindictive prosecution of enemies, but they had been abandoned in the mother country because they represented an open invitation to law enforcement officials to misuse their power. It was too easy for the official holding such a warrant to use the authority to search and seize to harass and intimidate his enemies — personal and official. Some British officials in America did misuse the warrants in that fashion to disrupt the businesses of Americans who irked them.

Parliament quickly followed with another punch, the much-hated Stamp Act of 1765. Among its provisions was one stipulating that any violation of the act would be tried in the new dominion vice-admiralty court. Since the Stamp Act was not an act to regulate trade, but an act to raise funds, the colonists saw the act as depriving them of the right to trial by jury in an entirely new area.

There was immediate uproar in the colonies over the Stamp Act. Mobs took to the streets. One in Boston even broke into the home of the deputy register of the court and burned court records. The Boston *Gazette* viciously attacked the Act for taking away the colonists' "darling privilege" of trial by jury.

Time would prove that in practice the judges in the vice-admiralty courts were not the toadying hacks the colonists thought. Most were honest enough (too honest, perhaps, for American merchant-smugglers). Few cases reached the newly-structured admiralty courts, and most people had little direct awareness of them. Most offenses were still handled by American courts, with American juries. At all events, the Stamp Act was eventually repealed.

But the principle behind the act irked the Americans. The King and Parliament were summarily stripping the colonists of rights they had long held as Englishmen, and as Americans. Increasingly, Americans came to believe that there was only one way, so they thought, to prevent further erosion of long-held judicial traditions — revolt.

Their irritation smoldered and when it came time a few years later to declare independence, there was little doubt that the King's alleged judicial offenses would find their way into the document that declared it. After final victory and the abolition of the hated admiralty courts, the colonists once again established a judiciary, one free of the shadow of the King.

The main body of the Constitution would decree:

"The trial of all crimes, except in cases of impeachment, shall be by jury; and such trial shall be held in the state where the said crimes shall have been committed..."

No longer were Americans to be forced to travel long distances to have a day in court, or be denied the opportunity to have their case heard by a jury.

Pro Patria

The first Man that either distributes or makes use of Stampt Paper, let him take Care of his House, Person, & Effects.

Vox Populi;

We Dare

Colonists were discouraged from complying with the Stamp Act by warnings such as the one above. Samples of the "fatal Stamp" are shown at top.

The Bill of Rights — the first amendments to the Constitution — also made sure that police and other law enforcement officials in America would not be able to terrorize citizens with punitive search and seizure.

"The right of the people," the Fourth Amendment specifies, "to be secure in their persons, houses, papers, and effects against unreasonable searches and seizures shall not be violated . . . ."

No warrants were to be issued except when there was "probable cause" to believe that evidence related to a crime would be discovered. And, even then, the warrant would have to specify "the place to be searched, and the persons or things to be seized."

The Bill of Rights also illustrates another difference between the new American and the old British, systems of justice. The British Constitution is unwritten, and its precedents appeared to the Americans to be too easily alterable by the whim of the individual judge. Americans intended to have things written down, and spelled out.

No American was to be held for trial on charges that could involve the death penalty (or for other "infamous crimes") unless he had been indicted by a grand jury; no American was to be tried twice for the same crime. No American could be "compelled to be a witness against himself," or be "deprived of life, liberty, or property without due process of law."

"In all criminal prosecutions, the accused shall enjoy the right to a speedy and public trial . . . to be informed of the nature and cause of the accusation; to be confronted with the witnesses against him; to have a compulsory process for obtaining witnesses in his favor, and to have the assistance of counsel for his defense . . .," the listing of basic American judicial rights continues.

Even in small civil suits, the right to trial to trial by jury was guaranteed.

"Excecessive bail" was not to be required; "excessive fines" were not to be imposed; "cruel and unusual punishments" were banned.

•

And what of the old courthouse, proudly standing in the midst of High Street? After many courts moved to the State House (Independence Hall) in 1735, the courthouse lost much of its prestige. But it remained as a symbol of the early judicial heritage of the city until 1837, when it was torn down.

The history of the building is easily traced. The more difficult, and important, question is whether the spirit of reverence for an American way of justice, out of which the courthouse was constructed, still continues. ★ ★ ★

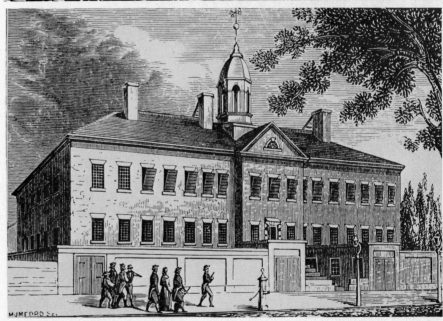

Philadelphia's convict population grew right along with the city, necessitating steadily expanding penal facilities. The city's first place of incarceration was a five-by-seven-foot cage, which was made in 1683, and which is not shown. Later, prisoners were housed in jails located in the middle of Market Street, between Front and Second Streets (top); on the southwest corner of Third and Market (middle); and then, by the 1770s, in the infamous Walnut Street prison at Sixth and Walnut Streets (bottom).

The Rights of Americans

The moment at which Hamilton stood to defend the New York on the grounds that English libel law was unconstitutional is depicted in this diorama.

Andrew Hamilton Speaks For the Defense

By Franklin S. Roberts

It reads like a second-rate television plot.

The honest but naive pawn in a small-town power struggle stands trial for a crime he *did* commit against the incumbent political machine. The stacked judge and jury begin the motions of hearing the case and pronouncing sentence.

Suddenly—as a ripple of excitement sweeps through the crowded courtroom—the Great Lawyer from the Big City rises to declare that he will present the case for the defense. In response to the secret entreaties of the Good Guys, it develops, he has been persuaded to step out of semi-retirement to battle again against injustice.

Yet that's the way it actually happened in the fall of 1735. A legal drama unfolded that would change English common law, and preserve an infant free press in America. The decision in the case would help the principle of freedom of the press and expression, and provide a personal triumph for the lawyer from the big town, and, in fact, produce the term "smart as a Philadelphia lawyer." This was the trial of New York printer

John Pete Zenger; the Philadelphia lawyer was Andrew Hamilton.

The leading actors in our play were all men who had come to make their fortunes in the new land. There the similarity ends.

Zenger, the immigrant German printer who stood trial for seditious libel in 1735, had lost his father during the difficult sea voyage to little old New York. A 13-year-old boy, barely proficient in English, he was apprenticed to a printer. Through industry and ambition he built a small but profitable printing business.

When the town was divided by political turmoil, he would agree to print an opposition newspaper for the foes of the new English governor of the colony. The profitable piece of business would secure Zenger's place in history — but only after eight months of incarceration in the dungeons of Federal Hall.

William Cosby, who in 1732 became London's new man in the governor's chair of New York province, was typical of many of the colonial administrators sent out from London. He ruled with a crude and heavy hand,

The issue in the Zenger trial was freedom of the press. One man said of the Philadelphian's summation: "If it is not the law, it ought to be."

and his prime interest in the New World was replenishing a fortune squandered in England.

Andrew Hamilton, an immigrant like Zenger and the hero of our drama, came from obscure origins. It's believed that he was born in Scotland in the latter half of the 17th century, and shipped out for Virginia about age 20. He appears to have had some formal education, and he may have had troubles at home or with the law that prompted him to leave.

In those times, many young men came to America to find a new life.

What we do know is that the young Scot found employment teaching classical studies to proper young Virginia gentlemen-to-be. His own education also continued. He took interest in the study of law with a fellow Scot named MacKemie, and the two young men taught themselves from available books. Soon they were active practitioners of the law.

Hamilton now began his move up the ladder of life. In 1706 he married a young widow of means with well-placed connections in Maryland.

Within two years Hamilton's prosperity enabled him to purchase a large estate along the Chester River in Maryland. As a solid citizen and a man of outspoken convictions, he won election to the Assembly, an honor he would also enjoy in Pennsylvania and Delaware.

News of the talented and successful young lawyer reached even to Philadelphia, the great city of the colonies. In 1712 the Penn family sent representatives to seek Hamilton's advice on a complicated matter involving title to the "Lower Colonies," as Delaware was then known.

Hamilton seized the opportunity to increase his fortunes and to move into one of the most lucrative areas of colonial law — real estate. But recognizing the limitations of a self-taught lawyer in a question which would resolve the southern boundaries of Penn's grant, he decided to go to England for formal legal training.

Late that year he sailed for London, was admitted to Gray's Inn, the oldest and most popular of the Inns of Court, and a year later returned to America.

The new advisor to the powerful Penns moved to join his patrons. Hamilton chose a fitting residence on the southwest corner of Third and Chestnut Streets, and Philadelphia soon found it had a new pepperpot to digest. Captain Charles Gookin was one of the first to know.

Gookin, a soldier scarce noted for his diplomacy or abilities, was Pennsylvania's English administrator. Hamilton's opinion of Gookin, and indeed of most politicians, was not high. As the *American Mercury* would note in Hamilton's obituary: ". . . He was no friend to power, as he had observed an ill use had been fre-

quently made of it in the colonies, and therefore was seldom on good terms with governors."

To be specific, in 1717 Hamilton was indicted by Governor Gookin's grand jury for "wicked, opprobrious and reproachful words . . . spoken . . . of the Honorable Charles Gookin, Esq., Governor of the Province of Pennsylvania."

It seems the governor objected to such Hamilton statements as, "Damn him. If I ever meet the damned dog Gookin out of the province in which he has command, or any other convenient place, . . . by the Eternal God, I will pistol him. He deserves to be shot or ripped open for what he has done already."

But if Hamilton had a talent for making enemies, he also attracted those who valued ability and energy. That same year of 1717 he became Pennsylvania's attorney general in the new administration of Sir William Keith, a friend of the Penns, who also happened to be a brilliant and enlightened colonial servant of the British.

In 1732, Governor William Cosby's arrival in New York had been greeted with optimism by the 10,000 citizens who lived, crowded together, on the southern tip of Manhattan Island. But within months, Cosby's heavy-handed ways had split the populace into two camps. A Popular Party organized to oppose the new governor's crude and greedy appetites.

The first confrontation came when Cosby demanded that New York's council president return half his salary to him as governor. This was, in fact, a tradition, but one not always observed. The council president, a stubborn and independent Dutch merchant named Rip Van Dam, refused unless Cosby gave Van Dam and the council half the benefits Cosby received from England as governor. Van Dam knew a bargaining position when he saw one. He was perfectly willing to return half his council income of 2,000 British pounds, if, in return, he could share Cosby's 6,500 pounds.

Infuriated by the challenge to his royal authority, Cosby ordered his attorney general to indict Van Dam. He then directed the provincial court to hear the case. But Chief Justice Lewis Morris, a Popular Party stalwart, defied the governor, and declared that the court had no jurisdiction in the matter. Cosby promptly sacked Morris and replaced him with a henchman.

Morris, one of the wealthiest and most influential men in New York, fought back. Joining with Van Dam and others excluded from the governor's clique controlling political appointments, land grants, and other financial rewards, Morris ran for and won election to the State Assembly and the New York City Council.

Now Cosby was faced with the strongest opposition party in the history of the province. Popular Partyites dogged his every move and cried foul each time they caught a royal hand in the cookie jar. They discovered an illegal gift of 1,000 pounds to Cosby for influencing legislation. They disclosed an act of near treason when Cosby permitted a French sloop, based in unfriendly Canada, to provision in New York port.

Stung by these disclosures and the growing strength of the Popular Party, Cosby employed New York's lone newspaper, as well as his controlled courts, to abuse his enemies.

By threat and government payouts, Cosby turned William Bradford's New York *Gazette* into a paper that was later correctly alleged to be "a paper known to be under the direction of the government, in which the printer of it is not suffered to insert anything but what his superiors approve of, under the penalty of losing 50 pounds per annum and the title of the King's Printer for the Province of New York."

Bradford had flirted with fame before. Some years earlier a Boston youngster traveling south came into his shop asking for an apprentice job. He replied that he had no openings but told the young man to check with his son, a printer in Philadelphia. And so Ben Franklin headed south.

To gain their own voice, Morris and his associates invented a new weapon in New York politics — an opposition newspaper.

The inaugural issue of the *New York Weekly Journal*, America's first political newspaper, appeared November 5, 1733. Its impact exceeded the fondest hopes of its creators, and it quickly became a powerful weapon of "invective and satire against the Governor."

The *Weekly Journal* was printed and published in the modest print shop of John Peter Zenger. What Zenger owned he had earned the hard way.

The small band of impoverished German immigrants with whom Zenger arrived in 1710 took whatever work they could find. With the family breadwinner buried at sea, Zenger's widowed mother apprenticed John Peter to New York's public printer, Bradford.

Zenger faithfully served his eight years of apprenticeship, then left for Maryland to be that colony's public printer, arriving a few years after Hamilton had left for Philadelphia. Zenger soon returned to New York, but this time as Bradford's partner. Then, within a year, in 1726, he proudly set out his own shingle as master printer.

Disposed toward the Popular Party's principles, but an innocent in politics, Zenger was delighted with the added business the *Weekly Journal* brought his presses. Dutifully he printed the anti-Cosby essays composed by Morris, Van Dam and the other opposition leaders. The essays were accompanied by all manner of satiric advertisements representing Cosbyites as lost spaniels, wayward monkeys, and the like.

Cosby raged that "open and implacable malice against me has appeared weekly in false and scandalous libels printed in Zenger's *Journal*" attempting to prejudice the minds of a "deluded and unreasonable mob."

The Popular Party replied that in a constitutional monarchy criticism by the press is a necessary safeguard against those unlawful ministers who were beyond the reach of ordinary legal action.

The second edition of the *New York Weekly Journal* carried a manifesto on the freedom of the press: "For if such an overgrown criminal, or an impudent monster in iniquity, cannot immediately be come at by ordinary justice, let him yet receive the lash of satire, let the glaring truths of his ill administration, if possible, awaken his conscience, and if he has no conscience, rouse his fear, by showing him his deserts, sting him with shame, and render his actions odious to all honest minds."

The editorialists of the *Journal* sounded even a further warning, that " . . . the loss of liberty in general would soon follow the suppression of the liberty of the press, for it is the best preservative of the whole. Even a restraint of the press would have a fatal influence. No nation ancient or modern ever lost the liberty of speaking, writing or publishing their sentiments, but forthwith lost their liberty in general and became slaves."

Cosby's mouthpiece, the *Gazette*, responded to the manifesto with a statement extolling the virtues of the English law of libel, the major restraint on the freedom to print.

In the English-speaking world of the 18th century, seditious libel had been defined as any printed statement critical of a government officer's official conduct. The question of the truth of such statements was irrelevant.

With public sentiment on Zenger's side, the Popular Party was willing to test the concept and, in the process, attack Cosby's rule in open court. Zenger would be the foil. His press was kept humming with new attacks, charges and invective.

•

Cosby did not disappoint his enemies. In 1735, he ordered his attorney general to take seditious libel action against Zenger. Stymied briefly when the grand jury would not indict Zenger, and when the sheriff refused to obey orders to burn copies of the offending *Journal*, Governor Cosby was nonetheless ultimately able to have Zenger arrested and jailed.

There he languished for almost eight months, Cosby choosing to ignore a writ of *habeas corpus* to extract a further measure of revenge on the hapless Zenger.

Whether Zenger's patrons wanted to make bail or preferred to see martyrdom increase support for the Popular Party is another question.

What Zenger felt, huddled in the dank little cell in Federal Hall, seemed only a matter of concern to himself, his wife and his children. He might have earned his freedom by pleading guilty. But he seemed to sense the enormity of the question. Persuading his wife to keep the printing business alive, he accepted his fate and the advice of his patrons.

Finally, in August of 1735, Zenger was brought to trial. The scene: Federal Hall, where, half a century later, George Washington would become the first President of the United States.

Chief Justice James DeLancey, his associate judge and the prosecutor of the Supreme Court of the Province of New York were all Cosby tools. They did their best to control the selection of a jury from the court book of freeholders.

Numb. XXIII.

THE
New - York Weekly JOURNAL.

Containing the freſheſt Advices, Foreign, and Domeſtick.

MUNDAT April 8th, 1734.

New-Brunſwick, March 27, 1734.
Mr. *Zenger*;

I Was at a public Houſe ſome
Days ſince in Company with
ſome Perſons that came from
New-York: Moſt of them complain'd of the Deadneſs of
Trade: ſome of them laid it to the
Account of the Repeal of the *Tonnage
Act*, which they ſaid was done to gratify the Reſentment of ſome in *New-York*
in order to diſtreſs Governour *Burnet*;
but which has been almoſt the Ruine
of that Town, by paying the *Bermu-*

three Years there has been above 300
Perſons have left *New-York*; the Houſes ſtand empty, and there is as many
Houſes as would make one whole Street
with Bills upon their Doors: And
this has been as great a Hurt as the
Carrying away the Money, and is oc-
caſioned by it, and all degrees of Men
feel it, from the Merchant down to the
Carman. And (adds he) it is the in-
duſtrious Poor is the Support of any
Country, and the diſcouraging the poor
Tradeſmen is the Means of Ruining
any Country. Another replies, It is
the exceſſive High Wages you Trades-

*What Hamilton (top) was defending was the right of
the contributors to Zenger's* New York Weekly Journal
to attack New York Governor William Cosby.

'His oratory shattered the silence. In a passionate summation which appealed to the hopes of men, rather than to the law, Hamilton won the battle for twelve minds.'

Seated imperially above the burghers of New York and the probably still somewhat confused Zenger, the bewigged officers bade the proceedings commence in the name of the King. The packed courtroom stilled. Zenger was clearly guilty, but the script had to be played out.

It was then, to the surprise and delight of the populace — and to the chagrin of the royal court— that the great Philadelphia lawyer, Andrew Hamilton, rose to declare himself Zenger's defender.

Legal experts will tell you that Hamilton argued the "law of the future." Indeed, more than a century later, with never a passing reference to Hamilton's arguments at the Zenger trial, Lord Campbell's Act of 1843 would bring English law into harmony with the Philadelphia lawyer's charge to Cosby's "controlled" New York jury.

At the outset of the trial, Hamilton asked for the privilege to prove the truth of the allegations against Cosby, his argument being that if true they were justified. The court refused him the privilege of arguing the merits of the libel law. The only course left was to persuade the jury, at peril to themselves, to deliver a "general verdict" based on both the law and the facts.

As Hamilton rose to address the jury, the eyes of the crowded courtroom shifted from the glowering Chief Justice to the man from Philadelphia. In the hush of the room the unspoken question for Zenger's supporters was: could Hamilton's words bring ordinary men to defy the vindictive Cosby, as well as the law of the day, which clearly required a guilty verdict?

His oratory shattered the silence. In a passionate summation which appealed to the hopes of men, rather than to the law, Hamilton won the battle for twelve minds. As one who heard Hamilton's historic speech would later remark, "If it is not law, it is better than law, it ought to be law, and will always be law wherever justice prevails."

Courageously, in the face of Cosby's court and not so subtle powers, the jury returned a verdict of "not guilty."

New York went wild. A cheering torch-lit procession escorted Hamilton to the Black Horse Tavern, where, to the accompaniment of endless toasts, Hamilton was saluted and presented with gifts.

Soon, in London, the press and legal community would give considerable debate to the legal precedents of the trial.

More important for Americans of 1735, slowly moving toward ideas which had yet to find public expression, the verdict prevented an infant political press from being struck down and, perhaps, postponing the date of independence. ★★★

Schools Opened the Way to Success —and Salvation

By Kathy Nagurny

America in 1776 was probably the most literate nation on the face of the earth, thanks both to the growing American faith in education, and the widely held belief that everyone ought to be able to read the Bible.

As the sky gradually lightened over Philadelphia on January the nineteenth, 1776, the new thermometers that rich people found amusing showed a very serious five degrees. Icicles formed on the end of downspouts, and the water in the horse troughs had frozen to the bottom. During the night it had snowed like it would never stop, blowing in out of the north, but at some point in the hours just before dawn the snow had stopped, and the wind had blown colder. A crisp white blanket now covered Philadelphia's narrow dirt roads and cobblestoned pavements; more icicles had formed on the window panes of the small, squarish brick houses that lined the streets and alleys. The sky was gray and overcast.

Inside their home on an alley off Third Street, John Jones, his wife Sarah, and their two children, Samuel, 14, and Elizabeth, 10, were awakening. Quickly the two children dressed. Samuel pulled on his tan buckskin britches, checked shirt, and red flannel jacket. Elizabeth wore a simple frock over her petticoat. They ate their breakfast of porridge, pulled on their coats, and headed out the door for school.

In warmer weather, the children often sang as they walked. (One of the songs went, in part, *"With satchel and shining morning face, Creeping like a snail — unwillingly to school."*) But today, as a knifing wind whipped fiercely through Philadelphia, they trudged quietly. Samuel was walking to a cold, drafty two-story brick building on Arch, just beyond Fourth Street that had been built as a chapel a quarter-century earlier, and which now housed his school.

The institution was one of several private secondary schools in the city that taught promising youngsters on a semi-scholarship basis, which was the only way Samuel could have afforded to go to school.

Samuel's father, a journeyman in a pewter shop, had not this kind of an educational opportunity, and watching Samuel leave each morning filled him with pride and hope — the eternal hope that the unfulfilled dreams of the father will see fulfillment for the son. And truly, anything seemed to be in Samuel's reach.

Jones could easily see his son becoming a rich merchant, a lawyer — or any-

One lad became something of a legend when he leaped up after his whipping, said it didn't hurt at all, and yelled, "Hooray for leather crackers."

thing, through schooling. He cherished with pride the awareness that not only did the sons of the Philadelphia elite attend the school, but the rich landowners in other colonies also sent their sons to Philadelphia to attend the school in preparation for admission to one of the great universities of Europe. Indeed, the distinction between a college and secondary school was much less clearly defined at the time, and already the Philadelphia school was expanding its curriculum and becoming a college itself.

Likewise, Elizabeth's mother had always wished as a young girl that she might have been able to go to one of the dame schools that Elizabeth now attended, where a woman of some educational attainment offered instruction. The dame schools were strictly profit-making enterprises and offered no scholarships. Elizabeth's education was one of the family's few luxuries.

Viewed on a world-wide scale, the idea of a workingman's children going to school at all was a novel idea. Statistics are hard to come by, but a number of historians have asserted that America was very possibly the most literate nation on the face of the earth in 1776. (Some amend that to apply only to America's white — or non-slave — population.)

Unquestionably, knowledge of the basic skills of reading and writing was unusually widespread in a nation that by the standards of the world at the time qualified for the category we today call "underdeveloped." Partly this was due to the fact that many of the Protestant sects that had come to America seeking refuge believed that each man must find his own personal part to God through the Scriptures. Such belief carried with it the corollary that members of the faith had to be able to read the Scriptures, and, hence, anything else.

But part of it was the already burgeoning American faith in education as the way to opportunity for everyone.

And it seems probable that Philadelphia, the premier city of America and the continent's intellectual center, led all of the other cities of the colonies in providing for the educational needs of its citizens.

The idea of free public education for all had not yet arrived in America (or anywhere else, for that matter) in 1776. But the city even then provided support for the school that Samuel attended, and for two "free" or "charity" schools — one for girls and one for boys. They were virtually open to all who chose to attend them.

In addition, there was a large number of church-related schools, affiliated with, variously, Quakers, Anglicans, Presbyterians, and Lutherans, among others. The latter two denominations even had a hand in running the city-financed schools.

The differing philosophies and traditions of these religious groups continued as separate strains within the overall pattern of education. The Quakers, for instance, while firmly of the belief that children should be taught the traditional "Three Rs," were skeptical of the advantages of more advanced forms of schooling, being fearful that such learning tended to make a person unduly proud.

And let it be said that among some elements of the population, particularly in the German community, anything more than the most rudimentary book learning was almost in disrepute. Bayard Taylor included a German saying in his *Pennsylvania Farmer,* which went: "Book learning gets the upper hand, and work is slow and slack; / And they that come long after us will find things gone to wrack."

Intermixed with all this were the schools set up by women (or "dames"). Also, some of the very wealthy families, particularly landowners in the countryside, employed tutors for their children. Particularly in the South, the wealthiest landowner in an area would sometimes hire a schoolmaster and establish a school on his plantation that the children of other members of the gentry in the area would send their children to.

In the city, "schoolmen" sometimes

Interior of the Old School House built by Letitia Penn in 1705. Washington's army used it as a hospital.

The Rights of Americans

offered night classes in everything from the genteel subjects of Latin and Greek to more utilitarian, almost vocational, classes in surveying, bookkeeping, and accounting. In point of fact, though, many of these teachers were poorly qualified, and closed up their schools as soon as something better came along, like the chance to operate a store. The average institutions of this type operated for a year or so. Enrollment also tended to be an informal affair for the students, who would join and depart the classes on no fixed schedule.

One such school, offering courses in applied mathematics and navigation, among other courses, advertised immodestly in the *Pennsylvania Chronicle* during 1767 that its programs were "a grand source of riches and power."

•

Most all of the schools, though, were characterized by the implicit belief that the business of learning was a serious affair.

Rules that students abided by in church-sponsored and private schools, like the academy Samuel attended, were quite stringent.

Samuel Jones, for instance, was instructed to arrive on time, to walk across the wooden floor to his wooden desk by the wall in a quiet and sober manner.

Elizabeth, as she entered the private residence of her teacher nearby, where her classes were conducted, acted with the same decorum.

". . . And on entrance of the master," one historian wrote about local colonial schools, "all shuffling of the feet, scrougeing, hitting of elbows and whispering disputes were hastily adjusted, leaving a silence which might be felt. Not a mouse seemed to stir."

Typically, a school consisted of one room lined with windows and pegs where students hung their coats and jackets. A tiny stove stood in the center, surrounded by circles of desks. The younger boys (and the girls if the school was coed) sat at the inner circle, facing the heat, while the older students sat on the outside.

The large teacher's desk in the middle of the classroom rested on a platform, leaving no doubt as to who ran the school.

The competence of the instructors varied. Some, to supplement their low incomes, would maintain a side business, like pen-making, in school. One unidentified Philadelphian who attended school here around 1776 wrote that his instructor had all his students stand up to read from the Bible while he made pens. "He did not perceive," the student wrote, "that for three or four months we had been reading the same small passage over and over again."

Moreover, many schools were just too overcrowded to teach. It was not unusual for a teacher to supervise as many as 150 pupils. It's perhaps not surprising then, that from time to time, despite the aura of sternness, some students got out of line. To annoy the more lenient masters and disturb other classmates, troublesome children would stir up clouds of dirt from the two to three-inch-thick dirt floor that lined many schools.

None of this unruliness prevailed, however, in young Jones' classroom. Samuel's teacher, the Reverend Francis Alison, maintained what was, in truth, a national reputation for his mercurial anger. Alison was reportedly much like a predecessor at the Academy, David I.

Creating a University

By Janet Novack

The University of Pennsylvania was never intended to be an urban institution. As founder Benjamin Franklin proposed in his 1749 tract, *Proposals Relating to the Education of Youth in Pennsylvania*, an academy should be located in the country to allow for students' "running, leaping, wrestling and swimming."

But when the Academy of Philadelphia, Penn's forerunner, was constituted in 1749, the 24 Philadelphia social leaders who founded it insisted the school be located in the city so they could closely supervise their pupils in everything from business to marriage.

Luckily, a suitable building, the Whitefield Chapel, stood at 4th and Arch Streets. It had been constructed by Christians of several sects who were inspired by the preacher George Whitefield, and who had hoped to entice Whitefield to stay in Philadelphia. The building had been intended to house a charity school, but enthusiasm had waned and the project was faltering. The Academy trustees took over the building, assuming the obligation for the charity school, and in 1751 the Academy, together with its stepchild, the Free School, opened.

Though Franklin, the craftsman, had envisioned a utilitarian curriculum, the Academy conservatively emphasized Greek and Latin, with the status of English reflected in the lower pay of its masters. The school was distinguished from other academies of its day, however, by its non-sectarian orientation.

The school had its problems. The Academy's first master, George Price, was removed after three years for his "intemperate drinking of strong liquors." But waiting in the wings was a young, impressive Scotsman and Franklin friend, Dr. William Smith, who became the first important leader of the college.

In 1755, the Academy obtained a more ambitious charter from the state proprietors, adding the title of "College" to the school, and elevating Smith to a "Provost" and the school's masters to "professors." Later the development of a medical school would make possible the Academy's eventual designation as a "University."

The Academy's student body, which numbered about 100, followed a rigorous routine of study in colonial days, with every afternoon devoted to the classics. Benjamin Franklin's own grandson, when enrolled in the school, complained in a letter home that the curriculum left him no time for lessons in fencing and dancing. Students unprepared for class were fined, heavy punishment for the fledgling scholars.

Finances were a continual headache. The College often operated at a deficit in the early years, but was unable to raise its tuition from a rather modest four pounds a year for fear of losing its students to competing institutions. During the 1750s money for the school was raised through a lottery. Later, more sophisticated fund-raising drives were launched.

With so many of the city's most prominent citizens involved in the College, it was perhaps inevitable that the school should become enmeshed in local politics.

Provost Smith was involved in several political skirmishes with the Quaker-dominated state legislature, and aligned himself with the pro-Penn proprietary party, against the party led by Franklin, which Franklin liked to refer to as the party of "Popular Liberty." In 1758, Smith spent three months in prison for libeling the state assembly, but continued to lecture on Moral Philosophy to 12 pupils in his jailhouse cell.

Franklin and Smith's differing politics led to the dissolution of their friendship, and the two exchanged insults in the Letters to the Editor sections of local publications.

Even though Smith and others were viewed with suspicion by the revolutionaries (some of the trustees were in fact Tories), the College's involvement in the Declaration of Independence was impressive. Nine signers were associated with the school. In May 1775,

Dove, whose sarcasm and ill-temper were described by one student in this way: "He was called Dove ironically, for his temper was that of a hawk, and his was the beak of a falcon pouncing on innocent prey."

Other stern educators flourished in local schools. One whipped daily and hourly with a hickory club with leather thongs attached to one end. Another had a row of rods of different sizes, which, with ugly humor, he termed his "mint sticks."

Yet one other, nicknamed Tiptoe Bobby, always carried a raccoon's tail slightly weighted at one end. Tiptoe would throw this — with sudden accuracy — at the offender, who meekly returned it to his instructor and received a fierce whipping with a butt-end of rawhide with strips of leather at the smaller end.

All in all, the most famous disciplinarian may have been John Todd, who around the time of the Revolution was 60 years old and taught in the Friends' School, at Second and Chestnut Streets. He had such a passion for incessant whipping that, after reading accounts of his ferocious discipline, manners and words, a court proclaimed the only explanation for his violence and cruelty was that of insanity.

At least one student, though, not only endured, but prevailed, after a fashion, under Todd's regime. The student's name was George Fudge, and he became a legend in his own time.

One day Todd seized Fudge, and after strapping him with his usual gusto, while still breathless with rage, Todd inquired unsolicitously, "Does it not hurt?" To the astonishment of the other students, and Todd himself, young Fudge replied, "No! — Hurray for Leather Crackers!"

Fudge was immediately thrown off Todd's knee, and as he sprawled on the floor, Todd shouted: "Intolerable being! Get out of my school. Nothing in nature is able to prevail upon thee — not even my strap."

During Revolutionary times, many instructors were redemptioners and exported convicts. And frequently newspapers like the *Pennsylvania Gazette* printed advertisements like this: "Ran Away: A servant man who followed the occupation of a Schoolmaster, much given to drinking and gambling."

One boy, John Lacey, who attended a private school here about the same period Samuel Jones did, later wrote: "The master of my school could neither read nor write correctly," wrote Lacey, "... knew nothing of grammar and it was not expected he could teach it to others ... grammar was never taught at any school I went to . . . ."

Even alumni of Samuel's school, widely considered the best in the city, did some grumbling. Alexander Graydon, who attended school there for four years in the late 1760s, said: "A little Latin, and but a little, was the chief fruit of my education. I was tolerably instructed in the rudiments of grammar, but in nothing else. I wrote a very indifferent hand and spelled worse than I wrote. I knew little or nothing of arithmetic."

The subjects varied considerably in the different dame schools, although etiquette was always highly emphasized. Rich girls could study piano, dance and even the sciences, while less well-to-do girls like Elizabeth Jones were simply satisfied with such electives as cooking, needlepoint and basic reading.

Teaching materials in the different schools tended to be similar. The Jones children, like others, first learned the principles of reading from the hornbook, a small, thin piece of wood resembling a paddle.

A sheet of paper containing the alphabet in large and small letters, some simple syllables such as ca, ci, co, cu, etc., and the Lord's Prayer were placed on it.

William Smith

The University about 1770, and William Smith, the first important leader.

the Continental Congress, attending the College's commencement, heard students offer decidedly pro-independence graduation addresses.

From 1775, the College's facilities were intermittently commandeered by troops, and the College discontinued all classes in June 1777, just a few months before the British occupied the city. Though the Provost resumed classes in 1778, the school was never to be the same.

Internal Pennsylvania politics and the questionable allegiances of many of the trustees led the state legislature in 1779 to reorganize the College into a state university with several state officials as trustees. Provost Smith's reign was temporarily ended.

Then in 1789 the state legislature did an about face, and reinstated the old trustees. By 1792, the institution assumed a new status as the University of Pennsylvania.

After a century of expansion in the central part of Philadelphia, the University moved to the west bank of the Schuylkill River in 1872. Today's Penn's sprawling, 250-acre West Philadelphia campus serves over 10,000 students and numbers among its alumni leaders in both the adademic and nonacademic world. Penn's most famous ex-students, interestingly, never stayed to graduate, including President William Henry Harrison, journalist I. F. Stone and actress Candice Bergen.

Some things haven't changed much in 200 years. The University still has difficulty balancing its yearly operating budget, now almost $280 million, and so, in the Franklin tradition, recently embarked on a major fund-raising drive.   ★ ★ ★

The Concord School House in Germantown was built in 1775 on a corner of the Upper Germantown Burying Ground.

This page was covered with a transparent sheet of horn, and both paper and horn were fastened to the wood by narrow strips of metal held by tiny handwrought nails. At the two upper corners were crosses, and a recitation from this device was commonly called "reading the crisscross row."

The hornbook usually had a perforated handle and it could be conveniently carried in the child's hand by a string, hung at his side, or worn around his neck.

Elizabeth's teacher ordinarily pointed to the letters with a quill or knitting needle while the "infant scholars" in her class read them aloud. Sometimes, the teacher had the older pupils shout their ABC's, spell out prayers and recite the crisscross row in a lusty chorus.

Elizabeth and Samuel, like other youngsters, moved on from the hornbook to such texts as *The New England Primer.* The *Primer* had crude little marginal pictures done in lead engraving. Its passages often rhymed, as in: *"He who*

(9)

17. Bite not thy bread, but break it, but not with slovenly Fingers, nor with the same wherewith thou takest up thy meat,

18 Dip not thy Meat in the Sawce.

19. Take not salt with a greasy Knife.

20 Spit not, cough not, nor blow thy Nose at Table if it may be avoided; but if there be necessity, do it aside, and without much noise.

21. Lean not thy Elbow on the Table, or on the back of thy Chair.

22. Stuff not thy mouth so as to fill thy Cheeks; be content with smaller Mouthfuls.

23. Blow not thy Meat, but with Patience wait till it be cool.

24. Sup not Broth at the Table, but eat it with a Spoon.

Would-be gluttons were urged to reform, in this page from a text on manners.

ne'er learns his ABC's, forever will a blockhead be."

Another book that had been in use was George Fox's *Instructions for Right Spelling, and Plain Directions for Reading and Writing True English.* Among the quainter items included in this little tome was a long section devoted to the "signification of Names in Scripture," and another section on "weights, measures, and coyns" mentioned in the Bible.

The spelling words were not given in lists, but were underscored in sentences like this: **"Jezebel** was a bad **Woman** who killed the **Just,** and turned against the **Lord's Prophets** with her attired **Head** and painted **Face peeping out of the Window."**

When Alison taught spelling, he'd give the students more than just spelling practice. First he would tell them what word they were going to spell. Then he would strike his whipping strap loudly on the desk as a signal to begin, and the whole class would spell out the word in chorus, one syllable at a time. Alison's ear was reportedly so acute that he could detect whether any student had erred or faltered. If this happened, he demanded that the delinquent scholar who made the mistake step forward. If none did, he would keep the entire class until, by repeated chorusing of long, difficult words, he was satisfied that universal accuracy had been achieved.

Cocker's Arithmetick, one of the older math texts still in use, showed a mathematician surrounded by a wreath of laurel on its frontispiece, and resembled the math texts of today in many ways. After a brief introduction to addition, subtraction, multiplication, and division, it focused on the vagaries of problem solving.

"If four yards of cloth cost twelve shillings," one problem read, "what will six yards cost?"

Like spelling, arithmetic was also taught with textbooks. Alison had "sum-books," which were chock full of rules and problems.

Frequently teachers would simply have the students copy the problems out of their books onto their slates without explanation or commentary, and then arithmetic over and over until it was error-free. But the better teachers, like Alison, would write out tables of measures, or rules from the sum books, on a sample paper, that would then be passed around for his scholars to write down — and remember.

Writing was closely associated with math, since arithmetic books often devoted several pages to penmanship. Samuel and Elizabeth used quills to write. The rest of their writing paraphernalia included a knife or razor to sharpen the quills, and pounce, the fine powder that prevented the ink from spreading. Texts that survive show that the school children of the time were scribblers, filling the margins with assorted notes and comments.

Besides scribbling, the only other opportunity to practice writing was during penmanship lessons.

There were no written tests. Samuel, like other students, remained ungraded, but often Alison asked him to approach his desk or lectern and recite orally, or display his work for praise or correction.

From year to year, the program of instruction did not change much, and Samuel and other students must from time to time have felt that they were simply reciting the same lessons and doing the same work over and over again. Figuring when a student's schooling was over was a subjective process in many instances.

Ex-student Graydon recalled that "one boy finally thought he had Latin enough, and his father thought so too, and was taking him from school ... Another was of the opinion that he might be much better employed in a counting house, and thus rid himself of his scholastic shackles."

Usually four years of secondary school was considered sufficient, with most students finishing up around age 18, give or take a couple of years. (The age for starting school was similarly indistinct. There was no kindergarten, and there were, of course, no compulsory attendance laws. Typically, a boy from a middle-class family might go to school for the first time at age six or seven.)

Those students that continued on into the college curriculum at Samuel Jones' school—and they were still few in number—studied more Latin and Greek, philosophy, logic, math, literature, astronomy, biology, and trigonometry, among other subjects. Most of these students were aiming at careers as clergymen.

Ordinarily school schedules were reasonably well planned out. Each day included a two-hour noon recess during which the students returned home for lunch before completing a school day that was somewhat longer than today's. There was also, of course, a summer vacation.

Samuel, Elizabeth and their friends couldn't know it at this point, in January of 1776, but less than a year later they were going to get an unscheduled interruption of their studies. On Dec. 2, 1776, the city's revolutionary Council of Safety ordered that "the schools be broke up, and the inhabitants engaged solely in providing for the defense of this city, at this time of extreme danger . . . ."

The British were coming. ★★★

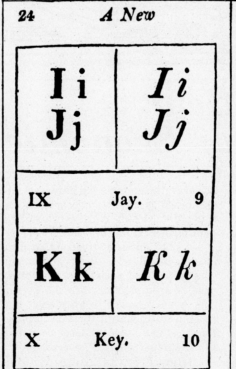

The "old math" of 1776 wasn't actually that different from arithmetic texts in use in our own times.

Etiquette was a principal subject at many Philadelphia schools, particularly the "dame schools" for young ladies.

Even learning the ABCs was infused with a disciplinary message: "K was a Key that lock'd up bad boys."

The Rights of Americans

Still a Question:
What Are Our Economic Rights?

By Edward Schwartz

On July 27, 1776, a committee working on a draft of the Pennsylvania constitution reported out a Bill of Rights with a final article stating as follows: "An enormous proportion of property vested in a few individuals is dangerous to the rights, and destructive of the common happiness of mankind; and therefore every free state hath a right to discourage possession of such property."

It was an unusual article. For the most part, property rights had been considered absolute, particularly by the upper classes. To their dismay,

however, the commercial elite was outnumbered in this state constitutional convention, losing consistently to the poor farmers from the west.

As one conservative spokesman later complained, "Must gentlemen, who have ruled society for a century past, be trampled down to the level of common mechanics in an instant and be obliged to consult their humors before they can have the least chance of filling a department of government?"

Ultimately the proto-populist amendment was removed from the state constitution, along with some other measures the farmers had rail-

roaded through in 1776, including a unicameral legislature which the agrarian western part of the state could continue to dominate at the expense of the Philadelphia merchants.

Today, many interpret these early economic conflicts as debates over *laissez-faire* capitalism. Thus, we can read that in opposing mercantilism, Americans favored an unregulated "free enterprise" system wherein the market would determine supply and demand in accordance with a just natural law. We are further told that the revolutionaries were demanding not a republican government, but no gov-

Unlike the French or Russian revolutions, the American Revolution was basically political, rather than social or economic. Yet right from the beginning Americans argued about what was in it for them.

ernment at all — at least no government that would dabble in economics.

Unfortunately, a careful reading of the period suggests that this analysis is quite wrong. Each side in the colonial era — farmers, workers, merchants — sought governmental support for its specific economic demands. Farmers called upon public authority to break up large landed estates; workers sought political support for efforts to control wages and working conditions within specific crafts; merchants solicited public involvement in capital formation and in stimulating economic growth.

The solution to the competing demands, then as now, was elusive. Early democrats at first were hopeful that the independent states would preserve the "natural equality" that a simple, agrarian economy seemed to provide. That seemed reasonable in the America of 1776. J. Franklin Jameson observed in *The American Revolution Considered as a Social Movement* that "from the pastures of Maine to the rice-fields of Georgia, America was almost absolutely rural, and her people were almost wholly devoted to agriculture. . . .

"Political democracy came to the United States as a result of economic democracy . . . this nation was to be marked by political institutions of a democratic type because it had, still earlier, come to be characterized in its economic life by democratic arrangements and practices," he continued.

Thomas Jefferson hoped that "for the general operations of manufacture, let our workshops remain in Europe . . . The loss by the transportation of commodities across the Atlantic will be made up in happiness and permanence of government."

Beyond these familiar observations offered in *Notes on Virginia* in 1785, Jefferson also confided to John Jay in a letter written the same year that "Cultivators of the earth are the most valuable citizens. They are the most vigorous, the most independent, the most virtuous, and they are tied to their country and wedded to its liberty and interests by the most lasting bonds. As long, therefore, as they can

find employment in this line, I would not convert them into mariners, artisans, or anything else."

Thus, the earliest American dream was an agrarian dream — the vision of a new land, evolving as a decentralized confederation of relatively small communities, preserving equality in its separate states, united in the worship of a just God. Where subsequent generations would debate the distribution of wealth, these first Americans worried about the pace and character of economic development itself.

Consistent with this perspective — the view that "an enormous proportion of property vested in few individuals is dangerous to the rights, and destructive of the common happiness of mankind" — post-Revolutionary farmers demanded the elimination of entail (whereby a large landowner was required to bequeath his land intact); they also brought about the end of primogeniture (whereby all land passed from the father to the eldest son). Both were long-standing traditions brought from England.

The farmers called for the break-up of the large Tory estates but there is debate as to whether or not this was accomplished. Jameson, when he wrote 50 years ago, was convinced that a redistribution of land did take place, and "had extensive social consequences." Among these was the securing of "peasant proprietors" as the centerpiece of the new economic system, an "innumerable multitude" that would fascinate Alexis de Toqueville 60 years later with its "rarity of lofty ambition."

More recent researchers have suggested that the situation was not quite that simple, and have argued that what happened after the Revolution in the redistribution of Tory lands was that rich Patriots got richer, and poor Patriots became relatively poorer.

Be that as it may, it is unquestionably true that the small landowners sought to break up concentrations of both land and capital. As early as 1784, foreshadowing the major conflict of Jefferson's and Jackson's administrations, Pennsylvania agrarians were able to revoke the charter of Robert Morris's Bank of North America. "The Junto have actually the command of all the money in the state, by means of their bank," a contemporary critic charged.

Industrial workers also sought a

Alexander Hamilton:
No laissez-faire

Robert Morris:
His charter was revoked

The Rights of Americans

kind of equality through craft guilds, authorized by government to set both the wages and conditions of their work. The Carpenters' Company, established in Philadelphia in 1724 "for the purpose of obtaining instruction in the science of architecture, and assisting such of their members as should be in need of support," set the precedent in this field.

By 1800, similar companies existed in every industry throughout the Northeast. Indeed, certain trades — porters, carters, butchers, and bakers — were even licensed as public utilities are today. Moreover, they were regulated. Richard B. Morris notes in *Government and Labor in Early America* that in New York, "when it appeared in 1791 that the cartmen were charging extortionate fees and in many cases operating without a license, the city authorities revoked all licenses and reorganized the carters into companies of 40, each under the supervision of a foreman." Hardly the workings of a *laissez-faire* economy.

●

The merchants and entrepreneurs of the new nation were, however, more interested in economic growth than in promoting equality. In fact, they were outspokenly in favor of more economic inequality. Alexander Hamilton, Washington's secretary of the treasury, functioned as the first spokesman for this segment, suggesting in 1791 that "manufactures" would "furnish greater scope for the diversity of talents and dispositions, which discriminate men from each other."

But Hamilton's plans were not *laissez-faire*. Quite the contrary, his plans called for the closest possible cooperation between government and business in the development of the continent, by whatever means of financing seemed necessary. These economic development plans became crucial issues in the early presidential campaigns, and were a major reason why Thomas Jefferson, the egalitarian, defeated John Adams, who had sought to continue Hamilton's program during his term in office.

Another of the enduring ironies of American history, however, is that Jefferson's time in office constituted a period of tremendous economic growth.

Capitalism was finally able to secure a firm location in the American ideology by changing its approach to the electorate. Instead of Hamilton's crass advocacy of increasing the "distinctions" between Americans, it was promised that the results of economic growth under capitalism could be "acres of diamonds" available equally to all.

Our mystic faith in corporatism would come only later in a more "scientific" age, where citizens would speak to one another only of their needs, and where the "common happiness of mankind" would become whatever private growth permitted it to be.

★ ★ ★

'The earliest American dream was an agrarian dream . . .'

The American Mind—1776

The American Mind

Now we plunge into the shadow world that exists between ideas and reality. At different times in history, men have interpreted the relationship between man's powers of reason and fate's succession of events with varying degrees of certainty. Tom Paine, for one, claimed to have little trouble understanding the way of the world. "My own line of reasoning," he wrote, "is to myself as straight and clear as a ray of light."

Writers in our own time especially have claimed a less laser-like degree of perception. Kurt Vonnegut, for one, has suggested that everything that occurs on earth is engineered by the denizens of the distant plant Tralfamadore for the Tralfamadoreans' own ends.

Nonetheless, it is possible to see the creation of the American nation as the culmination of trends that had begun as the West emerged from the Dark Ages — or earlier.

Ideas That Ignited the Revolt

Chapter One:

Wherein a gentleman from Virginia sequesters himself in a house on Market Street to write down the intellectual basis — if any — for the Americans' treason.

By Bob Lancaster

The horseflies from the nearby stable probably bothered him. And the heat and humidity of a torrid Philadelphia summer. And homesickness. He was always miserable with guilt whenever he was away any length of time from his sickly wife, who seemed constantly on the verge of miscarriage.

And although he was a professional lawyer and an amateur everything else, he was above all a writer. And every time a writer enters his workroom and spits on his hands, somebody has said, he starts a losing, depressing struggle with his body and his mind. He was known to suffer at times like these from diarrhea and migraine headaches.

And this piece he was working on was pure treason and that had to be on his mind. He knew the sentence that was being passed on other convicted traitors in the empire: "You are to be drawn on hurdles to the place of execution, where you are to be hanged by the neck, but not until you are dead; for while you are still living your bodies are to be taken down, your bowels torn out and burned before your faces, your heads then cut off, and your bodies divided each into four quarters, and your heads and quarters to be then at the King's disposal; and may the Almighty God have mercy on your souls."

So the sweat and the anxiety weren't just from the heat and the homesickness. This project was explosive, and it might very well blow up in their faces — his and the other delegates', who would sign it when they'd finished haggling over it and tampering with his prose. The tension of producing the document gave him sleepless nights, and made him into a compulsive eater who constantly nibbled at sugar cookies and green pears. He drank gallons of hot tea each day — despite the fact that it was considered highly unpatriotic to drink that beverage.

There wasn't any precedent for this thing he was trying to write, either. In the British Empire, if you didn't like the way things were going, you worked to get them changed. The British system was time-honored, world famous for its flexibility and adaptability. Sure, it was a long slow process to get the ministries and Parliament to respond to your grievances, but that stability was one of its virtues. It was the best system in the

world, and you didn't just pick up your marbles and say you were starting your own new game.

But that's what he was doing up there in the second-story parlor of the friendly German bricklayer's little house. Despite the horseflies, the heat, the homesickness, and visions of an executioner handing him his own guts, Thomas Jefferson was trying to knock out a declaration of independence.

He needed to get God and history on the side of revolution. He needed the weight of revered ancient thinkers and enlightened modern thinkers. He needed to make a credible case that what they were thinking about doing would be legal according to the best traditions of English law, and that it was absolutely neces-

Thomas Jefferson: Mother-hater?

sary in order to preserve the exalted principles that their forefathers had fled to a wild dangerous continent to establish.

Like harried writers will do, he dragged in bits and pieces of stuff he'd written on other occasions for different purposes, but he "turned neither to book nor pamphlet" for inspiration or comforting quotes. "All its authority rests," he would say later, " . . . on the harmonizing sentiments of the day."

There are those who wink and exchange knowing nudges when you start talking about the American Revolution being built on a solid intellectual foundation. Fancy ideas and noble ideals didn't prompt the Revolution, they say. That's just so much window dressing to hide the real cause of the rebellion.

Some Marxist historians will tell you that the Founders, for all their high-toned spoutings, were really just an alliance of bourgeois capitalists and slave-holding aristocrats sore that the government had tightened up a little on them, and eager to insure their longstanding economic advantages by assuming complete political control.

Some Freudian interpreters seem to see the Revolution, on the other hand, as some kind of externalized mass identity crisis, everybody invited, admission free. They stress such obscurities as the unusual number of revolutionary leaders (like Jefferson, Washington and Patrick Henry) who were just kids when their fathers died, and who, in several instances, didn't get along all that well with their mothers. And they point, nodding gravely, to the extensive use of the simile — even by conservatives like Edmund Burke and Pennsylvania's reluctant revolutionary John Dickinson — comparing the colonists to children treated unfairly by their father-king and mother-country.

Well, it's true that there's capitalist pig and spoiled brat written all over the American Revolution — much more so than there is gentleman and scholar. You don't have to look any farther than Tom Paine, raising hell all up and down Chestnut Street, to see that.

Paine's pamphlet *Common Sense* was just a diatribe, aimed at the lowbrows and dismissed by the sophisticated Harvard-educated John Adams as a "crapulous mass." And yet it probably converted more Americans to the cause of independence than any learned tome, or treatise, or oration. It was worth a hundred preachers, a thousand lawyers, and all the professors in the colonies put together.

Among its converts was George Washington, who, according to James Thomas Flexner's authoritative biography, didn't read much besides agricultural manuals before he got hold of *Common Sense* in January of 1776.

The meanest, most effective thing about *Common Sense* was the mad dog way Paine went after King George III. Now the psychohistorian would probably trace that bristling hostility back through old Tom's rumored impotence and his cuckoo marriages, and find the origin of it in his lingering grudge against his old man for having forced him as a boy into the dreary, futureless family business of whittling whalebone into corset stays.

(In the same way, historian Fawn Brodie decided that Jefferson's first truly revolutionary piece of work — his *Summary View of the Rights of British Americans* in 1774 — "may well suggest deeply felt grievances against his mother and perhaps even long buried and distorted resentments against his dead father.")

And the capitalist-pig advocates might argue that Paine's hatred of the king (and therefore monarchy) stemmed from an experience even further removed from the age of reason and the rights of man. Paine had been a minor tax-collector in England in 1773 and had led a lobbying campaign to get Parliament to give him and his colleagues a paltry little salary boost. Parliament didn't come across. And Paine concluded bitterly that the reason was that "the King, or somebody for him, applied to have his own salary raised a hundred thousand pounds a year, which being done, everything else was laid aside."

If Jefferson said he didn't do any research in writing the Declaration, Paine went him one better in tracing the origins of the ideas in *Common Sense*. He said he just thought them all up. He said he didn't read books (true) and didn't get his ideas from listening to other people's opinions (a lie).

"His mind was empty of the cultural and political traditions that inhibited educated contemporaries against change," David Freeman Hawke has written of Paine. "Ignorance, which carried lesser men into dark, narrow and bigoted lives, freed Paine's lively intellect to look at the world in a fresh way."

You could have dallied around the city during that summer of '76 and picked up plenty of other indications that the festering mood of revolution didn't have anything to do with a lot of guys having burnt a lot of midnight oil over the current Great Books of the Western World.

If you'd asked Franklin, he might have told you what he reported later in his autobiography about his lifelong "aversion to arbitrary power." Did it stem from his vast reading or from his having rubbed elbows with nearly every big-name egghead of the age? Nah, he didn't think so. He figured it went back to the beatings his older brother James had given him when he was a teenage printer's apprentice to James at the *New England Courant* in Boston.

Or Sam Adams. He was well-educated in the classics, particularly the Romans, and even took his motto from Ovid: "Take a stand at the start." But he knew that when it came to beating the bushes for revolution, you had to throw the classy stuff out the window and turn demagogue. "A master of propaganda," Samuel Eliot Morison wrote of him, "he realized that the general run of people prefer drama and ritual to a well-argued exposition."

Philadelphia had no fewer than 77 bookstores in 1776, but it was an oasis of colonial erudition. Historian Daniel Boorstin estimates that a majority of the citizens of Virginia weren't even literate enough to write their names. And although the early colonial settlers had made public education a first priority, formal schooling was mostly a lick-and-a-promise proposition. Franklin had had one term of elementary instruction at age 10, and that was it. Patrick Henry, who was putting on such a big show, had become a lawyer after six weeks of legal training.

Ignorance of book-learning wasn't anything to be ashamed of, either, in the minds of a lot of the colonists. They might have reminded you of the advice that William Penn had given his children back in the good old days: "More true knowledge comes by meditation and just reflection than by reading; for much reading is an oppression of the mind, and extinguishes the natural candle; which is the reason of so many senseless scholars in the world."

•

Such as that would have convinced you, I suspect, that if these guys were building their revolution on an intellectual foundation, it was a foundation that was opportunistic, derivative, slapped-together and about as smooth as a buggyride down Front Street. Certainly, the Founders didn't go about the job of developing a revolutionary rationale in the orderly, systematic way of the "senseless scholars" in the Old World.

They nailed together anything that seemed to fit — economic or psychological, legal or scientific, ancient or modern, poetic or rabble-rousing.

And they really didn't have much choice, because the European systems of political philosophy, unlike tulip bulbs, weren't something you could just boat across the Atlantic and expect to prosper in the alien soil. "Too much of the best elaborated thinking of the European mind," Boorstin says, "added up to proof that America and its novelties were impossible."

The Americans knew better. They'd spent 150 years coping with those impossible novelties and they'd learned a few things. They'd learned that you can rig up a fairly unobnoxious workable government without a detailed, streamlined political theory to work with. They'd found ways of staying in touch with the Creator without having to follow the tortuous routes prescribed by the formal overseas theologies.

But they'd generally had too much work to do to go head-to-head with the back-home intellectual establishment. The pleasures of philosophy — as known to, say, self-pitying old Dr. Johnson in England or to the En-lightenment forward-marchers in France—were an uncommon luxury on the frontier. So while they still dressed up their broadsides with quotes and gleanings from the Old World authorities, they were really more inclined to think in the practical terms you'd expect from veteran stump-grubbers with Indians for neighbors and a curious eye on the wild hills to the west.

Washington, for instance, when he wasn't fighting Indians, was designing plows, or figuring out that there were 13,411,000 grains in a bushel of timothy. John Dickinson had the good sense to call his collected political treatises *Letters from a Pennsylvania Farmer* instead of "Letters from a Philadelphia Lawyer," which would have been more accurate. Jefferson and Franklin and Paine weren't inventors for nothing. The American

Free Library of Philadelphia

Franklin's Poor Richard ". . . cribbed freely from the classics, the Enlightenment tomes, the continental scientists, satirists, poets, and journalists . . . ."

turn of mind, which would turn out Thomas Edisons and Henry Fords rather than Isaac Newtons and Albert Einsteins, had already appeared.

The most popular American character of the time was Poor Richard, the fictitious know-it-all in Franklin's enduring almanac. Poor Richard cribbed freely from the classics, the Enlightenment tomes, the continental scientists, the English legal sages, the English satirists and poets and journalists. Even the cogitations of Franklin's old saddlebur Cotton Mather weren't off limits to him. He made all these borrowings distinctly his own, twisting them around until they were something better than they had been, and meantime he kept a watch on the weather and an ear cocked for gossip and good jokes. That was America taking shape.

"I would not have you be too nice in the choice of pamphlets you send me," Franklin wrote to a London bookseller in 1744. "Let me have everything, good or bad, that makes a noise and has a run." He already knew then that Americans he sold the books to, or shared them with, didn't define themselves by imported systems of thought — so they wouldn't be intimidated or undone by any books the fellow might send, however unorthodox or irreverent. They'd find something useful in them somewhere.

So if there was in Tom Paine a kind of eloquent ignorance — the dead solid opposite of Penn's "senseless scholar"—there was in old Ben a kind of sophisticated intellectual innocence. You can see that quality best in his electricity experiments, which were the product of a wacky common-sense genius, but which were scientifically valuable only as long as he didn't know what the "respectable" European physicists of the time were doing and thinking. And it was that quality that caused Franklin to be regarded, on both sides of the ocean, as the archetypal American, the greatest of the self-made men.

More than in anyone else, the deep and devious and varied intellectual influences that brought on the revolutionary generation came together in Franklin, even if they were largely obscured by his homespun clothes, his homespun wit, and his homespun style, which unassuming country boys have used ever since to fox the slickers right out of their socks.

But Jefferson had more going for him than any

jerry-built strung-together American pragmatism as he flopsweated over the Declaration up there in his muggy aerie on Market Street. Otherwise his handiwork might have had no more lasting importance than the perpetual-motion machines that various screwball colonial "inventors" were building and whooping about all the time.

He drew from the "sentiments of the day" and the vitality of the frontier environment, all right, but even if he didn't consult any books directly, he had an unbelievable number of them lurking on the fringes of his mind.

Jefferson was only 33 years old at this time, but if there was a book available in the colonies that he hadn't read, it was a cinch he either didn't know about it or had his order in. When a colleague had asked him to prescribe a reading regimen for someone serious about improving his mind, Jefferson had responded by telling him the kinds of books he should have read and pondered before 8 a.m. each day. He had invented the swivel chair so that he could read all day beside a bay window at Monticello without having to get up and re-

Rome Was a Model for Law, Style — and Decline

The popular view in America has always been that Americans in 1776 looked back to the glory that had been Greece for their inspiration.

But this is something of a misconception. It is possible to say that in taking up the torch of individual liberty the Americans were choosing to carry the sacred fire of western civilization, which did in fact trace back to ancient Athens.

And it is undoubtedly true that educated Americans had read Plato, and other Greek writers, often in the original Greek. But Jefferson and John Adams, at least, confided to one another in letters that they were both unimpressed with Plato.

The Americans also read Homer's *Iliad* and *Odyssey*, but Homer wrote long before the golden age in Athens. The most popular piece of writing among Americans from around that later time was Xenophon's *Anabasis*, an account of difficult and perilous travels through Asia Minor with a lost battalion of Persian infantry.

Instead, it was to Rome that the Americans looked, both for inspiration and as a model in which to see their current situation. The Americans did not see themselves as citizens of tiny city states, as the Greeks had been. They were, instead, citizens of an empire, the greatest empire, in fact, since Rome.

And the Americans believed (correctly as it would ultimately turn out) that the empire they were in was on the decline,

just as the Roman Empire had been. Even as Jefferson was writing the Declaration of Independence in Philadelphia, Edward Gibbon in London was starting his monumental history, *The Decline and Fall of the Roman Empire*.

A major selling point for independence was the idea that Americans need not, and ought not, stay aboard the sinking British Empire.

To be sure, the Americans found more in Rome than a blueprint for imperial disaster. They admired Roman law and political organization. They also found sources of inspiration in, for instance, the successful prosecution of the corrupt Cataline by Cicero.

They admired not only Cicero's success, but reasonant brilliance of his rhetorical interrogation of the hapless Cataline, who was apparently scheming recklessly for some way to foil Cicero's prosecution. Cicero, thanks apparently to some superb detective work, learned of Cataline's plot against his own life, and confronted Cataline with the information on the floor of the Senate.

According to one historical account, Cataline blanched with fear and fury as Cicero disclosed further details of the assassination plan "which Cataline had fancied secret in his own guilty breast."

Cicero drew the noose of his summation closed with a magnificently measured interrogatory: *"Quosque tandem abutere, Catalina, patientia nostra?"* ("How much longer, Cataline, will you

abuse our patience?")

Cataline fled, but was apprehended and executed, along with several of his co-conspirators, at Cicero's order, without a trial.

Gaius Sallustius Crispus (Sallust) and Publius Cornelius Tacitus, two historians who wrote critically of Rome during the first century after the birth of Christ, were also admired by the Americans not only for what they said, but for how they said it. Sallust's writings are chock full of intriguing character sketches, exciting speeches, and charming digressions on the times and customs. Tacitus was one of the greatest prose stylists who wrote in the Latin language.

Despite the constant fascination with what caused Rome's fall, the reasons remain very much under debate, as does the question of what, if any, the Roman experience has for our own time.

Some thinkers of our own era, including Bertrand Russell, have suggested that the decline of Rome paralleled the decline the influence of Greek thought in Roman society.

"The supreme role of Rome," Russell writes, " . . . has been one of transmitting a culture older than, and superior to, its own. This was achieved because of the organizing genius of Roman administrators and the social cohesion of the Empire. Not even the barbarian invasions were able to destroy this cultural basis beyond repair."

" . . . What these Roman writers had in common was that they hated and feared the trends of their own time, which they considered decadent and oppressive . . ."

Homer: Popular Greek

Publius Cornelius Tacitus: Superb prose stylist

Gaius Sallustius Crispus: Critical historian

Marcus Tullius Cicero: Cataline's accuser

Free Library of Philadelphia

adjust the position of the chair to catch the light.

When Jefferson was only 28, a young friend had asked him for a reading list of works he considered essential, and the list Jefferson worked up must have blown the poor guy's mind. It would be easier to tell you what wasn't on it than what was. Many of the works on that list strongly influenced the American mind directly or indirectly, and were either actively or insidiously at play in the revolutionary deliberations of Jefferson's fellow delegates to the Continental Congress. Mar-

shaled by that Congress and its man in the upper room, the moral and intellectual power in those works would guy and buttress the American Revolution.

Chapter II: The Bible
Jesus didn't talk much about Justice, so they looked to the Old Testament.

Jefferson, having succumbed to the vague deism fashionable in Europe, was already ambivalent toward organized religion and violently hostile to the concept of the established church — that is, a state-supported and financed religious arm.

But he really was, nonetheless, a student of the Bible. It was on his list of essentials. And while he was writing the Declaration of Independence, the Good Book was crucial in a political way to his purposes. He knew that Bible-pounding preachers had played a key role in triggering the revolutionary mood. They had done so out of a suspicion that a corrupt political ministry back in England, already cracking down on the colonies with restrictive and punitive legislation, was also plotting to augment and extend the power of the established Anglican church in order to narrow the colonists' religious freedoms. If his Declaration was going to mean anything after he got it written, Jefferson also had to get it signed — and the signatures of clergyman-delegates like the Presbyterian Rev. John Witherspoon would be instrumental in getting public support behind the thing.

Because even if Jefferson was himself religiously adrift, most American colonists in 1776 were, and always had been, professing Christians who looked to the Bible for guidance in times of crisis. Ever since the Pilgrims had come over to set up a community that would be a model of Christian virtue, like a City on a Hill, Americans had viewed themselves as latter-day heirs to the biblical Israelites — a people who had a special covenant with God. Their black slaves would pick up on this, easily identifying with the plight of the Jews in bondage under Pharaoh, but since the WASP Americans at the time of the Revolution weren't slaves, they had to search the Scriptures for more appropriate biblical parallels.

One text they homed in on was the Book of Esther. In that minor Old Testament fragment, they found the story of Queen Esther's husband, mighty King Xerxes, being deceived by an evil minister named Haman. This Haman had finagled his way into a position of great influence with the king, and he loved to lord it over the peons. Haman became enraged when a virtuous Jew named Mordecai wouldn't bow down to him, so he contrived to persuade the king that all the Jews in the kingdom must be killed.

This sounded awfully familiar to the American colonists. King George III was also an out-of-touch monarch — so they believed — who was being manipulated by a haughty power-hungry gang of ministers led by Lord North. The colonists recalled too that Franklin had been over to London and had masterfully argued the case for their relief. He hadn't given an inch under the withering interrogation of the scheming ministers. He had refused to bow down. The colonists assumed that this had enraged Lord North and had convinced him to redouble the oppressive campaign against them. They found the parallels compelling — George III as Xerxes, Lord North as Haman, Franklin as Mordecai, themselves as the Jews.

They must have also found it encouraging that the biblical story had a happy ending. Haman's plot was thwarted and he was strung up on the gallows he had prepared for Mordecai. There was no question whose side God had been on.

But with the Bible, as with everything else they read, the Americans were relentless pragmatists. And while they pondered the Book of Esther, they chose to ignore the ominous possibilities in the more familiar New Testament story of Herod the Great ordering the Slaughter of the Innocents when he perceived a threat to his authority in one of the outlying provinces.

Chapter III: The Ancients
A selective reading of certain Romans was very helpful to the American cause.

Most Americans in 1776 who had received any formal schooling at all had learned Latin and Greek as youngsters. The emphasis was on the Latin, although Jefferson rejoiced more than once that he knew Greek well enough to enjoy Homer without having to depend on Alexander Pope's labored translations of the *Iliad* and the *Odyssey*. In any case, Americans then knew classical literature much more extensively than Americans do now.

But they knew some parts of it better than others. Bernard Bailyn, in *The Ideological Origins of the American Revolution,* says that what really gripped them and shaped their view of ancient history was "the political history of Rome from the conquests in the east and the civil wars in the early first century B.C. to the establishment of the empire on the ruins of the republic at the end of the second century A.D."

Their knowledge of this period, Bailyn says, came from several authors who either anticipated or lived through the decline of the Roman republic. Plutarch and Livy were two of them, but the Americans really dug Tacitus, Sallust, and Cicero. (All five of those writers were on that reading list Jefferson had compiled.)

What these Romans had in common — again quoting Bailyn — was that they "hated and feared the trends of their own time," which they considered decadent and oppressive, and that they "contrasted the present with a better past."

So did the American revolutionaries who thought corruption had eaten away the moral fiber of the overextended British empire. "They saw their own provincial virtues — rustic, and old fashioned, sturdy and effective — challenged by the corruption at the center of power, the threat of tyranny, and by a constitution gone wrong," Bailyn says. "They found their ideal selves, and to some extent their voices, in Brutus, in Cassius, and in Cicero, whose Catilinarian orations the enraptured John Adams, aged 23, declaimed aloud, alone at night in his room."

Cicero was certainly in the back of Jefferson's mind while he was writing the Declaration.

Cicero lived from 106 to 43 B.C. His father was just rich enough to give him the best education available, as was true of Jefferson. And, like Jefferson, he was tutored first in classical literature and then in the law. Like Jefferson, he became a lawyer, and like Jefferson as he toiled over the Declaration, he took on the establishment in his mid-thirties, in 70 B.C., by bringing suit against an influential senator who had been a crooked provincial official in Sicily.

In his indictment, Cicero showed how this bounder had sold appointments and decisions, had lowered tax assessments for bribes, had made off with public statuary, and, among other hijinks, had given an entire city's revenues to his mistress. Cicero's case for the prosecution was so overwhelming that the defendant's aristocratic lawyer coughed discreetly behind his hand and disappeared into the woodwork before even offering any evidence in his client's behalf. Cicero didn't have to deliver the summary speeches he'd prepared, but he published them, and 18 centuries later they still served as exemplary briefs against corruption by government officials sent out to work the provinces. When Jefferson was drawing up his brief against George III, he had a dazzling model to work from.

In his political writing, Cicero favored a republic, with powers separated and strong checks and balances in force. He did some hard thinking about how a society can steer a safe course between the Scylla of tyranny and the Charybdis of mob rule. He saw the connection between those two dangers in a famous passage whose implied warning wasn't lost on the Americans but which seems to anticipate with eerie accuracy how the French Revolution of 1789 would end up with Napoleon, and how the Russian Revolution even later would, for all its hopes and pains, bring on Joe Stalin. This is the passage, from Cicero's *De Re Publica*:

"Everything in excess is changed into its opposite . . . For out of such an ungoverned populace one is usually chosen as leader . . . someone bold and unscrupulous . . . who curries favor with the people by giving them other men's property. To such a man, because he has much reason for fear if he remains a private citizen, the protection of public office is given, and continually renewed. He surrounds himself with an armed guard, and emerges as a tyrant over the very people who raised him to power."

But it's worth mentioning again that the Americans were building an intellectual foundation for their revolutionary politics out of bits and pieces. They'd take a bolt from Esther, and reject a scrap from Matthew. In the same way, they found use for much of Cicero and threw out the rest. They liked his defense of natural rights based on the citizen's willingness to submit to reason, and his exaltation of law as an expression of reason. They skipped over his defense of executing rebellious dissidents without granting them the right of appeal. And when Cicero, in the crunch, sold out to Julius Caesar, the Americans looked the other way.

•

There was little writing in the ensuing 16 centuries that bore hard on the American Revolution. The Magna Carta in 1215 gave all Englishmen the rights of habeas corpus and jury trials. There was the hiatus of the Renaissance, whose artists depicted man in the nude, suggesting that underneath all our pretensions and ornamentations we're all equal. Martin Luther stole the holy fire and the Reformation, armed with Gutenberg's movable type, passed it down to everyday mortals, giving individuals the opportunity to bargain directly with God. But for the most part, the common people wore the collar of feudal politics and their champions were few and far between.

Chapter IV: Bacon and Descartes
Bacon had an idea: Why not forget everything except Aristotle?

Plow deep while the sluggard sleeps, Poor Richard counseled.

And there were some early tillers who, at the tail end of the feudal sluggishness, broke ground for the ideas which, when they came to fruition, Jefferson would harvest into the Declaration of Independence.

One of them was Francis Bacon, who was born in England in 1561 and who looked like a character on a cigar box.

Bacon was a minister to King James I of England, a hard-drinking bisexual to whom your family Bible is dedicated. When James took over in 1603 for the late lamented Queen Elizabeth I, he decided he was not only

Francis Bacon:
" . . . a sort of glorified John Ehrlichman . . ."

*Rene Descartes: He couldn't deny his own doubting;
"I think, therefore I am," he claimed.*

a king by divine right but actually a god, answerable only to God, and he proposed to rule the realm as such. This didn't go down well with the rising mercantile class and the English Puritans who had combined to get themselves strongly represented in the House of Commons. This antagonism set the stage for a prolonged civil war, which we'll get into later.

Now Bacon served as a sort of glorified John Ehrlichman to James, and when the shopkeepers and Puritans in Parliament decided, in the year the Pilgrims sailed for Plymouth Rock, to knock this uppity king down a peg or two, they chose discretion over valor and went after Bacon first. And they got him.

They convicted him of taking bribes. And since memoirs didn't sell in those days and CBS wasn't around to dole out interview money to disgraced politicians, Bacon was obliged to retire to his opulent estate where he became a philosopher and a scientist. He was first-rate in both roles.

His greatest contribution, for our purposes, was his conviction that human curiosity, aroused again after the Dark Ages hibernation, desperately needed a new method of science, a new way of discovering knowledge. Aristotle had tried once upon a time to gather together everything worth knowing, and ever since, men had been heaping systems and theories onto the floor that

Aristotle had built. The result was a big junkpile — what Bacon called "a medley and an ill-digested mass."

That mess had to be swept away. We had to start from scratch with the only trustworthy tools at our disposal — our powers of observation and our capacity to conduct scientific experiments — in order to build a reliable, uncluttered view of the world and of society and of men.

"Man, being the servant and interpreter of Nature," Bacon wrote, "can do and understand so much, and so much only, as he has observed, in fact or in thought, of the course of Nature; beyond this he neither knows anything nor can do anything . . . Human knowledge and human power (thus) meet in one."

Later that thought would be condensed to a slogan, "Knowledge is Power," which would become the battle cry of the Enlightenment, the broad philosophical movement of the 18th century whose most articulate political spokesman was Thomas Jefferson and whose finest political hour was the American Revolution.

In 1733, Voltaire, the great French lion of the Enlightenment, hailed Bacon as "the father of experimental philosophy." As such, Voltaire declared, Bacon had provided the scaffolding on which the scientific thinking of the later age was raised.

Bacon tried his best to be a scientist, and it seems fitting that the great precursor of the science that ultimately gave us deep freezes and TV dinners died in 1626, apparently of pneumonia which developed after he'd gotten chilled performing an experiment to see if a dead chicken could be preserved by stuffing it with snow. But he failed as a scientist because he never found the key to getting started in that new quest for knowledge that he'd called for.

That's because he got bogged down in his approach to the thing. The new method of science he came up with was really just a variation on the old inductive reasoning Aristotle had used. As Bertrand Russell explains Bacon's method, it "consisted in the drawing up of lists of things that shared a given quality under investigation, as well as lists of things that lacked it, and lists of things that possessed it in varying degrees. In this way it was hoped one would discover the peculiar character of a quality."

You're confused? Well, don't feel like the Lone Ranger.

Think of it this way. If Jefferson had used Bacon's method in trying to develop a rationale for the American Revolution, he would have started out by making up three lists:

On one list, he would have written down all the beefs that the colonists had with the king.

On the second list, he would have written down all the things about George III's government that the colonists were completely satisfied with.

And his third list would have contained an itemized account of those issues and political situations toward which the colonists had mixed feelings.

Then, or so the theory goes, he could have done a lot of cross-referencing and balancing off, and maybe fi-

THE FOUNDING CITY

nally have determined the truth about the real causes of the hubbub.

The infernal lists would have gone on forever, of course, and the Continental Congress, burdened with Bacon's method of reasoning, would no doubt still be in session—and we'd all be singing "God Save the Queen" before baseball games.

•

Over in France, meanwhile, Rene Descartes, a mathematical prodigy, was coming from a different direction at Bacon's basic problem of how to clear our heads of the Dark Ages mildew and make a fresh start in the quest to understand the world and ourselves.

His answer was suggested in a difficult but world-shaking little book called *Discourse on Method,* published in 1636, ten years after Bacon's death. Descartes proposed, among other things, to apply to philosophy the kind of deductive mathematical reasoning which Euclid had used in ancient Greece to deduce the principles of geometry, and which Copernicus had used in feudal Poland to figure out the earth's true place in the solar system.

Descartes thought mathematics suggested a simpler, more reliable way to go about stockpiling new knowledge than the use of Bacon's unwieldy device of comparative observation. Mathematics, he knew, is based on a few simple irreducible principles. It takes those principles for granted, using them as building blocks for more complicated mathematical formulas, and those can be combined and built upon endlessly to form the proliferating mathematical systems that made dropouts out of so many of us.

To apply that technique in other areas of thought, you must first, as Bacon had understood, throw out that old ill-digested mass of suspect knowledge. Take nothing on outside authority. Pare your assumptions about everything down to simple ideas that can't be broken down further. For Descartes, a fundamental idea of this sort was this: If he was determined to doubt everything, one thing he couldn't deny was his own doubting. He formulated that into the famous declaration: "I think, therefore I am."

That was getting down to the very basics. It was a place to start. He was a being capable of reasonable mental activity. That led him to certain other conclusions about his mind's capabilities and limitations. Building from those, he could confidently work up to some general principles of thought, and using those to test his perceptions of things, he could gradually develop a new understanding of the world and his place in it.

Bacon: Clearing Ground

The greatest intellectual undertaking of the Enlightenment was the encyclopedia put together by the so-called *"philosophes"* in France — an ongoing effort to draw together all human knowledge in the burgeoning scientific spirit of the time.

The editor, Denis Diderot, dedicated the work to Francis Bacon, calling Bacon the father of the Enlightenment. "At a time when it was impossible to write a history of what was known," Diderot wrote in his tribute, Bacon "wrote one of what it was necessary to learn."

Bacon's life was in a way a composite of the influences exerted on him by his mother and father. His mother, a devout Puritan, encouraged her precocious son to be a pious and solemn thinker. His father, who held the honorary and advisory position of Lord Keeper of the Privy Seal under Elizabeth I, wanted Francis to become a diplomat, and toward that end taught him the wheeling and dealing methods of politics.

Young Bacon entered Cambridge in 1573 at age 12, and by 23 had won a seat in Parliament and begun his first career — politics. He was reportedly about to be named attorney general by Queen Elizabeth when he committed the error of criticizing her tax policy.

Later he showed signs that he had learned that sincerity and honesty are not always the best policy. Bacon's close political associate and sponsor, the Earl of Essex, was a short while later tried for treason and the Queen appointed Bacon to be the prosecutor. Essex was hanged.

(One cannot help but wonder what emotions may have been at work in Bacon when, deep into his second career, he wrote his famous essay *On Friendship,* which still turns up in eighth-grade literature books today. Nothing, Bacon wrote, "openeth the heart but a true friend, to whom you may impart griefs, joys, fears, hopes, suspicions, counsels, and whatsoever lieth upon the heart to oppress it . . . .")

Bacon was never as close to Elizabeth, though, as he would be to Elizabeth's successor, James I, to whom he became advisor, confidant, and friend. ("It is a strange thing," Bacon later wrote, "to observe how high a rate great kings and monarchs do set upon this fruit of friendship of which we speak; . . . they purchase it many times at the hazard of their greatness . . . ")

Ultimately, that is, about the time James' enemies decided to go after Bacon, he had become Lord Chancellor, roughly the equivalent of being chief justice of the Supreme Court in the United States today. Bacon was charged with accepting bribes, which he admitted. (His defense was that he hadn't let the bribes influence his decisions.)

Bacon was fined 40,000 pounds, a stupendous sum, which he paid (and still apparently had a good deal left over. He continued to live in affluence). He was also sentenced to be confined in the Tower of London "at the King's pleasure." Luckily, it was the pleasure of Bacon's friend, King James, to turn him loose after serving four days.

Bacon was then free to begin thinking about what everything meant. If Diderot is to be trusted, Bacon did so very well indeed.

Descartes: Building Anew

Rene Descartes, who was born into the lower nobility in France in 1596, cannot be reckoned among the mental giants who had a powerful direct influence on the American Revolution. His influence was subtle and devious but nonetheless crucial.

Descartes' thought is maddeningly abstract. He was a mathematical genius — the inventor of analytical geometry — and as such most of his work was beyond the ken of most of the laymen of his time and even of later times. It's doubtful that either of colonial America's two great scientists — Ben Franklin and David Rittenhouse, both of Philadelphia—could have made heads or tails of most of his writing.

But they certainly had been affected by it.

Because, as a scientific thinker, Descartes provided the bridge between the haphazard and specialized scientific efforts of the ancients and the systematic and inclusive endeavors by later scientists like Sir Isaac Newton of England to deduce the rational, immutable principles that governed the universe.

Descartes' insistence on a rigorously scientific view of the world prepared the way for his scientist-heirs like Newton to prove to the popular satisfaction that nature really operated in reasonable, predictable ways, that supernatural explanations weren't valid.

Political thinkers soon began to suspect that if there were reasonable self-evident principles governing nature as a whole, then such principles probably applied also to nature's proudest creation, humanity, and to humanity's political schemes.

English political theorists like Thomas Hobbes and John Locke, relying on the rigorous systematic logic Descartes had prescribed, worked out detailed models of what they considered proper "natural" government. And it was at this point that the direct influence on the American political thinkers commenced.

As often happens with scientific geniuses, Descartes said that the outline of his entire philosophy simply spontaneously occurred to him one day when he was a youth. He was a soldier serving in Bavaria in the Thirty Years War, and he took refuge from the cold in a quiet countryside cottage that had a nice fire going in the tiled oven. He began to meditate there in the unexpected warmth and comfort, and the result was one of those epochal moments that changed history.

Descartes came to be recognized during his lifetime as the "father of modern philosophy," even though he was a quiet, shy man, a faithful Catholic who eschewed controversy and hesitated to follow up on the stunning implications of his work.

In 1649, Queen Christina of Sweden, an enlightened monarch anxious to learn philosophy and determined to learn it from the best, made Descartes an offer he finally couldn't refuse.

It turned out the Queen's schedule required her philosophy lessons to be taught at 5 a.m. each day, and such a dreary regimen in the cold predawn of a Scandinavian winter was too much for Descartes. After only a few weeks, he took ill. He died in February 1650.

One consequence of this method was that it put the individual — who had been pretty much kicked around for a thousand years — back at the center of the truth-defining process. His own reason was the ultimate smelter in which truth was extracted from the ore of experience and observation. If someone arose who claimed to speak with authority on any topic, anyone could challenge his conclusions by demanding to know, step by step, how he arrived at them.

There were implications here that Descartes hesitated to follow up — partly because he wasn't inclined to, partly too because he knew the Inquisition was giving Galileo a hard time just across the border for hanging around in this same general intellectual neighborhood.

One such implication was that the critical method might be used to challenge the legitimacy of a government. Claims to political power were, according to this method of arriving at truth, subject to rational analysis. Rulers simply couldn't proclaim themselves instruments of God or heirs of destiny. Politics should be traced back to its origins, and the various claims to authority justified step by step from the beginning. One of the first major modern thinkers to seize on that opportunity and obligation was Thomas Hobbes in England.

Chapter V: Thomas Hobbes
In nature, men's lives were "poor, nasty, brutish, and short," Hobbes said.

Hobbes published a book called *Leviathan* in 1651. It was, and is, one of the great, troubling books of the modern age. Jefferson didn't include it on his recommended-reading list, no doubt because he loathed every major conclusion in it. But even if he didn't know it (and he probably did), the book had a strong, if indirect, influence on him while he was writing the Declaration of Independence.

It's important to remember the situation that *Leviathan* grew out of. You'll recall that back in the early 1600s King James I declared himself a god called to rule by divine right, and that this angered the powerful contingent of shopkeepers and Puritans in Parliament, who showed their displeasure by packing Francis Bacon off to ice down dead chickens and change history.

The merchants had gotten their influence by getting control of more and more of the sceptered isle's money, and they were damned if they were going to tolerate a come-lately king claiming unrestricted authority to pick their pockets and spend their hard-earned cash according to his whims. And the Puritans, a dour crowd anyway, stubbornly denied the right of a king or anybody else to govern their modes of worship. Such conflicting claims to power had always been arbitrated by survival of the fittest; but both sides now had amassed considerable clout and weren't in any mood to budge.

Since neither side was strong enough to overwhelm the other, the issue seesawed back and forth for 50 years — a half-century marked by vicious power struggles, savage persecutions and a two-part civil war. James I's successor was publicly beheaded when the Parliamentary forces led by Oliver Cromwell temporarily got the upper hand, but the government was soon in disarray again, and as usual in such unsettled situations terrorism was rampant.

Hobbes grew up in this political climate, and the horrors he saw alarmed him.

What type of government would best be able to end the bloodshed, restore order, and create a lasting stability in the community? Everybody seemed to have an opinion, but Hobbes took on the task of working out an answer by the disciplined scientific process that Descartes had outlined.

Discard all the present arguments and opinions, Hobbes said. Doubt everything. Break down all the conflicting claims and current theories and see what you've got left. Find a basic starting point. All right, Hobbes said, since men obviously created government in the first place, then just as obviously men existed before governments did. So the question was: What were men like in this pre-government condition—in their natural state — and why did they feel compelled to impose governments upon themselves?

Relying on a few sketchy accounts of Indian life in the New World wilderness — and no doubt influenced deeply by the barbarities of the English civil war — Hobbes saw men in their natural state as violent predatory creatures who lived in constant fear of one another and whose lives were apt to be "poor, nasty, brutish and short." They were equals because they had an equal capacity to kill each other, and they had the instinct of self-preservation, and they possessed sufficient reasoning power to know they'd bloody well come up with some arrangement to save themselves from each other's depredations. So they formed governments which they

Voltaire: Philadelphia Fan

Voltaire, the French philosopher, may have been the most enthusiastic booster Philadelphia, and, in the larger sense, Pennsylvania, have ever had.

"Thy fields are fertile," he rhapsodized, "thy houses commodiously built, thy inhabitants industrious, thy manufactures highly regarded. An eternal peace reigns among thy citizens; crimes are almost unknown there; and there is but a single example of a man banished from the country . . . The wretch was no doubt possessed of the devil, for he dared to preach intolerance!"

Interestingly, Voltaire's admiring was done from afar. He never set foot in Pennsylvania.

He had wanted to come, though, and claimed that it was only fear of the sea, and the horribly unremitting seasickness voyages induced in him, that kept him on the terra firma of France. "If the sea did not make me unbearably sick," he wrote in his old age, "it is in thy bosom, o Pennsylvania, that I would pass the rest of my life. . . ."

Voltaire, born Francoise-Marie Arouet, was one of that breed of men so rare that the description sounds almost like a contradiction in terms — a French Anglophile. He lived at a time when the approach of English philosophers was diverging from that used by the philosophers of continental Europe.

The English thinkers were creating a system which concentrated on, and would ofttimes get bogged down in, the detailed applications of overall concepts. The continental Europeans, on the other hand, were devoting their energies to the construction of grand schemes that were often vulnerable to attacks based on specific nit-picking particulars.

Voltaire attempted to bridge the gap. He translated and made popular in Europe the writings — and discoveries — of Sir Isaac Newton, John Locke, and other Britishers. He also translated Penn's *Frame of Government* and praised its grant of civil liberties and religious freedom to Pennsylvanians.

Voltaire had gained much of his understanding of, and respect for, the British thinkers when he was exiled to England in 1726. His *Lettres Philosophiques* was in large part the result of his observation of religious tolerance in England.

Voltaire undertook to defend nearly any victim of religious persecution he heard of, including the torture of a French Protestant, Jean Calas, using some of the most scorching satire the world has ever seen. His efforts secured him a large popular following — and the bitter hatred of the French government, which believed, in that interesting way the French have, that persecution is an essential part of effective government.

It may have been, as the often repeated piece of hyperbole has it, that tyrants and bigots blanched at the mere mention of Voltaire's name. But it was Voltaire who had to scramble around Europe seeking a sanctuary from the wrath and recrimination of those he had offended. From 1754 until he made his final trip to Paris (where he died in 1778), he lived in Switzerland.

At the age of 82, two years before his death, Voltaire read the Declaration of Independence, and paid tribute to the promise of America. "You think what you like," he wrote proudly of the Americans, "and state it without anyone persecuting you."

He died encouraged, presumably, by the hope that across an ocean, in a land where he could never go, the ideals he had lived for would survive, perhaps even prevail.

empowered to control their destructive behavior.

Because individual men retain their dangerous natural tendencies, Hobbes thought, the government they create must be strong to be effective. It must be centralized and unfragmented. If it is expected to provide security and protection to the community, it must have discretion over practically all civil and religious liberties. Hobbes was evolving, as you can see, an apologia for an all-powerful sovereign—for political totalitarianism.

He went on in *Leviathan* to develop a comprehensive rationale not only for the political morality that underlies most modern political states but also for the cutthroat economic morality of much modern bourgeois capitalism.

"There is hardly a single bourgeois moral standard which has not been anticipated by the unequaled magnificence of Hobbes' logic," says political philosopher Hannah Arendt. "He gives an almost complete picture, not of Man but of the bourgeois man, an analysis which in 300 years has neither been outdated nor excelled."

From the point of view of the American Revolution, the most important thing about Hobbes' book was this: For the first time, a capable thinker had made a thorough scientific attempt to deduce the origins of political authority in a complex modern state, and had determined that government power ultimately rests on the consent of individual citizens.

His critics would attack most of Hobbes' other conclusions, but that one they'd leave alone—they'd use it, in fact, as a springboard for their more cheerful theories about human nature and the proper shape of just government.

Which brings us to John Locke, the patron saint of the American Revolution.

Chapter VI: John Locke
". . . Locke thought of people in their natural state as pretty decent folks . . ."

Jefferson included the complete writings of John Locke on that reading list of his, and the ideals he affirmed in that magnificent preamble to the Declaration of Independence were really a compact, beautifully-worded summary of the political principles advanced by Locke in his *Second Treatise on Government*, published in 1690.

Locke was born in 1632, the son of a Puritan who fought on the side of Parliament in the Civil War. During much of England's political strife, he was either in school — studying for the ministry first, and when that didn't work out, studying medicine and teaching Greek — or living quietly over on the Continent, teaching himself to become a liberal philosopher.

He returned to England for good only after the contending political forces had reached a lasting compromise, confirmed by the Glorious Revolution of 1688, which saw the peaceful accession to the throne of William and Mary in an atmosphere of tolerance and more widely distributed political power.

Library of Congress

Books from Thomas Jefferson's personal library.

In his *Two Treatises on Government*, Locke took up the challenge which Hobbes' book presented to this new political arrangement that was broader, looser, more tolerant, and more appealing to Locke than what Hobbes had prescribed. He acknowledged the value of Hobbes' trailblazing efforts that permitted him to consider people in their natural, pre-government state. He agreed that people were naturally free and equal in that state, and that it was by their common consent that government was formed.

But Locke didn't agree that people were by nature monsters. He wasn't intimidated, as Hobbes was, by vivid memories of the savage activities people were capable of when a tentative, weakened government let things get out of control. And where Hobbes hated and feared every manifestation of the church visible, Locke was a devout Christian with a redemptive view of human nature. He probably also had read more — and more accurate — accounts of what life was like among the American redskins.

So Locke thought of people in their natural state as pretty decent folks. And it wasn't just out of fear and desperation that they created governments. Rather, they were mainly interested in protecting their property interests. Locke defined property as what people create by applying their labor to the gifts of nature, but he added: "By property I must be understood . . . to mean that property which men have in their persons as well as goods."

That point needs elaborating.

Hobbes had viewed people as natural loners who came together in the first place only reluctantly — to form a government that would keep them from one another's throats. (Like the member nations of the UN, you might say.) Locke was willing to give what Mark Twain called the damned human race a little more credit. People were more reasonable and more sociable than Hobbes had thought, Locke contended. Among other things, their property interests had brought them together into communities — so society was an intermediate step between the lone savage and the political man.

Now as free, equal, reasonable creatures, people owned certain natural rights — as Cicero had said long before — and Locke enumerated those rights as the right to life, the right to liberty, and the right to the property contained in their persons and produced by the sweat of their brows. But in the commingling of society, there was likely to be confusion and conflict when individuals exercised their rights and pursued their various interests. So by unanimous consent, they created government to insure that nobody's rights would get trampled in the commotion.

But just because people gave over to the government certain powers, and became obligated to obey it, that didn't mean that the government now had the power to interfere with those basic individual God-given rights. In exchange for the powers the citizens granted to the government, they were entitled to guarantees that the government wouldn't overstep its legitimate authority.

Locke worried about the tendency of government to do that — to accumulate power at the expense of civil and religious liberties; to grow toward the totalitarianism that Hobbes had described and endorsed. Clear limitations should be put on it at the outset, Locke thought, to keep it in its place.

First, government should be fragmented, its powers separated among several branches. The legislative branch should be supreme, but it should be required to formulate laws in a proper, orderly manner, and apply them equally to all groups and classes of people. The legislature shouldn't be able to delegate its powers — that was the first step toward dictatorship — or to raise taxes without permission from the citizens or their representatives. The other branches of the government — which Locke defined less clearly — should be put in even stronger stocks.

Locke gave citizens one final guarantee against a government that betrayed them. Since the government existed only by their consent, they could withdraw that consent, dissolve the government, and form a new one. The British still do that after a fashion, when Parliament gives the administration in office a vote of "no confidence," thereby forcing the formation of a new administration. But the 18th century Americans, in what they saw as a much different political situation, construed Locke's guarantee differently. They saw it as justifying revolution. And it was for this idea — revolution as a moral, rational, responsible action — that Jefferson was up there in his room making a case.

Locke had himself offered one further thought. Not only could the citizenry as a whole withdraw its consent from a government turned oppressor; so could individual citizens. They were free to pull out of the agreement at any time and go off somewhere else in search of a government that suited them better. That freedom was largely what Jefferson meant by the "pursuit of happiness."

•

What Locke managed to do in his *Treatises on Government* was to justify in summary and compelling fashion a number of ideas and practices that had accompanied the European emergence from the Dark Ages.

The Dark Ages had been an epoch of stagnation and gloom. Ordinary people saw themselves as sojourners in a vale of tears, in a world that was really little more than a transitory proving ground for the hereafter. But the opening of a whole new world triggered a new optimism. No longer closed in by geography and fate, people began developing a new spiritual self-awareness, and they saw an opportunity for worldly advancement as well.

Nearly 200 years before Locke's book went to press, the Protestant Reformation lit the notion in the ordinary person that he might come to terms with God in his own way — and in probably more agreeable terms than he'd been offered before. And the ensuing attempts to extinguish that notion only convinced him of the need for a spirit of toleration, for a climate of live and let live.

The Dutch, who endured some of the most brutal religious persecution, were among the first to understand that. And once they won provisional national independence in 1609, they set up a regime celebrated for the freedom of conscience it permitted. It was no accident that among those who took refuge in Holland when their unconventional ideas got them in trouble elsewhere were the Massachusetts-bound Pilgrims, and later Rene Descartes, and later still, John Locke himself.

As commerce and industry revived with the opening of the New World, a middle class arose to chafe under governments that awarded virtually all political power to kings and distant emperors and titled aristocrats. Expanding and developing commerce would necessitate breaking up those outdated power monopolies. A redistribution of political power, based on property (as Locke would define it), seemed in order.

In short, people slowly began to believe that they could get to Heaven without being led by the nose, and that given the chance they could improve their earthly lot. They began to see the potential that each of them had to rise above circumstances by his own efforts. Knowledge was power and earned money was power, and only a contrived, self-appointed authority whose claims were suspect stood in the way of the exercise of that power.

They realized, of course, that law and order were essential to their progress, so they were willing to compromise with the government, to make haste slowly and gradually, to rebel only if their advance was blocked completely.

Even as Locke was deliberating these liberal concepts, American settlers were working to institutionalize them. Both the Pennsylvania Quakers and the New England Puritans were exercising that pursuit of happiness — which Locke would later proclaim as their right — by withdrawing from one government, in effect, and going somewhere else to set up a better one.

Penn had founded Pennsylvania on the policy of an unprecedented respect for those fundamental individual rights and liberties that Locke would hallow later. And if the New England Puritans tried to enforce a religious orthodoxy of their own, that freed them to

Locke: Declaration's Co-Author

One of the most difficult things about analyzing the Declaration of Independence is figuring out where John Locke ends and Thomas Jefferson begins.

Locke:

"Men being, as has been said, by nature all free, equal, and independent, no one can be put out of this estate, and subject to the political power of another, without his own consent . . . ."

Jefferson:

"We hold these truths to be self evident, that all men are created equal . . . that governments are instituted among men, deriving their just powers from the consent of the governed; that whenever any government becomes destructive of these ends, it is the right of the people to alter or abolish it . . . ."

Locke:

"Whosoever uses force without right . . . puts himself into a state of war . . . and in that state all former ties are cancelled, . . . and everyone has a right to defend himself and to resist the aggressor."

Jefferson:

"When in the course of human events it becomes necessary for one people to dissolve the political bonds which have connected them with another . . . a decent respect for the opinion of mankind requires that they should declare the causes . . . .

" . . . A long train of abuses and usurpations . . . evinces a design to reduce them under absolute despotism . . . it is their right, it is their duty, to throw off such government and to provide new guards for their future security . . . ."

Locke:

" . . . 'tis not without reason . . . (for a man to seek and join) in society with others who are already united, or have a mind to unite, for the mutual preservation of their lives, liberties, and estates . . . ."

Jefferson:

" . . . And, for the support of this declaration, with a firm reliance on the protection of Divine Providence, we mutually pledge to each other our lives, our fortunes, and our sacred honor."

The irony is that Locke was, in his own life, no practitioner of drastic action. The guiding principle of his life was tolerance. What his opinion would have been of the American Declaration of Independence, of which he was almost a co-author, is impossible to say. He had been dead for three-quarters of a century by the time it was written.

Locke grew up during the Civil War in England in which Cromwell's "roundheads" battled the royalist "cavaliers," and he eventually broke with both sides. Later, he went into exile in Holland, and lived there for a time under a pseudonym to avoid extradition. It was during this period that he wrote the first of his *Letters On Toleration* and the *Two Treatises On Government.*

His *Letters on Toleration* dealt mainly with religious toleration. "If any man err from the right way, it is his own misfortune, no injury to thee," he wrote. He also urged that no one be punished in this world "because thou supposeth he will be miserable in that which is to come."

---

concentrate on solving some practical problems of political organization — and the American revolutionists would profit immeasurably from studying the solutions they came up with.

A great deal has been written about how the 18th century European Enlightenment — spawned in part by Locke's political writings — influenced American thought during the era of the Revolution. But there's an element of the cart pulling the horse in that argument. Because no less an Enlightenment figure than Voltaire admitted that he drew his political inspiration from the principles promulgated into law in Pennsylvania in 1681 by William Penn.

In any case, Locke was able to articulate in a tight, pat political theory the liberalism that had swelled up over the preceding centuries. And when Jefferson finally started scribbling down the first part of the Declaration of Independence — the memorable and explosive preamble that became our national creed — he siphoned his principles directly from Locke's treatises on government.

All men are created equal; they are endowed with unalienable rights; these rights include life, liberty and the pursuit of happiness; it was to secure these rights

that governments were instituted among men; governments derive their just powers from the consent of the governed; when government becomes destructive of these ends men may alter or abolish it; and men have a right to institute new governments to effect their safety and happiness.

Straight down the line Locke.

Locke wrote something else that had a big impact on America. It was his *Essay Concerning Human Understanding,* also published in 1690. This essay is certainly not light reading for the commuter train, but all the brainier Founding Fathers wrestled with it from the time they were tykes, so we can't ignore it.

What it was, among other things, was an attack on the notion of innate ideas, which Descartes had picked up from ancient philosophy and reaffirmed. Locke was content to go along with Descartes' argument that the best method for building trustworthy knowledge was to start with a few basic ideas and reason our way cautiously upward. But he disagreed with Descartes about how we come by those basic ideas.

Descartes believed that we're born with them — that they already exist in embryonic form when we tumble forth from the womb, or at least that the poten-

John Locke argued in his Essay Concerning Human Understanding *that men are born with minds that are blank, and which are shaped by their environment.*

tialities for them are already determined.

Locke disagreed. Picking up on an argument first advanced by a French savant named Pierre Gassendi who had been moldering in his grave for decades, Locke contended that we're born with minds like blank sheets of paper. What determines the ideas our minds will have is the environment we grow up in.

That is, the sensations from the external world bombard this blank mind, and the mind, through reflection, combines and sorts these sense impressions and fashions them into ideas. The fancy philosophical term for this is "empiricism."

There was high-octane encouragement here for all those liberal hopes that had grown up out of the Dark Ages. If it's his environment that shapes a man, then by altering the environment in beneficial ways we should be able to help him turn out better. Political reforms, social reforms — these not only have immediate meliorating advantages, but also should produce cumulative long-term benefits. Progress. Toward a better world — if not for us, then for our posterity.

And the colonial Americans read a special message in the essay. Their New World environment, with all its novelties, seemed unique. And since they and their children were the ones who would be shaped by it — who would have to live with its consequences — they should have the right to alter it to serve their peculiar needs. To live under institutions and arrangements created by Old Worlders for Old Worlders would be unnatural and detrimental.

Paine had picked up those vibrations when he said it was crazy for a far-away island to be ruling a continent.

Chapter VII: The Law
The Americans argued that English common law allowed, even required, them to revolt.

So with Locke as his key, Jefferson managed in the first part of the Declaration to sketch us a creed, which included the right to revolution. But Locke had said that men were bound to obey their government until they had made a clear and convincing case that it had betrayed them. To Jefferson, a lawyer, that meant specifying the colonial grievances against the government point by point in a legal brief.

Maybe because of that business about their necks, their bowels and being hacked into quarters, the Ameri-

The draft of the Declaration of Independence showed plenty of evidence that the delegates had "haggled over and tampered with" Jefferson's prose.

The members of the Continental Congress were keenly aware that the penalty for the treason they were committing was death.

cans were extremely anxious to prove in the court of world opinion that their cause was justified not only by natural law but even by English common law.

In his famous speech to Parliament in 1775 urging reconciliation with the colonies, Edmund Burke mentioned the extraordinary American interest in the law. "In no country perhaps in the world," he said, "is the law so general a study. All who read, and most do read, endeavor to obtain some smattering of that science."

Burke understood the significance of that. In England, the details of the law were mainly known to, argued by, and interpreted by professional barristers. But in America a much larger percentage of citizens were landowners and so learned as much law as they could in order to guard their property rights. The country was crawling with lawyers — though many of them were amateurs and jacklegs — and Burke knew that such a people were likely to be united in a common understanding (or misunderstanding) of their legal rights.

Just as the Americans had developed speech patterns over a century that already sounded strange to the British ear, they had also developed — because of the absence of a professional lawyers' monopoly — an Americanized interpretation of the English law. Judges were often laymen and in the past had often found it necessary to bend and twist the law to make it serve the needs of frontier justice.

They could do that — and still consider themselves to be operating within the spirit if not the letter of the law — because English law wasn't summarized and organized in any intelligible way until 1753, when the 23-volume Viner legal encyclopedia was published in London. Until then, and even afterwards to a large extent, the colonists had relied mainly on the old, old legal opinions of Sir Edward Coke for their understanding of their legal rights and duties as Englishmen.

As a law student in 1762, young Tom Jefferson had written to a friend: "I do wish the Devil had old Coke, for I am sure I never was so tired of an old dull scoundrel in my life." But we know that Coke stuck with Jefferson, and made his presence felt in that hot fly-infested room where Jefferson was plugging away on his indictment of George III. So we ought to pay our respects to Sir Edward before moving on.

The dull old scoundrel was a big-name legal eagle in the late 1500s. He helped Elizabeth I separate Essex from his head, and also had a prosecutorial role in trundling hapless Sir Walter Raleigh off to rot in the Tower. But Coke's main interest to the Americans was his service during the reign of our inescapable old buddy King James I.

By the time James arrived on the scene in 1603, Coke was well on his way to a reputation as the great watchdog of English common law. He didn't hurt himself any in James' view with an opinion delivered in 1610 which rocked Parliament, and which was to become one of the enduring pillars in American law. In that opinion, cited by John Marshall to establish the right of judicial review 200 years later in the case of *Marbury v. Madison,* Coke wrote:

". . . It appears in our books, that in many cases, the common law will control acts of Parliament, and sometimes adjudge them to be utterly void, for when an act of Parliament is against common right and reason; or repugnant; or impossible to be performed; the common law will control it, and adjudge such an act void."

Historian Charles Beard numbers this opinion as among the three or four most important single intellectual influences on the American Revolution, and it's easy to see why.

Because much of the colonial outrage that brought Jefferson to his Philadelphia rendezvous with destiny was occasioned by a series of Parliamentary acts (like the Stamp Act) that the Americans considered unreasonable, repugnant, impossible to be performed, and contrary to their understanding of English common law.

King James made Coke chief justice of the King's Bench in 1613, apparently assuming that the dull scoundrel would serve him as a sort of semi-John Mitchell. But Coke fooled him. It was like what happened to Ike when he dredged up gray old Earl Warren to be *his* chief justice. As Will Durant describes it: "From being the King's man, he became the King's gadfly, condemning inquisitions into private opinions upholding parliamentary freedom of speech, and puncturing royal absolution with sharp reminders that kings are the servants of the law."

James tolerated this as long as any self-respecting, self-appointed god could afford to. After three years, he sicced his hatchetman Francis Bacon (you remember him) on old Sir Edward. Through Bacon's efforts, Coke was canned, but he wormed his way into Parliament and continued to snipe at the "royal prerogative." James sent him to the Tower a while to teach him some respect — or reverence maybe — but finally gave up and decided to endure him.

The damage — insofar as his future influence on the sassy American colonists — had already been done anyway because after the old scoundrel died in 1634, his opinions defending the common man's rights against invasion first by the Parliament and then by the monarch were collected and published in four volumes. These were the so-called *Coke Institutes* and American lawyers — pro, semi-pro and dabbler — would read them until they were sick of them.

Chapter VIII: Other Limeys
The Americans were listening to some Englishmen that the English ignored.

Bernard Bailyn, our best Revolution-era historian, thinks that maybe the most important intellectual influence on the Americans who decided to risk the executioner's vengeance in that summer of 1776 was another loose-knit group of Englishmen that many of us have never heard of. They were an assortment of Radical Whigs — journalists, historians, and sometime politicians — who did a lot of carping from the political sidelines in the early 1700s.

Among them were John Trenchard and Thomas Gordon, London journalists who teamed up to publish a weekly number called the *Independent Whig,* which appeared in book form in 1721, and a series called "Cato's Letters," also collected into a book in 1720.

These two guys were good, tough, talented, radical libertarian journalists like Tom Paine would be. They weren't as famous as the urbane journalistic duo of Joseph Addison and Richard Steele, from whose genteel essays in the *London Spectator* the adolescent Ben Franklin learned the elements of his prose style. But their indictment of moral corruption in English political life — and their highly readable concern for the threat that such corruption posed to the civil liberties won at such cost in the political storms of the 1600s — left a deep lasting impression on the Americans.

Trenchard especially harped relentlessly on the threat to liberty represented by a standing army in peacetime. "Unhappy nations have lost that precious jewel liberty," he wrote, because "their necessities or indiscretion have permitted a standing army to be kept among them." When the troops landed in Boston in 1768 in response to the Stamp Act disorders, the colonists remembered what Trenchard had written, and read it, and reread it with increasing anger and apprehension.

The same point was driven home in another work by one of these disaffected Whigs — Robert Viscount Molesworth's *Account of Denmark,* published in 1694. That was a casebook study of how modern Denmark, like ancient Rome, had succumbed to political corruption and then, with its moral guard down, had allowed a standing army to destroy its constitution.

Standing armies in peacetime — the issue bugged the Americans so much, they fretted about it so much and wrote so much about it that it got into our blood. It's touched off angry debates and controversies from time to time throughout our national history, right up to the eve of World War II.

Jefferson made it a priority item in his brief against George III in the Declaration of Independence.

A fellow traveler of these radical Whigs was Lord Bolingbroke, a reconstructed Tory, who had become an eccentric, bitter man after losing his chance for political glory as a young man by taking sides with a would-be king who didn't make it. Bolingbroke was a close friend to Jonathan Swift, and the influence showed in both Bolingbroke's journalistic and historical writing, which turned the political establishment every way but loose. John Adams blew his stack when Burke suggested around the time of the Revolution that nobody read Bolingbroke any more. Adams said he'd read Bolingbroke through five times, and considered his writing "most perfect."

But these guys were out of the mainstream. English politics in the early 1700s was lax and easy-going.

When the blockhead George I came from Hanover in 1714 to be England's king, he didn't know the first thing about English politics and he cared less. He hated London and went home a lot. He was more than happy to leave the chores of government to Robert Walpole, a friendly flatterer in Parliament who thus became England's first prime minister in the modern sense.

Walpole's administration stayed in power for decades — with minor interruptions like George II, who thought briefly of being a real king before deciding the hell with it — and its policy was by and large one of what Daniel Moynihan would have called benign neglect toward the colonies and almost everything else. These were sluggish political times in the old realm, and nobody could get very excited about much of anything.

Nobody but those rad-lib sideline critics who, with nothing more pressing at the moment, worried that complacency itself was a grave threat to a free people. A lulled citizenry would quickly lose its chance to keep a small band of ambitious ministers who had assumed great power from slipping off into corruption, and then it wouldn't be long before liberty dissipated and slowly disappeared. To keep the air charged, these critics proposed all sorts of liberal reforms — everything from universal manhood suffrage to full freedom of the press.

There wasn't much of a market for their line in the homeland, but the American colonists were all ears. They not only stayed alert for signs of a corrupt ministry encroaching on their liberties but also gave respectful thought to those reform proposals, and incorporated most of them into their politics when they finally got the chance.

So while it had to cross the ocean and smolder a spell, the torch lit by those radical little-known English dissenters did manage to get itself passed on. It too provided some of the illumination for the homesick man with stomach trouble, writing there in a stuffy Philadelphia room with horseflies for company, putting the finishing touches on what was to become the most electrifying document of the age. ★ ★ ★

Tom Paine Brings It All Back Home

The task of making the ideas of the Revolution clear to the mass of Americans fell to an erstwhile corset staymaker who claimed that he thought it all up himself.

By Edgar Williams

Let the names of Whig and Tory be extinct; and let none other be heard among us, than those of a good citizen; an open and resolute friend; and a virtuous supporter of the RIGHTS OF MANKIND and of the FREE AND INDEPENDENT STATES OF AMERICA.
—Thomas Paine, *Common Sense*

To borrow historian W. E. Woodward's line, Thomas Paine was the godfather of America. He made untold thousands of Americans from Georgia to New Hampshire a proposition they couldn't refuse.

More accurately, Paine articulated a proposition that had been in the back of the minds of many Americans for some time, ideas half-formed and misty and only dimly perceived: Everything that might have led to reconciliation between Britain and the colonies had been said, to no avail; therefore, the only solution for the colonies was independence, a new nation.

Paine said it, simply and directly, in what historian Eric Foner, in his book, *Tom Paine and Revolutionary America*, has termed "one of the most remarkable political pamphlets in the history of English writing" — a thin volume of 47 pages containing about 25,000 words, titled *Common Sense*, brought out in Philadelphia in January 1776.

Americans bought the pamphlet, which sold for a modest two shillings. It was a publishing success roughly equivalent to *Jaws* in our own time. And they bought Paine's argument. Before winter gave way to spring, *Common Sense* had fanned the smoldering fires of liberty throughout the colonies to full flame.

And the godfather of America had inspired the Declaration of Independence.

As Woodward has said, the pamphlet, 120,000 copies of which were sold within three months after it first appeared, " . . . struck a string which required only a touch to make it vibrate. The country was ripe for independence, and only needed somebody to tell the people so with boldness and plausibility."

How it was that Paine, an erstwhile corset staymaker, should have been the man to do this is yet another of the enduring little mysteries of the American Revolution.

He claimed never to have read books, and yet it can be argued that he was the

Thomas's Paine's Common Sense *was a smash best-seller in 1776.*

man who focused diffuse intellectual fires that had been burning for centuries into a ray hot enough to ignite men to action.

Nothing he had done before — and he had never been successful at anything — gave a hint that he possessed such powers.

And the things that he would do after the American Revolution would almost earn him a guillotining at the hands of the French revolutionists, and would cost him the friendship of some of his closest friends in America.

Simply stated, the fact of the matter appears to have been that through some transmogrification of the laws of chance and circumstance, Thomas Paine became, for a few years in the 1770s in America, the right man in the right place at the right time.

He was a born hell-raiser, a rebel by instinct. He had a deep-seated hatred of royalty, the nobility, the British Parliament — the whole British scheme of things, in short. He was the type of man, found in every generation, who is always opposed to the existing authority, regardless of what it happens to be. To employ Woodward's trenchant observation, "If Paine had drowned while crossing a river, it would have surprised no one if his body had floated upstream."

Whatever his shortcomings, Paine was indisputably an incandescent rebel who was able to radiate that incandescence so that its glow is reflected in others. There is a special place in oblivion for rebels who through the centuries have failed utterly to convince anyone of anything because their vituperations were so shrill as to have been unintelligible to those they tried to rally to a cause. This has been particularly true of rebels who have endeavored to make their thrust with the written word. Few have been convincing, because they have been blown away by the storm of their own emotions.

But Paine could write. He possessed literary poise, which was passing strange for one who had had only seven years of formal education and never had been a journalist until he came to Philadelphia from his native England late in 1774, shortly before his 38th birthday. As a writer, Paine really was a natural.

Moreover, Paine wrote in homely words, in the English of the people. Simplicity and force, as Woodward points out in his biography, *Tom Paine: America's Godfather,* were the vital principles of the man's creative literary work. Paine reasoned that if an argument did not carry force and conviction, there was no point in printing it; and if it were so intricate in style and expression that only the highly educated could understand its full import, most of its possible readers were excluded.

Most of the political writings of Paine's time were both ponderous and pompous. As a matter of vanity, authors felt impelled to quote freely from Plutarch and Ovid, from Horace and Lucretius, even if they were arguing nothing more important than the right to keep a green-grocery open an extra hour on Saturday night.

But Paine used no quotations from the classics in *Common Sense.* Nor did he employ words that could not be comprehended by the average person. And while some of his sentences were lengthy, by today's literary standards, they were not involved contrivances which practically required a compass to navigate.

Paine opened with a savage attack on the constitution of England:

"... I draw my idea of the form of government from a principle in nature which no art can overturn, namely, that the more simple anything is the less liable it is to be disordered, and the easier repaired when disordered; and with this maxim in view I offer a few remarks on the so much boasted Constitution of England. That it was noble for the dark and slavish times in which it was erected, is granted. When the world was overrun by tyranny the least remove therefrom was a glorious rescue. But that it is imperfect, subject to convulsions, and incapable of producing what it seems to promise, is easily demonstrated."

He went on to denounce the whole notion of the historical legitimacy of the monarchy, beginning with the accession of William the Conqueror seven centuries earlier: "A French bastard landing with an armed banditti and establishing himself king of England against the consent of the natives, is in plain terms a very paltry rascally ... (origin.) It certainly hath no divinity in it."

Paine minced no words in his assault on the principle of hereditary rule: "One of the strongest natural proofs of the folly of hereditary rights in kings is that nature disproves it, otherwise she would not so frequently turn it into ridicule by giving mankind an *ass* (the italics are Paine's) for *a lion."* And: "Of more worth is one honest man to society, and in the sight of God, than all the crowned ruffians that ever lived."

Did Americans owe allegiance to King George III? No, Paine cried, labeling the monarch a "hardened, sullen-tempered Pharaoh" who had shown himself to be not the father of his people but "the Royal Brute of Great Britain."

Turning to a discussion of independence, Paine considered and then demolished the arguments for reconciliation. Inasmuch as Britain was the "parent country," was it not ungrateful for the colonists to rebel? No, Paine answered: "... the more shame upon her conduct. Even brutes do not devour their young, nor savages make war upon their families."

Moreover, Paine insisted, "Europe, and not England, is the parent country of America. This new world hath been the asylum for the persecuted lovers of civil and religious liberty from every part of Europe."

Was America weak in comparison to Britain? Quite the contrary, Paine asserted. "There is something absurd in supposing a continent to be perpetually governed by an island."

Would independence involve America in war with European powers while depriving it of British protection? Replied Paine: "France and Spain never were, nor perhaps ever will be, our enemies as Americans, but as our being the subjects of Great Britain."

Paine's arguments were general in character. He did not go deeply into the legal and political aspects of the dispute between the colonies and Britain. There was, for example, no mention of the Stamp Tax or the Intolerable Acts. To have discussed various grievances in detail, Paine knew, would have distracted the reader from the main issue.

To the conservatives who were pushing for reconciliation, Paine said, "Ye know not what ye do." And: "Ye that tell us of reconciliation, can ye restore to us the time that is past? Can ye give to prostitution its former innocence? Neither can ye reconcile Britain and America. The last cord is now broken."

Government in an independent America, Paine said, would be simple and law would be king. There would be equality of representation and annually elected assemblies. The business of the assemblies would be purely domestic; all other matters would be left to the Continental Congress. Paine also called for a constitutional convention to draft an American Magna Carta, "fixing the number and manner of choosing members of Congress, members of assembly, with their date of sitting, and drawing the line of business and jurisdiction between them."

Toward the close of *Common Sense,* Paine called for a declaration of independence:

"Were a manifesto to be published setting forth the miseries we have endured ... declaring at the same time that not being able longer to live happily or safely under the cruel disposition of the British court, we had been driven to the necessity of breaking off all connections with her ... such a memorial would produce more good effects to this continent than if a ship were freighted with petitions to Britain ... let a day be solemnly set apart for proclaiming the charter ... "

Then Paine gave his idea of the meaning of American independence: "We have it in our power to begin the world over again ... the birthday of a new world is at hand." Having stated that, he almost lyrically broadened the struggle over the rights of the colonists into a contest with meaning for all mankind:

"O! ye that love mankind! Ye that dare oppose not only tyranny but the tyrant, stand forth! Every spot of the old world is overrun with oppression. Freedom hath been hunted round the globe. Asia and Africa have long expelled her. Europe regards her as a stranger, and England hath given her warning to depart. O! receive the fugitive, and prepare in time an asylum for mankind."

•

Common Sense was the first book in our history to reach the whole American public. Probably it was read, in whole or in part, by every adult who could read at all; it was even read aloud to illiterates. The adjutants of regiments in the Continental Army read parts of it to troops drawn up on parade. George Washington observed that it was "sound doctrine and unanswerable reasoning."

As historian Merrill Jensen has observed, it is impossible to estimate how many persons were converted to the cause of independence by *Common Sense*, but contemporaries agreed that its impact was enormous. After the Revolution, Edmund Randolph wrote that "this pamphlet put the torch to combustibles," and that because of *Common Sense* perhaps a majority of Virginia counties instructed their delegates to the Virginia convention in May to vote for independence.

And in the judgment of the eminent South Carolina historian, David Ramsey, the pamphlet "... in union with the feelings and sentiments of the people ... produced surprising effects. Many thousands were convinced and led to approve and long for a separation from the Mother Country. Though that measure, a few months before, was not only foreign from their wishes, but the object of their abhorrence, the current suddenly became so strong in its favor, that it bore down all opposition. The multitude was hurried down the stream. ..."

There is an old journalistic truism that the ultimate test of a piece of expository writing is not the accolades it receives but the amount and type of criticism it evokes. Or to put it another way, if you

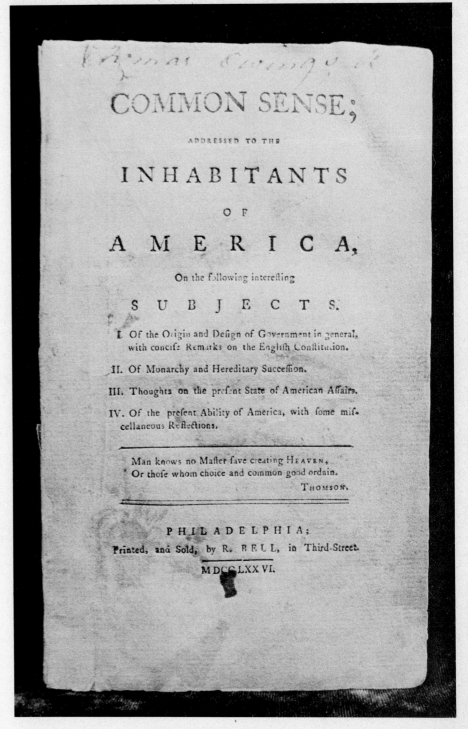

COMMON SENSE;

ADDRESSED TO THE

INHABITANTS

OF

AMERICA,

On the following interesting

SUBJECTS.

I. Of the Origin and Design of Government in general, with concise Remarks on the English Constitution.

II. Of Monarchy and Hereditary Succession.

III. Thoughts on the present State of American Affairs.

IV. Of the present Ability of America, with some miscellaneous Reflections.

Man knows no Master save creating HEAVEN, Or those whom choice and common good ordain.
THOMSON.

PHILADELPHIA;
Printed, and Sold, by R. BELL, in Third-Street.
MDCCLXXVI.

don't draw blood you have failed to accomplish your purpose.

Measured by that yardstick, *Common Sense* was again a thumping success.

The pamphlet was denounced by many, including the Reverend William Smith, whose "Cato" attacks appeared in the *Pennsylvania Gazette*, but the major pamphlet printed in reply was *Plain Truth* by James Chalmers, a Maryland landowner who later became a Loyalist.

As "Candidus" he attacked the author of *Common Sense* (whose identity was unknown to the general public until some time in the spring of 1776) as a "political quack," and defended monarchy and the English constitution. He charged, like many other opponents of independence, that without the control of the Crown, "our constitution would immediately degenerate into democracy" and that the history of "democratical or popular governments" was one of warfare, internal rebellion, and constant repression of the rich by the poor.

Even John Adams, his nose out of joint because, he claimed, *Common Sense* was simply "a tolerable summary of the arguments which I had been repeating again and again in Congress for nine months," dashed off a pamphlet in which he took Paine to task for his ideas on government which Adams also considered "too democratical."

Indeed, many of the ideas expressed by Paine in *Common Sense* had been put forth earlier by Adams and many others. For, although Paine contended that he "never studied other people's opinions" and that his views in *Common Sense* were entirely original, the fact is that he was simply a good journalist who listened intently to others and, when the proper time came, was able to crystallize what he had heard.

This is not to disparage Paine. For no other man of the time could have brought the whole galaxy of revolutionary ideas into coherent form as he was able to do. Historian Woodward gives us a clear picture of what Paine did: "The situation may be compared to a chemical process where several diverse elements are brought together to form a single compound. They are all present but they will not unite until a catalyst is added to them. The catalyst in this case was Thomas Paine."

It was Dr. Benjamin Rush, the patriot physician of Philadelphia, who in the autumn of 1775 suggested to Paine that he write a pamphlet broaching the subject of independence. It was Rush who found a printer, one Robert Bell, who would publish the pamphlet, and it was Rush who suggested that it be titled *Common Sense* rather than *Plain Truth* (the title later seized upon by the anti-Paine Chalmers), as Paine wanted to call it. As Paine progressed with the work, it was read by Rush and scientist David Rittenhouse. But contrary to claims made by James Cheetham, one of Paine's first biographers, neither Rush nor Rittenhouse did any of the writing. *Common Sense* was pure Paine.

•

To understand what drove him, it is necessary to go back to Paine's beginnings in England. From early childhood in the village of Thetford, Norfolk, about 70 miles northeast of London, where he was born January 29, 1737, he seemed bent on making a career of failure.

An indifferent student, he dropped out of school at the age of 13 to apprentice himself to his father's craft of staymaking, the manufacture of whalebone stays for corsets. At 16, he ran away from home to serve aboard a privateer, but he

soon returned, and by 1756 he was working as a journeyman for a staymaker in London.

In 1759, Paine married Mary Lambert, a maid employed by the wife of a shopkeeper. She died less than a year later, and there were reports that her death was due to "ill-usage" by her husband. These reports have never been substantiated, however. Paine did have faults, but he was not a cruel man.

Paine couldn't — more likely, wouldn't — make it as a staymaker. In 1762, therefore, he took an examination for — and won — a job as a low-level exciseman, a collector of excise taxes. After three years in that job, he was fired for committing the not uncommon offense of "stamping his whole ride" — that is, filing a report without in fact having examined the goods involved.

There followed three years of near indigence for Paine, who tried to get back into staymaking but found that no one would employ him. Then he taught school for a time, at the magnificent salary of 25 pounds a year — a poverty-level figure.

Finally, in 1768, Paine swallowed his pride and wrote a humble letter of apology to the Excise Board for his previous infraction. He was restored to the post of exciseman and assigned to the town of Lewes, Sussex, where he met and married Elizabeth Ollive in 1771. When the two separated late in 1773, Elizabeth paid Paine 35 pounds as part of the agreement by which he left her house and was reported to have told friends that the marriage never was consummated. The obvious supposition was that Paine was impotent. But all Paine would ever say concerning the separation was "It's nobody's business but my own. I had cause for it but I will name it to no one."

In addition to collecting taxes, Paine operated a tobacco shop and grocery which he mismanaged so badly that he soon was deep in debt. Further, to punish him for his leadership of a movement to win higher salaries for excise tax collectors, the Board of Excise abruptly notified him in March 1774 that he had been discharged.

So Paine was a failed husband, a failed tax collector, a failed staymaker and a failed merchant. At age 37, he had no future in England. Like many another Englishman in similar straits, he decided to seek a new start in America.

Paine went up to London and sought out Benjamin Franklin for advice. Franklin advised him to seek his fresh start in Philadelphia. Of all American cities, Franklin said, Philadelphia offered the best opportunities for newcom-

ers from abroad. He gave Paine a letter of introduction to his son-in-law, Richard Bache, a Philadelphia merchant, and advanced him money to pay his passage.

The immigrant arrived in Philadelphia on November 30, 1774, aboard the ship *London Packet*. He was seriously ill, having contracted "putrid fever" (later identified as typhus) during the nine-week voyage. Once here, however, Paine was nursed back to health by Dr. John Kearsley Jr., one of the city's best known physicians — and every bit as much a Tory as Paine was a radical.

It was a great irony. Tom Paine, who had failed at everything he had undertaken in England, was destined to become the patriot-pamphleteer of the American Revolution, the godfather of America. And Kearsley, the man who saved his life, was to be imprisoned as a Tory activist and die behind bars before the war ended.

Once Paine recovered his health, Richard Bache began introducing him around. Paine was presentable — not the dirty, drunken near-derelict pictured by some anti-Paine biographers. True, he was a two-fisted drinker, but he was not a drunk. He kept himself clean and his attire was reasonably neat. He was, in fact, a decidedly ordinary-looking man except for his fine eyes, which had a piercing brilliancy. He was 5 feet 9 inches tall, slender, and possessed of a prominent nose. He looked, in fact, more like a friendly family physician than a hellraiser.

Through Bache, Paine met Robert Aitken, a Philadelphia printer who had just launched a new publication, *The Pennsylvania Magazine*. Aitken hired Paine as editor. Paine did more than edit. He wrote most of the contents of the magazine under such fanciful names as "Aesop" and "Vox Populi."

From the start he expressed an outspoken radicalism that frequently alarmed Aitken but boosted circulation. When Paine took charge of the publication, the circulation was about 600 copies a month, nearly all in Philadelphia; within three months the magazine had nearly 2,000 subscribers, some as far away as New Hampshire and South Carolina.

By mutual agreement, Paine and Aitken parted company in mid-1775. Paine desired complete editorial freedom in espousing the revolutionary cause, and Aitken had begun to rein him in — not because he disagreed with Paine, but because he was under increasing pressure from a strong bloc of the city's shakers and movers to muzzle the upstart newly arrived from England.

PLAIN TRUTH;

ADDRESSED TO THE

INHABITANTS

OF

AMERICA,

Containing, Remarks

ON A LATE PAMPHLET.

entitled

COMMON SENSE.

Wherein are shewn, that the Scheme of INDEPENDENCE is Ruinous, Delusive, and Impracticable: That were the Author's Asseverations, Respecting the Power of AMERICA, as Real as Nugatory; Reconciliation on liberal Principles with GREAT BRITAIN, would be exalted Policy: And that circumstanced as we are, Permanent Liberty, and True Happiness, can only be obtained by Reconciliation with that Kingdom.

WRITTEN BY CANDIDUS.

Audi et alteram partem. HORACE.

Will ye turn from flattery, and attend to this Side.?

There TRUTH, unlicenc'd, walks; and dares accost
Even Kings themselves, the Monarchs of the Free!
THOMSON on the Liberties of BRITAIN.

PHILADELPHIA:

Printed, and Sold, by R. BELL, in Third-Street.

MDCCLXXVI.

James Chalmers, writing under the pseudonym "Candidus," denounced Paine in his pamphlet, Plain Truth.

George III: Paine attacked him maliciously, calling the monarch a "hardened, sullen-tempered Pharaoh . . . the Royal Brute . . . ."

And thus it was that when Dr. Benjamin Rush approached Paine in the early autumn of 1775 with the suggestion that a pamphlet broaching independence be written and published, Paine was ready.

•

After writing *Common Sense,* Paine went on to write *The American Crisis.* It was a series of papers, the first of which, written in December 1776 when the outlook for the patriot cause was grim, began with the immortal words: "These are the times that try men's souls." In England in 1791 he wrote *The Rights of Man,* the earliest complete statement of republican principles, setting forth the fundamental ideas on which America was founded.

Then Paine went to France to become a pamphleteer for the French Revolution. Typically, he wound up swimming against the tide, and it almost cost him his life. He joined the most revolutionary party there was, and yet when the Revolution was accomplished he found himself at odds with it over the editorial tone of the government's pronouncements. Paine's fractious personality didn't help him.

The Robespierre clique, then in control, threw him in jail and gave him an early appointment at the guillotine. By a stroke of good fortune, Robespierre was beheaded first, and a new group of Revolutionary leaders, marginally more friendly to Paine, took power. Even so, Paine continued to languish in prison.

Gouverneur Morris, then the American ambassador in Paris, detested Paine and did nothing to obtain his release. Not until the arrival of the new American ambassador, James Monroe, was effective action taken to have Paine released.

One thing Paine accomplished during his 10 months in prison was to complete his pamphlet *The Age of Reason.* It was a plea for a rational approach to religion, but it got Paine the permanent tag of atheist. Actually, Paine was a deist. "I believe in one God, and no more; and I hope for happiness beyond this life," he wrote.

In 1803, Paine was back in the United States. In February, en route from Washington, D. C., where he had been the guest of President Thomas Jefferson, he stopped in Philadelphia to call upon old friends. Benjamin Rush, who had stood by Paine and encouraged him in years gone by, refused to see him. "His principles avowed in *The Age of Reason* were so offensive to me that I did not wish to renew my intercourse with him," Rush explained.

And when Paine died in virtual solitude on his farm near New Rochelle, N.Y., in 1809, Dr. Rush wrote of him: "He possessed a wonderful talent of writing to the tempers and feelings of the public . . . (but) . . . his vanity appeared in everything he said or did. He once said he was at a loss to know whether he was made for the times or the times made for him . . ." ★★★

Philadelphian Benjamin West startled the artistic world with this "modern dress" depiction of British General Wolfe's death at the moment of his heroic victory at Quebec.

By Patricia Tice

PAINTING

By an odd divergence of destiny, one of Philadelphia's great painters was with Washington at Valley Forge, while the other was with George III in London.

Colonial America promised opportunity to all except, perhaps, one particular type of man: the artist. No lords granted commissions; no societies sponsored exhibitions; no academies conducted classes. There were no great collections of classical or medieval art. There were no established churches seeking to glorify God through artistic endeavor. Indeed, there was in America a decided anti-aestheticism, a legacy of Calvinist thought, which distrusted beauty for beauty's sake. Any would-be artist also had to contend with a frontier-inspired ideology that demanded function, not form.

Similarly, men in America were more concerned with carving homes from the forest than with carving figures from stone. By 1776, only four examples of sculpture, apart from utilitarian work such as gravestones and figureheads, were to be found in America. One of these, a lead statue of George III, landed in a melting pot to be recast as bullets for Continental troops shortly after the outbreak of hostilities, reducing the American statue population to three.

The American environment was, at least initially, artistically chilly.

As the 18th century, and the colonies, matured, though, attitudes began to thaw. Prosperous merchants recognized the practical aspect of art. A portrait was, after all, a testimony to success, even if it was also a concession to vanity. Fourth-rate artists, unable to secure profitable business in Europe, drifted to America. Artistically uninspired, they plied their craft and produced tolerable likenesses.

Despite oppressive conditions, talented men, born and bred in these same American colonies, emerged as remarkable artists. The company includes Benjamin West, Charles Willson Peale, Gilbert Stuart and John Singleton Copley.

Pennsylvania claims the first two as native sons, both by birth and association. The lives of West and Peale, like their paintings, were extraordinary — and quite different.

Peale became a close friend of George Washington's, painting him many times — as a wealthy plantation owner before the war, as a general, and as President. He even brought his children to paint Washington. In one famous scene Washington found himself posing while Peale and four Peale children worked at their easels around the room. At this point another painter, Gilbert Stuart, whose paintings of Washington were also widely known (one appears on the dollar bill), arrived on the scene. Stuart took in the scene, smiled, and stepped quickly into the adjoining room where he told Martha Washington, in tones of mock alarm: "Rescue your husband! He's being 'Peale-d' to death."

West became a close personal friend of King George III, and was a co-founder of England's Royal Academy. But as the first American to win international artistic acclaim, he became a source of American pride and hope. And despite his close association with a monarch who was widely despised in his homeland, West always considered himself an American. Three generations of struggling American artists found their way to his London studio, including Copley, Stuart and Peale. He died in London, and was buried in St. Paul's Cathedral. But long before he died he had earned the title "Father of American Painting."

Here are the stories of these two extraordinary men, beginning with. . .

Benjamin West: "A Companion For Kings"

Seldom does man experience the rapid success that Benjamin West enjoyed. But then, it was clear from the beginning that Benjamin West was not an ordinary man.

On a warm September day in 1738, John West and his wife attended the Chester County Meeting, and on this particular First Day, an evangelist delivered a rousing sermon. After denouncing the sin-stained Old World, he proceeded, in stirring terms, to proclaim the greatness vouchsafed by God for the virtuous New World. And in the midst of this religious fervor, Mrs. West, then advanced in pregnancy, was stricken with labor pains.

To all, the coincidence was obviously fraught with Divine Revelation. The preacher concurred, and with emphatic solemnity, declared that a child sent into the world under such remarkable circumstances would prove "no ordinary man."

Actually, as the excitement subsided, so did the contractions. Benjamin West actually arrived two weeks later, on October 10. But the expectations of greatness adhered to him nonetheless — and they were not in vain.

As a young boy, Ben West was so inspired by the beauty of his infant niece, asleep in her cradle, that he seized pen and ink and hastily sketched a portrait. His delighted parents encouraged his talent. Mrs. West's indigo dye served for blue colorings; local Indians taught West to blend yellow and red pigments; and the family cat provided the bristles for his first brushes.

A relative named Pennington admired the sketches and brought West to Philadelphia, where he met the English painter William Williams. As Benjamin watched Williams lay paint to canvas he listened to tales of European art treasures. More important, while in Philadelphia he discovered Richardson's *Essays* on art. Though the work merely described great paintings, it influenced West profoundly.

Museum of Fine Arts, Boston

Jaws, 1778

Philadelphians West and Peale had a rival — and colleague — in John Singleton Copley of Boston. A few years after West had achieved great acclaim for modern-dress portrayal of the "Death of General Wolfe," Copley set out to do West one better with this even more dramatic depiction of a shark attack that had taken place 29 years earlier in Havana harbor. Copley's patron was Brook Watson, the victim, who lost his right leg in the attack. (The leg was taken just before the moment depicted, close observers will note. The shark misses on this pass.) The picture did great things for Watson, who rode the fame it helped to induce to a seat in Parliament and a term as Lord Mayor of London, which was pretty good for a one-legged orphan. It also did great things for Copley. Copies of the picture were circulated throughout England and America, arousing lively debate wherever they went over its realism, or alleged lack thereof. Copley had never seen a shark, and portrayed a composite of different species, and added lips, which sharks don't have. Some critics were unimpressed; one dubbed the style "Neoclassic Horrific."

He returned to Springfield only to ponder the wonders of art. When a comrade asked, "What sort of trade was a painter?" West coolly replied, "A painter is a companion for kings and emperors."

His Quaker father, awed and perplexed at his son's increasing skill and ambition at a skill his co-religionists regarded as a dangerous addictive frivolity, called a special meeting of the Friends to help him confront his parental dilemma. One of the Wests' neighbors, John Williamson, rose to examine the fears now troubling the community. "It is true," he acknowledged, "that our tenets deny the utility of . . . art to mankind. But God has bestowed on the youth a genius for art. . . . What God has given, who shall

dare to throw away?" So it was agreed. One by one the women kissed the artist and the men prayed for Divine Protection.

And thus blessed, West launched his career. Wealthy Pennsylvanians sought him out to paint their portraits, paying West two to five guineas to do one, which was a handsome fee. One guinea was as much as a skilled workman earned in a week. But West's work was worth it. His canvases, unlike those of competitors, glowed with subtle animation and the soft blues characteristic of his early work. Painting heads grew monotonous, however, and West longed to paint grander themes.

The guineas were carefully saved that

'The extraordinary report of the arrival of an American presuming to call himself an artist jolted Roman society. Prominent citizens sought out this curiosity . . . .'

he might eventually see first-hand the masterpieces described in Richardson's *Essays*. But then merchant John Allen, on learning of West's desire to study in Europe, provided him with free passage to Italy.

The extraordinary report of the arrival of an American presuming to call himself an artist jolted Roman society. Prominent citizens sought out this curiosity. One of these amazed aristocrats reported that he had discovered "an artist who comes we do not know from where, and paints as we do not know how."

West's friend and biographer, John Galt, recalled, "The Italians, concluding that, as he was an American, he must, of course, have received the education of a savage, became curious to witness the effect which the works of art in the Belvidere and Vatican would produce on him . . . It was agreed that the Apollo Belvidere should be the first submitted to his view because it was the most perfect work . . . and consequently, the best calculated to produce that effect that the company were anxious to witness."

An entourage of 30 carriages escorted West to the Belvidere, and as the American approached the cabinet housing the Apollo, silence fell upon all. The doors were opened, West gasped and cried, "My God! How like it is to a young Mohawk warrior!" An interpreter quickly translated his remarks.

Initially the Romans were shocked at this barbaric comparison. But then they recalled Rousseau and the ideology of the Noble Savage. They became delighted, and the Quaker from Pennsylvania continued in his celebrity status.

West, on the other hand, was less than delighted with Italian painting until the artist Mengs introduced him to the rising Neoclassic school. In Neoclassicism, a revival of classical culture, West found moral themes worthy of his brush. Before long, he was elected to the academies at Parma, Bologna and Florence, and word of his success echoed across the Atlantic. West resolved to return to Philadelphia —after first visiting England.

West's debut into London society resulted more from his agility as a skater than as an artist. Art historian James Flexner described the meeting between West and Sir William Howe, the soldier who would command the British Army during the Revolution, and who had served in America during the French and Indian Wars, in this way: first Howe explained that when he had told his friends

of the brilliant skating he had seen during a trip to America, he had been accused of lying. Howe then begged the young Pennsylvanian and his American friends to give an exhibition.

West complied, winning the patronage of Howe's aristocratic friends. A newspaper commented: "There was never a more brilliant exhibition, ministers, lords, commons, all on the ice. Of the commons, Mr. West, the celebrated painter, and Dr. Hewitt were the best. They danced a minuet on their skates to admiration of spectators."

Greater honor lay in store. Archbishop Drummond, agreeing with West's belief that art should offer moral uplift, approached King George III and told him about West. The grave monarch grew interested in the colonial who shared his distaste for the licentiousness of London society, and summoned West to court. From their initial meeting, the Quaker and the king enjoyed warm friendship. Later, West delighted George III with his scenes of classical Rome, and was duly appointed Court Historical Painter.

By 1771, West had tired of classical history, and he turned to American history looking for new themes. The first one he tried was the death of General Wolfe. Until then, artists had immortalized all historical events by depicting their subjects in classical dress. Deviating radically from the style he once endorsed, West returned to a realistically American approach; he would paint his subjects in contemporary dress.

His plan for a "boots and breeches" composition aroused much criticism. George III, the Archbishop and his friends begged him to abandon the foolhardy scheme, but West held fast.

"The event," West argued, "took place on the 13th of September, 1759, in a region unknown to the Greeks and Romans and at a time when no such nations nor heroes in their costumes existed . . . the same truth that guides the pen of the historian should govern the pencil of the painter." His painting, forceful, dramatic—anticipating news illustration— was a huge success, bringing new direction to history painting.

As hostilities mounted between England and America, West remained staunchly loyal to his homeland. His frankness outraged the court, but, oddly enough, the monarch applauded his honesty. When a courtier criticized the

On July 4, 1776, there were exactly four pieces of sculpture in America. A few days later, when patriots finished with this statue of George III, there were three.

American, George III observed that "a man who did not love his native land could never be a faithful subject of another — or a true friend." This was not the attitude that the King took towards Americans in general, whom he regarded as children who were badly in need of a thorough thrashing.

In 1788, the shadow of insanity darkened their friendship as the King's behavior grew increasingly erratic. While examining one of West's paintings the King suddenly became furious. Fumbling with a pencil, he disfigured the canvas, shouting that a lion West had painted "looked more like a dog." Then, just as suddenly, the King regained his composure, and looked with horror at what he had done. Within a few weeks, however, the King's mental instability had become more pronounced.

West, a frequent witness to similar scenes, found himself excluded from court by a queen anxious to keep secret her husband's "symptoms of disorder." Queen Charlotte also intercepted West's letters to the King. The tortured monarch, in his occasional moments of sanity, wondered at West's apparent desertion. "Who," he exclaimed, "would have thought he could be one of them?"

Deprived of royal patronage and harshly censured, West found himself bankrupt at 72. But the generosity which had contributed to his financial hardship had also prompted him to donate a painting to the Pennsylvania Hospital back in America. The work, entitled "Christ Healing the Sick," became more famous, once it arrived, than all his previous work. As a result, West became wealthier and more famous than ever.

In 1820, nine years later, at the age of 81, the revered artist died.

Charles Willson Peale: "...The Ingenious Mr. Peale..."

"**I** admire you," wrote Thomas Jefferson, "in the variety of vocations to which you can give your attention. I cannot do this."

The man to whom Jefferson humbly deferred was Charles Willson Peale, and the variety of Peale's vocations was impressive indeed. At 13, he had begun his apprenticeship to a Maryland saddler. At 20, he owned the shop. Shortly, he branched out into upholstering, clock and watch repairing, and silversmithing. Then, upon seeing a poorly wrought painting, he instantly concluded that he could do better. Everyone was amazed when Peale succeeded—except, of course, Peale himself.

Peale resolved to master the newly discovered occupation. He began by bar-

Charles Willson Peale painted this self-portrait in 1823, when he was 82, to commemorate the opening of his museum of natural history.

gaining with a successful artist whose work he would soon surpass: John Hesselius. The deal was one saddle for "permission to see him paint a picture." Hesselius agreed, and after several sessions allowed Peale to paint one half a face while he painted the other half.

Unfortunately, Peale's enthusiasm for plunging into a variety of enterprises also led him into debt, and almost into a debtor's prison. As the sheriff knocked on the front door, Peale slipped out the back, pausing only to gather his brushes. The fugitive found refuge with his sister Elizabeth and her seafaring husband, Bobby Polk. The latter invited Peale to

sail with him on a voyage to New England, and the aspiring artist gratefully accepted.

It was to be an advantageous trip, for in Boston Peale became acquainted with a young artist named Copley who advised him on painting. As Peale recalled, "Mr. Copley's picture room was a great feast to me." For the first time in his life, Peale saw a competent artist at work.

When Peale returned to the Polk home, he strategically presented paintings to two of Maryland's leading citizens —Charles Carroll of Carrollton and Judge Bordley. The two recipients were immediately certain that Maryland had

Out In The Woods, Artists Were On Their Own

By Lita Solis-Cohen

European painting traditions spread outward from their centers in Europe, wrote American art historian Edgar P. Richardson, "like ripples growing fainter as they crossed the broad Atlantic, changing as they strike upon a distant shore, yet still discernible and recognizable until they vanish into the silence of the forest."

But there were artists at work out in those forests. Even as the Benjamin Wests, Charles Willson Peales, John Singleton Copleys, and the like were embarking for London, these folk artists were hard at work using their homespun skills and imaginations to depict their visions on on paper or canvas, engrave them on copper plates, or paint them on furniture and other household objects.

"Bethlehem of Pennsylvania" Bethlehem Chamber of Commerce

Collection of Mr. and Mrs. Peter Tillou/courtesy William Benton Museum, U. of Conn.

Jacob Maentel, an itinerant German-born artist, did this painting of a Pennsylvania schoolmaster and two of his pupils (left).

A fraktur birth certificate for William Kehres, who was born in Schuylkill County (right).

produced another Benjamin West, who was by now being lauded as the "American Raphael."

Something," decreed Judge Bordley, "must be done for Charles."

Before long, the very creditors who had hounded Peale were contributing funds to send the artist to London. Peale sailed in 1766.

The passage was typically tedious but Peale amused himself first by making a violin, then by learning to play it.

As soon as the ship docked, Peale hastened to West's studio. West, learning of Peale's arrival, flew down the stairs without stopping to lay down his brushes. The established artist installed

Peale in his own studio and continually worked at cheering his homesick compatriot.

West, still under the influence of Mengs, futilely tried to convert Peale to Neoclassicism's smooth, idealistic forms. The American predilection for realism, however, remained rooted in Peale, who eventually evolved his own highly personal style.

One year passed and Peale longed to return to his wife and family. Since there had been little change in his work, West advised another year's study. In his typical fashion, Peale "was not content to learn one way, but engaged in the whole circle of arts." After the second year

passed, again with only minor development, West agreed; it was time for Peale to go home to Annapolis.

Peale never attained the renown Carroll and Judge Bordley envisioned, but his portraits delighted his patrons. While his figures often betrayed faulty proportions, the canvases were animated with the artist's own warmth and good humor. Rather than merely painting the person, Peale strove to portray the personality. Not surprisingly, the better Peale knew his sitter, the more pleasing the portrait.

Business steadily increased, especially after Copley sailed for Italy in 1774, removing Peale's prime competitor for carriage trade portraiture. Two years

A sketch of George Washington, done by a Pennsylvania woman in 1796 (left).

Portrait of one of the prominent women of the Moravian colony (right).

There is perhaps no greater evidence of human beings' artistic urge than the efforts made by these Americans on the frontier to bring into their lives creations of beauty.

One of the first paintings done in Pennsylvania was Peter Cooper's "Southeast Prospect of Philadelphia," a primitive, almost cubist depiction of a pink city of brick homes with toy-like boats in the foreground. It is the earliest known view of any American city.

Most pictorial art in early America sprang from religious need for decorative or commemorative art. For instance, John Valentine Haidt began his work as the official painter of the Moravian Church in Bethlehem in 1754.

Another form of religious art was "fraktur," the decoration of documents, such as certificates of baptism, confirmation, marriage, and death, with a combination of artful printing and decorative symbols. It is in effect a continuation of the art of the illuminated manuscript which had been turned out by monks during the Middle Ages, an art form that was killed off by printing.

But fraktur wasn't used just on documents; its patterns of hearts, tulips, and unicorns were also applied to the flat surfaces of chests and cupboards.

The end of the Revolution marked the beginning of an explosion of artistic activity in America, particularly of non-religious art, as itinerant portrait painters crisscrossed the landscape painting likenesses of the citizens of the new republic for nominal fees in oil and watercolor. These artists also turned out farm scenes, alms houses, and other views. One, Edward Hicks, made a personal specialty of biblical "Peaceable Kingdom" scenes, in which lions and lambs, among other animals, lie down together in peace. ★ ★ ★

later, Peale and his growing family left Annapolis for the greener pastures Philadelphia afforded.

Determined to found a dynasty of American artists, Peale converted his brothers James and St. George into painters. (James later became the most successful miniature painter in America.) Nor did he rest there. While most fathers were inscribing births into family Bibles, Peale noted family events in Pilkington's *The Gentleman's and Connoisseurs' Dictionary of Painters.*

He named nine of his 17 children after painters—Raphaelle, Angelica Kauffmann, Rembrandt, Rubens, Sophonisba Angusciola, Rosalba and Van Dyck, as well as two who were named after Titian, the first of whom died in infancy.

War interrupted the artist's plans. The "thin, spare, pale-faced man," as Peale described himself, enlisted in the Pennsylvania militia and rose to the rank of captain. He participated in crucial battles of the war at Trenton, Princeton and Germantown. Recollecting the retreat of the exhausted, half-frozen — but victorious — American army from Trenton with its Hessian prisoners, Peale remarked to Jefferson, "I thought it the most hellish scene I ever beheld."

While others languished at Valley Forge, Peale was, as always, busy with a variety of activities. He discussed medicine at length with Dr. Benjamin Rush, and experimented with a telescopic rifle with David Rittenhouse, and painted George Washington.

No one knows for sure how many depictions of Washington he made at Valley Forge because they are still coming to light. (The most recent one to be found was painted on blue-striped bed ticking; the lack of supplies at Valley Forge also affected painting canvas.) In addition to the most famous one, which depicts Washington leaning nonchalantly against a cannon while what is supposed to be the Battle of Princeton rages in the background, Peale did at least 40 miniatures of the general and many other standard-size portrayals.

Clearly, Peale foresaw that Washington was going to have considerable popularity in the new nation, the continued existence of which must have seemed to others a chancy proposition during the winter at Valley Forge. Peale, toting his easel, literally stalked the tall leader around the encampment.

But Peale did not neglect his military duties. When his men were hungry, Peale found food. When his men were shoeless, he made moccasins. A soldier commented, " Peale fit and painted and painted and fit."

"Having now become unfortunately popular," the Committee of Safety promoted the artist and gave him what might have seemed a plum assignment confiscating Tory property. Peale, however, did not enjoy it. In his diary he lamented the "disagreeable tasks" he had been given during the "most disagreeable part of my life." So contrite was Peale when a Loyalist's desk was damaged during a search that the artist himself paid to have it repaired.

Peace finally came and Peale gladly dropped his military duties to design a mind-boggling spectacle celebrating the Paris Peace. His plan included the construction of a 20-foot arch and two 15-foot arches covered with transparent paintings lighted from behind by more than 2,100 candles. At the appropriate moment, fireworks were scheduled to explode as a large mechanical figure of "Peace" slid down a nearby rooftop to land on the central arch.

Unfortunately, a firecracker ignited prematurely, setting fire to the arches, to the paintings, and to Peale.

After he recovered, he planned another arch — without fireworks this time — for President Washington's triumphal entry into Philadelphia. "The ingenious Mr. Peale," as he was called, constructed a bridge bedecked with laurel. Angelica Kauffmann Peale, also bedecked with laurel, operated a device which dropped a laurel wreath upon the unsuspecting President's head. To everyone's gratification, the device worked.

Though Peale was still painting, he grew increasingly interested in science. He discovered the works of such European scientists as George Saint-Hilaire, Cuvier, Lamarck, and Latham, and began corresponding with them. In 1786, the *Pennsylvania Packet* announced that "Mr. Peale, ever desirous to please the public . . . will make part of his house a repository for natural curiosities."

One of these curiosities was the angora cat Franklin brought back from Paris. After it died Peale endeavored to preserve the animal. After failing, he added a chemistry lab to his studio and delved into taxidermy.

A visitor, describing the specimens which were displayed against painted backdrops of their natural habitats, exclaimed, "Mr. Peale's animals reminded me of Noak's ark . . . but I hardly conceived that even Noah could have boasted a better collection."

The apex of Peale's career as a naturalist came in 1801 when a New York farmer stumbled upon the prehistoric bones of a mastodon. Peale and his son Rembrandt rushed to the scene to organize America's first scientific expedition. President Jefferson assisted his friend by ordering the secretary of the Navy to provide pumps.

After carefully studying his discovery, Peale assembled two 15-foot skeletons in his Philadelphia museum. In its honor, Rembrandt Peale held a dinner party inside one of the rib cages, squeezing in 13 people, a walnut table and one Patent Portable Grand Piano. In the issuing merriment, one guest could not resist toasting the "boney parts of Europe."

(Those readers who did not get the above pun should read it again, keeping in mind the fact that Napoleon's star was on the ascendancy in Europe.)

Peale eventually installed his menagerie in Independence Hall, where American naturalists flocked to study in America's first museum.

●

In his pursuit of science, Peale all but abandoned his brush. Rembrandt Peale, returning from West's studio, showed his father new techniques which rekindled Peale's desire to paint. The resulting work shows a smoothness and sophistication which earlier paintings lacked. Several of his most distinguished canvases were executed after the age of 80. Unquestionably America lost a potentially great painter to gain a great naturalist.

Nonetheless, Peale's contributions to American art were considerable. As one of few artists working in America at the time of the Revolution, he kindled interest in art. He nourished that interest by founding the Pennsylvania Academy of Fine Arts.

His variety of accomplishments marked him as a product of the Enlightenment. Peale himself said of his time and his career, "This was an age of discovery, every experiment . . . helps expand the mind to make man better, more virtuous and liberal." ★★★

THEATER

The show went on, despite claims that plays were "a most powerful engine for debauching the minds and corrupting the manners of youth," and that theaters were "the House of the Devil."

By Arthur Sabatini

In mid-April 1754, an acting group advertised as the "London Company of Comedians," under the direction of Lewis Hallam, traveled from New York City to open a season of stage plays.

The actors, who had already encountered opposition to their trade in other cities, were well aware that they would have to contend with the staunch Quakers and other religious factions in Philadelphia who regarded plays as sinful and actors as "inlets of vice."

Nevertheless, they obtained permission from Governor James Hamilton to stage plays that "offered nothing indecent or immoral"; rented William Plumstead's warehouse on Front Street (Plumstead was an ex-Quaker turned Anglican who relished the chance to rile his old church); and braced themselves for a controversial season in Philadelphia.

They were not disappointed. Before opening night, an angry writer in the *Pennsylvania Gazette* railed against "the infamous characters of the actors and actresses" and their "inhumanely impudent dances and song" which "polluted and debauched" the minds of the audience. The Quakers, German Lutherans, and Presbyterians wrote more letters, organized protests, and petitioned the governor to prohibit the "dreadful view of the ruinous effects of passion let loose" on the stage.

But it was all to no avail for, despite disturbances inside and outside the theater, the show went on. The plays that

The Southwark Theater, opened in 1766, was denounced by the Quakers as a "dangerous school of vice."

liar compromise gave Douglass six months to build his theater and produce plays. The compromise solution, of course, did not satisfy the righteous, but the rest of Philadelphia enjoyed a total of 80 performances that season. Denny left office before his order took effect.

The plays performed included a variety of the more entertaining offerings from the contemporary London stage as well as several Shakespearean selections. Such plays as John Gay's *The Beggar's Opera*, Colley Cibber's *The Provok'd Husband*, and *George Barnwell* by George Lillo were among the most popular productions. Often the plays were edited to make them more lighthearted and less objectionable for American audiences. Shakespeare was performed in the expurgated versions then fashionable in London. (The original text was regarded as too racy.) By all accounts, plays were attended by a mixture of people who desired, and got, a night's worth of music, fun, and theatrical diversion.

The theater built in 1759 was only a temporary structure and Douglass went elsewhere when the government edict took effect. Seven years later he returned to Philadelphia, after successfully playing in all the major East Coast cities, and constructed what was to become the first permanent theater in America. It was to be called the Southwark Theater and was built at Fourth and Cedar (South) Streets in a suburb of the city reported to be "inhabited by people of circumstance."

Of course, when the good Quakers again heard of the return of Douglass and his "dangerous School of Vice," a se-

evening were Rowe's *The Fair Penitent* and Garrick's *Miss in Her Teens*, both of which were reported to have been received "with universal applause" by "a numerous and polite audience."

At the end of the performance came a brief epilogue on the state of the theater, which began:

> Much has been said in this
> reforming age,
> To damn in gross the business
> of the stage;
> Some for this end, in terms
> not quite so civil,
> Have given both plays and
> players the Devil . . .

Indeed, the theater had experienced severe pressures in that "reforming age." Yet, looking at the debates, it is apparent that conflict over the theater reflected the social, political, religious, and intellectual complexities of colonial Philadelphia.

On the one hand, the conservative and politically influential Quakers, Presbyterians, and, later, Lutherans and Baptists tried to exert their authority over every facet of life in the city while, on the other hand, the more liberal Anglicans, aligned with free-thinking aristocrats and intellectuals, wanted the city to expand and develop on all fronts.

The conflict reached a crisis point again in 1759. (There hadn't been any plays since the London company had braved Quaker wrath in 1754; and, before then, the only known theatrical records happenings consisted of "a player who

had strowled hither to act as a comedian" on the outskirts of the city in 1723, and in 1749, a performance of Addison's *Cato* by the Murray-Kean Company, also in Plumstead's warehouse.)

In April 1759, then, David Douglass and his American Company secretly gained permission to build a theater on Society Hill in Southwark. When news of the proposed construction became known, an enormous amount of opposition grew.

The combined religious sects called the theater "the house of the Devil" and petitioned Governor William Denny to outlaw what they considered to be "a most powerful engine of debauching the minds and corrupting the manners of youth." Caught in an uneasy political dilemma, the governor, backed by his Council, decided in June to outlaw the theater — but the order wasn't to go into effect until January 1, 1760. This pecu-

During the British occupation of Philadelphia, Major John Andre kept alive Philadelphia's reputation as a theatrical center. This is a self-portrait.

The magnificent Chestnut Street Theater, at 4th and Chestnut Streets, modeled after the Theater Royal in Bath, England, opened in February, 1794.

ries of protests and condemnations began that lasted intensely for the next two years. Arguments against the theater were heatedly aired in public places, in churches, and in the newspapers (one was the *Pennsylvania Journal,* whose masthead unashamedly displayed a bare-breasted woman that no one objected to). Unlike in the past, however, no laws were passed against construction and by November 1766 the Southwark Theater was ready to open.

The seasons from 1766-1768 at the Southwark Theater are widely considered to have been the most brilliant and significant in colonial American history. During that time, the theater came to be recognized as an undeniable aspect of American culture. A regular and sizable audience grew who, thereafter, not only defended the stage against its adversaries but began to thoughtfully and critically respond to actors and plays. Moreover, the ambitious Douglass and his versatile company expanded the repertoire of plays for Americans and also produced the first play by a native American, *The Prince of Parthia* by Philadelphia-born Thomas Godfrey.

The theater itself was built of crude brickwork and its exterior was painted a dull red. It measured 95 by 55 feet and was described in 1786 as "an ugly ill-conceived affair outside and inside. The stage was lighted by plain oil lamps without glasses. The view from the boxes was intercepted by large square wooden pillars supporting the upper tier and roof." The building was used as a hospital during the Revolution and lasted until 1821 when it burned down.

Plays at the Southwark were advertised in several papers before the performance which usually began at 5 on a Monday, Wednesday, or Friday afternoon. In addition to the featured play an "afterpiece" or short farce was performed. Music, juggling acts, or dances took place as interludes during the theatricals. In short, the emphasis was on providing as full an evening of entertainment as possible for the audience.

Yet, even while the theater was growing in the city the stubborn opposition from religious groups continued. Not only were actors and actresses attacked, but those who attended the theater were accused of consorting with the very Devil in this "synagogue of Satan."

One actor became so disgusted with the treatment he was receiving that he wrote, "I am quite tired of plodding for-

ever in this confounded Quaker Town. Plague take it!"

A regular theatergoer also complained to the righteous, saying, "O you poor, blind, hard-hearted people, to condemn others because they do not see as you do."

Another writer wittily argued against the claim that the theater taught little, by noting, "The art of seducing a maid is perhaps no other way to be gained than by the theater."

And so the debates went, back and forth, no doubt doing more good than harm to the prospering theater.

As the years passed, though, opposition to the stage gradually faded and "readings" and amateur productions began to occur in a few of the city's academies. Douglass and the American Company, which was the only professional acting group in the colonies, had developed a strong following in the city and were welcomed back each season by patrons who expected the best in theatrical entertainment. From 1768 until 1774 the Southwark presented Philadelphia with an ever-widening range of plays.

•

By the 1770s, it was becoming all too apparent that serious issues were confronting the colonies. Responding to the temper of the times, Douglass offered the first American production of *Julius Caesar* and the great Shakesperian tragedy was an almost instant success.

The success may have rested more on the play's political implications—a tyrant is overthrown in it — than for its theatrical execution. One critic noted, "Our playbills promise to exhibit to us the noble struggles for liberty of those renowned Romans, Brutus and Cassius, tho' poor (actor portraying) Cassius was so deficient in his Latin as to call Publius 'Puppylies' throughout the whole piece."

Another significant event occurred in 1772 when Douglass staged George Cockling's *The Conquest of Canada, or The Siege of Quebec*. It was an extravagant production that featured soldiers, sailors and actual battle equipment for the performance. Apart from its theatrical impact, the play had a clear message: war with England was inevitable.

In October 1774, most of this theatrical activity came to a temporary end. The Continental Congress, meeting in Philadelphia and seeking to get the country on a war footing, passed a resolution that, among other things, was aimed at discouraging "every species of extravagance and dissipation, especially all horse-racing, and all kinds of gaming, cock-fighting, exhibition of shows, plays, and other expensive diversions and entertainments."

Though the resolution was successful in halting performances by professional actors (most of whom had fled the country), the theater was kept alive by numbers of British soldiers who staged plays while they were stationed in the city. As mentioned earlier, the Southwark Theater was used as a hospital; but when it was no longer needed for that purpose, General Howe's soldier-thespians took it over and produced such plays as *Douglass* by John Home, *The Constant Couple* by George Farquhar, and Shakespeare's *Henry IV*. Perhaps the most famous participant in these theatrics was Major John Andre, who, in 1780, would be hung as a spy for his part in arranging Benedict Arnold's treachery.

After the Revolution, the theater had almost as much difficulty establishing itself as it had back in the 1750s. The reason for this was a law passed in 1778 which prohibited plays in the city. Initially, the law was strictly enforced, but by 1784 the managers of the Southwark Theater found that they could get around it by offering plays as lectures, operas, or "Spectaculum Vitae."

As a result, the large and hungry theater-going public in Philadelphia attended such productions as: "a moral and instructive tale as exemplified in the history of the Prince of Denmark" *(Hamlet)* and a "comic lecture in five parts of the pernicious vice of scandal" *(The School for Scandal)*. Plays so titled continued at the Opera House, Southwark (as it was called during that period), until the law was repealed in 1789 and a whole new era for the theater began.

The opening of the magnificent Chestnut Street Theater at Fourth and Chestnut in February 1794 introduced new excitement to American theater. The new theater, modeled after the Theater Royal at Bath, England, reportedly held about 1,500 spectators in both a huge pit and boxes three tiers high. By all accounts it was the most spectacular theater in all the United States and, immediately after its opening, full productions of plays, operas, and ballets were undertaken. It became the showcase for the greatest actors of the day as well as Philadelphia's own symbol for elegance and culture. ★ ★ ★

LITERATURE

This somewhat saucy account of one of the things Americans were doing when they weren't out taming the wilderness deals with mature themes in a mature manner. Some members of your family may find it objectionable. Read on . . .

By Larry Swindell

God and the Devil tended to dominate the thought — and the reading — of Philadelphians in particular and Americans in general throughout the colonial period. The new settlers were terrified by both the Celestial Being and the Stoker of the Fires down below; but, if anything, they were rather more fascinated by the fellow with the forked tail.

But unquestionably the transplanted English folk swung both ways in their reading habits. In the late 17th century, the well-read folk of the Puritan-bred Massachusetts Bay Colony might at least have pretended reading of Michael Wigglesworth's frightening sermon in verse, *The Day of Doom,* but tucked under aprons of leather or linen was Thomas Morton's *New English Canaan,* read furtively for vicarious delight.

They knew about sin but had precious little opportunity to experience it, and *New English Canaan* with its provocative report on the lascivious doings around the maypole at "Merrymount" filled that void. Morton's composition provided our first literary scandal.

A vagabond who briefly found adventure in the early Massachusetts settlement of Quincy, Thomas Morton worked a Barnum-like promotion of the bawdy entertainment revolving around his maypole, and wrote of the frolics for English consumption. The enraged Pilgrim Fathers deported Morton to the mother country, where he was promptly hauled into prison for his salacious writings, but he had effectively initiated the Plain Brown Wrapper tradition that has been one of the hardiest conventions of our reading, if not of our literature.

New England Canaan had "underground" success in the colonies well into the 18th century, then was supplanted by other scabrous material that lacked literary stature, but possessed the sure-fire credentials for notoriety. Looking backward, it would appear that Piety arrived in New England with the *Mayflower,* but that Sinfulness was a passenger on the next incoming boat.

Our accepted early literary history is vulnerable to the revisionists. The first critical accounts were authored not by colonists but by Englishmen, and the textbooks have continued to emphasize what was the "best" in early American writing, or in any event what was most influential philosophically, intellectually, and politically. That tells us little about what the Americans were reading, or, perhaps even more meaningfully, of what they most *wanted* to read.

It is certainly true that colonial America was remarkably literate, and that there was no grave shortage of reading material. But even as it was revolving

Philadelphia illustrators later depicted Washington Irving's tale of Revolutionary America, Rip Van Winkle. *Maxfield Parrish's is at left; N. C. Wyeth's at right.*

into Revolutionary America, it had almost nothing in the way of a proud literary tradition to call its own. This was still true in 1776 and throughout the official term of the armed conflict, and for some years afterward. Nobody seemed distressed by this cultural shortcoming, or even to acknowledge that anything might be lacking.

Before the English colonization of America, an aboriginal cultural legacy was inhabited in music and art, and in oral narrative, but not in literature. No primitive epic of American Indian life was discovered in a written form, or transmitted in an English prose version Even later when Longfellow ostensibly reprised an Indian legend of the Great Lakes region, the metric scheme for *The Song of Hiawatha* was adapted from an obscure ballad of Scandinavian origin.

So our national literary saga began in the operative sense at Jamestown and Plymouth. Surely the first authors of note were Captain John Smith, the dashing self-styled hero of the Virginia mission, and the Pilgrim Fathers' estimable governor, William Bradford. Smith was his own fanciful chronicler, and acceptance of the Pocahontas legend is still mainly a matter of willingness to take his

Washington Irving

word for it. Bradford possessed a certain stylistic grace, as Smith also had; yet Bradford's *History of Plimouth Plantation,* charting the colony from its founding in 1620 to 1646, was not even discovered and published until more than 200

years later, so it had no meaning for the newly conceived United States.

Our first "respectable" poet —Anne Bradstreet, author of *The Tenth Muse Lately Sprung Up in America*— was English-born but came of age in the Massachusetts Bay; yet scholars, not the public, nurtured her slender historical reputation. Her poems had only limited circulation and sales in New England, while on the other hand, the aforementioned *The Day of Doom* was America's first runaway bestseller (second only to the Bible throughout the colonial period).

Yet this sermonistic tome was found lacking in artistic merit from the very beginning, in the discernment of well-lettered persons. Wigglesworth, a Puritan minister, wrote *The Day of Doom* as a long sermon about Judgment Day, when sinners would get their comeuppance in Hell for, among other transgressions, their failure to have been baptized. *The Day of Doom* may be seen as a kind of easy-reading equivalent to Jonathan Edwards' later, and more rhetorically imposing, *Sinners in the Hands of an Angry God.* But Edwards, while indubitably a giant in the shaping of philosophical thought during the period, was hardly a regular reading reference of the common people.

Nor, indeed, were such later titans of political philosophy as Thomas Jefferson and his ideological opposite, Alexander Hamilton, both of whom were accomplished polemicists on stylistic terms, as was also John Adams. Their theses were addressed in King George's most eloquent English, but it remained for a raffish ne'er-do-well named Thomas Paine to conjure eloquence in the everyday language of the people and to connect with their thought through the document whose substance reflected its title: *Common Sense.*

Benjamin Franklin was the great public figure of the late colonial period, before he came to be revered as the grand old man of the new republic. The first *Poor Richard's Almanack* appeared in 1733 and was an annual occurrence for 25 years. It was popular to a degree of graduating into folklore, but its homespun maxims were hardly the stuff of literature.

Franklin's great *Autobiography* was that, but it remained unfinished at the time of his death in 1790 and did not attain publication until the following year. Then its sale and its impact—at least immediately — were both counted disappointments, attributed to the book's being *too* literary.

For the lay reader in young America, there was a considerable distance between what passed as good writing and what satisfied him as good reading. Despite every notion that the literate Yankee was a sobersides preoccupied with political thought, he often read for the sheer pleasure of reading; and that was not regarded as a frivolous pastime.

The birth of a new American nation had occurred while a great age of English literature was drawing to a close, and Americans shared in it. The formidable figure of that age was Samuel Johnson, very nearly Ben Franklin's identical contemporary, and the completion in 1775 of Dr. Johnson's great *Dictionary of the English Language* vitally influenced the colonists by stabilizing the language they shared with stay-at-home Britishers who had chosen not to cross the Atlantic to the New World.

The English language had been running riot, changing drastically from one century to the next for want of a substantial authority for its usage and pronunciation. Compare the English of Chaucer's day, say, with Shakespeare's. But the Johnsonian achievement occurred in the nick of time, to preserve the legacies of Shakespeare, Marlowe and Ben Jonson, and of Milton, Pope, and Dryden.

The pre-Revolution colonists nurtured this legacy with their own classical scholarship, and the new dictionary functioned as a unifying effect for the strikingly dissimilar versions of American English.

In *America in 1750: A Social Portrait*, Richard Hofstadter emphasizes the vexing frustration that could befall a New Englander attempting conversation with a Southerner. It would have been more difficult then than now because, while American regional accents, inflections, and dialects have persisted into our own time, American English achieved an essential unity in the second half of the 18th century. This gave impetus to the unity of thought which, in turn, was the catalyst for independence. But we did not immediately seek independence in our literature. We became, in fact, even more obliged to England, reacting to the sudden and immense popularity of the relatively new form of prose narrative called the novel.

Although Cervantes' *Don Quixote* and lesser European novels were accorded some scholarly attention in the fledgling American colleges, the reading passion of literate commonfolk was the novel written by Englishmen about their scepter'd isle and its inhabitants. Even after the Declaration of Independence fostered the entirely radical idea that all men were created equal, and after the Revolution's denouement banished what had been shaping up as a genuine American aristocracy, many rank-and-file Americans still kept reverie for a society offering royalty, nobility, and other traditional trappings of the fairy tale.

They devoured the English novels that related the often amorous adventures of lords and their ladies, of innocent kitchenmaids under siege of noblemen's leers. The novels most popular in America were those that also regaled England: Samuel Richardson's *Pamela* and *Clarissa;* Henry Fielding's *Tom Jones* and *Joseph Andrews;* Tobias Smollett's *Humphrey Clinker* and *Roderick Random;* and Laurence Sterne's *Tristram Shandy* and *Sentimental Journey.* Americans were also titillated by Defoe's earlier *Moll Flanders* and continued to relish his *Robinson Crusoe*, which addressed itself to the adventuring American spirit.

But for all these estimable works, there were scores of sleazier imitations in their wake, and these, too, entertained American readers of 1776 and for some time afterward.

And even when amateur American writers began to produce their own phosphates in the sentimental and picaresque genres, there was a curious reluctance to employ their own landscape as scenic backdrop. Americans who had never seen England wrote novels of London balls, of affairs of the royal court, of land and sea military exploits featuring larger-than-life English heroes rather than American ones.

When the success in England of Horace Walpole's *The Castle of Otranto* in 1765 initiated the "Gothic" vogue for eerily romantic melodrama, it was no less successful in America; and again there were many American imitators, but the

The Library Company of Philadelphia was one of the first libraries open to tradesmen and others not part of society's elite.

James Fenimore Cooper

setting remained English by obligation, since there were no American castles. (The notion that life in the mother country was and ever shall be somehow more refined than our own persists here to the very present, exemplified by the success of one of the better-known titles of the late R. F. Delderfield—*God Is an Englishman.*)

William Hill Brown's *The Power of Sympathy,* published in 1789, was the first fully-fleshed novel that is unmistakably American, for its depiction of recognizable native types and its employment of local scenes, primarily Boston. It was more than ordinarily successful.

But *Charlotte Temple,* issued two years later, was a phenomenon for American readership. A best-seller until Civil War times, this little-known but once much-loved romance outsold any of James Fenimore Cooper's still famous bonanzas. Amateurishly written by Susanna Haswell Rowson, *Charlotte Temple* is the prototypical novel that cannily gives it to the American reader both ways. Oh, it has redeeming social value! In design it is a morality fable, but its commercial packaging had rather more to do with sex raising its altogether irresistible head.

Charlotte Temple is the tragic and curiously touching account of an innocent English girl adrift in wicked New York. Perhaps not surprisingly, Miss Rowson's most imaginative writing is contained in the (numerous) scenes of debauchery — the inevitable "good parts" for which the book was passed around, its scarlet pages becoming dog-eared in the process.

The novel had the additional appeal of being based on the actual case of one Charlotte Stanley who lies buried in New York's Trinity Churchyard under a tombstone now inscribed with the name of "Charlotte Temple." It was true life adventure.

That book had a Connecticut equivalent in Hannah Foster's *The Coquette,* published in 1797 — another fictionalized case history of one who died in illegitimate childbirth. (The scoundrel in this instance was at least rumored to have been Aaron Burr, that resourceful fellow.)

To whatever degree morality may have persuaded the composition of such fiction, these works are tied to the commercial tradition that now embraces lasciviously the legacies of Grace Metalious, Jacqueline Susann and their own imitators.

Aside from the reluctance of the early American novelists to explore characteristically American themes, there was also a sustained academic resistance to the very idea of an autonomous American literature. Powerful voices, most notably Longfellow's, were convinced that America's cultural barbarism would be enlarged if a literature calculatedly our own were allowed to develop. He preached that homage to the British example should continue.

America's actual declaration of literary independence would be deferred until 1871, when Walt Whitman's impassioned prose essay, *Democratic Vistas,* settled the issue philosophically for all time. "American English" was then on the threshold of its ultimate liberation by Mark Twain. Yet once this break was made it was possible to trace back a strain of distinctly American literature, unfettered by and unobligated to any other, that had been taking nourishment, almost clandestinely, for exactly an even century.

American literature's keynote address may have been given in the Princeton commencement in 1772, when two remarkable students introduced a poem of their own collaboration, called *The Rising Glory of America.* They were Philip Freneau and Hugh Henry Brackenridge, each remarkable in his own way toward the formulation of our literature in its national character.

Freneau became "the poet of the Revolution" and came near to achieving greatness and recognition as America's first major poet. (Even now he is deserving of reevaluation.) Brackenridge's long and varied career included a five-volume

sequence of novels initiated in 1792 and collectively titled *Modern Chivalry* — then an American prose work unprecedented for ambitiousness of design.

Francis Hopkinson, a signer of the Declaration of Independence, exhibited flair as a political satirist in *A Pretty Story,* published in 1774 under the pseudonym of Peter Grievous. But America's first writer of prose fiction to earn high regard abroad was the sturdy Philadelphian Charles Brockden Brown — also our first professional man of letters.

Brown, who was five years old when the Declaration was signed, produced all of his novels between 1797 and 1801, and is now seen as a true master of the Gothic novel, most notably for *Wieland* and *The Transformation.* The critic George Snell sees Brown as the oracle of the Apocalyptic tradition that includes Poe, Melville, and, most recently, William Faulkner.

Washington Irving, generally acknowledged as America's first great writer of prose, similarly is the prophet of the Temperamentalists: Hawthorne, James, Wharton, Cather, Hemingway, Fitzgerald, Wolfe and Steinbeck. Fenimore Cooper is the architect of native historical romance, while the Realists have no marked American beginning prior to Howells and Twain — but influences are easily seen in the early legacies.

•

Throughout the progress, there has been not-always-peaceful coexistence between "serious" and "popular" literature, and to our own time the bestsellers seldom represent what are also our most artistic literary accomplishments. The die for this dubious condition was effectively cast in the days of the Founding Fathers.

The dispute actually endures: Some of our own eminent literary critics remain persuaded that current English literature is still somehow "better" than our own, besides relegating our legacy to subordinance beneath France, Germany, and Russia.

Yet we have taken the initiative in terms of literary world influence. Even the English now prefer most American fiction to their own, if not our poetry. We embrace other traditions but are sincerely proudest of our own accomplishment. Even as we furtively read the latest Harold Robbins aphrodisiac, we continue to mine Bellowses and Updikes and Doctorows; and two centuries later, we can give confident assurance to Philip Freneau and Hugh Henry Brackenridge that America's literary glory is still rising. ★ ★ ★

THE FOUNDING CITY

MUSIC & DANCE

The organ, Pastor Falckner wrote, "would not only attract and civilize the wild Indian, but it would do much good in spreading the Gospel truths among the sect and others . . ."

By Marilyn Kochman

Sunday evening strollers walking down Third Street past the home of Governor John Penn in the spring of 1776 were charmed by the sweet strains of music seeping out from the front room. Penn himself would probably have been performing on the violin, accompanied by Francis Hopkinson, a future signer of the Declaration of Independence, on the harpsichord, with the instrumental or choral assistance of other members of Philadelphia's elite. The music was that of the then popular European masters — Handel, Bach, Corelli, and Purcell.

Music stores and music teachers flourished in Philadelphia. By 1760 it was possible to obtain instruction in any known instrument, and voice lessons were being offered in "singing schools" for individuals or groups. Signor Gualdo and Michael Hillegas both operated stores selling German flutes, harpsichords, violins, hautboys (oboes), guitars, mandolins, and other instruments. The two proprietors also strung instruments, repaired them, and performed other musical services.

Dancing was immensely popular. The "polite part of society" danced the formal minuet and the "contre-danses," as those dances in which the participants stood in lines facing each other. The famed dancing assemblies, large balls open "by subscription only," had been in existence since 1748.

Nor was organized musical activity confined to the well-to-do. The "commonality" enjoyed singing the popular folk songs of England, Scotland, Ireland, and Germany, to which new verses — often with a satiric political message —were constantly being added. They also danced to jigs and rollicking "hipsesaws."

A foreign visitor observed: "Girls and women are fond of dancing, which is one of their greatest pleasures. The women like it almost as much as the men. They indulge in this pleasure either in the morning . . . or in the evening from the end of the day far into the night. Dancing is less a matter of self-display than it is of true enjoyment."

In short, music was yet another area in which colonial Philadelphia asserted its pre-eminence in North America. It was neither an easy — nor a universally applauded — achievement. The city's Quakers were staunchly opposed to making a joyful noise unto the Lord, or anyone else. At the yearly meeting in 1716, members of the Society of Friends were enjoined from "going to, or being in any way with plays, games, lotteries, music, or dancing."

But it was probably already too late to stop the trend. Members of other religions, who would shortly be coming in a flood, regarded music as an integral part of their religious observances. The Rev. Justus Falckner, pastor of the Swedes' Gloria Dei church in Southwark, had sent back a request for an organ shortly after his arrival in

The regular Order of the Minuet continued.

To the Honourable Mr Belasyse, and the Honourable Miss Belasyse, Daughter to Thomas Viscount Fauconberg, and my once honoured Scholar Catherine Viscountess Fauconberg, this PLATE is most humbly inscribed by their Honours very much obliged Ser. Kellom Tomlinson

1700. The organ, he contended, "would not only attract and civilize the wild Indian, but it would do much good in spreading the Gospel truths among (the members of) . . . the sect and others by attracting them . . ."

Philadelphia was the landing place for several different religious sects whose zeal was, in fact, focused in musical expression. In 1694 a small group of mystics settled in caves along the banks of the Wissahickon, where they became known as "The Hermits of the Wissahickon" because of their solitary lifestyle — but, oh, how they could harmonize.

Their leader, Johannes Kelpius, was an avid hymnist and many of his followers were musicians as well. Kelpius wrote that during the voyage to Philadelphia "we . . . had prayer meetings and sang hymns of praise and joy, several of us accompanying on instruments that we had brought from London."

The Ephrata Cloister, which was established in 1720 in what is now Lancaster County, also made music an integral part of its religious experience. Conrad Beissel, who led this group of Seventh Day Baptists together with Peter Miller, didn't allow his lack of familiarity with traditional music theory and harmony hold him back as a composer — he devised his own.

Beissel set forth his principles in his *Dissertation On Harmony,* and sought to spread them by establishing choirs and singing schools. His theories on music went beyond the superficial aspects of composition and performance; he also devised special diets for different kinds of singers.

For one reason or another, it worked. Most Ephrata members were, by all accounts, good singers, and many became amateur composers using Beissel's musical system. Ultimately they had a repertoire of about 1,000 hymns.

The Moravians who settled in Bethlehem in 1741 under the leadership of their bishop, Count Zinzendorf, were a religious group that was very enthusiastic about music, and they added something to their hymn renditions that set them apart from the others: brass instruments. Trombones, in particular, were used in brass choirs on festive occasions, and to announce the death of community members.

The Moravians also had a congregation in Philadelphia, at Broad and Race Streets. When John Adams had occasion to visit Philadelphia's churches during his attendance at the First Continental Congress in 1774 he described the singing of the Catholics and Methodists as "exquisitely soft and sweet," but he tempered his praise by noting that it was "the finest music I have heard in any society except the Moravians."

By the time of Adams' visit every religious sect in the city — except, of course, the Quakers — had an organ. Christ Church, the principal Episcopal church in the city, had received its in 1728. St. Joseph's, the first Catholic church, had one in 1748. The Moravians actually had two.

The decline of Quaker influence in the city had been paralleled by a rise in non-religious musical activity as well. The first professional music teacher in Philadelphia was apparently a woman. In 1730 the *Pennsylvania Gazette* included an advertisement which stated that a Miss Ball, "lately arrived from London," was available to teach "writing and French —likewise, singing, playing the spinet, dancing, and all sorts of needlework."

By 1749 Miss Ball was facing competition from a John Beals, who was advertising in the paper that he could teach "violin, hautboy, German flute, common flute, and dulcimer by note."

(The story of the dulcimer is one of the more fascinating sidelights of American music. Today it is an integral part of the mountain music played by people of Scots-Irish descent who established communities in the hollows of the Blue Ridge Mountains and elsewhere. The instrument was, however, unknown in the British Isles.

(Folklorists with the Smithsonian Institution have recently discovered some old dulcimers among the Pennsylvania Dutch, and hypothesize that these Germans brought the dulcimer with them from the Rhineland, where it was known. Then, for some reason, the Germans stopped playing it in the New World — though not before they had passed it on to other settlers who were moving through Pennsylvania and on down the Shenandoah Valley toward the Blue Ridge.)

The flute was apparently a popular instrument, and by 1753 another teacher, Robert Coe, was announcing by advertisement that he had a new, easy method for learning the instrument. His method was the very thing, he averred, for "some gentlemen (who are) afraid to undertake it by reason of its taking more wind than they could well spare."

The key part of Coe's method was a new mouthpiece he had invented, which, in either the tin or silver model, "does not in the least alter the tone of the flute" which sounds "as if blown by the nicest lips."

The city's first dancing teacher had actually preceded Miss Ball by a year in announcing to the city his availability for lessons. Samuel Perpoint advertised in the *American Weekly Mercury* that he taught both "the art of dancing and the use of the small sword."

And when, in 1738, a Mr. Bolton arrived in the city proclaiming himself ready and willing to instruct in this "polite art" he found himself facing a number of entrenched competitors, including Theobald Hackett, who taught "all sorts of fashionable English and French dances" to all comers.

The Dancing Assemblies were established in 1748 by John Swift, an English merchant who came to the city, and who was also well known for his political activities. In the early versions, young love was guided by a gambling spirit. One visitor to the city chronicled the lottery-like procedure by which partners were selected:

"A master of ceremonies presents to the dancers folded billets which each contain a number," and each of the young people had to find the member of the opposite sex with the corresponding number. "Thus it is fate which decides the partner which one is to have for the whole evening."

To sort of load the deck the dances became increasingly exclusive, as the sponsoring parents endeavored to make sure that there was a minimum possible chance that their offspring would get to spend an entire evening with a person from a background that was undesirable in one manner or another, with all of the possible untoward repercussions that could involve.

Politics was one of the lines along which this exclusiveness was begun. Loyalists were often excluded from the affairs during the Revolution (except, of course, during the British occupation of the city in 1777-1778, when the discriminatory policies were reversed).

A December 1780 issue of the *Penn-*

SONG III.

Francis Hopkinson — lawyer, poet, writer, inventor, and composer — dedicated one collection to unmusical George Washington, who lamented: "I can neither sing one of the songs, nor raise a single note on any instrument . . ."

sylvania Packet contained an article headlined "A Hint," which was somewhat more than that. The author said that "it is expected that no man who has not taken a decisive part in favor of American independence will, IN FUTURE, intrude on the Dancing Assembly of the city; such characters are either too detestable or too insignificant . . ."

It's easy to understand how a Tory might feel uncomfortable at one of these Assemblies. "The dances, like the toasts we drink at the table, have some relation to politics," reported the same visitor who had chronicled the method of choosing partners. "One is called the Success of the Campaign; another, the Defeat of Burgoyne, and a third, Clinton's Retreat."

The theatrical fare also included a lot of music, such as "ballad operas," which consisted of spoken texts with songs interspersed, and musical farces, such as *Hob in the Well*, which was sort of *The Fantasticks* of its time (around 1754). Several operas were performed in the Southwark Theater before the Revolution, including

Theodosius and the then very popular *Beggars Opera* by Gay-Pepusch.

Philadelphian Andrew Barton wrote the first American opera, *The Disappointment*, which was printed in 1767. The two-act comic opera included 18 songs, among them "Yankee Doodle."

Concerts of chamber music had been held in private homes from very early in the city's history, and the first concert in a public hall was held on January 25, 1757, in the Assembly Room of the State House under the direction of a John Palma. The tickets, which were obtainable at the London Coffee House, the city's business and trade center, cost one dollar. Little else is known about the event, except that it was apparently not wildly popular. One more concert was advertised later that year, but that was the last one for several years.

Professional musicians were not considered at the time to be "gentlemen," and it was the amateur musicians who set the tone for the artistic development that Philadelphia experienced.

Benjamin Franklin's music stand.

One of these was Francis Hopkinson, who was a lawyer, politician, poet, writer, and inventor, as well as harpsichordist, organist, and America's first

One of the hit tunes of the Revolution was "The Yankey's Return From Camp," better known as "Yankee Doodle Dandy." It wasn't just a pleasant little nursery rhyme; one of the verses began: "I see another snarl of men, a-digging graves, they told me . . . ."

The YANKEY's Return from CAMP.

FATHER and I went down to camp,
  Along with Captain Gooding,
There we fee the men and boys,
  As thick as hafty-pudding.
    Yankey doodle keep it up,
Chorus.   Yankey doodle, dandy,
  Mind the mufic and the ftep,
    And with the girls be handy.
And there we fee a thoufand men,
  As rich as 'Squire David;
And what they wafted every day,
  I wifh it could be faved.
    Yankey doodle, &c.
The 'laffes they eat every day,
  Would keep an houfe a winter:
They have as much that I'll be bound
  They eat it when they're a mind to.
    Yankey doodle, &c.
And there we fee a fwamping gun,
  Large as a log of maple,
Upon a ducid little cart,
  A load for father's cattle.
    Yankey doodle, &c.
And every time they fhoot it off,
  It takes a horn of powder—
It makes a noife like father's gun,
  Only a nation louder.
    Yankey doodle, &c.
I went as nigh to one myfelf,
  As 'Siah's underpining;
And father went as nigh again,
  I tho't the deuce was in him.
    Yankey doodle, &c.
Coufin Simon grew fo gold,
  I tho't he would have cock'd it:
It fcar'd me fo, I fhrink'd it off,
  And hung by father's pocket.
    Yankey doodle, &c.
and Captain Davis had a gun,
  He kind of clap'd his hand on't,

And ftuck a crooked ftabbing iron
  Upon the little end on't.
    Yankey doodle, &c.
And there I fee a pumpkin fhell
  As big as mother's bafon,
And ev'ry time they touch'd it off,
  They fcamper'd like the nation.
    Yankey doodle, &c.
I fee a little barrel too,
  The heads were made of leather,
They knock'd upon't with little clubs,
  And call'd the folks together.
    Yankey doodle, &c.
And there was Captain Wafhington,
  And gentlefolks about him,
They fay he's grown fo tarnal proud,
  He will not ride without 'em.
    Yankey doodle, &c.
He got him on his meeting clothes,
  Upon a flapping ftallion,
He fet the world along in rows,
  In hundreds and in millions.
    Yankey doodle, &c.
The flaming ribbons in their hats,
  They look'd fo taring fine, ah,
I wanted pockily to get,
  To give to my Jemimah,
    Yankey doodle, &c.
I fee another fnarl of men
  A digging graves, they told me,
So tarnal long, fo tarnal-deep,
  They 'tended they fhould hold me.
    Yankey doodle, &c.
It fcar'd me fo, I hook'd it off,
  Nor ftop'd, as I remember,
Nor turn'd about 'till I got home,
  Lock'd up in mother's chamber.
    Yankey doodle, &c.

native secular composer. As a member of the first class at the College of Philadelphia, a precursor of the University of Pennsylvania, Hopkinson had performed the "Masque of Arne" in concert on the harpsichord as an exercise in oratory. He later played the organ at Christ Church and St. Peter's, and instructed children in psalmody.

Benjamin Franklin was an amateur musician. In that field he is perhaps best known for his improvements of the glass harmonica, originally called the "glassychord." The instrument, which had been known to the Persians at least since the 14th century, consisted basically of glasses filled with water, which emit a sweet, clear tone when the rim is rubbed by the glassychordist's finger.

Franklin changed the shape of the glasses so that they resembled a nest of bowls, which were skewered on a central rod and set horizontally in a case. The rod was then rotated by a spinning wheel-like foot lever. The player then touched a moistened finger to the rotating bowls.

Legend has it that once the device was perfected, Franklin roused his wife from a sound sleep to hear a midnight concert. She initially believed that it was the voice of angels — or so the story goes.

The art of playing the glassychord leads at best a fugitive existence today at amateur nights and the like, but it was considered quite something at the time. Mozart and Beethoven composed pieces for it.

Franklin also played the guitar, harp, violin, and sticcado-pastorale, an instrument made out of glass rods.

•

Two of Philadelphia's musical entrepreneurs, at least, are worth more than a passing mention.

Giovanni Gualdo hadn't intended to open a music store. He had arrived in the city in 1767 intent on opening up a wine cellar. It wasn't until that effort proved unremunerative that he moved into the music business. Soon it was a thriving business, and Gualdo had in his employ a music teacher and a music copy boy, who would copy out single compositions from the music books for people who didn't want the whole book. Being a composer himself, Gualdo offered to "arrange music for every kind of instrument," and organized concert series throughout the colony.

Signor Gualdo's principal rival in the music store business was Michael Hillegas, who later became treasurer of the United States. ★★★

THE FOUNDING CITY

Patriot Capital
or Tory Stronghold?

Patriot Capital or Tory Stronghold?

A lot of this chapter will be regarded by many Americans as seditious, if not downright treasonous. We aren't used to the idea that the Loyalists may have had a point or two on their side of the argument.

But the goal isn't sedition. Instead, the purpose of this chapter is to destroy the idea that decisons were somehow simpler in that earlier era. They weren't, and Thomas Paine wasn't kidding when he said that those were the times that tried men's souls.

The decision to delare for independence wasn't arrived at easily — except in the case of professional radicals and perennial misanthropes. As Lord Acton put it: "The point at issue was a very subtle and refined one, and it required a great deal of mismanagement to make the quarrel irreconcilable."

Benjamin West's depiction of "Penn's Treaty With the Indians" contains several anomalies, including the fact that there probably was no treaty. The clothes and buildings are also inaccurate. As the painting indicates, much about Penn was misunderstood a century later.

First Phase: Penn's Dream Dissolves

By Willard S. Randall

Late on the crisp autumn afternoon of October 4, 1779, an angry crowd of armed Philadelphians and militiamen with fixed bayonets stormed a handsome brick house on the southwest corner of Third and Walnut Streets.

The mob, busily rounding up Quakers all day, now was intent on killing or capturing James Wilson, signer of the Declaration of Independence, and several of his friends, for reasons that were probably never clear.

That such an assault could take place only three years after Wilson helped found the new nation, and less than a century after William Penn planted his peaceable kingdom in Philadelphia, underscores the complete political revolution that had transformed the seeds of the first American democracy into a tangled wilderness of bitter party politics.

James Wilson: Mob's target . . .

And it is only by understanding the full sweep of colonial Pennsylvania politics that reasons for the turn toward Revolution by many of the city's leaders — and the turn away from Revolution by a large number of others — can be properly deciphered.

It was not a simple situation. In its first century, Philadelphia was wracked constantly by political strife, rigged elections, corrupt officials, patronage schemes, riots and near-riots in a city politic as disruptive as any before or since.

What the God-fearing had conceived of as a Holy Experiment had become anything but that by the third quarter of the 18th century.

That the city became the birthplace and first capital of the United States is one of the enduring ironies of American history.

Patriot Capital or Tory Stronghold?

George Fox: Quaker visionary . . .

Chapter I:
Dream Meets Reality

The Holy Experiment, as the Quakers were fond of calling the colonization of Pennsylvania, began auspiciously enough.

Thirty years after Quaker firebrand-founder George Fox faced west from a hilltop in England and had a vision of a new way of life across the Atlantic, his ideas were turned into the reality of a mass exodus of Quakers from England to the banks of the Delaware by William Penn.

What brought prosperous English, Welsh, Dutch, Swiss and Irish farmers and merchants to the junction of the Schuylkill and Delaware Rivers was the dream of peace and harmony in a commonwealth where toleration of all forms would be extended to settlers, and where prosperity would, they believed, be its natural outgrowth.

More than 15,000 Quakers had suffered in the foul dungeons of England in the decade before the Holy Experiment began, because of their faith.

Now they poured west over the ocean in long convoys of ships, placidly enduring decimating outbreaks of smallpox as they faced the unknown life in the new land along the Delaware.

They arrived to find a scene of almost unimaginably stirring pastoral beauty, a land as rich and green as any they might have imagined. The contrast with the fetid cities and squalid little towns that they had left behind — whose filth and poverty would astonish a visitor named Benjamin Franklin a century later — must have been profound.

They were greeted by Swedish settlers who lived in cabins with distinctive herringbone-patterned log walls.

Quickly, before winter set in, the Quakers assembled similar cabins, or, if they arrived too late in the season, took up housekeeping in caves dug into the high bluffs along the Delaware.

Many of these caves were ready for occupancy, since they'd been used first by Indians, and then by Swedish settlers over the past 50 years. The Quakers improved them by building log fronts and chimneys. Later these caves would become Philadelphia's first sailors' bars and brothels.

More than 100 ships loaded with immigrants arrived that first year of English settlement. In the fall convoy came the household and distinguished personage of the province's proprietor, William Penn, known in England as a radical troublemaker, but hailed in the new colony (for a few years at least) as a great protector and law-giver.

Penn exulted at the beauty and bounty of the river valley: "And thou, Philadelphia, the virgin settlement, named before thou wert born," he wrote. "What love, what care, what service and travail has there been to bring thee forth, and to preserve thee from such as would abuse and defile thee!"

In a less stentorian note home to England he added, "The soil is good, air serene and sweet from the cedar, pine, and

William Penn as a young man; tragedy lay ahead.

Founder's Odd Reward

No sooner had William Penn planted his idealistic "seed of a nation" in the rich soil of Pennsylvania than he was called back to England to begin a 25-year struggle to keep the colony and his personal fortune out of the clutches of his enemies.

During his two-year absence from England, the Proprietor's rivals for the forested wilderness between New York and Maryland had been busy at the court of Charles II conniving to strip Penn of his royal charter.

In the years before King Charles died in 1685, Penn lived in London and worked hard at court, not only to keep Pennsylvania in Penn family hands but also to represent the interests of all religious dissenters in the British Isles.

As the spokesmen for the dissenters, he was able to secure pardons for no fewer than 1,200 Quakers and assorted nonconformists suffering in England's prisons.

Yet his prominence made him a conspicuous target for the intrigues of the court. By openly preaching toleration of all religions, he was accused, among other things, of high treason and worse yet, of being a tool of the hated Jesuits.

When Catholic King James II came to the throne, Penn, who tried to get along

sassafras, with wild myrtle of great fragrance. I have had better venison, bigger, more tender, as fat as in England.

"Turkeys of the wood I had of 40 and 50 pounds weight. Fish in abundance, especially shad and rock (fish). Oysters are monstrous for bigness. In the woods are divers(e) fruits, . . . and flowers that for colour, largeness and beauty excel."

Penn apparently wasn't exaggerating, for other Quakers noted in letters home that passenger pigeons were as thick as low-flying clouds, and could sometimes be knocked down with clubs.

What nature didn't provide free, the Swedes provided at a reasonable mark-up: a 30-pound turkey cost a shilling, or about $1 in today's market; an entire deer cost two shillings; a bushel of corn slightly more.

"We have peaches by cart loads," reported Penn. "The Indians bring us seven or eight bucks of a day. Without rod or net we catch abundance of herrings, after the Indian manner, in pinfolds (a kind of net). Geese, ducks, pheasants are plenty."

Penn proclaimed his Frame of Government to the new settlement for the first time at a tavern in Chester — even though one of the "Greate Laws" in it forbade "the drinking of toasts." It was the first of many ironies that would characterize the Experiment, but these weren't to show up until later. It was, on its face, a remarkable document.

Penn was himself a political refugee. He had twice been jailed at Newgate for publicly preaching the Quaker faith, and Penn had spent almost two decades as a

writer and speaker formulating his ideas on how to govern the new province.

He had consulted many times with the leading English political philosophers, John Locke and Algernon Sidney, and rewritten his Frame of Government — which would be the constitution for his colony — at least 20 times. It represented the most far-reaching advance in terms of civil liberties since the Magna Carta, and formed the basis for the Declaration of Independence.

Penn, while reserving the right to sell about 20 million acres of land and remain titular head of the province under the Frame, gave virtual control to the Assembly, a piece of popular democracy that quickly met for three days in December 1682 to ratify Penn's plan.

The Assembly was given control over the pursestrings, to determine how tax revenues were to be spent and to dispense the resultant jobs and such business as printing and advertising. While Penn gave himself power to make laws, it was with the advice and consent of the governed, who elected representatives to the Assembly every year.

The liberal document also eliminated capital punishment except for murder at a time when there were 200 capital offenses in England. The Frame also granted full religious toleration, a pre-

with everyone, became his close friend, a fact that was used against him in the bloodless Glorious Revolution that brought the Protestant King William to power. Penn was formally accused of carrying on a treasonable correspondence with the deposed King James. He demanded a public trial before the King and Privy Council and was acquitted.

Nevertheless, still distrusted, he was stripped of the governorship of Pennsylvania in 1692. For the next two years, Pennsylvania was ruled by the governors of New York.

Penn's personal life was no less trouble-filled. His first wife, Gulielma, died in 1694, his son Springett shortly after that. Remarrying, Penn learned too late that his second wife, Hannah, disliked the rustic life of Pennsylvania almost as much as his daughter, Letitia, did, a fact that cut short their last sojourn to the colony, which took place between 1699 and 1701.

Penn found little to give him satisfaction in Pennsylvania in any event. The seeds of unrest had been sown side by side with the seeds of democracy; both royal and proprietary officials clashed with Quaker leaders from the start. Three times in 20 years, Penn had to rewrite the charter of Pennsylvania to meet the varied demands of the new residents. Still unsatisfied, the royalist faction among Pennsylvanians was pressing hard to have Pennsylvania taken from Penn and annexed by the crown by 1701. Again, Penn had to return to London to fight for his proprietorship.

Within three years, Pennsylvanians had almost totally rejected Penn's authority. Royalists in the Assembly obstructed all Penn's legislation, and only Penn's constant presence at court kept him from losing the colony.

To add financial injury to political insult, the ungrateful inhabitants of Pennsylvania refused to pay rent for the lands Penn had sold them. By this time, bilked out of his fortune by a business partner in London, Penn really needed the meager 500 pounds in annual "quitrents," as such payments were called.

This first widespread American rent strike was the final insult for the long-suffering Penn. He would quietly endure nine months in prison for debt, but could not take the ingratitude of his Quaker beneficiaries in Pennsylvania.

"The undeserved opposition I meet from (Pennsylvania) sinks me in sorrow, and I cannot but think it hard measure that while that proved a land of freedom and flourishing to them, it should become to me by whose means it was made a country, the cause of trouble and poverty."

By 1711, his paternal patience at an end, he added, "I once had reason to expect a solid comfort from the services done so many people. Did the people really want anything of me in the relation between us that would make them happier, I should readily grant it."

But by then the Holy Experiment had faded. Penn was considered just another grasping absentee landlord, ignored in his old age both at home in England, and in his woodland paradise of Pennsylvania.

The last six years of his life proved the most bitter of all: between 1712 and 1718, he was stricken with a long series of apoplectic seizures that left him crippled and simple-minded, an invalid with few lucid moments.   —WSR

The FRAME of the

GOVERNMENT

OF THE

Province of Pennſilvania

IN

AMERICA:

Together with certain

L A W S

Agreed upon in England

BY THE

GOVERNOUR

AND

Divers F R E E - M E N of the aforeſaid
PROVINCE.

Tobe further Explained and Confirmed there by the firſt
Provincial Council and *General Aſſembly* that ſhall
be held, if they ſee meet.

Printed in the Year M DC LXXXII.

The title page of William Penn's "Frame of Government."

Loyalists and patriots were both forged in the heat of Pennsylvania's partisan and seamy politics. Indeed, the process of revolution had to be slowed while the state's political fabric was torn apart.

Penn debarks from the "Welcome."

cept that led to immigration not only from Europe, but from the despotic Puritan colonies of New England, where Quakers had been hanged for their missionary zeal.

Another point of difference with already-established American colonies was Penn's view of how to deal with those first Philadelphians, the Indians. While there is no evidence he signed a formal treaty with them in 1682, he is said to have studied their language and customs with more sympathy and fair-mindedness than his successors, a fact that would ultimately do more harm than good to the Indians.

(All things considered, they would probably have been luckier to have discovered, right off the bat, the chicanery and fast-dealing that would come to characterize their dealings with the white men, including most particularly Penn's successors. As it was, they were lulled into a false sense of safety.)

The city's "undefiled" status, about which Penn had rhapsodized on arriving, was to be short-lived. Pennsylvania politics was born kicking and squalling, as rural farmers jostled with their urban brethren for more power and funds, beginning a struggle which continues annually today, three centuries later, under only slightly changed conditions in the state legislature in Harrisburg.

The realities of power politics quickly pressed in from the outside, too. Inside two years, the 300 houses and 1,500 inhabitants of Philadelphia stirred the jealousy of Lord Baltimore, who held the next colonial franchise to the south, and who pressed a claim at the court of King James in England for all of Pennsylvania.

Penn had to leave the colony, not to return for nearly 20 years, to defend his interests in person.

He was to learn another bitter political lesson from his absence: his interests and his ideals in Pennsylvania were sharply eroded before he could return.

Inside those years, the number of crimes punishable by death was expanded to 20 as criminals deported from England found their way into the homes and pockets of the thriving Quaker merchants and artisans.

Political disharmony increased. At first a trickle of Church of England adherents joined the Quaker colony, then more and more, until they comprised a voting bloc against the Quakers.

Penn's agents found themselves rebuffed when they tried to collect quitrents, the annual rental on ground that Penn had already sold them. Quitrents would remain an issue for 75 years, until Penn's grandson was finally paid off.

But the basic cause of division was money. Almost immediately, the Assembly sought the power to print money whenever it could find a need, and sometimes when there was no good reason. The main reason was that the Assembly, under the complex fiscal machinery of the day, earned interest on currency issues, which its members spent to hire political friends, and to provide themselves with sundry other emoluments.

As early as 1706, the Assembly began lobbying for a suitable building for its

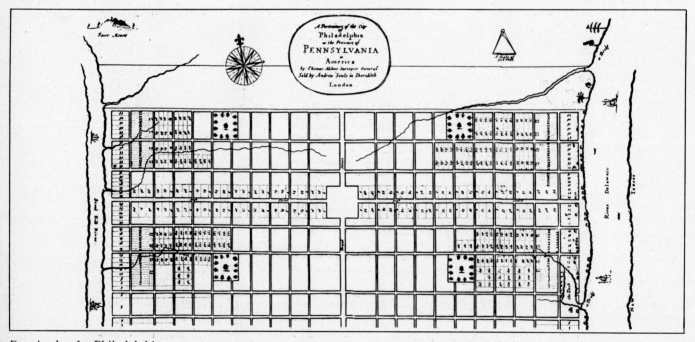

Penn's plan for Philadelphia

THE FOUNDING CITY

august deliberations, but it would be 30 years before the state house, now Independence Hall, was erected. The lawmakers, meanwhile, had to content themselves with carrying out most of their business in taverns, a circumstance that apparently didn't do a thing for the moral tone of their deliberations.

A Digression: The Indians Learn A Lesson

The first serious problem the politicians created was their handling of the Delaware Indians. Generously, the Indians had agreed originally to allow the white men to extend their settlement "as far as a man can walk in a day and a half."

But the Indians had made the deal with William Penn, not his sons, John and Thomas. In 1737, the brothers, in exchange for a guarantee of protection of the Delawares against their rivals, the Iroquois, invoked this agreement in one of the shadiest land swindles on record.

(Just how it was that the pacifist Quakers intended to offer meaningful protection to the Indians in the event of attack is another of the intriguing little unsolved mysteries of Pennsylvania history.)

Hunting up the three hardiest and fastest-walking woodsmen in the colony, the Penn brothers put them to work practicing heel-and-toeing while hired work parties cleared a path through the forests. On the appointed day, the Penn relay team quickly outdistanced the Indian escorts and finished their strolls at a dead run. As a result, the Penns extended their holdings 67 miles, probably quadruple the distance the Indians had intended.

Chapter II: The Anti-Pennites Govern

By 1737, the wealthy Quaker merchants of Philadelphia controlled Pennsylvania politics, and the Penns were left with few prerogatives other than vetoing legislation that might cost them money. For 28 years, from 1736 to 1764, the anti-Penn "Anti-Proprietary Party" controlled the Assembly. Most years, the elections were uncontested.

By 1740, though, the Philadelphia Quakers were a minority in Pennsylvania outnumbered by Mennonites, Amish, Dunkards, Moravians and Scots-Irish Presbyterians. Somewhat to their own embarrassment, they found themselves forced to resort to trickery to keep control of the colony. Their principal device was to deprive the poor and the more recent immigrants of the vote until they had property worth 50 pounds sterling,

Free Library of Philadelphia

John Penn: "... reserved in his manners, and very near-sighted ..."

The Grandson's Tale

John Penn's story is almost the reverse of that of his grandfather, William Penn.

Where William Penn was a forceful character who made both intense friendships and lasting enmities. John was a well-meaning neutral character who was neither loved nor hated by those around him. An acquaintance recalled him only as being "of the middle size, reserved in his manners, and very near-sighted."

And where his grandfather's career had started with great hopes, and ended in poverty, ill health, and unhappiness far from his Pennsylvania, John Penn's was quite the opposite.

He started badly, with an inauspicious marriage he was forced to renounce, then suffered through some difficult times as Pennsylvania's last colonial governor before the Revolution, but he ended up happily at ease on his estate on the Schuylkill.

It is yet another of the fascinating ironies of history that the Revolution made John Penn rich, probably beyond his wildest expectations; it made him in particular much richer than establishing a "peaceable kingdom" in the wilderness had ever made his grandfather.

John Penn was born in 1729, the first of Richard Penn's four children. After his repudiated marriage to a young lady named Cox in England, he was sent with a tutor to study at the university in Geneva, where he stayed from 1747 to 1751.

He alternated sojourns in England and Pennsylvania, until 1773 when he returned to become the last Penn to serve as governor. Along the way he had married Ann Allen, a Philadelphia girl.

He seemed to greet the prospect of independence with surprising equanimity.

He was arrested and placed on parole by the Continental Congress for several months in 1777. But that body, ultimately unable to figure out just why they had arrested him in the first place, released him.

In 1778, he and the other descendants of William Penn were granted the right to retain their personal lands and estates, and paid the staggering sum of 130,000 pounds as compensation for the appropriation of their unsettled holdings.

When he died in 1795, at 67, he was buried at Christ Church. — *Tom Peters*

Irish and German settlers are shown serving as bearers for Indians and Quakers, while Benjamin Franklin, at left, looks on.

being refused ... drink ... they went back enraged to the election grounds. There they fell heavily with their clubs upon the Germans and others, beating off the former, as many as 500 ..."

Next the sailors attacked the stairs, up which the voters had to pass, and on which adherents of the anti-Penn Quaker party headed by Isaac Norris customarily stood to buttonhole voters before they entered the polling place.

"There was a great trial for the stairs," Peters reported, "... the ship carpenters clubbed together to make it their own, which they accomplished."

•

But such efforts had no substantial or lasting effect. The Penns were not even able to exploit the fact that the Philadelphia Quakers were breaking up into two factions at this point.

Isaac Norris, a wealthy merchant who

which was the price of well-developed, good-sized farms. Until the Revolution, the western counties of Pennsylvania, where the majority of settlers was forced to settle for cheap lands, were seriously underrepresented in the Assembly.

It was also no real trick to keep the later immigrants at each other's throats, and incapable of joining together to outvote the English Quakers. Most of the Swiss-German settlers had serious political differences built into their rival sects.

When, from time to time the "Pennsylvania Dutch" decided to get their act together and assert themselves, it was usually to support the Quaker faction that was resisting the power of the Penn family.

The Penns, while in eclipse, were not above using some unsavory surreptitious tactics to try to reduce the voting power of the anti-proprietarian combine.

Richard Peters, the secretary to the Proprietors, described, without editorial comment, one such effort that occurred during the election of 1742. It was an effort to keep the turnout down through methods that haven't fallen totally into disuse in some South Philadelphia wards even today:

"Young Joseph Turner (apparently a Penn henchman) gathered the sailors, to the number of 40 or 50 persons, at an open lot over against Christ Church. Thence they made an assault on the courthouse, on some of the electors (voters) there.

"Thence they went to Chestnut Street, and by a back way to the Indian King Inn on High (Market) Street, where,

The English as Bunglers

George III depicted with the tokens of his power.

By the eve of the Revolution, Benjamin Franklin had spent 17 years in England arguing the American case, and he was at the end of his rope.

When he heard that his old friend, Joseph Galloway, had proposed to the First Continental Congress a Plan of Union between England and America that was basically the same as a plan he had put forward two decades earlier, he wrote a dangerously candid letter that reflected the effect of his long stay in England:

"When I consider the extreme corruption prevalent among all orders of men in this old rotten state, and the glorious public virtue so predominant in our rising country, I cannot but apprehend more mischief than benefit from a closer union."

A natural tendency exists when studying the American Revolution to consider mainly the events that occurred in America. Yet it is probably true that what happened in England was more important — or, to be more precise, what *didn't* happen in England.

The basic characteristics of British policy toward America and its problems were profound indifference, amazing ignorance, and suffusing corruption — all of which was mixed, at precisely the wrong time, with some truly impressive stupidity. The result tended to be that little, in a positive sense, was done.

In 1763, England had, to its own vast surprise, bested France and Spain in an epoch-long struggle by following the maxim of its great wartime leader, William Pitt: "When trade is at stake, you must defend it or perish."

Yet in 1775, when trade was even more at stake in the widening rift between England and America, King George III not only refused to call back the ailing Pitt as prime minister — and Pitt was probably the only man who could have reconciled England and America — he also ignored Pitt's dictum. Instead of following a pragmatic mercantile policy

emulated the elegant lifestyle of an English country squire at Fairhill, his country estate, led the dominant faction.

A much smaller Quaker party, less worldly and more concerned with maintaining the purity of the Quaker faith, was led by Israel Pemberton, "King of the Quakers."

While Pemberton and his adherents held that virtually all participation in politics was un-Quakerly, Norris and his party believed that Quaker religious interests could only be maintained if Quaker political power was strong — even if achieving the latter occasionally meant abridging the former.

However, even Norris wasn't willing to abandon Quaker pacifism, and because of this a crisis was coming that would end Quaker dominance of Pennsylvania affairs.

Chapter III:
Indian War

All through the years of the Holy Experiment, French and Indian depredations along Pennsylvania's borders had been creating a conundrum for the Quakers: how to offer protection without taking to arms. As Scots-Irish settlers moved farther west into Indian country, inviting more and more attacks, the crisis of conscience grew ever more acute at the Quaker meetinghouse at Fourth and Arch Streets.

Adroitly, in early Indian wars, the pacifist Quakers had avoided voting direct appropriations for war by earmarking them "for the Queen's use," or for the "purchase of grain," a turn of legislative phrase that could be loosely construed to include grains of gunpowder.

But these bits of hypocrisy weren't sufficient to assuage the new immigrants suffering Indian raids in the hinterlands and, by 1755, the commonwealth was on the brink of civil war.

As the French and their Indian allies occupied Fort Duquesne and British General Edward Braddock organized his expedition against it, the issue became unavoidable, and before the Quakers could agree to a solution, events had outrun them: Braddock was dead, the English slaughtered and the French and Indians were advancing against the Pennsylvania settlements.

To complicate matters, even when the Quakers finally voted 50,000 pounds for defense, the Penns refused to contribute unless their lands were exempted from the tax.

This created a formidable new adversary for the Penns. Not even the King of England was exempt from land taxes in time of war, fumed one Philadelphia politician who had remained independent through the years of wrangling. His name was Benjamin Franklin, and at this critical moment he stepped to the foreground in Philadelphia politics with a salvo at the Penn party:

"Vassals must follow their lords to the wars in defense of their lands," he stormed. "Our Lord Proprietary, though a subject like ourselves, would send us out to fight for him, while he keeps himself a thousand leagues remote from danger.

"Vassals fight at their lords' expense," Franklin continued, "but our lord would

aimed at maximizing trade with the American colonies, he was intent on "punishing the child (America)."

Englishmen in general, moreover, had little sympathy with American tax protests, like the Boston Tea Party. The British landed gentry, which controlled Parliament, was paying 15 percent of its income in taxes, with part of that money going to pay off loans incurred during the French and Indian Wars to protect the Americans. American complaints about a piddling three pence tax on tea were incomprehensible. The average Englishman cheered the repressive measures taken against America.

Their enthusiasm for repression was fed by their view that the average American was a frontier lout, skinning and trading wild animal skins, living in a log fort, and picking his teeth with his hunting knife; in short, a decidedly second-rate citizen that should be put in his place.

"Sir," Dr. Samuel Johnson said, quite possibly in the hearing of his old crony Franklin, "they are a parcel of convicts, and if they get anything short of hanging, they ought to be content."

The once-irresolute king began more and more to believe his own memos as he issued detailed orders for putting down the growing troubles in America. On receiving news of Lexington, he wrote: "With firmness and perseverance, America will be brought to submission. America must be a colony of England or be treated as an enemy.".

Historian Edward Gibbon, who sat silently in Parliament all through the Revolution, wrote later that "the executive power was driven by the national clamor into the most vigorous and repressive measures." Gibbon, who was completing his monumental work, *The Decline and Fall of the Roman Empire*, considered Americans, to the extent that he considered them at all, to be the Visigoths of the period, threatening the protectors of Western civilization — the British.

America could not win, England's warriors chorused: "They are raw, undisciplined, cowardly men," snorted the Earl of Sandwich, corrupt head of the navy.

To be sure, there were pro-Americans in Britain. In general, they were not listened to. Few thought it significant that Sir Jeffrey Amherst, hero of the last French and Indian War, refused the command of British forces in America, declining to fight his American cousins.

All the rhetoric of Edmund Burke, Charles James Fox, William Pitt and the fiery John Wilkes on the side of peace with America was wasted. When the key vote was taken in Parliament on the Boston Port Bill, the bill that unleashed the war machine, it was a lopsided 270-78 for repression of America.

"This is the day, then," Edmund Burke intoned ironically on March 31, 1774, "that you wish to go to war with all America in order to conciliate that country to this."

Saddened, Benjamin Franklin would write to his old friend, Member of Parliament William Strahan, ending his last letter before the war, "You are now my Enemy, and I am,
Yours,
B. Franklin."

—*WSR*

Delegates to the Continental Congress leaving Carpenters Hall.

have us defend his estate at our own expense! This is not merely vassalage, it is worse than any vassalage we have heard of; it is even more slavish than slavery itself."

Franklin's outburst, his open break with the Penns who had helped him raise money for his Academy of Philadelphia (later the University of Pennsylvania) and for Pennsylvania Hospital, came at the perfect time for the Quakers. They now had a powerful new ally — to whom they promptly abdicated (or perhaps the better phrase would be "passed the buck").

In August 1755, Franklin had set about forming a new party in the Assembly separate from the Quakers and the Penns. The Quakers had decided to put an end to their Holy Experiment rather than openly aid and condone war. By declining to stand for reelection, they turned over control to Franklin's group, becoming, in effect, Franklin's silent partners as he declared war on the rampaging French and Indians.

Among his allies, Franklin had won a young lawyer named Joseph Galloway to his cause. Together, they would dominate Pennsylvania politics down to the time of the Revolution, at which point these two friends would come to a tragic parting of the ways.

When their first aim — expelling the French — was accomplished, Franklin and Galloway set about expelling the Penns from all their remaining semblances of power. Galloway took control of the Assembly as Franklin journeyed to England as the Assembly's agent to lobby at the court to have Pennsylvania made a crown colony on the grounds, spelled out in the Charter of 1681, that the Penns should forfeit the colony if they failed to administer it properly.

For six years, Franklin maintained his fruitless campaign, each year winning reelection to the Assembly in absentia as Galloway kept up the constant pressure on the Penns. Ironically, he would not meet political defeat until he had returned to Philadelphia and achieved what at first seemed to be his greatest triumph.

Chapter IV:
The Paxton Boys

The French and Indian Wars drew to a close, but sporadic fighting continued in western Pennsylvania.

In the winter of 1764, along the Susquehanna River near Lancaster, a group of frontiersmen calling themselves the Paxton Boys fell on 20 peaceful Conestoga Indians, long since converted to basketweaving and Christianity by Moravian missionaries, and massacred them.

When the survivors sought sanctuary in Lancaster jail, the Paxton boys pursued them, broke into the jail, and, as the townspeople and British garrison stood by, slaughtered the Indian old men, women and children.

Buoyed by this great success, the Paxton Boys determined to march on Philadelphia to press the already antique demands of the rural farmers for more power in the commonwealth government.

The first to surrender was Governor John Penn, who turned over the task of defending the city to Franklin as soon as he got wind of the impending attack.

He did, at least, pick the right man. Franklin, outraged by the massacre of the Indians, had been attacking the Paxton Boys in print even before they had turned their attentions toward Philadelphia.

Franklin was now determined that if these lawless killers meant to indulge in the politics of confrontation, he would give them all the confrontation they could handle.

Soon, earthworks were thrown up around the British barracks in the Northern Liberties and Franklin's Associators, heavily armed with artillery, ringed the city and began digging in. They were aided for the first time by shirt-sleeved Quakers manning muskets and trowels.

Inside two days, Franklin was ready. Riding out to meet the Paxton Boys on Germantown Pike, Franklin, Galloway and Daniel Roberdeau coolly convinced them to turn around and ride home. Before they meekly headed west, the Paxton Boys handed Franklin a petition

The Best—and Worst

In Philadelphia's colonial era, its best and brightest citizens often became its mayors, while the worst dregs of the British Empire usually became the Commonwealth's governors, which is not to say that the the office of mayor was especially sought after.

Indeed, the first man appointed mayor of Philadelphia, Griffith Jones, paid a stiff 30-pound fine in 1703 rather than serve his term in the city's top office.

Under Penn's Charter of Privileges, Philadelphia, still a small town, was a borough ruled by a municipal corporation. The mayors were elected by the select members of the corporation for one-year terms. In essence, it was a private club. About the only requisite of being mayor was to be able to throw a bash for your fellow members. Philadelphia's mayors invented the political dinner, among other things.

The mayoral selections, nonetheless, ranged from good to excellent. The first Philadelphian who would take the job was Edward Shippen, a transplanted Bostonian who had embraced Quakerism at the time of his first marriage, and done a jail term for his faith before joining Penn's Holy Experiment.

Shippen also claimed the distinction of serving as mayor, city council president, and governor simultaneously when there was a shortage of politicians that year.

Among Philadelphia's more notable colonial mayors were James Logan, who seemed fonder of his 2,500-volume collection of books than of exerting himself as mayor, and William Allen, better remembered as the founder of Allentown than for any contribution to Philadelphia government.

Despite its uselessless, the office somehow attracted perennial incumbents: Thomas Griffitts served four terms between 1729 and 1738, Thomas Lawrence four terms between 1728 and 1754.

The early mayors concerned themselves with an assortment of weighty matters. In December 1704, Mayor Griffith Jones rammed through a legislative package providing for the winter feed and shelter of the town's two bulls. He then called for a census of all cattle owners, and ended his bovine-related parliamentary *tour de force* by granting a franchise for a slaughterhouse.

If the mayors were a sociable lot, the governors appointed by the Penn family were quite the opposite. They didn't get along with anybody, it seemed.

Governor John Evans distinguished himself mainly as a barroom brawler. On July 1, 1704, he and his good friend William Penn Jr. helped a group of young gentlemen severely beat up the town constable and town watchman at Enoch Storey's tavern.

requesting more representation in the Assembly.

Franklin's popularity proved fleeting, however: within months, he would be defeated in his bid for reelection to the Assembly.

This came about as the result of a variety of factors. Although John Penn had been eager enough to let Franklin handle the Paxton affair in 1764, the fact of the matter was that Penn had returned to Pennsylvania from England four years earlier for the express purpose of putting some kind of curb on Franklin's influence.

John Penn was neither particularly charismatic or bright, but he was able, by simply being present in the colony personally, to become a power center of sorts.

And in the election of 1764, he was abetted by an unlikely ally: the previously non-political Israel Pemberton. Pemberton had decided that he was ever more opposed to the idea of royal government — which is what Franklin was seeking — than he was opposed to John Penn.

The Quakers were also, by some strange process of logic, irked at Franklin because he had induced them to take up arms against the Paxton Boys, even though they hadn't had to use them.

Two other long-standing points of vulnerability were exploited to the hilt in the campaign, and both helped to rank the election of 1764 as one of Philadelphia's least admirable.

One "highlight" of the campaign was the publication by William Smith, provost of the Academy of Philadelphia and a Penn lackey, pointing out that William Franklin, by now appointed the royal governor of New Jersey, was an illegitimate son of Benjamin's, having been delivered of a serving girl named Barbara, who was kept by the elder Franklin in a house in Burlington, N. J., not far from the governor's official residence.

This attack didn't appear to have bothered the Franklins — father or son. William came over to help his father by passing out drinks in Germantown.

Germantown was the right place to be passing out drinks. Franklin's opponents had also dredged up Franklin's unfortunate reference to the Germans as "Palatine boors" in a speech 20 years earlier.

(Franklin's speech was, in fact, an interesting example of the kind of bigotry that was abroad in the commonwealth. He made the reference in the course of advocating a limitation on the immigration of Germans, whom he saw as threatening the Anglo-Saxon traditions of Pennsylvania.)

But the election probably most deserves its infamous reputation for the fact that in it John Penn introduced political patronage as a method of influencing elections. He dispensed lucrative justice of the peace commissions to those who were willing to help him get the anti-Franklin bandwagon rolling.

Together, all of the efforts were availing. Franklin finished 13th in a field of 14.

However, the party he headed continued to control the Assembly, and Franklin was sent back to England as the agent for the Assembly.

Franklin himself shrugged off the defeat in at least one piece of correspondence as "quite a laughing matter."

Chapter V: A New Issue Arises

By 1765, Philadelphia's political interests were falling more and more into line with other colonies, who were unifying to resist new British taxes on imports. And it was a conservative Philadelphia lawyer, John Dickinson, who became the leading spokesman for the opponents of British policy in America.

In 1767, Dickinson, a rich socialite, published his closely reasoned *Letters from a Pennsylvania Farmer*, a strong statement on the rights and liberties of English subjects that made him the leading spokesman for the colonists' point of view for many years.

Before he was overshadowed by Thomas Jefferson and John Adams, Dickinson led the verbal resistance to British imperial policy in America. Although moderate compared to the Boston patri-

Free Library of Philadelphia

Mayor Edward Shippen:
Made up for a shortage of politicians . . .

Free Library of Philadelphia

Mayor James Logan:
Preferred books to government . . .

His successor, Charles Gookin, feuded with the Assembly from the moment he arrived. The Assembly refused to pay his salary or living expenses, insisting Penn was rich enough to pay his own governor. Gookin eventually had enough. In 1717, he kicked a judge who crossed him, then walked out on an Assembly meeting and left the province in a huff.

His successor, Sir William Keith, was typical of the arrogant, useless career courtiers sent from England. After enriching himself at the public trough, he deserted his wife and daughter in Philadelphia and went back to write a bad history of Virginia before he died broke in London.

—WSR

Was It Democracy—or Mob Rule?

If the Revolution was fought to preserve freedom of the press, how does one explain the incident in the fall of 1775 when a group of armed Americans rode into New York, entered the print shop of newspaper publisher James Rivington, smashed his presses, and carried away his type — all because he spoke out for Loyalism?

If the Revolution was fought for freedom of religion, how does one deal with the decision of the Continental Congress to put prominent Philadelphia Quakers in what was, in effect, a prison camp in Virginia?

If the Revolution was fought for freedom of speech, why did opposition to the Congress become a crime?

And, most perplexing of all, if independence was to be declared in order to assure for all Americans the rights of "life, liberty, and pursuit of happiness," why did so many Americans — in Philadelphia and elsewhere — have to live their lives during much of the Revolutionary era in more or less constant fear of mob violence?

There is no easy answer. It was wartime; reasonable men could, and did, conclude that extremism in the cause of liberty was not a vice. Draconian means seemed, to many, to be justified by the prospective ends.

Yet the truth appears to remain: if the Revolution brought out some of the best in Americans, it also brought out some of the worst. Let's examine an episode from Philadelphia in 1775. Try to imagine: which side would you have fought on?

•

In August of 1775, George Schlosser, a member of Philadelphia's Committee of Safety, caught William Conn, a dry goods merchant and a Loyalist, doing something wrong. He caught him selling British-made cloth after the Continental Congress' ban on the sale of British goods had gone into effect.

Conn asked attorney Isaac Hunt to represent him during the court proceedings instituted by the committee, and to try to get his confiscated goods back. Hunt agreed. All things considered, it was probably a mistake.

Before a crowded courtroom, in stifling heat and humidity, Hunt launched into a bitter attack against the authority of the Committee. The Committee demanded that Hunt apologize, accusing him of arrogance and impudence, and drop his suit. Hunt declined on both counts. Sterner measures appeared to be called for.

Hunt was seized, according to research by Richard Ryerson of the University of Pennsylvania, and dumped into a horse-drawn cart, and taken from intersection to intersection, while a rag-tag fife-and-drum corps following behind played "The Rogue's March." At each corner he was called upon to make — and made — an apology for his arrogance.

As the procession crossed Market Street, going south along Front, a shot rang out. It came from the third floor window of the handsome, three-story brick house owned by Dr. John Kearsley Jr., a respected Philadelphia physician. Kearsley himself, infuriated at the way the mob had been treating Hunt, had fired the shot. No one was hit.

The crowd rushed into the house, smashing windows and destroying furniture, and seized the hot-headed doctor, skewering his hand with a bayonet and hitting him several times in the head. The disheveled doctor, "foaming with rage and indignation," his hair still bloody from his wounds, replaced Hunt in the cart, and the mob continued its tour. Onlookers pelted Kearsley with fruit and stones.

At one point the doctor demanded a bowl of punch, which was provided, and which he "drained of its contents before he took it from his lips," then presumably continued his tirade against his tormentors. The crowd at one point demanded that he be tarred and feathered — an atrocious torture — but less inflamed minds prevailed. He was returned, alive, to his vandalized home.

There's an irony in the fact that some years earlier a young ship's passenger, stricken with typhoid, and bearing a letter of introduction from Benjamin Franklin, had been brought to Kearsley's house, where he was nursed back to health. The man's name was Thomas Paine.

Kearsley was ultimately imprisoned by the American rebels for his Loyalist writings, and died in the York, Pa., jail.

—*Richard S. Dunham*

---

ots, he was considerably to the left of Joseph Galloway, who actually ruled Pennsylvania during Franklin's long absence.

The two men exemplified the middle-of-the-road stance of most Philadelphians in the years before the outbreak of hostilities in New England. Galloway favored peace with England no matter what the price, seeking at most a more favored footing for Americans; Dickinson favored conciliation, without English control.

It was this coalition, which took in Franklin, Dickinson, and Galloway before the break with England became imminent, that would be split apart. These men would find themselves forced slowly, but inexorably, to oppose long-time friends who had been political allies for decades.

Popular discontent over British policies was growing in Philadelphia, first during the disputes over the Stamp Act, a short-lived British effort to collect revenues in America to pay for the British effort in the French and Indian Wars, and then during the contretemps over the tax on tea.

In 1772 an anti-Galloway faction had done surprisingly well at the polls in the assembly elections, and in October of 1773 some 8,000 Philadelphians showed up at a meeting to protest the arrival of the British East India Company's sloop *Polly* with a shipment of tea consigned to two firms of Philadelphia Quaker merchants — T. & I. Wharton and James & Drinker.

The captain was given one day to refill his water casks and buy food before returning to England.

Still, the waters of the Delaware — unlike Boston harbor — were not polluted with English tea.

Chapter VI:
Congress Convenes

By the time the First Continental Congress was convened in Philadelphia, a neutral point midway point between the northernmost and southernmost colonies, Galloway and the conservatives had lost control of the Assembly — yet they were still powerful, and dominated the Pennsylvania delegation.

But the selection of the newly-built Carpenters' Hall, a tribute to the leather-apron-wearing artisans of Philadelphia, over the conservative stronghold at

the State House was a symbolic victory for the Boston radicals.

Moreover, the presence of Samuel Adams and John Adams in Philadelphia had a strong influence on working-class citizens, who increasingly banded together, first into revolutionary committees, and then into militia regiments.

By masterful manipulation within the Congress, the radicals first isolated Galloway from the other members of the conservative coalition — and then disgraced him. And once the forces of moderation were undone in Pennsylvania, similar courses of events took place in New Jersey and New York.

Revolutionary sentiment really began to roll in pacifist Pennsylvania. By spring 1776, the moderates counselling conciliation with England began to lose their grip on city politics.

Fearing violence and destruction, the Quaker-dominated populace had moved slowly. But on May 20, 1776, the radicals called a town meeting to coincide with the opening of the Assembly. Some 4,000 people stood in the rain in the State House yard, listening to speeches and cheering for independence.

They would be back again in July.

Rapidly now, the radicals took power. When the duly-elected members of the Pennsylvania Assembly failed to show up to begin the session later in 1776, the radicals called an extra-legal constitutional convention, established a provisional revolutionary government, and required "test oaths" of allegiance as a requirement for voting.

Barred from taking oaths under pain of expulsion from their faith, most Quakers and many of the Swiss-German sects were disenfranchised — which is what the revolutionaries intended.

The point was moot, however, since the radicals were so afraid their constitution would be defeated that they didn't call for a referendum until two years later.

Epilogue: Dangerous Brush With Extremism

For the first two years of the war in Philadelphia, there was little civil government. As early as December 1776, as the British swept across New Jersey.

A strong body of militiamen and soldiers was mustered in Philadelphia to meet the threat of the Paxton Boys.

Congress declared martial law and installed Israel Putnam as military governor. After the British left, Benedict Arnold, wounded at Saratoga, unenthusiastically took the post.

But the atmosphere of suspicion pervading the city after the British evacuation only worsened as the war dragged on, and food and clothing became extremely scarce, at least for the average man.

By late 1778, the Continental dollar had been devalued to the point where it had about 1/40th of its original purchasing power. It was, as the expression went, "not worth a continental." German farmers in outlying counties refused to sell their crops for this almost worthless currency.

Both the British and American Armies had plucked the city's orchards and gardens clean, and the only food to be found in the winter of 1778-79 was that hoarded by merchants in warehouses, until it was sold to the French fleet, whose quartermasters could offer gold.

In reaction to these events, anyone suspected of war profiteering, or refusing

A cortege of weeping British officials bears the coffin of the Stamp Act. The dog (at left) adds his own comment.

THE FOUNDING CITY

to sell provisions to the American Army for depreciated dollars, was branded a Tory by the radical committees ruling the city, and risked beatings by the ever more radical mobs.

Even Robert Morris, the man most responsible for keeping the Army paid and supplied throughout the war, came under suspicion, and twice had to appear publicly to try to clear his name.

By May 1779, prices had soared to four times their prewar level and mass hysteria threatened to sweep the city. Feeding on the suspicion, the radicals used it as a campaign device to cover for their inept handling of the economy.

On Monday, May 24, the radical revolutionary committees, in a scene ominously foreshadowing the tactics of the French Revolution only ten years later, called a mass meeting in the State House yard after days of stirring up the city, cursing merchants, and threatening to break into offices and storehouses.

At the meeting, a large crowd listened as the now-General Daniel Roberdeau, the man who had helped calm the Paxton Boys 15 years earlier, harangued his listeners: "The dangers we are exposed to arise from evils amongst ourselves. I scorn, and I hope every citizen scorns, the thought of getting rich by sucking the blood of his country; yet alas, this unnatural, this cruel, this destructive practice is the greatest cause of our present calamities.

"I have no doubt but combinations have been formed for raising the prices of goods and provisions, and therefore the community, in their own defense, have a natural right to counteract such combinations."

In the virulent campaign that followed Roberdeau's speech, merchants were beaten and harassed and Quakers were chased through the streets repeatedly.

The occupation of the city that summer by the American First Artillery Company only added to the tensions. On July 1, 1779, the company published a statement in the *Pennsylvania Packet:*

"We have arms in our hands and we know the use of them. . . . We will see the virtuous, innocent and suffering part of the community redressed, and endeavor to divest this city of the disaffected, inimical, and preyers on the vitals of the inhabitants, be their rank or station what it may."

It was only a short step to the inconclusive attack, eight days before the first election under the revolutionary rule, on signer James Wilson's house.

Oddly, though, the attack on the Wilson house did not become the beginning

Free Library of Philadelphia

Benedict Arnold, military governor of Philadelphia, used his pistols when necessary.

of a chain of radical terror episodes, as would occur in France. There were other incidents, to be sure. Two days after the attack on Wilson's home, Arnold, the military governor, was accosted by a mob, but he fired a couple of shots with his pistols, and the mob retreated.

But it was as if the radical explosion had misfired, or gone off prematurely. The radicals themselves tended to regard what happened in much the way men regard accounts of their activities on a previous night while under the influence of spirituous beverages. "Did we do that?" they seemed to ask themselves.

The mob violence was clearly a political embarrassment. In his explanation to

the Assembly, a radical leader passed it off as "the casual overflowing of liberty." It unquestionably served to compound the radicals' problems. Not only did they appear to be unable to stabilize the state's economy, provide food for the populace, or come up with pay for the army —now it appeared that they couldn't even keep the peace.

Even though the radical party was able to carry the elections of 1779, the next sequence of events saw the political initiative in the city pass to the city's leading conservative businessmen. These businessmen came to gather in a meeting at the London Coffee House on June 8, 1780, and hammered out an ingenious,

Patriot Capital or Tory Stronghold?

pragmatic solution to the major problems.

First they agreed to form a private bank that would raise money to pay bounties to men who enlisted in the American Army, and provide the soldiers with sufficient rations and rum.

Then, within the next three days the merchants subscribed 270,000 pounds of hard British currency, an awesome sum, with which they purchased flour, beef, pork, sugar, coffee, and salt. These provisions then went into military and civilian distribution channels, and had the effect of sharply reducing food prices.

The radicals lost their grip on local politics as it became clear that the long-distrusted merchants had saved not only the army, but the commercial life of the city and its inhabitants, who now began to spend more time eating and less time running amok in the streets.

Philadelphia again became politically one of the most moderate of the American cities.

Just the same, its government would never be as the city's founder, William Penn, had fondly dreamed a century before that it might become: " . . . a part of religion itself, a thing sacred in its institution and end." ★★★

Continental currency, source of the phrase "not worth a continental."

The British Came – And Were Welcome

They not only came, they also saw, and if they didn't conquer, they at least had a good time. The British occupation of Philadelphia wasn't exactly a trial by fire.

By David Markowitz

First came the light horse . . . in clean dress uniforms and their bright swords glittering in the sun. After that came the foot, headed by Lord Cornwallis. Before him went a band of music, which played a solemn tune . . . called 'God Save Great George Our King.' "

And so through the eyes of one citizen did the British enter Philadelphia early on the late summer morning of September 26, 1777. General Washington's army had departed, ultimately for the wintry refuge of Valley Forge, and the revolutionary American government had fled.

Many of Philadelphia's citizens had also departed before British General Sir William Howe's army arrived, fearing reprisals against supporters of the Revolution. The Quakers, quietly apprehensive, preferred to stay, hoping to remain neutral. The Loyalists — and there were many — welcomed the British with open arms, hoping for a long occupation.

A large number of Philadelphians viewed the occupation as relief from arbitrary restrictions imposed by the Continental Congress, whose authority was not generally accepted. In the summer preceding the occupation, Congress had ordered all private stores of food and other materials removed beyond the city limits. Homes and shops were searched, and seizures were made with empty promises of future compensation. Civilians had become angry at continental troopers' petty larceny and officers' impressment of horses, wagons, and blankets.

Nor had all Philadelphians necessarily been overjoyed with the congressional fiats banning horse racing, cockfights, dancing, the theater, and other entertainments on the grounds that there was a war going on.

And so, as the British marched up Second Street, Philadelphians were in no mood to resist. In return, the British had no intention of rocking the boat.

A Philadelphian who was 10 years old at the time later recalled: "Several of them (the British) addressed me thus: 'How do you do, young one?' 'How are you my boy?' It was in a brotherly tone that seems still to vibrate on my ear. Then they reached out their hands, and several caught mine, and shook it not with an exulting shake of conquerors, as I thought, but with a sympathizing one for the vanquished."

Observed another citizen, "It was a solemn and impressive day, but I saw no exultation in the enemy, nor indeed in those who were reckoned favorable to their success."

Immediately after marching into the city, the British quietly set about solving their first major problem, the quartering of troops. A large part of Howe's army was quickly settled on the city's open squares. The remaining troops encamped along the road to Germantown.

Officers prepared to move into more appropriate quarters. Empty homes, previously occupied by revolutionaries, were requisitioned without consulting the missing owners. For lodging in houses still occupied, the owners were generally politely consulted, and not imposed on.

Wrote Elizabeth Drinker in her diary on October 6, "An officer called this afternoon to ask if we could take a sick or wounded captain. I put him off by saying that as my husband was from me I should be pleased if he could provide some other convenient place. He hoped he had given no offense and departed."

But some other officers searching for lodging were not quite as cordial. One officer was so perturbed when denied quarters that he shattered the front door in pieces with his sword. Another, after being granted his request for lodging, refused to allow the owner entry through the front door, permitting the man to enter his own house only by the back alley entrance.

Accommodating an officer was not as simple as quartering one man. They traveled "en troupe." One major arrived with three servants, three Hessians, three cows, two sheep, two turkeys and several fowl.

Sometimes an initial antipathy was replaced by a feeling of mutual admiration. Recalled one woman,". . . the reception of one old officer was opposed to the utmost of civil resistance, . . . (but he was) as intent on gaining admission as he would have been of urging on the surrender of a fortress.

"The family formed a terrible idea of him, and thought they should have a more uncomfortable time with such a blustering inmate, but by degrees this subsided, and they became so pleased with him that 'Captain Scott' was quoted as authority by them upon every occasion."

In conclusion she said, "The officers very generally, I believe, behaved with politeness to the inhabitants, and many of them upon going away expressed their satisfaction that no injury to the city was contemplated by their commander. They said that living among the inhabitants, and speaking the same language made them uneasy at the thought of acting as enemies."

Which is not to say that the sojourn of the British Army in Philadelphia was free of unpleasantness. Reported the *Pennsylvania Gazette:* "All the favor shown us is the liberty of being plundered as friends to the Crown and not as rebels, and of starving in the streets instead of starving in a gaol."

One woman recalled that near the British encampments hardly a wood or a fence was left standing and many wooden buildings were destroyed.

All of the furnishings of the State House — Independence Hall — were used for firewood, and some of the paneling was torn off to keep the stove fires

British General Sir William Howe: A surprisingly popular conqueror . . .

Patriot Capital or Tory Stronghold?

British newspapers often published cartoons supporting the complaint of British soldiers serving in America that they were underpaid.

going for the five companies of British artillery quartered on the first floor.

Americans taken prisoner by the British at the battles of Brandywine and Germantown, or when the American Navy was caught still on the wharf when the British moved into Philadelphia, were housed on the second floor of the building.

The able-bodied prisoners were in the council chamber and in the committee room, while the wounded lay on pallets in the long gallery. The conditions, especially right at the start of the occupation, were crowded and miserable.

An American officer, Persifor Frazer, wrote a letter about conditions that was carried to General Washington by his wife, complaining that "many of us were here for six days without having any provisions served to us, and for many weeks after our allowance did not exceed from four to six ounces of salt pork (a day) and about half a pound of very ordinary biscuits per day."

These rations were later supplemented, however, by food that was brought to the prisoners by local women, "without which we must have all inevitably perished," Frazer says. The women may also have helped with the nursing of wounded, some of whom had received no medical attention at all, according to Frazer, during the first month of captivity.

Frazer had other complaints. "The windows were also nailed down, though the smoke occasioned by a stove below stairs in the guard room, and the badness of the chimnies has been for many days ... almost intolerable," he continued.

Frazer and another prisoner both gave accounts — as if it were a scandal — of an episode in which one of the captured American officers ordered a Negro janitor employed by the British to sweep out the Americans' quarters. When the black man refused, the officer tried to hit him, at which point a British guard stepped in, brandished his bayonet, and threatened to run the captured American through.

"A certain Capt. Hogg refused to punish ... (the) Negro ... " one of the amazed accounts continued, "but in direct words said that the Negro was as good as any of us."

When the Americans returned to the city, the building was a wreck and a pesthole. A William Hurrie was paid as amount roughly equal to a year's rent for an average house to clean the place out, paint it, and accomplish other necessary repairs.

The task took him from June 26 to August 17, and his bill included the cost of several quarts of whisky that had apparently helped bolster his crew of workmen during the task.

The bell that would become the Liberty Bell was also returned to the State House tower after the occupation from its hiding place in Allentown. All of the city's bells had been removed out of fear that they would be melted down by the British to be made into bullets.

●

For the record, General Howe issued before his army's arrival a proclamation guaranteeing security and protection to those who remained quietly in their dwellings. A leading Tory, Joseph Galloway, announced no provisions should be taken from "well-affected citizens."

But most often British officers looked the other way when confronted with any reports of looting.

The officers, in fact, were not above

doing a little of it themselves. A young French painter named du Simitiere who was in Philadelphia at the time the British were preparing to evacuate the city paid a surprise visit on Major John Andre, who was living in Benjamin Franklin's home.

Du Simitiere was amazed to find Andre busily engaged in packing up some of the books from Franklin's library. Andre was not dissuaded by the young Frenchman's expressions of outrage. In fact, in addition to the books he took with him a portrait of Franklin by Benjamin Wilson that he had taken a fancy to.

Andre's larcenous activities, however, contrasted sharply with the punctilious propriety with which General Knyphausen, a Hessian, took care of John Cadwalader's home.

Knyphausen was a small, sharp-featured man who became widely known in Philadelphia during his stay there for

A British Grenadier

his elaborately courteous manner, including his way of bowing deeply when greeting strangers on the street.

Prior to his departure, the German general summoned Cadwalader's agent to the home, and presented him with an inventory of the items in the home, indicating that nothing had been removed or disturbed — not even a single bottle in Cadwalader's extensive wine cellar.

Then Knyphausen further amazed the agent by presenting him with a payment — rent for the period he had spent in the house. Cadwalader at the time was one of Washington's officers, and had led one of the echelons attacking the Hessians at Trenton the previous winter.

•

There were, though, more serious problems for the citizens than the widespread plundering — at least at first. The scarcity of provisions and the poor state of the economy caused numerous hardships.

At the outset of the occupation, civilians found provisions hard to obtain and high in price. British currency was scarce and unfamiliar. No one, needless to say, would take the Continental money printed by the Congress, which had retreated first to Lancaster, and then to York. Although Pennsylvania colonial currency was supposed to be legal tender, many merchants refused it as well.

The city was largely cut off from the countryside. The Continental Congress and the Pennsylvania Assembly declared that anyone bringing fuel or provisions into the city would be liable to punishment by death, and detachments of troops guarded the approaches to the city.

Therefore, at first, frequent raids were made outside the city to supply provisions. Sympathizers aided the raiders.

General Washington had some success in dismantling the flour mills in the Wilmington region, seriously hindering the British. He was even more successful in cutting off traffic from the countryside, and down the Schuylkill.

But eventually the superior British forces opened the Delaware, and ships arrived from England. Dry goods again became plentiful, and by New Year's business was as active as ever. One British officer reported in his letters that "when we had been in the city but four weeks, and the ships arrived from New York, everything became as lively, even livelier, than in peacetime."

An American woman informed a correspondent: ". . . everything is gay and happy, and it is like to prove a frolicking winter."

By his EXCELLENCY
Sir WILLIAM HOWE, K. B.
General and Commander in Chief, &c. &c. &c.

PROCLAMATION.

WHEREAS It is expedient for the Security of the Inhabitants, the Suppression of Vice and Licentiousness, the Preservation of the Peace, the Support of the Poor, the Maintenance of the nightly Watch and Lamps, and the Regulation of the Markets and Ferries, with other Matters in which the Oeconomy, Peace, and good Order of the City of Philadelphia and its Environs are concerned, that a Police be established; I do therefore constitute and appoint JOSEPH GALLOWAY, Esq; SUPERINTENDENT GENERAL, assisted by three Magistrates of the Police, to be hereafter appointed, with Powers and Authority to make such Orders and Regulations from Time to Time, as may most effectually promote the salutary Ends above proposed, and to nominate and appoint such a Number of inferior Officers under them as may be found necessary to carry the said Orders and Regulations into Effect: And that their Authority shall extend in and over the Country lying between the Rivers Delaware and Schuylkill, and within the Chain of Redoubts from River to River: And I do hereby enjoin and require all Persons whatever, to pay due Obedience to the SUPERINTENDENT GENERAL, Chief Magistrates, and all others acting in Authority under them, in the Execution of their Duty, and all military Officers commanding Guards, to aid and assist them where it shall be found necessary.

Given under my Hand at Head-Quarters in Philadelphia, this 4th Day of December, 1777.
W. HOWE.

By his Excellency's Command,
ROBERT MACKENZIE, Secretary.

PHILADELPHIA, Printed by JAMES HUMPHREYS, Junr. in Market-Street, between Front and Second Street.

So it was. The troops, for the most part, had little to do, in terms of military duties. One sergeant wrote: "Our two battalions of light infantry gave the covering parties for the wood-cutters in front of the lines, (and that was) . . . the only duty we did."

The British, however, having conquered the city by force of arms, were not about to give themselves over to terminal ennui. The officers busied themselves with a series of theatrical productions, and a whirl of social life developed in the city, while Washington and his men were enduring Valley Forge.

The "other ranks" filled their free time with general fraternizing with the city's inhabitants. The city's taverns were "well-attended," says one historian.

Horse racing was revived during the occupation, with races being staged out in the area north of the city that the British had cleared as a sort of "no man's land."

The officers also sought to keep the men gainfully employed as stagehands for the theatrical productions, and in the construction of assorted pavilions and other structures that figured in the officers' dances and other entertainments.

The highlight of the lively social season was the famed "Meschianza," a huge entertainment staged by General Howe's officers on May 18 in honor of the commanding general's departure for England.

A month later the British occupation ended on a note of utter anticlimax. The British marched out as the result of a strategic order to consolidate British forces at New York. Many of the Tories followed them.

Philadelphia's last nine months as a city of the British Empire were over. ★ ★ ★

Patriot Capital or Tory Stronghold?

John Pemberton

Quaker modesty and reticence, which forbade portraits, also cost the Quakers their power and influence.

Benjamin Chew

The Quakers Didn't Go to War — But They Lost

The Quakers sat out the American Revolution. They did not sign the Declaration of Independence. Most of them refused to fight in the war or to recognize the Continental Congress. None of them took a hand in writing the Constitution.

It seems, in some ways, an odd stance. Certainly the Quakers had no great love for the British ministry or king. As Philadelphia's leading merchants, they were as upset as their fellow countrymen by English attempts to squeeze taxes from the colonies, and they joined heartily in all the preliminary measures of resistance.

Some fifty Quaker merchants, for example, signed the non-importation agreement to defeat the Stamp Act of 1765. But their influence on Philadelphia's growing resistance movement was a conservative one. When the act was repealed, Bostonians and New Yorkers lit great bonfires and burned effigies of the King. Quaker-dominated Philadelphia, in contrast, celebrated the event by quietly sending King George a dignified declaration.

This same tempering influence operated again in 1773, when the English attempt to force tea on the colonies precipitated the dramatic act in Boston harbor.

In Philadelphia, the consignees of the tea were two Quaker firms — T. & I. Wharton and James & Drinker — and, like their Boston counterparts, they refused to accept the shipment. It was typical of Quaker Philadelphia, though, that the tea was neither dumped nor burned, but carefully consigned back to London.

John Dickinson, the well-known "penman of the revolution," probably exemplifies the Quaker attitude during the pre-war period. An articulate lawyer, he wrote nearly every important pre-revolutionary state papers — the appeals to the King and English people and the Declaration of Rights. His *Letters from a Pennsylvania Farmer* of 1767-68 gave the legal and historic basis for American claims.

But in 1776, John Dickinson refused to sign the Declaration of Independence. "He would have preferred to continue appealing for justice from the English people. He would have waited to take advantage of a change of English ministry, of the hundred ways of solving a problem and securing honorable claims, of a resistance stopping short of arms," one historian explains.

When the movement for independence overwhelmed the prudent and circumspect Quakers, and the war began, Philadelphia's monthly meetings admonished their members to "be quiet and mind your own business," and to stay clear of all the "commotions," a favorite word of the Friends.

Their pacifism, of course, set them solidly against war. They believed in resistance only by peaceful means, and the key statement of the Declaration of Independence — that people have a right to violently overthrow oppressive governments — was not a view they shared.

Thus, Friends refused to recognize or support in any way the new Continental Congress. They would not fight for it, pay taxes to it, use its money or pledge allegiance to it. But, on the other hand, neither would they assist Britain in "the unrighteous means taken to conquer rebellious Provinces." They would stay out of the whole business, giving no aid or comfort to either party.

Friends who strayed from this position were "read out of meeting." One of the first to go was Thomas Mifflin, who later became a general and then governor of Pennsylvania.

An estimated four or five hundred other Philadelphia Quakers also joined up with the American Army or helped the Congress to finance the insurrection.

Disowned by their meetings, some formed a new group — called the Free Quakers, and built the small meeting house that still stands at Fifth and Arch Streets. Differing from other Quakers only in not disowning people for military service or other related transgressions, Free Quakers died out by 1820. Betsy Ross, the putative flag maker, was the last surviving member.

Also "read out" were about 20 Quakers who fought with the British Army.

The vast majority of Quakers, maintained strict neutrality, a position which spelled Tory to avid American patriots and subjected some of the Quakers to severe suffering. The most serious actions against the Quakers began in 1777, when the British Army approached Philadelphia.

That fall, the nervous Continental Congress advised the Council of Pennsylvania to arrest those Philadelphians "who have not manifested their attachment to the American cause," most notably "a number of persons of considerable wealth who profess themselves to belong to a society of people called Quakers."

The Council quickly (and arbitrarily) arrested about 40 people, among them such prominent Friends as the Pembertons, the Fishers, Thomas Wharton and Henry Drinker.

There was no trial, no hearing. The 40 were hurried into confinement, their houses were searched and their desks broken into during the search for compromising papers. A promise to remain in their houses was demanded of them. In effect they were under house arrest.

When the 17 Quakers in the group and three others protested the arrest as an outrage, they were banished to Winchester, Virginia, where they were kept in nominal confinement through the winter — all at their own expense.

The group was released in the spring, with something of an apology, after their wives appealed to General Washington.

Those Quakers who remained in the city didn't fare much better. The windows of some Friends' homes were broken with stones; they were hooted at in the streets. Others were jailed and their property confiscated. The meetings' estimates of property loss suffered by their members amounted to 50,000 pounds by the end of the war, roughly equivalent to half a million dollars today.

More importantly for the long run, the Quakers lost power and influence during the Revolution. Though they acknowledged their reconciliation with the new American government in 1787, their refusal to participate in its founding, and the bitterness against them for their neutrality, placed them outisde the mainstream of American political life. Never again would the Quakers dominate Philadelphia.

Contemporary historians differ in their judgements of the early Quakers. E. Digby Baltzell, in his book *The Philadelphia Gentlemen*, accuses them of irresponsibility:

"To have refrained from participating in the series of stirring events which took place in Philadelphia between 1776 and 1787 was to have missed one of the greatest opportunities for statesmanship in world history."

On the other side, Historian J. William Frost, curator of the Quaker collection at Swarthmore College, supports the position of the early Friends. "Who can say that if more Americans had been of the Quakers' mind, all that was secured by war could not have been secured by diplomacy? The U. S. might have been able to separate peacefully from England, as did Canada and Australia, and the bloodshed and bitterness avoided.

"I don't find the Revolution a cause for celebration. It has given us a legacy of violence and militarism which is still very much with us today."—*Julia Cass*

Henry Drinker

James Pemberton

John Parrish

Parade of the Knights of the Burning Mountain on the lawn of the Wharton Mansion.

"... So Elegant an Entertainment"

'... amidst all
the criticism
no one disputed
the fact that
it was one
incredible party . . .'

The Meschianza was different things to different people.

One of Philadelphia's young lovelies remarked wistfully after it was all over, "We never had, and never shall have again, so elegant an entertainment in America. . . ."

John Andre, the dashing young British major who thought up the full day in May full of medieval games, dancing, and dining to celebrate the departure of British General Sir William Howe, regarded the whole thing as a terrific success. "The most splendid entertainment ever given by an army to its general," said he.

But others were less enthused. A Quaker lady remarked caustically in her diary, "This day may be remembered by many for the scenes of folly and vanity."

Abigail Adams, when accounts of what the Philadelphians had been up to reached her in New England, was frosty. "An outrage on all decency," she told one correspondent, adding that it was her understanding that the gowns of the women were so low-cut that the women looked like so many "nursing mothers."

Nor were people back in England necessarily delighted by the reports of the gala extravaganza for a general who had not, after all, won the war, and who, in fact, had seemed perfectly happy to peacefully co-exist with Washington's army, which had been only a few miles away at Valley Forge all winter.

"Our officers were practicing at the dice-box," one London editorialist penned, "when they should have been storming towns, and crushing the spirit of rebellion." He continued with a tasteless reference to Mrs. Joshua Loring, who had provided General Howe with female companionship during the winter in Philadelphia:

"The harlot's eye," he wrote, "glistened with wanton pleasure at the general's table, when the brightness of his sword should have reflected terror in the face of the rebel."

The occasion was, in fact, the method chosen by Howe's officers, who had followed him through the victories at Long Island, Brandywine and Germantown, not to mention a very pleasant occupation tour in Philadelphia, of demonstrating their dissatisfaction at his having been recalled.

The "brilliant farewell," another British officer wrote home, "was doubly dear to (the) commander, for it expressed (the) . . . belief that the ministry had wronged him."

Yet, amidst all of this criticism, no one disputed that the Meschianza (from the Italian, meaning "to mix") was one incredible party.

The attention to detail was meticulous. Andre designed special invitations, or tickets, to the affair, which showed a shield emblazoned with a sunset seascape, and bearing the legend, *Luceo Discendens Aucto Splendore Resurgam*. This, freely translated, means, "Departing I shine; I shall arise again in added splendor." Tomorrow, it was implied, would be another day for General Howe.

The affair itself began on the afternoon of May 18, 1778, with a "grand regatta." All of the British officers, selected American guests, and almost every unattached young lady in Philadelphia, gathered at Knight's Wharf on the Delaware to begin the trip down to the Wharton mansion.

(Not all of Philadelphia's marriageable young ladies were there, however. After a discussion with a delegation of leading Quakers, Edward Shippen had forbidden his daughters to attend. The young ladies, who had prepared their gowns, and whose names had been listed on the programs, were reportedly inconsolable. And, in addition to the young ladies of Philadelphia, two British officers invited dates down from New York for the occasion.)

The guests and officers sat in barges and galleys, which were, in turn, surrounded by other boats bedecked with flags. Leading each of the three divisions of this parade of vessels were flatboats on which a band was playing. The oarsmen rowed "regular to harmony" with the music, according to impresario Andre. The shore was teeming with spectators.

On arriving at the wharf near the mansion, the assemblage passed through lines of grenadiers and cavalry.

This cordoned corridor led to a lawn, about 150 yards square, which, surrounded by soldiery, was to be the scene of the afternoon's entertainment — a jousting tournament between the Knights of the Burning Mountain and Knights of the Blended Rose.

The ladies were seated in canopied grandstands and both the stands and the ladies were decorated in the colors of the appropriate team. Young ladies who accompanied a Knight of the Blended Rose, for instance, wore flowing robes of white silk, which were open in front to the waist. Their waists were cinched with a six-inch-wide pink sash, sprinkled with spangles.

In the center of things was Peggy Chew, daughter of the former Chief Justice of the Province, who was reigning as "Queen of the Tilt."

After much sounding of trumpets and saluting of ladies, seven armored Blended Rosers on gray chargers caparisoned in red and white charged headlong against seven Burning Mountainites clad in black and orange armor, and astride black horses.

Andre provides us with this account of what ensued: "The knights, . . . encountering in full gallop, shivered their spears. In the second and third encounters they discharged their pistols. In the fourth they fought with their swords. At length the two chiefs, spurring forward into the centre, engaged furiously in single combat 'til the Marshal of the Field, Major Gwyne, rushed in between the chiefs, and declared that the fair damsels of the Blended Rose and Burning Mountain were perfectly satisfied with the proofs of love, and the signal feats of valor given by their respective knights. (He) . . . commanded . . . that they should instantly desist . . ."

The knights and ladies then proceeded to the ballroom of the Wharton mansion, where refreshments were served. (The Whartons, incidentally, were not present. Thomas Wharton, along with a number of other prominent Quakers, had been arrested by order of the American Congress, and marched to Winchester, Va., where they were being held in custody.)

Andre had painted the walls to resemble rose-pink Siena marble, and bedecked the hall with pale blue drapes, mirrors, pink ribbons, and artificial flowers. The floor was painted blue, with a design of golden circles.

Dancing began, and continued until 10 p.m., when the windows were thrown open, and a display of fireworks began. At midnight, supper was announced. Large, concealed folding doors were swung back to disclose an elegantly set, and brilliantly candlelit, supper table, attended by 24 black slaves in oriental dress.

Dancing and gambling at a faro table continued until 4 a.m. The only untoward moment occurred when two small units of American troops attacked British fortifications north of the city while the dancing was in full swing.

But calm was preserved at the Meschianza, where the ladies were assured that the fusilade was in honor of the occasion.

—*Kathy Nagurny*

The young lady models the coiffure designed by Major Andre.

The Meschianza invitation shows Howe's sun setting— to rise again.

Once to Every Man and Nation...

By Edgar Williams

I t's possible to generalize, to an extent, about what sorts of people remained loyal to the King, and which chose to cast their lot with an independent America.

"Almost all persons who enjoyed public office under the Crown became Tories," J. Franklin Jameson noted in his book, *The American Revolution Considered as a Social Movement.*

One reason was that officeholders had, by definition, a vested interest in maintaining the status quo, which included their relatively handsome salaries for not particularly burdensome governmental duties.

But there was another factor at work as well. These officials had taken an oath to support the King, and in the 18th cen-

... But what to decide? Which was the good, and which the evil side? For this difficult choice, each man had to look into his own heart. Honest and reasonable men found different answers there.

tury a man's pledge was worth somewhat more than it often appears to be in our own time.

When a band of American soldiers encountered two young men on a New Jersey road who were en route to join a Loyalist brigade, the Americans simply exacted a pledge from the men that they would not do that, and turned them loose.

It was almost as predictable that colonial merchants would favor independence, a fact that undermines any attempt to use Marxist analysis on the American Revolution. While the Revolution would have profound effects on the social structure of America, it did not begin as a class struggle.

The reasons for the merchants' tendency toward Whiggery — the Revolutionaries were known as Whigs — was pragmatic enough. One of the most potent underlying causes of American discontent with royal rule had been Parliament's attempt to limit and control American trade.

Rev. Jacob Duche

John Dickinson

Benjamin Rush

Americans were proscribed from making many items, from trading with foreign powers, and from expanding beyond the Appalachians — all factors that hurt the merchants.

And it was the affluent merchants who were the most annoyed by the persistent and bothersome—if never very successful — English attempts to curtail smuggling and to collect tax revenues from the Americans to at least partially defray the cost of the joint British-American war effort against the French and Indians.

The aristocracy — the landed and affluent — did different things in different places. In Boston, the 1,100 Loyalists who sailed away with Howe when he evacuated the city probably included a majority of the established aristocracy of that commonwealth.

But in Virginia, the plantation owners not only joined the Revolution, but provided most of its important leaders — George Mason, George Washington, Peyton Randolph, Thomas Jefferson, James Monroe.

Until Andrew Jackson was elected President in 1825, it seemed to be almost a requirement for the job that one be a member of either the Virginia aristocracy or the Adams family.

The irreverent have noted, however, that the Virginia planters were usually deeply in debt to English creditors.

The richer farmers in general, Jameson believes, did tend to be Loyalists, as did members of the Church of England.

On the other hand, "the debtor class was, as was natural, and as has been true the whole world over, mainly on the side of Revolution," he states.

Most lawyers were Whigs, though probably fewer of the richer lawyers were for the Revolution than was the case among the more impecunious members of the bar. Doctors probably broke down in much the same way.

Colonists who had recently arrived were more likely to be Loyalists; Scots were, by reputation, pro-English. No one is sure about the Irish. Some authorities think they were the backbone of the Revolution, that the bulk of Washington's army spoke Gaelic. Other studies have indicated that colonists born in Ireland were more likely to be Loyalists than colonists born in England. But, Jameson adds, in Pennsylvania "where the proportion of Irish or Scots-Irish population was greatest, it was unquestionably their influence that carried the state for independence."

Younger men were more likely than old to espouse the Revolution — but the Franklins were not the only exception to that rule.

Many factors played a role. Becoming a Whig required that one associate oneself with such outrageous demagogues as Sam Adams and Patrick Henry, whose incompetence at everything they had laid a hand to was notorious.

Even persons who thought America was being badly mistreated by England, or who believed with all their heart that the national destiny required independence, might have been hard to stomach the radical rhetoric of democracy and equality being mouthed by some of the Revolutionary leaders.

And times were not bad in America. The system under which the colonies had operated for 150 years had not failed.

But finally each American had to make his or her own decision. And the reasons may have been as numerous as there were Americans.

On the following pages are the stories of the moments of decision of a few Philadelphians.

Benjamin Franklin

Joseph Galloway

Charles Thomson

Patriot Capital or Tory Stronghold?

Franklin Under Fire

Franklin's love of the British was shattered when Lord Wedderburn called him a criminal. It was an unfortunate choice of words.

It is an article of faith among most historians that Benjamin Franklin did not opt for independence until July 1775, two months after the convening of the Second Continental Congress, at which Franklin was a delegate from Pennsylvania.

Not so. Franklin made up his mind on Jan. 29, 1774, as he stood motionless and silent in "The Cockpit" — the floor of the meeting place of the Privy Council of Lords in London — and took a ferocious tongue-lashing from Alexander Wedderburn, Solicitor General of England.

In his diatribe before a glittering assemblage of British notables, Wedderburn charged Franklin with every crime from theft to the plotting of a revolution to set up an American republic. Wedderburn demanded that Franklin be removed from his office as deputy postmaster general for America, and alleged that Franklin was "so possessed with the idea of a Great American Republic that he may easily slide into the language of the minister of a foreign independent state."

Franklin, attired in a dress suit of Manchester velvet, remained impassive throughout.

Interestingly, Franklin was not, at the time, in favor of independence for America. Quite the contrary. What he foresaw was a natural and gradual transfer of power within the British Empire from the British Isles to America. As a consequence of its natural and inevitable growth, America would, he believed, eventually become the tail that wagged the dog.

The American colonies should simply bide their time, he believed, taking advantage of Britain's weak moments to demand ever wider privileges and powers for themselves. Britain, he pointed out in letters home, was deeply in debt, and when another war came, the situation would become desperate. "Then is the time," Franklin counseled, "to say, 'Redress our grievances!' ... Our claims will then be attended to, and our complaints regarded."

Franklin had great love for England. He actually saw ahead to the time when England would need America standing beside her — and believed that would be America's proper role. Remember, Franklin urged, "that this Protestant country — our mother, though lately an unkind one — is worth preserving, and that her weight in the scale of Europe, and her safety in a great degree, may depend on our union with her."

So why was Franklin standing before the House of Lords, and sustaining this torrent of abuse? It's a complex story, involving some purloined letters.

Readers should perhaps be forewarned that Franklin's conduct in the episode may not appear unblemished when judged by the standards of a post-Watergate morality, though Franklin himself never doubted his own rectitude, and was unable to understand those who did. Franklin believed that his ends justified his means.

The proceeding that occasioned Franklin's appearance before the House of Lords was a petition from the Massa-

A nineteenth century artist painted this depiction of Benjamin Franklin's moment of humiliation before the Privy Council of the House of Lords. Franklin listened silently—then made his choice.

chusetts legislature calling for the removal from office of Thomas Hutchinson and Andrew Oliver, the governor and lieutenant governor, respectively, of that colony.

Hutchinson, in particular, was a breed of man who was to be found widely in America in the 1770s, but who most history books ignore. He was a man of unblemished integrity, widely acknowledged brilliance, and imbued with a great love for the American land in which he was born — but who also believed that America should be subject to British rule. Logic and order required it.

Hutchinson and Oliver were both intransigent in their belief that the British Parliament held absolute supremacy over the colonies — meaning, among other things, that they considered the cry "No taxation without representation" to be utter nonsense.

In its petition, the radical-controlled Massachusetts legislature charged that the two sought to "suppress the very spirit of freedom" and had formed a conspiratorial cabal "to raise their own fortunes and advance themselves ... not only to the destruction of the constitution and

charter of this province but at the expense of the rights and liberties of the American colonies."

But the hearing, held in the midst of the furor created by reception of news of the Boston Tea Party, resulted in a vote of confidence for Hutchinson and Oliver. And Franklin was tarred as "seditious" and "ruthless."

What got Franklin into the bind was his acquisition in December 1772 — by means that never have been satisfactorily determined — of letters written by Hutchinson and Oliver to Thomas Whately, a former secretary to the British Treasury under George Grenville. Franklin sent the letters to Thomas Cushing, speaker of the Massachusetts legislature, telling Cushing that the letters must not be copied, but could be shown to the proper people.

Franklin always claimed that his sole purpose in returning the letters to Boston was to clear the British ministry of the blame the colonists had wrongly heaped upon it and restore tranquility between the colonies and England by making scapegoats of the "very mischie-

vous men" who could now be seen in the letters to have "laid the foundations of most, if not all, our present grievances." To wit, Hutchinson and Oliver.

The letters, in which Hutchinson in particular argued vehemently that the government should assert more vigorously its authority over the colonies, were intended to serve only as a basis for the legislature's petition. But in June 1773, the letters were leaked, probably by Samuel Adams. Soon, the letters, suitably edited to make Hutchinson and Oliver look as bad as possible, began appearing in newspapers throughout the colonies.

The news of the publication of these presumably stolen private letters created an uproar in London. Franklin, then colonial agent for Pennsylvania, Georgia and Massachusetts, wrote to Cushing that his role must be kept secret or his usefulness in England would be at an end. But in December, when a brother of Whately accused another man of stealing the letters, and the two fought a duel, Franklin published a statement that he alone was responsible for securing the letters and sending them to Boston.

Dickinson's Dilemma

Although John Dickinson, also a wealthy Philadelphia lawyer, was by conviction almost as conservative as Galloway, he opted for independence when all the chips were down. This came about despite the fact that he had worked in the Continental Congress against passage of the Declaration of Independence.

John Dickinson was a complex personality, and different aspects of his character were placed at war with one another by the need to decide for or against independence. Perhaps he had too much of the spirit of compromise for Revolutionary times. Many reviled him, but he was always his own man.

Unquestionably, Dickinson was a patriot. During 1767 and 1768 he had written a tough-minded pamphlet, *Letters from a Farmer in Pennsylvania to the Inhabitants of the British Colonies,* in which he argued convincingly that while the British Parliament had the right to regulate trade in the colonies, it did not have the right to raise revenues in the guise of duties on trade. He was hailed, as a result, as "the penman of the Revolution."

But Dickinson was opposed to violent resistance. He worked tirelessly to find some way of resolving the conflict through conciliation.

It wasn't until after the Declaration that Dickinson came to his moment of decision. "The lines have been drawn," he told his wife. "I am an American, and America has set its course. Now I must help my country reach safe harbor."

Whereupon John Dickinson, the man who had opposed the Declaration, took up arms and fought valiantly for independence in the War of the Revolution.

After the national Constitutional Convention of 1787 and the Delaware Constitutional Convention of 1792, in both of which he played a vital part, Dickinson retired. He died in Wilmington on February 14, 1808, at the age of 75. ★ ★ ★

Thus it was that he was called before the Privy Council hearing on the petition.

And, as Wedderburn flogged him verbally before a brilliant assemblage of high clergy and members of the nobility, Franklin made up his mind that reconciliation now was impossible.

He made this clear in two letters he wrote the next day. In one, to his friend Joseph Galloway in Philadelphia, Franklin wrote that if the ministry had really been interested in reconciliation, as they had professed to be, they should have thanked him for the opportunity he had given them "... but they chose rather to abuse me, an opportunity I shall never give them again."

The other letter was to his son, William Franklin, the Loyalist governor of New Jersey, in which he stated bitterly that "as of yesterday" he had had his fill "of the corruption of this government." He entreated his son to "get out of government" and to "become a gentleman farmer." He had been dismissed as deputy postmaster general, Franklin wrote, and soon would be returning to America "to do whatever it may be that I can do for my native land."

Franklin never forgot that day in 1774.

On Feb. 6, 1778, at the signing of the treaty of alliance between the United States and France, the Comte de Vergennes, the French foreign minister, complimented Franklin on the appearance of the suit of Manchester velvet he was wearing.

"I have worn it only once before," Franklin said. "That was four years ago on a day of humiliation. I made a vow then that I would not put on this suit again until the day I felt certain my country was assured of absolute and unlimited independence. Today is that day." ★ ★ ★

Governor Thomas Hutchinson (with mace of office) and his lieutenant governor (without wig) flee a Boston mob after letters purloined by Franklin were published in Massachusetts.

THE FOUNDING CITY

Joseph Galloway Gets a Message

Joseph Galloway was a longtime friend of Benjamin Franklin's, and the friendship obviously ran deep. For, although the two wound up on opposing sides in the conflict, Franklin never could bring himself to denounce Galloway. For decades they had fought together in the political war of the colonies. As comrades, they had brought to power the forces opposing the Penn family proprietorship of the commonwealth.

Galloway was a wealthy Philadelphia lawyer and an ultra-conservative who opposed separation from England, although he favored stringent measures for compelling the British government to redress the grievances of the colonists. As a delegate to the First Continental Congress in 1774, he had fought vigorously for his beliefs. And in the Pennsylvania Assembly in early 1775 he had courageously carried on the fight.

But his courage could carry him just so far. And one night in February 1775, he underwent a traumatic experience that set him on the road toward becoming a virulent and proscriptive Loyalist. His mind was made up after he found on his doorstep a box containing a hangman's noose and a note that read: "Hang yourself, or we shall do it for you."

Initially Galloway said that such threats had only made him more determined "to oppose those lawless measures" being passed by the Second Continental Congress that he believed were inciting sedition.

But at the very least the threat coincided with Galloway's realization that his power to influence the Congress was coming to an end.

A short time later, Galloway was requested to draft a message for the governor, but while he was away doing so the rest of the committee he was on met and adopted a more militant message than Galloway had proposed.

Galloway called the action "one of the most dirty and scandalous measures which ever was transacted in public life."

Historian Merrill Jensen notes that "despite the justice of his charge, the house adopted the committee's version by a vote of 22-15."

In May, Galloway asked to be excused from serving as a delegate to the Second Continental Congress. The request was granted and, ironically, Galloway was succeeded by Franklin, who had just returned from England. The most effective spokesman for loyalty was replaced by the arch-schemer for independence.

After independence was declared in 1776, Galloway fled to the protection of the British Army in New York. When the British occupied Philadelphia in 1777, Galloway returned to serve as the city's civil administrator under Gen. Howe. Forced to flee Philadelphia again when the British evacuated the city in 1778, Galloway went to England, where he lived out his life in unhappy exile. ★★★

Rev. Duche's Conversion

Ever since he had delivered the opening prayer at the third day's session of the First Continental Congress, the Rev. Jacob Duche had been one of Philadelphia's most ardent and eloquent Patriots. He was chaplain to both Congresses. On July 19, 1775, on the first national day of prayer, he had delivered a fiery sermon at Christ Church, where he was rector, excoriating Great Britain for the wrongs she had done to her colonies in North America.

But now it was after nightfall on October 7, 1777, and Duche was in jail. The British had occupied Philadelphia, and Duche had been incarcerated as "a dangerous radical." Pacing in his cell — cold, alone, and quite afraid — the clergyman considered his plight. And then, perhaps in a flash, the idea occured to him.

He could switch sides.

Next morning, Duche asked for, and was granted, an audience with Sir William Howe, commander of the British forces. He could not stand another night in prison, Duche said, and would do anything to avoid being returned to his cell.

"I take it, then, that you have seen the error of your ways," Howe said.

"I have been in grievous error," the clergyman replied. "But I have never renounced my allegiance to the Crown."

"In that case," Howe said, "you doubtless wish to make amends."

Indeed so, Duche said.

And Howe capitalized immediately on the clergyman's change of heart.

On Oct. 8, at Howe's bidding, Duche sent a letter to Gen. Washington, then with his army in Montgomery County, northwest of Germantown. He urged the commander-in-chief to desert "a degenerate cause." He also begged Washington to "represent to Congress the indispensable necessity of rescinding the hasty and ill-advised Declaration of Independency" and to "recommend, and you have an undoubted right to recommend, an immediate cessation of hostilities."

All this from a man who, in his first prayer before the Congress on Sept. 7, 1774, had invoked the Deity to "defeat the malicious designs of our cruel adversaries."

All this from a man who had thundered from his pulpit on the first national day of prayer: "Alas! If arms must decide the unnatural contest, and Heaven should even smile on our righteous cause, our success cannot be purchased without many a tear, on the part of the victor as well as the vanquished .

All this from a man who on July 4, 1776, after the Declaration had been proclaimed, had enthusiastically complied with a request by the Congress that all references to the Crown be extracted from the Anglican prayer book.

When the British evacuated Philadelphia in May 1778, Duche fled to London. After the Revolution, he made overtures to Washington and others that he be permitted to return. "My heart is in America and I long for my beloved Philadelphia," he wrote in one such plea.

In 1792, Duche finally was permitted to come back to his native city. His property had been confiscated by the Pennsylvania Assembly, and shortly after his return to Philadelphia he was partially paralyzed by a stroke. He died in 1792, a broken man.

Benjamin Rush wrote of Duche: "He was much disordered in the evening of his life, with a tendency to palsy, and with hysteria. He sometimes laughed and cried alternately all day."

Dr. Rush Hears Gunfire

Close by the bridge in Concord, Mass., a monument is emblazoned with these words by Ralph Waldo Emerson:

By the rude bridge that arched the flood,

Their flag to April's breeze unfurled;

Here once the embattled farmers stood,

And fired the shot heard 'round the world.

To the modern ear the sentiment seems tritely hyperbolic. A "shot heard 'round the world" — how poetically presumptuous.

Maybe so. Yet the story of Dr. Benjamin Rush's moment of decision indicates that the reverberation of the fusillade at the bridge did reach at least as far as Philadelphia.

But we are getting ahead of our story.

While the brilliant young Philadelphia physician was completing his medical education at the University of Edinburgh (M.D., 1768) and his residency at St. Thomas' Hospital, London (1768-69), he enjoyed arguing with British colleagues. The issue, of course, was the controversy between Great Britain and the American colonies concerning taxation of the colonists by Parliament.

"I came off rather well," Rush wrote later. "My attachment to political justice

Free Library of Philadelphia

was much increased by my adopting republican principles."

Returning to his native Philadelphia late in 1769, Rush began the practice of medicine and served as a professor of chemistry at the College of Philadelphia (later to become the University of Pennsylvania). He also continued his arguments. Soon he was writing essays for the newspapers in favor of the American cause, though carefully stopping just short of advocating independence.

During the First Continental Congress, Rush had numerous delegates as patients, and as guests in his home. One was Patrick Henry, whom Rush inoculated against smallpox. But although he was privy to details of many of the actions of Congress, Rush still took no outright stand.

Then, in the spring of 1775, the Massachusetts countryside resounded with gunfire, and the shooting war was on. When Rush heard the news, he knew what he must do.

"I (had) continued as a spectator of the events which passed in our country in the winter of 1775," Rush wrote. But, he continued, "the battle of Lexington gave a new tone to my feelings, and I now resolved to bear my share of the duties and burdens of the approaching Revolution. I considered the separation of the colonies from Great Britain as inevitable.

The first gun that was fired at an American cut the cord that tied the two countries together. It was the signal for the commencement of our independence . . ."

One of Rush's first major contributions to the war effort was his close association with — and constant encouragement of — Thomas Paine as that famous firebrand wrote the pamphlet that was to be called *Common Sense*. Rush found a publisher for the pamphlet, a clarion call for independence which converted thousands to the patriot cause.

Rush had no opportunity to vote for the Declaration of Independence, since he was elected to the Continental Congress on July 20, 1776, but he signed the Declaration on August 2, 1776, and served the Revolutionary cause. ★ ★ ★

Thomson: Born To Rebel

It has been said — only partly in jest — that Charles Thomson, the only secretary the First and Second Continental Congresses ever had, chose the side of American independence the day he was born in 1729 in County Derry, Ireland.

Thomson, who was brought here at the age of 10, and went on to become first a teacher and then a successful importer, was a radical by disposition. He was scrupulously honest (the Delaware Indians named him "The Man Who Tells the Truth") and he abhorred anything that smacked of tyranny.

The actual moment of decision for Thomson doubtless occurred in 1765 when news of enactment of the Stamp Act by Parliament reached Philadelphia. That was the first occasion offered him; if an opportunity to take a rebel stand had come earlier, it's likely he would have taken it.

Franklin wrote to Thomson, regarding

Free Library of Philadelphia

passage of the act: "We might as well have hindered the sun's setting. That we could not do. But since the sun is down, my friend . . . let us make as good a night of it as we can. We may still light candles."

To this, Thomson replied: "Be assured the Americans will light lamps of a different sort than those you contemplate."

Thomson proceeded to organize the Philadelphia unit of the colonies-wide Sons of Liberty, a secret organization dedicated to fighting the Stamp Act.

Thomson made no secret of his hatred of British tyranny. The people of America, he said, must band together and throw off the British yoke. He said this in a city where peace-loving Quakers held the political reins at the time, and where even a suggestion of revolution was regarded as treason.

Joseph Galloway, probably Thomson's bitterest enemy, labeled Thomson "one of the most violent of the Sons of Liberty in America." Other observers have termed him "the Sam Adams of Philadelphia."

When the First Continental Congress was called in 1774, Galloway led a successful fight to keep Thomson from being named a delegate from Pennsylvania. But Galloway couldn't prevent an "arrangement" achieved by Sam Adams, John Adams, and John Dickinson the night before the Congress convened. That "arrangement" resulted in Thomson's being named secretary of the Congress — a post he held for the next 14 years.

Having faithfully recorded all the actions of Congress, having observed the wheeling and dealing of the delegates through all those years, Thomson was the logical man to write the political history of the Revolution.

This he refused to do.

In his autobiography, Benjamin Rush wrote of Thomson:

"He was once told in my presence that he ought to write a history of the Revolution. 'No,' said he, 'I ought not, for I should contradict all the histories of the great events of the Revolution, and show by my account of men, motives and measures, that we are wholly indebted to the agency of Providence for its successful issue. Let the world admire the supposed wisdom and valor of our great men. Perhaps they may adopt the qualities that have been ascribed to them, and thus good may be done. I shall not undeceive future generations.'"

Or, as a later historian observed: "The human frailties of Thomson's contemporaries were such that he thought it better not to say it."

If "The Man Who Tells the Truth" couldn't tell all the truth, he would tell nothing. ★ ★ ★

A Short Treatise In Defense of Loyalty

By Willard S. Randall

In the tense winter of 1775-76, as British warships blockaded New England and ragtag American armies invaded Canada, thousands of peace-loving Philadelphians agonized over the terrible choice forced upon them by the abrupt outbreak of war.

A majority of Pennsylvanians and New Jerseyman, it now seems evident, either were at first opposed to war or sided with England. They were not immediately, or easily, converted to the Patriot cause that was so popular in New England and Virginia.

It would take seven years of civil war, punitive measures, American victories, Hessian plundering, and British blundering before the vast majority would swing their support to the new American nation.

In the meantime, thousands would flee to the British strongholds of New York and Canada; entire regiments of New Jersey and Pennsylvania troops would fight on the British side; and many thousands of other persons in this region would attempt to stay neutral and remain at home until the outcome of events could be more clearly envisioned.

In the end, many of the wealthiest, best-educated and most gifted citizens — doctors, lawyers, merchants, farmers, and sea captains, as well as large numbers of farmers, artisans, able-bodied seamen, laborers and their families — would flee the towns and villages flanking the Delaware River to go into exile.

At war's end, they would crowd their belongings onto ships escaping to England, Bermuda, Canada and the Bahamas, safe from the wrath of old neighbors and friends, to begin again — rather than renounce their allegiance to England and its king.

Vilified and persecuted as "Tories," they called themselves the Loyalists; but actually, they were merely the political conservatives of a day when dissent from

George III

the popular radicalism was not tolerated. In truth, America began with a one-party system, and the loss of these conservatives would ultimately cause many of the severe problems that plagued the early life of the new American republic.

Nowhere, except perhaps in solidly-Loyalist New York City, were there to be found more Loyalists than in Philadelphia in 1776, and nowhere were they so hounded and persecuted as in Pennsylvania and New Jersey. And yet, for a short season on the eve of hostilities, it had appeared that moderate Philadelphia and its loyal majority would prevail.

The Loyalists of Philadelphia and New Jersey, acting in concert under the leading figures of Joseph Galloway, speaker of the Pennsylvania Assembly, and William Franklin, governor of New Jersey, very nearly pulled off a separate peace, in fact, with England.

But that moment was to come briefly, and it would follow a decade in which the Loyalists had been victimized and put on the defensive by a decade of well organized mob violence. It had

begun with the Stamp Act Crisis of 1765. At that time, New Jersey's stamp commissioner, William Coxe of Burlington, came to Philadelphia to get away from the Sons of Liberty on the other side of the river. When he did so, there were more Sons of Liberty — or "Sons of Despotism," as the Loyalists considered them — waiting for him with a choice between tar and feathers, or signing an oath that he would not sell the troublesome stamps.

Coxe, recommended for the job by Pennsylvania agent Benjamin Franklin, was unable to rent a house because he could not guarantee it wouldn't be torn to pieces by the mob, as had already happened to stamp officials in Boston. He forfeited his 3,000-pound bond of office and returned home to Burlington a broken man.

At first, the only apparent victims of anti-English sentiment were royal officials such as Coxe, but slowly the suspicion of Tory sentiment spread to communicants of the official English church and its preachers, the Anglican clergy.

Many of the leading Episcopal preachers around Philadelphia, such as the Rev. Jonathan Odell of St. Mary's in Burlington and the Rev. George Panton, rector in Trenton, would become outspoken Loyalists and would end their days in exile in Canada.

They were religious Tories whose motto was "Fear God and honor the King," and they early came under attack from Patriot preachers, especially the English-hating Scots-Irish Presbyterians who dreaded the established Anglican church, and who raised the specter — horror of horrors! — of Anglican bishops in Philadelphia and Burlington.

With the onset of shooting, anti-Tory activity accelerated. As late as 1775, even as the Continental Congress sat behind closed doors deliberating at the State House on Chestnut Street, Philadelphia had been considered, by outsiders at

Patriot Capital or Tory Stronghold?

least, a place of relative sanctuary for loyal subjects of the King. But this changed.

In his journal, Boston Loyalist Samuel Curwen tells of taking refuge from the Boston mobs in Philadelphia — only to be greeted by a Philadelphia mob, demanding he recant his Tory views. He refused and fled to England to sit out the war.

Another Loyalist who blundered into Philadelphia in May 1775, was Major Philip Skene, who, on landing at the Market Street Wharf, announced that he was the newly-appointed governor of Ticonderoga and Crown Point and Surveyor of the Woods. Hoots and jeers swept the assembled crowd that watched him clapped into Walnut Street Jail by order of Congress. Unfortunately for Skene, two weeks earlier the 43-man force of Benedict Arnold and Ethan Allen had taken Ft. Ticonderoga at dawn without a shot "in the name of the great Jehovah and the Continental Congress."

But by this time, the Loyalists' best moment of opportunity had come — and gone. It had occurred during a few warm fall days in late September and early October 1774.

It appeared then that the First Continental Congress might avert war by compromise and conciliation and establish a new relationship with Great Britain. While Patriots drilled outside, Loyalists held out the olive branch.

On September 28, 1774, Joseph Galloway, the most powerful man in Pennsylvania in the absence of his old partner, Benjamin Franklin, rose in the Carpenters' Hall and delivered a long and closely-reasoned Plan of Union with Great Britain, worked out that summer with Governor Franklin of New Jersey.

The plan itself wasn't anything terribly new. As early as 1698 William Penn had proposed a scheme whereby a separate legislature of American colonies would be represented in Parliament. At the Albany conference with the Iroquois Indians and the governors of the major colonies in 1754, Benjamin Franklin had worked out a similar plan together with Massachusetts governor-to-be and leading Loyalist Thomas Hutchinson.

The Albany plan had called for a union of the colonies under a president-general appointed, and paid, by the king. It also included a grand council of delegates from each colony with legislative power subject to the approval of the president-general and the Crown.

Galloway's plan was virtually identical, but had the unfortunate wording of creating "an inferior and distinct branch of the Britsh legislature," words that

Wherein we note that all Americans were not rebels, and inquire as to whether it might have been better for world history if none of them were.

An illustrator's depiction of Loyalists fleeing to Canada.

grated on the ears of New England representatives who considered themselves already at war with the repressive Parliament.

During most of the First Continental Congress, Galloway had held sway. His "Olive Branch Petition" to the King was already en route to England in the Loyalist hands of Richard Penn. But this latest scheme drove Sam Adams and the other radical partisans to extreme measures.

First, the New England delegates led a successful drive to table the measure six colonies to five (two colonies didn't vote). Then they went to work outdoors, stirring up the Philadelphia citizenry to a point that cowed conservative Philadelphians and moderate delegates to the Congress. By October 22, a few days after Galloway received the broad hint of a noose in a box, the radicals could vote to expunge all trace of the moderate proposal from the journals of Congress, despite the fact that it had come within a single vote of adoption.

After the final humiliation of being coerced into serving on the committee to expunge the minutes, Galloway retreated to his estate in Trevose, removing himself, the most potent Loyalist in American politics, from contention. When the British marched across New Jersey in December 1776, he openly joined them.

For five years, he would go on writing and publishing Plans of Union. One of them even reached the King, who is rumored to have looked at it for a minute or two, and then put it aside.

Even before Galloway left, Congress had passed a measure that constituted the first open campaign against adherents to the Crown in Philadelphia. On October 20, the Articles of Association were approved, pledging that all importation from England would cease effective December 1, and that the slave trade would cease by the same date; Americans were to stop consuming all British products and various other foreign luxuries by March 1, 1775, and an embargo of all English, Irish and West Indian exports would go into effect the following September 1.

Not only did these articles cut deeply into the predominately conservative-controlled trade of Philadelphia's merchants, but they also worked other hardships as well as the new republican Puritanism made its debut in this heretofore cosmopolitan city. The English ritual of tea was the first victim, but even more disconcerting was the ban on horse-racing, gambling, plays and "other expensive diversions and entertainments."

Congress, in mourning for the death of English liberty, began stripping away American liberties.

Still, the Loyalists waited, waited for the clampdown of British authority they expected momentarily — but which did not come. Instead, the Congress-backed mobs rigidly enforced the Association rules. Anyone, private householder or merchant, who disobeyed the Articles ran the risk of having his business boycotted, his name and address put in the newspapers, and resultant visits of mobs disturbing his peace. Attempts to form counter-associations for free trade were quickly broken up.

When the Second Continental Congress was meeting in early 1776, the Loyalist politicians in New Jersey made one last, foredoomed attempt to undercut the drive for independence. Congressional hawks had been unable to crack the conservative New York-New Jersey-Pennsylvania coalition. The principal reason remaining was the active and popular Governor Franklin of New Jersey, who had called together the colony's Assembly in Burlington in January to make a plea for moderation:

"It is not for me to decide on the particular merits of the dispute between Great Britain and her colonies, nor do I mean to censure those who conceive themselves aggrieved for aiming at a redress of the grievances. It is a duty they owe themselves, their country and their posterity.

"All that I could wish to guard against is the giving any countenance or encouragement to a destructive mode.

"You have now pointed out to you, gentlemen, two roads, one evidently leading to peace, happiness and restoration of the public tranquility — the other inevitably conducting you to anarchy, misery and all the horrors of a civil war."

Many leading Jerseymen, including future president of Congress Elias Boudinot, were still wavering, undecided. In February 1776, Boudinot went to a secret meeting and was shocked by the incendiary 90-minute speech of the Rev. John Witherspoon, president of Princeton University and soon-to-be delegate to Congress, which made a case for violent insurrection.

When he went home, Boudinot recorded in his journal that he had been "at my wit's end to know how to extricate myself from so disagreeable a situation ... two or three gent(lemen) of the audience came to me and desired that I would inform the doctor, that if he proceeded any farther they would not be answerable for his safety ... out of 36 members, there were but 3 or 4 who voted for the Doctor's proposition, the rest rejecting it with great warmth."

Against this backdrop, Governor Franklin prevailed on the Assembly to instruct its delegates to Congress against independence, and instead petition through him to the King for redress of grievances — in other words, to open bilateral talks between New Jersey and England.

When the Assembly agreed, the alarmed Congress dispatched delegates to Burlington to argue against a separate peace. The Assembly wavered and fell into line with the other rebellious colonies — "not wanting to appear singular."

Angrily, Franklin sent off the petition anyway, but the moderate Middle States coalition was broken. Quickly,

Provincial Congresses were formed in Pennsylvania and New Jersey to take power, and to send pro-independence delegates to the Continental Congress. On July 2, 1776, they voted for independence and war with England.

Governor Franklin received a special message from the King and Parliament offering limited grounds for negotiation under incongruous conditions. Even as he read it, a huge British task force sailed from England to subdue the rebellion. Congress decided Franklin's efforts had been treasonous — "in direct contempt and violation of the resolve of the Continental Congress" — and ordered his arrest.

•

The passing of a Declaration of Independence was a bitter blow to Philadelphia's Loyalists. That the movement had spread from a handful of Boston radicals in 1768 to all thirteen colonies in eight years was incomprehensible.

No longer could they remain neutral. The active partisans of revolution saw to that. All who were not openly for independence were against it. No fence-straddling was allowed.

To flush out and convert the Tories, the new Committees of Observation and Inspection imposed fines on anyone not joining the rebel militia.

Merchants and shopkeepers were forced to accept the rapidly-depreciating Continental money, even if they could not pay their own bills with it.

And the committees systematically barred Tories and neutralists, which meant the Quaker, Mennonite, Amish and Moravian majority, from practicing law, running drug stores (where Patriots might be poisoned) and from holding any jobs connected with the courts.

There were other difficulties. Unfortunately for the wavering Loyalists, the British commander, Sir William Howe, did not point out the distinction between Loyalist and Patriot to his Hessian mercenaries. They plundered and raped indiscriminately; to them, all Americans looked alike, and this was part of the business of war.

Still, strangely, there were no Loyalist countermoves, no open attempts to resist. The Loyalists did not even vote in local elections where they might have overturned the radical minority. In all Pennsylvania by July 1776, Galloway would note later in a cross-examination before the House of Commons, there was not one Loyalist association.

A major reason was that every American was, by now, awaiting the outcome of the British military campaign unfolding in New York and New Jersey.

While the Americans were beaten back

Patriot General Israel Putnam dealt sternly with Loyalists while he commanded Philadelphia. "Old Put" is depicted here in a famous episode in which he escaped from a British patrol.

one state would be deported to the backwoods of the next state, where plentry were eager to keep a close eye on them.

One covered wagon train of exiles, including 17 leading Philadelphia Quakers, was stoned as it passed west by a roundabout route through Reading on its way to western Virginia.

Not until his striking victories at Trenton and Princeton in December 1776 did Washington break his long public silence on the treatment due the Loyalists: All persons who had accepted Howe's recent offer of protection were either to retire within the British lines or take an oath of allegiance to the United States.

From that moment on, Loyalists had to make their decision and risk the consequences, and the neutralist Quakers and Pennsylvania Germans had to risk, because they could not take oaths for religious reasons, being branded and treated as Tories.

The years of open persecution began.

Now the Committees of Safety began clamping down on recruitment. Loyalists who refused military service were fined, sometimes in odd ways. Christopher Sauer, young Loyalist editor of the *Germantown Gazette,* had his desk taken out from under him.

Others, including a number of Quakers, were dragooned into service in the militia.

Early in 1777, Pennsylvania began to enforce test oaths of allegiance to the Congress. Unless Pennsylvanians took the oath, they could not travel more than one mile from home, they could not vote, their houses were searched, and their arms and personal papers seized. They could not hold office, collect money, or take any legal action of any sort without pledging allegiance.

In a ruthless suppression of civil rights, they could not adopt or serve as guardians for children, dispose of their own property, serve as executors for estates, buy, sell, or transfer property, convey gifts, serve on juries or as clerks, notaries, or sergeants-at-arms.

As early as 1776, certain professions were closed to them; they could not be doctors, surgeons or lawyers, either.

Informants against suspected violators were numerous, and for good reason: half the fines for discovering violations of the test laws were given as a bounty to the person bringing charges.

What helped to feed this atmosphere of suspicion was a careful Radical Party campaign of wild propaganda. The Russians were coming — 50,000 Cossacks to be exact — hired by the King to crush

across Long Island, out of New York City and down through northern New Jersey, the Loyalists waited ... waited — then joined ranks, rising in the wake of the British advance to revenge themselves on the crumbling American rebellion.

The American rebels became alarmed. As General George Washington's small army retreated toward the Delaware, General Israel Putnam was sent to Philadelphia to clamp martial law on the city. All known Loyalists were to be rounded up and deported to the hinterlands, where they could not incite likeminded citizens or join the British advance.

At first, where rebel committees and mobs were less active, many Loyalists had managed to survive and carry on their lives. But as the British rolled up military successes and menaced Philadelphia, the reign of terror heightened.

As the British, reassured that thousands of Loyalists would flock to their standard by optimists such as Galloway, moved on Philadelphia through the Tory strongholds of Maryland and Delaware, the Patriots were rounding up and deporting the Tories at a rapid clip.

Since the back-country was, by and large, Patriot-dominated, the Tories of

the revolt. In truth, King George had tried to hire some Russian troops before turning to his fellow German princes for hirelings, but Empress Catherine the Great felt she had enough trouble of her own, and declined.

The British occupation of Philadelphia was the signal Loyalists had long awaited: nearly 2,500 of them came into the British lines in Philadelphia from Maryland, Delaware, Pennsylvania, and New Jersey.

As Washington drilled his motley army in Valley Forge, the British drilled newly-formed Loyalist regiments. Two of them — the Volunteers of Ireland and the Pennsylvania Loyalists — would distinguish themselves in the South in the next few years. Under Lord Rawdon, the Volunteers of Ireland would help win the greatest battle of the war at Charleston, then quick-march to raise the long siege of Fort Ninety-Six on the Georgia-South Carolina frontier.

Both Pennsylvania Loyalist regiments would take part in the devastating rout of the Americans at Camden, S.C.

At Brandywine and Germantown, the Loyalists played key roles. Hancock's Bridge, in Salem, N.J., their growing reputation as ruthless guerrilla warriors was enhanced by surrounding a houseful of sleeping Patriot militia and slaughtering them in their sleep.

The Loyalist brigades never, perhaps, achieved the sort of success they were capable of because they were treated by the British with much of the same sort of arrogance and high-handedness that had started the war in the first place.

Symbolically, the British always referred to the Loyalist units as "Provincial Corps," and were loath to trust them to take the field on their own against their fellow Americans.

When the Loyalist were turned loose, they were savage and often successful soldiers. Simcoe's Rangers turned portions of New Jersey into a wasteland; Tarleton's legions scourged the South cruelly, if you were a Patriot, or with marvelous efficacy, if you were a Loyalist.

It's a stunning fact that more than 50,000 Loyalists fought with the British during the war, and at the end of the Revolution there were slightly more Loyalists under arms than there were Patriots.

Revenge became the watchword of the Loyalists now. While the polite Quaker ladies did their bit, sewing uniforms for the new Loyalist recruits, the embittered Loyalists rounded up suspected rebels and threw them into the Walnut Street Jail.

Since the jail's windows had been

shattered when a British warship exploded in the Delaware in October 1777, it was cold inside the jail and in equally-unglazed Pennsylvania Hospital, where the lunatics had been turned out to make room for American prisoners.

There was also a food shortage and little firewood and none too little British cruelty, and some 2,000 American prisoners died that winter in British custody, feeding the hatred that would sweep the city as soon as the British left.

In May 1778, after a splendid farewell party, the British did desert the Loyalists of Philadelphia.

At the time of the British evacuation, John Potts, one of the first 13 Pennsylvanians declared traitors by the state, had described the mood in Philadelphia as "depressed," noting that the remaining Loyalists had "their confidence in the British Government destroyed" by the evacuation and had "abandoned themselves to a lethargy very nearly bordering on despair.

"They say they cannot be certain of, possessing the fruits of their labor, and they publicly declare that they would rather suffer their ground to remain uncultivated . . . than have their property taken from them by Commissioners or Quarters Masters who will pay them in paper money, which depreciates so fast that no man knows what value to affix to it."

Some 3,000 Loyalists thought it better to go to New York with the British, but many, despairing of British victory, and ready to face the worst, stayed behind.

The worst came soon enough. All through the occupation, the Patriot committees had been keeping careful lists of collaborators. Now a blacklist of 490 names was published. Loyalists on it surrendered or were rounded up to stand trial for treason.

However, in part because there were few witnesses willing to come forward, all but nine Loyalists were acquitted or released with fines and parole.

The gallows at Centre Square was kept busy that summer as Loyalists and American deserters were strung up as "examples." Two of the executions particularly stirred Loyalist Philadelphians, and demonstrated that not all the Tories and Quakers had lost their will to protest.

While treason was considered a capital offense on both sides, the anti-Loyalist rage ran so deep that summer that two Quakers, Abram Carlisle and John Roberts, who had merely been conscripted to serve as scouts for the British and guards at the city gates, were condemned to hang.

Carlisle, a carpenter, and Roberts, a miller from Lower Merion, were tried by

This allegorical sketch by Benjamin West, entitled "Reception of the American Loyalists in England," depicts Britannia's mantle being spread over the arriving Tories by figures representing Religion and Justice.

the Court of Oyer and Terminer, Judge Thomas McKean presiding. Although the juries found them guilty, most of the jurors petitioned for mercy for Roberts, and all recommended reprieve for Carlisle.

Five clergymen and 387 Philadelphians petitioned for a reprieve, including many leading Patriots. Nevertheless, the Pennsylvania Executive Council, dominated by Thomas Paine, Joseph Read, and Charles Willson Peale, was unmoved. They considered it necessary to terrorize the Quakers, and appease the popular bloodlust for reprisal against British sympathizers.

On November 4, 1778, the sentence was carried out. James Humphreys, editor of the *Pennsylvania Ledger,* would flee to New York after witnessing the scene, where he would write to Galloway in England:

" . . . Poor Roberts and Carlisle have been wantonly sacrificed. They were walked to the gallows behind the cart with halters round their necks, attended with all other apparatus, which makes such scenes truly horrible. . .

"Poor Carlisle, having been very ill during his confinement, was too weak to say anything; but Mr. Roberts, with the greatest coolness imaginable, spoke for

some time . . . they both behaved with the utmost fortitude and composure.

"After their execution, their bodies were suffered to be carried away by their friends — and Mr. Carlisle's body buried in the Friend's Burying Ground."

The amazing fact, which Humphreys saves for last, and remarks on almost matter-of-factly, is that more than 4,000 people followed the funeral procession.

The execution of Quakers drove others out soon enough; Samuel Shoemaker fled, leaving behind vast amounts of property to be confiscated by the Patriots to help support their war machine. machine.

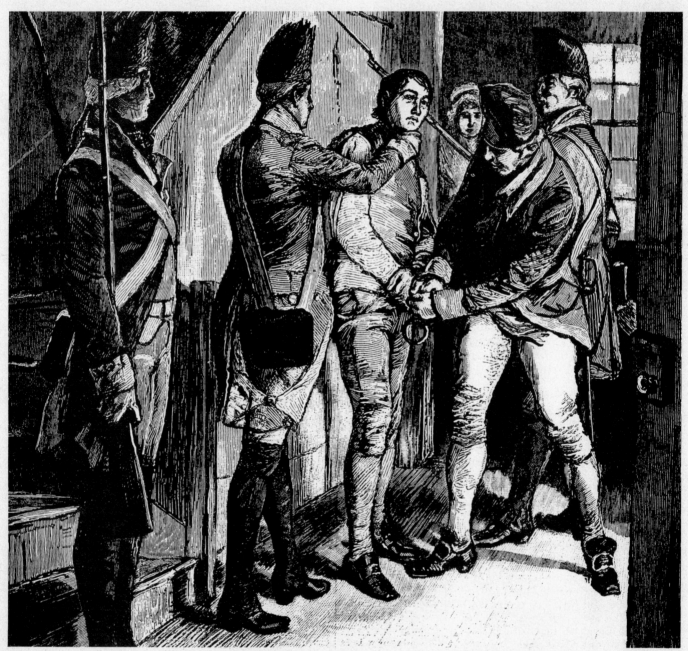

Stern British disciplinary measures, exemplified by the arrest of a colonist in his home, pushed many fence-sitting colonists into the Patriot camp.

THE FOUNDING CITY

Loyalism Lives!

When a writer told the late Catherine Drinker Bowen, a great biographer whose own Quaker family was persecuted in Philadelphia during the Revolution, that he was researching the Loyalists, her eyes lit up.

"Ah," she said, "that is the last great untold story of the Revolution."

Until recently, the story had been the target of a historical cover-up on a scale that vastly exceeds anything of recent memory.

John Adams said, a few years after the war, that the Loyalists had "seduced" fully one-third of the American people. Ever since then, historians have been whittling down that estimation by an honest man who had no reason to flatter the strength, or importance, of his enemies.

But lately, a handful of honest historians, including Dr. James Mooney, director of the Historical Society of Pennsylvania, and his father-in-law, Dr. Robert East of the City University of New York, have begun sorting through Loyalist diaries and documents seeking to tell the somewhat embarrassing story of the Loyalists.

Usually, people dealing with Loyalist history keep quiet about their work, though more and more of late they have summoned up the courage to speak. During a series of lectures by distinguished professors conducted at Independence Hall last year, John Beeson, a professor of history at Cheyney State College, startled the assemblage by standing to ask a speaker if the Americans were really as put upon as they liked to make out.

He himself suggested that perhaps a national paranoia was at work, causing Americans to feel that somehow they were being had. Not content with that, he went on to say that unless Americans came to appreciate that the choice between independence and the "imperial viewpoint" was hard, the Bicentennial would "degenerate into a simplistic, jingoist charade."

There was no applause, but then neither was Beeson clapped in irons.

Philip Katcher: Latter-day Loyalist

Some latter-day Loyalists are armed, though not especially dangerous. Philip Katcher, a magazine editor at Chilton Press, has formed and now commands the "1st Battalion of Pennsylvania Loyalists," a 23-man unit which has participated in about 10 Revolutionary War re-enactments over the past year.

Katcher recalls with particular relish the group of Girl Scouts who came up to him at Valley Forge and asked, "Aren't you the bad guys?"

"I told them, 'No, we're the good guys.' They just sort of stammered and walked away," he recalls.

Neo-Toryism is often laced with whimsy. Gary Christopher, a researcher at the Historical Society of Pennsylvania, who himself belongs to a British military group for re-enactments and who frequently lectures on the Loyalists, passes out bumper stickers that read, "Bring Back The Monarchy in '76."

The *Tory Torch*, a newsletter of Loyalist persuasion published in Richmond, Va., includes in its latest issue advice on how to remove tar and feathers. It also urges present-day Tories to avoid crowds ("Crowds are a major source of mobs") and even to steer clear of "lone strangers" with "dyspeptic expressions" especially if they are carrying "large truncheons."

There is, perhaps, no more fascinating inquiry in history than that expressed by the question: "What if . . . ?"

What if — the British had won? Beeson, for one, suggests that for starters there might not have been a Civil War. Slavery was abolished in the British Empire in 1833, a circumstance that would have defused a major source of friction between the American north and the American south.

An Anglo-Saxon colossus astride the Atlantic, he suggests, might have intimidated the Kaiser, obviating World War I and, with it, World War II.

The possibilities of this game are, of course, endless, and anyone can play.

Beeson takes some of the fun out of it, though, by saying that in truth he believes "if ever an event was inevitable, it was the American Revolution. If it didn't happen in 1776, it would have happened in 1800, or 1805. The power relationship had changed, and something had to happen."

Between 1779 and 1782, some of the best estates, business houses, warehouses, shops, large and small farms were seized from Loyalists and sold, more often than not, to leading Patriots.

Portraitist Charles Willson Peale personally and forcibly evicted Grace Galloway from her mansion at Sixth and Market, pushing the woman into a carriage. The house was then turned over to Pennsylvania President Joseph Read. Later it was deeded to financier Robert Morris, and it eventually became the official residence of President George Washington.

The Rev. Jacob Duche's house would be sold at a most reasonable price to Chief Justice McKean. Patriot John Dunlap, printer of the Declaration of Independence and Radical politician, would buy Galloway's Boon Island property and Alexander Bartram's house, as well as the properties of Loyalists Joe Evans and Joseph Grieswold.

The infamous General Joseph Wilkinson, later a traitor himself, would be rewarded for his military services with Galloway's Trevose estate.

But many smaller pieces were constantly auctioned off, indicating that many of the Loyalists who left were smallholders and artisans owning rowhouses or three-acre plots of pasture and small farms here and there around the city.

To be sure, the Loyalists in some cases richly deserved the distrust and persecution they were receiving. Some were spying for the British — just like the Americans suspected. Oddly, though, the patriot drag net tended to miss these real spies.

Consider Joseph Stansbury, Second

Some Came Back...

The case of Matthias Aspden, Philadelphia merchant, illustrates as well as any the dangers of seeking simple explanations of the Loyalist versus Patriot imbroglio.

In 1776, Aspden fled to New York, seeking the safety of that British-occupied city. He gave up an income of 2,000 pounds annually from his business — a fortune at the time — and fled farther — first to England, and then to Spain — before coming home after the war had ended.

How did the patriots in Philadelphia respond to his return? With outrage and vengeance, one might suspect.

And some did. Aspden's life was threatened, and he fled the city again. But on April 1, 1785, he wqs granted a full pardon by the Pennsylvania Assembly. He came home, and lived reasonably happily in the town that was his home.

The anomalies of the way in which Loyalists were treated after the war seem almost incomprehensible to us today, and no doubt reflect the conflicting emotions and passions that attended the issue at the time.

The same legislators who were capable of voting retributive and confiscatory punishments against long lists of Loyalists, were also capable, it appears, of looking at an individual case and thinking, "There, but for the grace of God..."

There were some very intriguing instances. Christopher Sauer, for example, eventually returned to Philadelphia, and one of the little unanswered questions one would give a lot to know the answer to is this: After his return, did Sauer continue to draw the 40-pound annual pension he had been awarded by the British for his invaluable espionage services in their behalf during the Revolution? If he did, did any of his neighbors ever suspect the source of his income?

A past record of Loyalism did nothing to enhance one's political popularity in the young nation, of course, but some erstwhile Tories achieved high office in spite of that blemish in their background.

Edward Shippen 4th, a London-trained lawyer and prominent Loyalist, was initially stripped of his judgeship and deprived of his practice by the rebels. He moved from the city to his country home at the Falls of the Schuylkill.

When the British occupied the city, he moved back to his townhouse, and was friendly with many of the British officers, among whom his accomplished and beautiful daughters were most popular.

Shippen remained when the British returned, and his daughters entertained American officers. Peggy Shippen married the American military governor, Benedict Arnold, and after Arnold turned traitor, Peggy returned to the city for a visit. However, she encountered so much bitterness that she shortly returned to England, and remained there with Arnold for the rest of his life.

Yet despite his avowal of Loyalism, his open fraternization with the enemy, and his close link to America's premier traitor, Shippen became chief justice of the Supreme Court of Pennsylvania in 1799.

Another lawyer, Benjamin Chew, who had been raised a Quaker but had converted to Anglicanism, was arrested by order of the Continental Congress in 1778 along with others who had refused to support the rebel cause. He was kept in custody for 10 months, before being allowed to return.

Yet in 1791, he became president judge of the High Court of Errors and Appeals.

The persons who had been the principal leaders of Loyalist resistance, though, were not allowed to return, especially if they had attractive land holdings that appealed to a prominent patriot.

The petition of Joseph Galloway to be allowed to return wasn't approved by the Pennsylvania legislature, and so the man who had once been the speaker of that body died in England, an unhappy exile, always longing to come home.

Street bookseller, who made frequent trips up to British-held New York. While he was eventually deported for trading with the British, no one realized at the time that the books he carried contained the codes for the correspondence between John Andre and Benedict Arnold, the beginning step in Arnold's treachery.

And Christopher Sauer, who had fled to the British lines during the Battle of Germantown, became a leading British operative. When he reported that American troop strength was down to 3,000 at one point, the British staff stupidly scoffed at the report — and lost forever its chance to crush the rebellion.

It was true.

Those Loyalists and neutralists who dared stay behind, including the Quakers, were galled by the final victory at Yorktown, especially by the fact that they were forced to participate in the "Illumination," the proclaimed lighting of candles in all windows to celebrate the victory.

Anna Rawle, stepdaughter of Samuel Shoemaker, had remained in Philadelphia after her parents had taken refuge in New York. In her diary for October 24, 1781, she recorded: "It is too true that Cornwallis is taken" and noted "long conversations we often have together on the melancholy situation of things."

On October 25 she wrote, "I suppose, dear Mammy, thee would not have imagined this house to be illuminated last night, but it was. A mob surrounded it, broke the shutters and the glass of the windows. ... (There was) none but forlorn women here ...

"We thought the mob were coming in ... but it proved to be Coburn and Bob Shewell, who called to us not to be frightened, and fixed lights up at the windows, which pacified the mob ... after three huzzas, they moved off.

"Even the firm Uncle (William) Fisher was obliged to submit to have his windows illuminated, for they had pick axes and iron bars with which they had done considerable damage to his house. In short, it was the most alarming scene I ever remember."

Even in victory, the Americans kept up the pressure, and it would be many years before the hostility subsided. Many Loyalists did not wait for further signs they were unwelcome.

James Humphrey, former Philadelphia newspaper editor, took ship to Port Roseway, Nova Scotia, and set up shop for the *Nova Scotia Packet & General Advertiser,* but in the bare winter in that forlorn refugee settlement of cabins and sails and starving children, he had to peddle food and liquor between editions to survive.

One of his better-off neighbors was Robert Appleby. Born a wealthy Philadelphian, Appleby led 142 former Philadelphians to the refugee city south of Halifax. But his resources were depleted; he soon would end up serving five months in debtor's prison.

John Green lost his business and home in Philadelphia and settled in Bermuda.

Some of the Loyalists returned to America. Most, though, went to England, where they underwent a long period of adjustment, during which they thought of themselves as expatriates who were merely sojourning in England until the rebellion was suppressed — and they could return to their native land.

They were not, for the most part, accepted by British society. "We Americans are plenty here, and very cheap," wrote Thomas Hutchinson, former governor of Massachusetts, who also urged his friends to drop the title "His Excellency" when writing his address, saying, "Everybody laughs at such things here."

The American Loyalists, according to Harvard historian Bernard Bailyn's book *The Ordeal of Thomas Hutchinson,* met together "in an unending series of teas, dinners, coffees, walks, and journeys, during which they talked over the latest news from home ... (and) organized to seek jobs, pensions, and compensation for their losses ... "

Hutchinson, as Bailyn depicts him, was a particularly tragic figure. He had been forced to flee Massachusetts after Benjamin Franklin's disclosure of letters he had written, while governor, to friends in England urging that the British take firmer action in America. Now in England he devoted himself to writing long, rambling tracts defending himself.

He became even more certain, Bailyn writes, that the British government had "not been seized by a desperate cabal intent on destroying liberty in America."

Instead he saw for himself now a government "paralyzed by inefficiency, consumed with self-doubt, almost totally innocent of purpose good or bad ... "

The man Franklin ruined agonized through the slow deaths, apparently by cancer, of his son and daughter, all the while longing for his home outside Boston, with its shady walks and lovely views of the countryside.

He died of a stroke in January 1781, a few months after hearing that he had been formally banished by the Massachusetts legislature, and that his lands were to be confiscated and sold. ★ ★ ★

Conflict: The Franklins Choose Sides

By Willard S. Randall

To many Americans in 1776, the Revolutionary War was really a painfully personal civil war that divided, even destroyed, their families. Some of the rifts would never heal.

Fathers and sons, brothers and sisters. In-laws and cousins would never see each other again after making the choice between loyalty to England or America.

The list of prominent families wrenched apart by conviction and the fortunes of war is long: Sir John Randolph of Virginia was loyal to the King while his son, Edmund, was a leading patriot; Samuel Quincy of Boston was a prominent Loyalist, while his son, Josiah, embraced the patriot cause.

But there was no more obvious example of the bitter choice brought about by Revolution than in the family of Benjamin Franklin of Philadelphia, whose son would lead the Loyalists in a bitter war of retribution after both men's attempts at peaceful negotiation failed.

Although William was born out of wedlock, the two men were extremely close, and the wounds they inflicted on each other were searing.

Benjamin Franklin had three children: a son, Francis Folger, and a daughter, Sarah, by his common-law wife, Deborah Read, and

American Philosophical Society

Seldom have a father and son been so close. Together they had worked at science, practiced politics, and cut a swath through London society. But William Franklin could never understand why his father was such a rebel.

William, his firstborn, whose mother's identity has never been determined for certain.

The elder Franklin openly acknowledged William, however, and, after the death of the other son, Frankie, at four of smallpox, indulged him as his only son and heir.

By the time Billy was 12, he had his own bay mare, a rare pet for a printer's son of that time.

At 16, Billy joined the militia and

became Captain William Franklin. He distinguished himself in the Third French and Indian War. Tall, handsome, distinctly resembling his father, he was as proud of his sire as his sire was of him.

Their most notable achievement together was in the field of science. In the open field at Seventh and Race Streets, it was William Franklin — not the small boy that is often depicted, but a six-foot, one-inch-tall man — who ran across what's now called Franklin Square with a kite in his hand during a thunderstorm.

His father, standing in a shepherd's shed, watched electricity dance down to the key on a string in his hand, proving that lightning and electricity were the same thing. Later, the father and son would receive honorary degrees together from Oxford for their work.

But not all of their ventures had been scientific. Some were political. As Benjamin Franklin's power in the Pennsylvania Assembly grew in the 1750s, he turned over the clerkship of the House to his son. William Franklin also wrote a stream of skillfully scurrilous pamphlets under the pen name of Humphrey Scourge that defended his father and vilified the opposition.

William did not get along with his stepmother, who no doubt resented the fact that his father kept her on a miserly household budget while he paid for fancy clothes for his son, who became a dashing figure in Philadelphia society.

Deborah was afraid of the water, too, and didn't make the trip to England in 1757 when Benjamin went as agent for the Pennsylvania Assembly. William did, and the six years of politicking, touring, and carousing in their fashionable flat in London undoubtedly brought the two even closer.

On his own, without the intervention of his father, William obtained appointment as the royal governor of New Jersey at age 32. His tenure there was the longest and one of the most progressive in the Garden State's history, lasting from 1763 to 1776.

Leaving England in 1762, William had only seen the British Empire at its best. With his father, he witnessed the coronation of the supposedly enlightened young ruler, King George III, a man more powerful than any person since Augustus Caesar.

Proud of his legal training in Philadelphia, and of having been admitted to the bar of the Middle Temple in London, William Franklin was a constitutional conservative glad to uphold the royal prerogative despite his Whig background. He was the model British-American subject, the inevitable Loyalist.

Governor Franklin ruled over the most tranquil and conservative of the colonies in the decade before the Revolution, and sometimes couldn't understand what the flap was all about.

On quite the other hand, Benjamin Franklin was to see the worst of England, whose national affairs went into a postwar decline after William left.

Though honored throughout Europe as a man of science, Franklin was systematically humiliated by the Tories in power in England. He came to scorn British nobleman such as the spiteful Lord Hillsborough, the venal Lord North, the cowardly Lord George Germain.

When he illegally opened confidential government correspondence between British colonial officials in Boston and the Crown officers, he was publicly tried before the Privy Council and fired as deputy postmaster general. This was a blow to the political fortunes of both father and son, and precipitated a stream of anti-British advice crossing the Atlantic from Benjamin to William. The stage was set for the final heated argument.

"Parliament has no right to make any law whatever binding on the Colonies," the elder statesman argued, while adding, "I know your sentiments differ from mine on these subjects. You are a thorough government man, which I do not wonder at, nor do I aim at converting you. I only wish you to act uprightly and steadily, avoiding that duplicity which adds contempt to indignation."

"Honored Father," William patiently responded on Dec. 24, 1774, "If there was any prospect of your being able to bring the people in power to your way of thinking, or of those of your way of thinking being brought into power, I should not think so much of your stay. But as you have had pretty strong proofs that neither can be reasonably expected, and that you are looked upon with an evil eye in that country, you had certainly better return."

When, in May 1775, Benjamin Franklin returned to a tumultuous welcome in Philadelphia, his son rushed to meet him and to take his own son, who had arrived with Benjamin, back to Perth Amboy.

There, for three days in August 1775, four months after Lexington-Concord and five months before Congress ordered Gov. Franklin's arrest as an enemy of the new nation, father and son met for the last time before the war.

It would be nearly 10 years before Benjamin and William Franklin met again to settle up accounts on a ship at Southampton, England, before parting company forever.

In the intervening years of war, William Franklin was held under house arrest for five months before he was ordered "led like a bear through New England," as he put it, from jail to jail until he was finally confined in chains underground in the notorious Simsbury Mines.

In the two years before he was exchanged, he was to lose his second wife, Elizabeth, who died in New York, literally of a broken heart; his papers and his furniture, which were destroyed in a fire; and his status as an American. He was declared an outlaw, and never dared return to America again.

Embittered that his father made no apparent attempt to aid him, and angered at his treatment by the Patriots, he organized the Board of Associated Loyalists and supervised its bloody raids on New Jersey and Connecticut. When he finally fled to exile in England, he was remembered as one of the most notorious Tories.

While his father would later confess that "nothing has ever hurt me more" than the breach with his only son, Benjamin Franklin went to his grave denouncing William, disinheriting him except for some worthless Nova Scotia land.

"The part he acted against me in the late war," Benjamin Franklin wrote in his will, "which is of public notoriety, will account for my leaving him no more of an estate he endeavoured to deprive me of." ★ ★ ★

The War

The War

In wartimes, and in accounts of them, a whole new set of rules goes into effect. War offers hero status to the sadistic and brutal, while it makes cowards of the sensitive and humane. Once battle is joined, the forces of Good can hope for no more than an even chance against those of Evil, assuming that it is possible to determine the difference.

Yet it is from war that our national legends come. There is something that stirs our souls — and not altogether ignobly — in picturing the American troops huddled in groups along the west bank of the Delaware on Christmas Day 1776, stamping their feet for warmth, while their commanders read Tom Paine's stirring words: ". . . the summer soldier and the sunshine patriot, will, in this crisis, shrink from the service of his country . . .tyranny, like hell, is not easily conquered."

And one cannot help but stand in awe of the steely resolve of Washington, who, on hearing that one unit had gotten its powder wet, instructed a messenger: "Tell them to use the bayonet. I am resolved to take Trenton."

THE GENERALS

Amateurs 'Out-Muddle' the Pros

What was the flaw of the British generals —Indecisiveness? Stupidity? Or were they simply the victims of the shifting tides of history?

By Edgar Williams

There is an article of faith, established centuries ago and held by succeeding generations of right-thinking Britons, that while British generals are expected to muddle, they also are expected to "muddle through."

In the American Revolution, the British generals — for numerous reasons, most of which still are neither clear nor convincing — proved excellent muddlers. But they were utter failures at muddling through.

To coin an awkward-sounding but nonetheless apt term, the generals of the American forces "out-muddled through" their British counterparts. The Revolution wasn't the kind of war in which victory was achieved; it was the other kind, in which defeat was evaded.

How did it happen? Even allowing for the disadvantages faced by the British command that had to transport and maintain an army across some 3,000 miles of ocean and re-establish military control over a vast geographical area with poor interior lines of communication, Britain should have won the war. She had control of the sea at the outset of the conflict and for years thereafter. The British military establishment was better organized than the establishment the Americans had to throw together hastily. Britain was superior in experience, training and discipline of officers and men. Britain possessed greater material resources.

Also, there can be no gainsaying the fact that the British were winning the war until the French came in on the American side.

Actually, it might be more precise to say that the Americans were losing the war until the French arrived. The Revolution was collapsing under the pressures of domestic quarrels — after all, the colonies were actually like 13 separate, small countries, loosely bound together in a flimsy federation — as well as from lack of supplies, worthless money, and creeping Toryism. The Americans were ablt to hang on mainly because the British generals failed to press advantages. In so doing, though, the British gave the Americans time to develop generals of their own who grew in experience and leadership qualities, and who achieved, if not brillance, at least highly commendable professional competence.

Or did the British generals fail because of overconfidence? After the war, Benjamin Franklin recalled that just before he returned to America in 1775, he heard Gen. Alfred Clarke, a British hero of the Seven Years War, boast at a party in London that he could solve the problem of rebellious America.

With only two thousand British grenadiers, Clarke boasted, he would "undertake to go from one end of America to the other, and geld all the males, partly by force and partly by a little coaxing."

Franklin noted that it was "plain he took us for a species of animals very little superior to brutes."

Such expressions were rather commonplace in the War Ministry in London, where remote-control generals could look at maps and determine that victory over a disorganized rabble in America would be easy. From these men, some experts have theorized, oozed an overconfidence that infected the generals on the field with the feeling that they could wrap up the conflict victoriously simply by occupying cities and letting the Revolution wind itself down to extinction.

The American Revolution was also a tough one for generals in that it represented a transition phase in the history of warfare. A military history textbook notes that "the professional military methods of the 18th century were more important in the revolution than popular legend admits . . . (But) at the same time the war was a portent for the future, presenting a new set of strategic and tactical challenges and opportunities that wouldn't be mastered until Napoleon did so.

Some historians argue that the war was an unwinnable one for the British because it was the first conflict of modern times in which an army was fighting not just an opposing army, but an entire people.

Louis B. Morton, professor of history at Dartmouth College, says, "You can't go through and say if this British general had done this, or this British admiral had done that, the British would have won the war. Even if the British had defeated Washington's army, that doesn't mean, for instance, that Virginia would have given up." Another army could have been drawn together from militia virtually overnight.

Once the colonies had decided for independence, Morton argues, no military force could reverse that course. ★★★

"Every Inch a General..."

It long has been fashionable among some members of the Intellectual Establishment, Division of American History, to put down George Washington as "the general who never won a battle."

For the sake of making a point, let us stipulate that Washington never won a big battle. Which is not to downgrade such victories as those at Trenton and Princeton. It simply is to underscore a great truth, to wit:

He took what the British correctly referred to as a "rabble in arms" at the outset of the Revolution and built it into the Continental Army. When that army showed signs of falling apart on occasion, it was Washington who, through sheer force of personality, patched it up and kept it functioning.

He dealt successfully with a dilatory and of times troublesome Congress. He dodged the slings and arrows of jealous subordinates who, usually for their own personal gain, sought to have him removed as commander-in-chief.

And he won the war.

There is no denying the fact that Washington's selection as commander-in-chief was based in part on political considerations. John Adams saw the wisdom of binding the South to New England's fortunes by choosing a Virginian to lead the army then encamped outside Boston. At Adams' suggestion, the choice fell upon Washington. It was a logical choice.

For one thing, Washington looked every inch a general. A big man — 6 feet, 2 inches, 200 pounds — and heavily muscled, he had a dignified manner.

To be sure, Washington's actual military experience had been relatively modest in accomplishment, and had occurred many years earlier. As a novice of 22, he had led an unsuccessful militia maneuver during the French and Indian Wars, skirmishing with the French near the Ohio River. Then he spent the next three years patrolling the western frontiers against the marauding Indians. In 1755, in the disastrous battle at Fort Duquesne, he was an aide to the ill-fated British general, Edward Braddock, Washington's courage, though, was certified by that battle. Despite having two horses shot from under him, Washington displayed remarkable coolness in action.

"He was," a comrade remembered, "like a bishop at his prayers."

General George Washington

Now, 20 years later, Washington was a wealthy planter and one of Virginia's delegates to the Second Continental Congress when the Congress, on June 15, 1775, followed Adams' suggestion.

He accepted with trepidation. Washington told Congress, "I do not think myself worthy of the command I am honored with," and later that same day he remarked to a fellow Virginian, Patrick Henry, "Remember what I tell you. From the day I enter upon the command of the American armies, I date my fall and the ruin of my reputation."

Such self-depreciation was not counterfeit. Washington was a man given frequently to self-doubt. But it is a mark of his character that he always was able to overcome it — possibly, some psychologists have suggested, because he was not above "ventilating" his feelings.

In so doing, however, he was selective. He confided in a few close friends and, most of all, in his wife.

Washington was an innately shy man, and that shyness often was mistaken for aloofness. But he had a tender side, as an incident that occurred in Morristown, N. J., in 1777, well illustrates.

Leading his troops through the town, Washington was welcomed by a large crowd. In the midst of it was a little girl crying because she could not see Washington. Washington reined in his big white horse and called out. "Bring the child to me." One of the men in the crowd complied. Gently, Washington lifted the child to the saddle in front of him and carried her a little way.

Washington's first view of his "army" when he took command at Cambridge, Mass., on July 2, 1775, would have discouraged many another man. The "army" was, in truth, little more than an armed mob. Washington worked long hours to whip the troops into shape, invoking stern discipline. When most of the enlistments ran out in December, Washington even succeeded in raising another army within cannon shot of the British besieged in Boston.

When it came time to take the offensive, Washington realized keenly his own lack of military experience on a large scale. He learned as he fought, and his early errors with consequent disaster grew steadily fewer. But, in the final analysis, it was the confidence that Washington inspired as a man, rather than his ability as a soldier, that made him the only man in America who could carry the Revolution to a successful conclusion.

The Shell-Shocked Leader

"Had Sir William Howe fortified the hills round Boston, he could not have been disgracefully driven from it; had he pursued his victory at Long Island, he had ended the Rebellion; had he landed above the lines at New York, not a man could have escaped him; had he fought the Americans at the Bronx, he was sure of victory; had he cooperated with the ... (northern) Army, he had saved it, or had he gone to Philadelphia by land, he had ruined Mr. Washington and his forces. But as he did none of these things, had he gone to ye Devil before he was sent to America, it had been a saving of infamy of himself, and of indelible dishonour to this country."

These searing words were written by Sir Henry Clinton, the man who succeeded Sir William Howe as commander-in-chief of the British Army in North America. They sum up one view of the strange general who, as historian Thomas J. Fleming has said, time and again seemed to make sure Washington would escape to fight another day.

There is, for example, Howe's failure to smash the half-starved, freezing American Army at Valley Forge during the winter of 1777-78, a historical mystery so baffling that it ranks as a classic. Howe was occupying Philadelphia with 20,000 well-fed and well-clothed troops. Just 22 miles away was Valley Forge, where Washington had 9,000 men at the beginning of the winter. Before the winter was over, 3,000 of them had deserted to the British. There were times when Washington had less than 2,400 men fit for duty.

Within a matter of a day or two, Howe might very possibly have surrounded the whole destitute outfit and driven them like a flock of captive sheep into Philadelphia with a concerted effort.

So why did Howe fail to deliver the crushing blow, preferring to luxuriate in Philadelphia with his mistress, Betsy Loring, whom he had brought along with him from New York (along with her complaisant husband)? The answer is locked in the generals' tombs.

Historian Sidney George Fisher theorized that Howe had determined on a policy of holding cities and fortified positions until the Revolution ended.

But historian W. E. Woodward has put forth a more imaginative — yet not illogical — guess.

"My guess," Woodward wrote, "is that Howe was suffering from a neurosis

General Sir William Howe

which was not understood at the time but which is now known as shell shock. I do not believe that he ever recovered from the deadly fire at Bunker Hill. He had an inward panic, I believe, whenever anybody suggested an attack on a line of American breastworks. So he circled about the Americans, taking sea voyages, retreating, standing still, doing anything to avoid out-and-out grappling."

The Battle of Bunker Hill on June 17, 1775, had been Howe's first fight with Americans. He had only recently arrived, together with Generals Burgoyne and Clinton, to assist General Thomas Gage in the besieged city of Boston, and, almost immediately, he was afforded the opportunity of seeing England's best regiments cut to ribbons by the entrenched Americans. Only the most frantic efforts on the part of Howe and his officers drove the battered Redcoats up the hill one last time to oust the rebels.

Howe wrote to his brother, Admiral Lord Richard Howe, that in the midst of the carnage "there was a moment I never felt before."

What was that moment? Was it the simple possibility of a defeat? Howe had experienced that before. The moment of Bunker Hill may indeed have been, as Woodward suggests, the beginning of an inward panic that changed Howe from the daredevil he had shown himself to be years earlier, when he led his brigade up the cliffs of Quebec to help Wolfe defeat Montcalm in the French and Indian Wars, to a hesitant leader.

Not long after Bunker Hill, George III appointed Howe commander-in-chief as successor to Gage. Subsequently, there were head-to-head clashes between Howe and Washington — Kip's Bay, Long Island, White Plains, Brandywine — in which the British always won, but in which Howe invariably failed to press his advantage.

In May 1778, Howe was recalled from America, and was succeeded by Clinton as commander-in-chief. Parliament ordered an investigation of Howe's conduct, but he was acquitted.

When the war was over, a military critic in England wrote: "I am of the opinion that any other general in the world than General Howe would have beaten General Washington, and any other general in the world than General Washington would have beaten General Howe."

General Greene: Ablest General Began as Private

His troops thought a limping officer was embarrassing; Washington decided that it wasn't

When Nathaniel Greene helped organize a patriot militia company known as the Kentish Guards in his native Rhode Island in 1774, he naturally assumed that he would be an officer. But his fellows refused to vote him a commission, on the ground that Greene had a stiff knee that made him limp. After all, how would it look for a crack military unit to have an officer who limped across the parade ground?

Greene's character is attested by his willingness to serve in the ranks. In spite of his 32 years and his position as the son of an affluent iron foundryman, he readily picked up a musket and began service as a private.

That action shaped Greene's career for him. In May 1775, when the Rhode Island Assembly decided to raise 1,500 troops and to defy the royal governor, the legislators, impressed by Greene's selflessness in agreeing to serve as a private — and, besides, finding no one as well qualified for leadership — appointed the erstwhile private to be brigadier general in charge of the force. A month later, Congress commissioned Greene a brigadier general in the Continental Army. And the man who had been rejected as an officer of a militia company was on his way toward becoming Washington's most competent general.

Greene served to the end of the war, rising to the rank of major general. As time passed, Washington came to rely on him more than on any other officer, of whatever rank.

Greene was a self-educated man. His father did not believe in education, so instead of sending young Nathaniel to school, he kept him at work in the family foundry. But the young man had a desire for learning that could not be defeated by the heavy work with hammer and anvil. He bought books, read them, and taught himself. By the standards of the times, Greene had a good education. He had a natural inclination for military life, and much of his reading was of detailed histories of military campaigns.

If Greene made any mistake as a general, it was his advice to Washington not to hold Fort Washington on the Hudson after the Battle of White Plains in October 1776. When the British stormed and captured the fort, the Americans lost nearly 3,000 men. Critics claimed that the costly defeat was unnecessary, and argued that Washington had listened too readily to Greene. But not long thereafter the critics were silenced by Greene's masterful handling of the troops under his command at Trenton and Princeton.

Greene again proved himself a team man in 1778 when Washington, alarmed by the sad condition of the quartermaster's department, asked Greene to become quartermaster-general. Greene didn't want the post, but he accepted it. For nearly two years he wore two hats, shaping up the quartermaster's department and commanding in the field.

Probably nothing sums up Greene's patriotism better than the letter he left for his wife when he set off for the American camp at Cambridge, Mass., in June 1775:

"The injury done my country, and the chains of slavery forging for posterity, call me forth to defend our common rights, and repel the bold invaders of the sons of freedom. The cause is the cause of God and man . . . I am determined to defend my rights and maintain my freedom, or sell my life in the attempt; and I hope the righteous God that rules the world will bless the armies of America."

John Burgoyne: False Modesty Wasn't His Style

This gambling man and sometime playwright had the odd idea that the war could be won with words

To borrow a line from Shakespeare, General John Burgoyne was the glass of fashion and the mould of form. A dashing figure, he had a way with women. A dramatist of some reputation, he had a way with words. And as a general, he had a way with tactics — when he put his mind to it.

Burgoyne's failing as a military man was that he often didn't. As he had demonstrated during the Seven Years War, he had the winning touch when the spirit of the warrior was upon him, but at other times he was a loser.

Burgoyne first set foot on American soil in the spring of 1775, shortly after Lexington and Concord, with the reinforcements sent to General Gage in besieged Boston.

"How many (British) regulars in Boston?" Burgoyne inquired.

"About 5,000," was the reply.

"What?" Burgoyne exclaimed. "Ten thousand peasants keep 5,000 King's troops shut up? Well, we'll soon find elbow room!"

Burgoyne convinced Gage that all that was needed to disband the rag-tag militia army at Roxbury and Cambridge was a proclamation, a proclamation so brilliantly written that the locals would see the folly of their uprising and sue for forgiveness. A man of no false modesty, Burgoyne said he was obviously the most qualified person to compose the proclamation.

In the proclamation, Burgoyne described the Lexington-Concord skirmishes as an outrage. It was preposterous for the King's troops to be attacked. Absurd, even. It shouldn't be done.

He ridiculed the militia and its "preposterous parade of military arrangement, affecting to hold the (British) army besieged."

"Gentleman Johnny," as Burgoyne

was called, never understood why the proclamation had precisely the opposite effect from that which he had intended.

It was not altogether surprising, then, that in 1777 Burgoyne would be the principal figure in a British military disaster. As part of a grand plan he had gone to London to help prepare, Burgoyne came down through the wilderness from Canada with a force of about 7,000. At the same time, Colonel Barry St. Leger was to work his way eastward from Fort Oswego with about 1,700, and General Sir William Howe was to march north from New York City with his army. In the neighborhood of Albany, the three conquering armies would meet and join hands.

Three things went wrong. First, St. Leger was defeated at Oriskany, N. Y. Next Howe, whose orders from the War Office in London were vague, decided to march south to capture Philadelphia, rather than north to help Burgoyne. And, finally, Burgoyne failed to prepare his forces to cope with the rigors of the northern wilderness. (He had, however, prepared himself. He brought along his mistress, the wife of one of his officers.)

On Oct. 17, 1777, Burgoyne, his food and ammunition exhausted, had to surrender to a superior American force under Generals Horatio Gates and Benedict Arnold. It was the first English army that had surrendered in many years.

Burgoyne returned to England, where he faced severe criticism for a while. But his charm overcame all, and eventually he turned to being a full-time playwright. One of his plays, *The Heiress,* written in 1786, is still performed occasionally in London's West End.

"Mad" Anthony: His Methods Brought Victory

His plan to assault Stony Point without gunfire— just "cold steel"—was considered crazy. It wasn't

Early in the Revolution it became a popular saying that "wherever (Anthony) Wayne goes, there is a fight, for that is his business."

Anthony Wayne was a good soldier, a born fighter. In terms of leadership, courage and command of the science of war, Gen. Wayne was surpassed by few generals of his time. Praised by Washington as "one of my most reliable generals," he had a penchant for succeeding where others were likely to have failed.

And while he was called "Mad Anthony Wayne," he was neither mad nor foolhardy. "Fiery" was the word for him.

Jenkin Lloyd Jones, writing of Wayne in a recently published book, *The Patriots,* explains the method to Wayne's alleged madness:

"They called him mad when he ordered the starved and ragged relics of the American disaster at Quebec to appear on the Ticonderoga parade ground with their hair powdered and plaited.

"But how better can you rebuild the spirits of the spiritless than by the appearance of polish and pride?

"They called him mad when he ordered Stony Point taken by cold steel, and threatened to kill the first man that fired a shot.

"But in a night so black that only the cockades of white paper distinguished friend from foe, what good would musket fire have been in the rush across the parapets?

"And at Green Spring on the James River when his Pennsylvania line fell into Cornwallis' trap and faced annihilation, it seemed a mad thing to order a great drum-beating, trumpet-blowing assault by 800 against 5,000.

"But how else could Cornwallis have been induced to snap open the trap and withdraw, fearing that the whole American Army had come up?"

Born and reared on an estate called "Waynesboro" in Easttown Township, Chester County, Anthony Wayne was a prosperous tanner by inheritance. By the circumstances of war, he was a soldier from January 1776. At the head of the Fourth Pennsylvania Regiment, which he had recruited, he was one of the few standouts in the feeble and clumsy Canadian campaign.

In 1777, he was raised to the rank of brigadier general and assigned to Washington's army, then operating in New Jersey. His self-confidence, always strong, had been increased by his survival of the hideous adventures of his first year in the army.

At Paoli on the night of Sept. 20, 1777, Wayne was attacked by a force much larger than his own, but handled his men with such skill that the British gained only a doubtful advantage. His critics — and as with any man of considerable ego, he had many — attempted to label the

skirmish the "Paoli Massacre," and accused Wayne of negligence. Wayne demanded a court-martial.

"As always," he said, "my planning was as careful as my execution was bold. Our loss was small in proportion to the striking force. I was not surprised by the attack, and I saved my guns. And I will uphold my argument personally at pistol point against anyone who would like to dispute me."

Wayne was acquitted.

He went on to further battlefield triumphs, and was retired from active service in 1783 as a brevet major-general.

He died in 1796, at Erie, Pa., when a wound he had received in Yorktown 15 years before suddenly flared up. The 52-year-old general told his recent bride, "Bury me on the hill beside the Flag."

The War

Lord Cornwallis: By Ironic Twist He Lost It All

The Patton of the British Army was caught in a trap not of his own making— and then it was all over

Lord Charles Cornwallis was the Gen. Patton of the British army. Where most of his colleagues chose to dawdle, Cornwallis was a general who believed in striking swiftly and moving ahead.

It is something of an unfortunate happenstance, then, that this man, accounted by most historians to have been the most capable of Britain's generals in the Revolution, is best known for his surrender at Yorktown, Va., in 1781, a defeat that precipitated British capitulation.

Ironic, too, is the fact that as a member of Parliament, Cornwallis had been an outspoken opponent of the tax measures for America that brought on the Revolution. On one occasion he denounced such measures as "reprehensible," and lauded the protesting colonists as "free Englishmen, such as we, who are simply standing up for their rights."

When the war came, however, Cornwallis, who had served in the Seven Years' War, placed himself at the King's service and was sent to America in 1776.

He served under Generals Howe and Clinton in the campaigns of 1776-79, acquitting himself with distinction. Named British commander in the South in June 1780, Cornwallis won a great victory over Gen. Horatio Gates, the hero of Saratoga, at Camden, S. C., in August. Then, after a lightning-strike victory over Gen. Nathaniel Greene at Guilford, S. C., he invaded Virginia in the spring of 1781.

Richard M. Ketchum describes Cornwallis as follows in his book, *The Winter Soldiers:* "He was only 38 years old, a strong, imposing man with a full face, large nose, and heavy-lidded eyes, one of which had a cast from a hockey accident at Eton . . . unlike most of his fellow officers, he took his profession seriously enough to have studied and worked diligently at it since his eighteenth birthday. He had traveled about in Europe with a tutor, who was a veteran officer, attended the military academy in Turin, and visited several German courts to observe their armies . . ."

But, after moving his forces according to successive and contrary instructions from Clinton, Cornwallis found himself besieged in Yorktown, unable to escape either by land or sea, he was compelled to surrender on Oct. 19, 1781, as a regimental band played "The World Turned Upside Down."

Somewhat surprisingly, despite his epochal defeat, Cornwallis remained in high esteem at home. In 1786, he was appointed governor general of India, where, before leaving office in 1793, he brought about a series of legal and administrative reforms, notably the set of regulations known as the Cornwallis Code. By paying

civil servants adequately while forbidding them to engage in private business, Cornwallis established a tradition of law-abiding, incorruptible British rule on that subcontinent.

Gen. Lafayette: Nobleman, 19, Comes To Fight

And it was all because of what King George's brother said about America to the officers' mess at Metz

It was one of the great ironies of the American Revolution that the young French nobleman, the Marquis de Lafayette, was inspired to come here to fight for the patriot cause by none other than the Duke of Gloucester, brother of King George III of England.

In August, 1775, the Duke was rattling around Europe on a pleasure trip. One of his stopovers in France was at Metz, where the officers of the army garrison invited him to dine at their mess. The Duke spoke freely of the revolution that had flared up in Britain's American colonies, and his views were directly contrary to those of his brother; the colonists were in the right, he said, and he wished them success.

Lafayette, only 18 but already a French army captain, listened attentively, and was stirred. Then and there he resolved to go to America and help the insurgents. It took time to overcome the objections of his family, but ultimately Lafayette went. Extremely wealthy, he purchased and outfitted his own ship, and on April 20, 1777, with a number of

fellow French officers, he sailed for America.

Silas Deane, one of America's two agents in France (with Benjamin Franklin), had promised Lafayette a major general's commission in the Continental Army. But when he reached Philadelphia on July 28, Congress, of foreign adventurers, gave him and his companions the brushoff.

Undaunted, Lafayette wrote a letter to Congress. The last paragraph read: "After the sacrifices that I have made in this cause, I have the right to ask two favors at your hands: The one is, to serve without pay, at my own expense; and the other, that I be allowed to serve first as a volunteer."

Apparently impressed, Congress did an about-face and on July 31 made the young nobleman, who had never as yet even heard the whine of a bullet on a battlefield, a major general in the service of the United States.

Benjamin Franklin also had a hand in the congressional change of heart. From Paris, Franklin had written to Congress, pointing out that Lafayette was "exceedingly beloved" by his countrymen and his presence in the Continental Army would have a good influence on U. S.-French relations. Franklin made the further request that Congress keep Lafayette out of dangerous situations. The news of his death would probably not be well received in France, Franklin noted.

But this last request could not be enforced by the Congress. Lafayette had come to fight.

On August 1, Lafayette met Washington for the first time at a dinner in Philadelphia. The young major general, still a month away from his 20th birthday, was virtually adopted by Washington, who named him to his staff. Lafayette received his baptism of fire at Brandywine and was wounded in the leg. He subsequently commanded troops in action under older generals.

Congress, swayed by ulterior motives, granted Lafayette a furlough in early 1779 to return to his native land. It was no ordinary furlough. The French alliance with America had not gone as well

as had been hoped, and Lafayette, who found himself a popular hero in France, smoothed over some misunderstandings.

More than that, as a living advertisement for the American cause, he joined with Franklin in urging the French to send over an army, accompanied by a fleet. When Lafayette sailed back to America in March 1780, he brought with him his king's assurance that a formida-

ble expedition would arrive by mid-summer.

Given full field command when he returned, Lafayette showed that, while he had done well as subordinate general in battle, he was not a top-flight commanding general. In the Virginia campaign of 1781, Lafayette and his entire force of 1,200 men narrowly escaped capture by Lord Cornwallis, owing to Lafayette's failure to understand the overall military situation. General "Mad Anthony" Wayne saved him in the nick of time.

But later in a subordinate role under Washington and French Gen. Rochambeau, Lafayette did an exemplary job of keeping Cornwallis from breaking out of the Yorktown peninsula.

Lafayette gave a new dimension to the traditional command stricture to look out for the welfare of the troops. Near the close of the war, his entire command was in rags. Lafayette requisitioned the quartermaster for new clothing, but was told that the army had neither clothing nor money at the time. So Lafayette went to merchants in Baltimore and purchased a new outfit for every man — some 1,400 in all.

As historian W. E. Woodward has put it: "A great and noble gentleman was the Marquis de Lafayette."

BRITISH

Lord Amherst: A Ruthless Man Sits Out the War

During an earlier tour of duty in America he had offered a solution for the Indian problem: genocide

When they held the American Revolution, Gen. Jeffrey Amherst declined to attend — even though he received invitation after invitation from King George III himself.

And we can only wonder whether the outcome of the Revolution might have been different had the tough, hawk-nosed general who had led British forces to victory in the French and Indian Wars, acquiesced to the King's entreaties.

For Amherst was not only a brilliant tactician; he possessed a quality, if such it can be termed, lacking in other British

generals who served in America — utter ruthlessness.

During the French and Indian War, for example, he had accepted the assistance of the Indians with reluctance. To Amherst, Indians were contemptible auxiliaries "more nearly allied to the Brute than to the Human Creation."

When the war ended, and the Indians could no longer play the English off against the French, he saw no further need of conciliating them. So in 1763, just before returning to England, he conceived a plan for exterminating the Indians.

Amherst's idea was to kill the Indians by spreading smallpox among them — and to spread it he proposed giving them blankets "inoculated with the disease." The blankets were to be given as presents, accompanied by smiles and expressions of good will.

Amherst wrote to Col. Henry Bouquet at Fort Pitt: "You will do well to try to inoculate the Indians by means of blankets, as well as to try every other method that can serve to extirpate this execrable race."

In reply, Bouquet wrote to Amherst on July 13, 1763: "I will try to inoculate

them — with some blankets that may fall into their hands."

In 1768, Amherst was notified through channels that it was George III's wish that he return to America and take up the governorship of Virginia. Amherst, who detested what he regarded as the primitivism of life in America, refused.

Then in 1774, with the tide of insurrection rising in the colonies, and with the First Continental Congress having convened in Philadelphia, the King sent for his most successful general to beg him to return to America as commander-in-chief with, as one modern commentator has put it, "an olive branch in one hand, while the other should be prepared to obtain submission." But Amherst once more refused to cross the ocean. He told the King he would rather resign from the army.

After Burgoyne's defeat and the surrender of his army at Saratoga, the King again appealed to Amherst to take up his old post. Twice, George held pleading audiences, and both times Amherst refused. Finally he did agree to continue as senior general on the staff, advising the government on the conduct of the war from a vantage point in London.

Why did Amherst decline appointment as commander-in-chief of North America? One theory is that he did not wish to fight against old friends and associates in America. Yet his correspondence with Lord Richard Howe shows that he had virtually no sympathy for the colonials.

Other historians maintain that Amherst refused the North American command because he could see no possibility of success. He is said to have told the King in his second audience that it would take a force of 40,000 to conquer America — an obviously impossible number in view of the renewed French threat to the homeland. But if he did not believe victory possible, why did Amherst stay on in England as senior general on the staff?

The most reasonable explanation, in the view of historian Francis Russell, is that Amherst remained in the War Office because he was then chiefly concerned with the defense of England against her European enemies.

Indeed, when France signed the alliance with America in 1778, Amherst, who had now entered the cabinet as acting commander-in-chief for Great Britain, suggested that all British troops be withdrawn from America. After that, he proposed, the revolution would be opposed entirely by means of a naval blockade.

In 1780, Amherst led troops against a London mob that might well have been handled by a few hundred constables. The mob was protesting passage of the Catholic Relief Bill, a modest enough measure designed to encourage Catholic support for the growingly unpopular American war.

Amherst took to the streets with his troops and put down the mob with his old ruthlessness, and his soldiers shot several hundred rioters before order was restored. It was Amherst's farewell appearance as a commander.

Von Steuben: The Baron Tells A Lucky Lie

He didn't "Prussianize" the Americans; instead, he Americanized Prussianism to fit a new kind of war

Friedrich Wilhelm Ludolf Gerhard Augustin, Baron von Steuben, stretched the truth when he volunteered to come to America to aid the patriot cause. It was a fortuitous fib. For if von Steuben hadn't told it, the Continental Army doubtless would not have had the services of one of the finest teachers of military history.

Von Steuben represented himself as a former "lieutenant general in the King of Prussia's service" when he actually was a retired captain of the general staff of Frederick the Great, having served in the Seven Years' War.

The falsification was rationalized by parties to it — including Benjamin Franklin and Silas Deane, who met von Steuben in Paris in the summer of 1777 and were impressed by the baron's widespread reputation as a master of the Prussian military system — on the ground that under his actual rank von Steuben would be given short shrift by the Continental Congress. Over the past

two years, Congress had hired all too many European captains who proved short on ability but long on desire for money and quick promotion. Ergo, von Steuben would have been viewed as just another mediocrity.

Congress was impressed not only by the credentials of the "lieutenant general," but also by von Steuben's waiver of all claim to pay. He asked only that his expenses be paid. Too, he proposed that if his services should contribute to the eventual success of the American cause, he then would be given such reward as Congress might see fit to grant him. If the cause should fail, he would make no claim whatsoever.

Congress accepted.

Von Steuben reported to Washington at Valley Forge on February 23, 1778, and the baron was appalled at what he saw. Not only was the army underfed and poorly clothed, but there was little or no organization. Yet von Steuben's discerning eye perceived that the men who endured the rigors of Valley Forge were the best of soldier material. Indeed, he thought, no European army could have held together under such hardships.

Impressed by the baron's judgment, Washington made von Steuben the army's first Inspector General, with the rank of major general. Von Steuben spoke little English, and was required to act through interpreters, but he was such a master of organization that within a remarkably short time the army began to look and function like an army.

Von Steuben was able to bring the

troops so far so rapidly because at the outset of the training regimen he had organized a model company and drilled the men in the movements that he was introducing. When he had progressed far enough with the model cadre, he extended the drill to the entire army, keeping the model unit about six lessons ahead.

The process whereby learning to march in step on a parade ground ultimately improves an army's effectiveness in battle has never been satisfactorily explained — and certainly not to the satisfaction of the men in the ranks. But somehow the process does work, and von Steuben proved it again.

Thus, von Steuben taught the army to

march in regular columns of twos and fours in uniform step, to fire volleys at regular command, and to use the bayonet effectively.

Von Steuben, according to an official U.S. Army history, "was also a pioneer in impressing on officers their obligations to the men they commanded. American officers, following British traditions, tended to regard their responsibility as only that of leading their men in battle."

Also, realizing the importance of skirmishers in a war such as this one, he organized elite companies of light infantry as part of every regiment, which the commanders could control separately.

The drill and discipline he imposed was rigorous, but von Steuben's trenchant good humor and his outbursts of profanity, virtually the only English he knew, delighted the soldiers and made the tough training more palatable. Moreover, von Steuben was not unalterably Prussian in his training methods. He was quick to recognize that the American soldier had to be told *why* he should do things before he would do them well, and the baron applied this philosophy to his training program.

While von Steuben subsequently led troops in battle, he never was given as much line command as he desired. Washington considered him far too valuable as a teacher.

When the war was won, von Steuben asked Congress for $60,000 in payment for his services — a not unreasonable sum in view of what he had done. But he was granted only an annual pension of $2,500. In the fourth year of the pension he died suddenly at age 65.

================== BRITISH ==================

Henry Clinton: A Sour Critic Gets His Chance

He was able to get the immovable British Army moving—but he couldn't figure out where to go

It might be said that General Sir Henry Clinton inherited not a military force, but a large stationary object when he succeeded Sir William Howe as commander-in-chief of the British Army in North America in May 1778. For Howe had spent the winter of 1777-78 doing nothing of military value in Philadelphia. The British Army was at rest and, in conformance with the classical principles of physics, tended to remain at rest.

Now, with Washington rebuilding the Continental Army after the awful winter at Valley Forge, it was decided that Clinton should take the British troops that had occupied Philadelphia to New York.

It took some doing, for Clinton had to figuratively recharge the batteries of soldiers who were not by any means a crack fighting force, who had grown almost indolent during the winter of leisure in Philadelphia. But the new commander was up to it and, by artful dodging of Washington's pursuing army, got the troops across New Jersey and to safety in New York, with only one near disaster at Monmouth.

Clinton was an able officer, who had served in the Hanoverian War. He came to Boston with Generals Howe and Burgoyne in 1775 and was Howe's second-in-command at the Battle of Bunker Hill. Clinton never forgave Howe for not following up that hard-won victory by an immediate advance on the American camp at Cambridge, which would surely have fallen.

"I pleaded with General William Howe to pursue the fleeing rebels," Clinton wrote later. "But he chose to ignore me. Had he ordered the advance, he had ended the Rebellion that very day."

Clinton had not had exactly a star-studded career here himself, however.

Early in 1776, Clinton and Admiral Peter Parker were ordered to lead a combined military and naval force into the South. Charleston, S. C., largest port in the southern colonies, had fallen to Patriot militia. The expedition was delayed, however; by the time Clinton and Parker got to Charleston, the Patriot bastions had been more than adequately prepared, and Major General Charles Lee had been detached from Washington's staff to direct the defense of the city. The British attack, on June 28, was beaten off.

In 1777, when Howe moved southward from New York with the capture of Philadelphia as his major objective, Clinton was left behind to command a small force, but it was only enough for a "starved offensive." Thus, when Burgoyne's northern army, moving down from Canada, ran into the trouble that eventually resulted in its surrender at Saratoga, Clinton did not even attempt to create a diversion until it was too late.

Clinton was an able officer, but he lacked the wide-screen vision necessary to command a far-flung operation, as witness his series of conflicting orders to Cornwallis that resulted in the latter's being cornered in Yorktown.

After Cornwallis's capitulation, Clinton resigned and returned to England.

THE WEAPONS

By Mel Greenberg

In this age of industrial warfare in which machine guns can destroy scores of human beings in minutes, in which tanks can roll through infantry lines, and in which wire-guided missiles with nuclear warheads can literally hit bulls-eyes from miles away, the warfare of the 18th century seems tame.

The firepower of the single-shot guns and cannon was tiny by comparison with today's standards; the closest thing to a tank was a man riding an all-too-vulnerable horse; and artillery accuracy was a very approximate affair indeed.

But for all that, there were ways in which the 18th-century battlefield was as terrifying, in its way, as modern war.

Consider this: The North Vietnamese used to refer to the F-111 fighter as "whispering death." The plane would come in at tree-top level, guided by radar, traveling ahead of its own sound wave. The only thing troops on the ground would hear before its bombs burst in their midst was a soft, almost inaudible, "whisssssssss. . ." Soldiers blasted to molecules by the bomb bursts literally never knew what hit them. On the 18th century battlefield, the soldier was acutely, even intimately aware of what might hit him — and what it would do to him if it did.

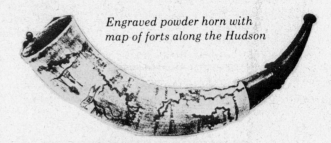

Engraved powder horn with map of forts along the Hudson

The roaring cannons of the enemy were in plain view, never much more than 1,000 yards away, because that was as far as they could shoot.

The roar of a musket volley filled the air with fire and smoke, and getting hit by a musket was like getting hit by a dum-dum bullet; the exit wounds were horrible gaping holes.

And infantry battles didn't remain long-range fire fights. The two sides fought hand-to-hand, eviscerating one another with long, triangularly bladed bayonets.

From the somewhat hazy distance of 200 years, the war of the American Revolution tends to take on a romantic, glory-tinged quality. It's important to keep in mind that for the soldiers who fought in it, it was hell.

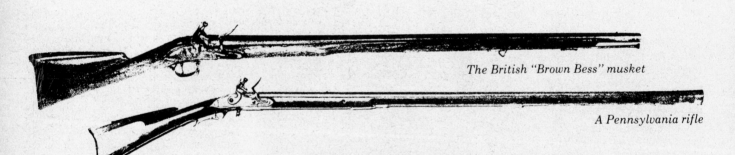

The British "Brown Bess" musket

A Pennsylvania rifle

Rifles & Muskets

The smooth-bore musket was the basic infantry weapon of the Revolution. The famous American rifle was in use by only a small percentage of the American units, and an even smaller percentage of the British troops.

Still there was a debate among militarists of the time as to which was the superior military weapon, and if a British officer had succeeded in gaining the attention of the British War Office to a fast-loading rifle he had developed, the entire course of the war might have changed.

Unquestionably the rifle was more accurate. British Major George Hanger, a weapons expert, analyzed the situation as follows:

"A soldier's musket, if not exceedingly ill-bored (as many of them are), will strike the figure of a man at 80 yards, it may even (do so) at 100 . . ." But at 200, he added, "you may just as well fire at the moon and have the same hopes of hitting your object."

On the other hand, Hanger said that "if an American rifleman were to get perfect aim at 300 yards at me standing still, he would hit me unless it was a very windy day. . ."

By the time of the Revolution, Pennsylvania gunsmiths had raised rifle-making to a fine art, hand-crafting beautiful weapons with curly-maple stocks and shined brass fittings. Their accuracy was legendary. There are accounts of frontiersmen putting eight consecutive shots into a five by seven-inch target at 60 yards.

The secret of the rifle was in its longer barrel, the inside of which had spiral grooves that caused the bullet to spin, and to travel much straighter than the tumbling musket ball.

But as a result the rifle required a bullet that fit much more tightly in the barrel than did a musket ball, and therefore took longer to load. Even though ramming powder and ball down the barrel of a musket was a complex, ten-command process, a veteran soldier could fire four shots a minute, much faster than a rifleman could load and fire.

And while the rifleman was reloading, the opposition would seek, often successfully, to run up and skewer him with a bayonet.

The Revolution wasn't a contest of technology. The weapons on both sides were basically the same. The big difference was that the British "Brown Bess" musket was somewhat heavier than the French "Charleville" musket that the Americans used. A bullet fired from the .79 calibre Brown Bess, it was said, could knock over a cow.

The muskets were fired by a flintlock mechanism. When the trigger was pulled, the hammer was snapped forward by a spring action. The hammer held a flint, and as the flint hit the metal cover of a powder-filled compartment, sparks were struck.

The sparks ignited the powder in the pan, which, in turn, ignited the powder inside the barrel, behind the bullet. (The interior of the barrel and the pan were connected by a small hole called a "vent.")

The big trick in musket marksmanship was to avoid flinching at the preliminary explosion of the powder in the outside pan.

One technological breakthrough did almost occur. British Lieutenant Colonel Patrick Ferguson developed a breech-loading rifle that could be loaded and fired as fast as a musket, and outfitted a light infantry company with them.

Luckily, Ferguson was wounded at Brandywine, and his company was broken up. He recovered, but before he could reorganize his riflemen, he was shot to death at King's Mountain.

There is an interesting irony in the fact that he was almost certainly killed by a well-directed bullet from an American rifle. Rifle-carrying American militiamen dominated the battle.

The Pistols

The pistol had not yet been perfected at the time of the Revolution. A British officer told of firing both of his pistols at an onrushing American, without effect. He would have been better off, he later commented, if he had thown the weapons at the man.

Nonetheless, most officers carried them, as did the few cavalrymen who fought in the Revolution, and sailors. (There was little cavalry because the British had trouble getting horses over to America, and Washington, even though he was himself an expert equestrian, was basically an infantryman who didn't understand or appreciate the use of cavalry.

In addition to being inaccurate, pistols also had a troubling tendency to explode in the user's hand. They were essentially sawed-off muskets, and took much time to reload. Even wielding a pair, an officer had only two shots.

Nonetheless, pistols were highly prized possessions. Washington carried one all through the war, and left it to Lafayette when he died.

They were also treasured booty. When a British major's horse threw him on the way back from Concord, the Minutemen who captured the horse presented pistols that were in the saddle holsters to General Israel Putnam. The pair of fine Scottish pistols is on display today in the Lexington museum.

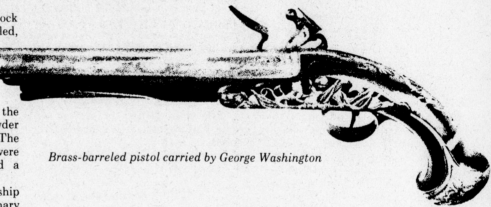

Brass-barreled pistol carried by George Washington

The Blades

The sword was no longer a standard piece of fighting equipment by the time of the Revolution, but there were plenty of them around, often serving as symbols of authority. In the British Army a regimental commander could decide who would be entitled to wear what. The arrangement on the American side was even more haphazard.

A sword could be something of a disadvantage. Americans, the riflemen in particular, did a lot of sniping, and it was simple enough to figure out that the people wearing the swords were officers, sergeants, or other non-commissioned officers. So wearing a sword was something like walking around carrying a large sign that read "Shoot me."

The most widely used British sword was called a "hanger," which was appropriate enough since it "hung" from a cross-belt that passed over the shoulder opposite the side on which the sword was worn. The typical hanger had a single-edged blade 24 to 30 inches long, with a hilt of wood, horn, or cast bronze. The hand guard was usually brass.

The blade was slightly curved, representing a compromise between the ideal shapes for offense and defense. When charging into a fray on the offensive, one could rip up one's enemy far more satisfactorily with a curved blade. But when on the defensive, the most effective way of halting a charging foe was to skewer him with a straight-bladed thrust.

British officer's "hanger"

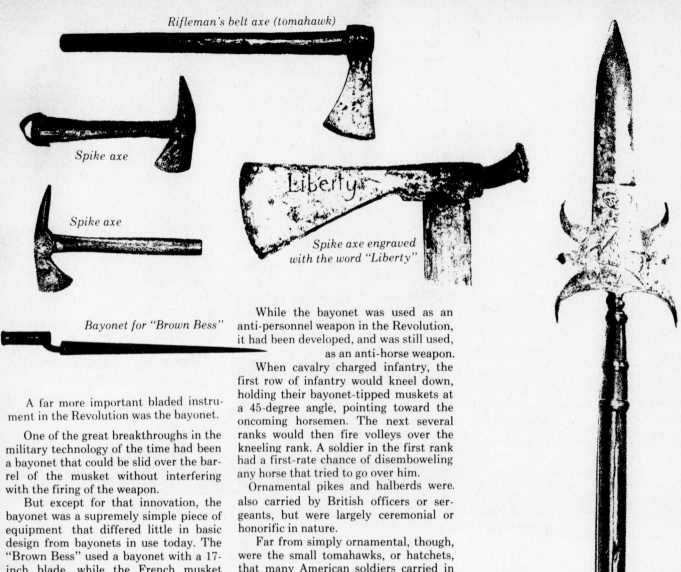

Rifleman's belt axe (tomahawk)

Spike axe

Spike axe

Spike axe engraved with the word "Liberty"

Bayonet for "Brown Bess"

Hessian halberd

A far more important bladed instrument in the Revolution was the bayonet.

One of the great breakthroughs in the military technology of the time had been a bayonet that could be slid over the barrel of the musket without interfering with the firing of the weapon.

But except for that innovation, the bayonet was a supremely simple piece of equipment that differed little in basic design from bayonets in use today. The "Brown Bess" used a bayonet with a 17-inch blade, while the French musket used by the Americans took a 14-inch blade. The French bayonet also had a more secure fitting device, though the American weapons based on the French design often didn't incorporate this feature.

While the bayonet was used as an anti-personnel weapon in the Revolution, it had been developed, and was still used, as an anti-horse weapon.

When cavalry charged infantry, the first row of infantry would kneel down, holding their bayonet-tipped muskets at a 45-degree angle, pointing toward the oncoming horsemen. The next several ranks would then fire volleys over the kneeling rank. A soldier in the first rank had a first-rate chance of disemboweling any horse that tried to go over him.

Ornamental pikes and halberds were also carried by British officers or sergeants, but were largely ceremonial or honorific in nature.

Far from simply ornamental, though, were the small tomahawks, or hatchets, that many American soldiers carried in their belts. The American habit of scalping British corpses, which was particularly prevalent during battles in the Mohawk Valley in the spring of 1778, escalated the level of brutality in the war significantly.

The Artillery

The three types of artillery pieces used on the battlefield of the American Revolution — guns, howitzers, and mortars — were all basically similar in the way they functioned. Powder and shot would be shoved down the barrel from the muzzle end, and then the weapon would be fired by igniting the powder through a hole at the back of the cannon.

The guns, or cannons, had relatively long barrels, and were designed to fire solid shot with a heavy charge of powder for maximum range and momentum. They ranged in size from small guns that fired four-pound shot to huge 32-pounders. They fired either solid balls, packages of smaller projectiles, or projectiles that consisted of two hemispheres connected by a bar or chain.

The guns could also fire powder-filled exploding shells, but the howitzer had been developed specifically for this new type of ordnance. It had a shorter barrel since less powder could be used with the explosive shells, and was designed to fire its shells at a higher trajectory. (Solid shot was fired more or less straight out, and would bounce around the battlefield until, hopefully, it damaged the enemy in some way.)

Mortars were short, squat devices that fired shells in a high arc over fortifications.

Tactics were simple. Usually a general would ask to place his artillery to the side, so that the enemy advance would, in effect, have to parade past it.

Every cannon crew sought to emulate the much-talked-about feat of the age in which a cannon ball knocked down a rank of 43 men as if they were so many ninepins.

At other times the cannon might be moved up with the front line of infantry to fire grapeshot at oncoming ranks of enemy troops.

Once the cannons were set in place, they weren't often moved. That was because the teamsters and horses that pulled the cannon were usually civilians hired on contract, and the teamsters tended to feel that their contracts did not require their presence on the field of battle while shots were being fired in anger.

While the cannons of the time could fire somewhat farther than 1,000 yards, it was difficult or impossible to tell where the cannon balls hit at distances beyond that distance, even with a spyglass. And if the gun crews couldn't tell where their shots were going, it was impossible to focus effective fire on the enemy.

One other piece of explosive ordnance was used on the battlefields of the American Revolution: the grenade. These were simply bombs with fuses that were lighted, and then tossed toward the ranks of the enemy, or over fort walls.

★ ★ ★

British cannon

This huge chain was stretched across rivers to obstruct enemy ships.

THE SOLDIERS

The Americans: They Could Shoot

By Richard S. Dunham

The American soldier complained about the food, his officers, his uniform, and the tedious training. But ultimately he prevailed.

The American soldier in the Revolution griped a lot, which is understandable because there was a lot to gripe about.

The food was not good. Each man was supposed to receive a daily ration of 1½ pounds of flour or bread, one pound of beef, fish, or pork, a pint of whisky or other spirits, and ½ pint of peas or beans, but usually they did not. Often the troops had to forage for themselves, and camps were often set up near rivers or streams where the men could fish.

Even when food supplies were relatively plentiful, of course, there were complaints about the cooking. "Here comes a bowl of beef soup, full of dead leaves and dirt," soldier Albigense Waldo griped to his diary. Many times the soldiers went days on end without fresh bread or meat. Horses and dogs were sometimes eaten.

And there were several episodes — not just during the winter at Valley Forge — when the army endured near-starvation. Another soldier recorded the following conversation as having taken place between an officer and two men seated beside a boiling kettle:

"Well, men, anything to eat?" the officer inquired.

"Not much," they replied.

"What are you boiling in that kettle?" the officer persisted.

"A stone, colonel," one replied. "for they say there is some strength in it if you can only get it out."

Pay was supposed to be a strong point for the Americans. Privates were to be paid $6.66 a month, the highest rate for that rank paid by any army in the world as the time. However, pay was distributed irregularly, and it was in Continental currency, which depreciated in value rapidly during the war.

To be sure, bounties, or bonuses, were paid to recruits when they signed up. A ten-dollar bonus was paid for a three-year enlistment early in the war, and later a land bounty of as much as 500 acres was added.

Officers also had complaints about the pay. General Henry Knox noted at one point that American captains were paid just five shillings a day, half what a British captain received. He reported that many officers were not very enthusiastic about the opportunity "of starving their families for the sake of being in the army."

One of the major problems facing the army was a shortage of qualified officers. The privates resented the efforts of the officers to assert authority, since the enlisted men believed, often correctly, that the officers were no more qualified at soldiering than anyone else. Also, often officers were elected, a process that wasn't always effective in nominating good military leaders.

Debates and discussion were held over everything in many units — over who was going to stand guard, who was going to clean the camp, or who was going to peel the potatoes.

Historian Christopher L. Ward noted this in giving his assessment of the attitude of the ordinary American fighting man:

"The privates were, as a rule, individualists, fiercely independent, undisciplined, insubordinate, disrespectful of their officers, inexperienced in warfare, and unconvinced of the necessity of unquestioning obedience to military command."

Trying to come up with something positive, he added that "as individuals they were generally able-bodied, hardy, sufficiently courageous, and they knew how to shoot. That is about all anyone could say for them."

Battles, as in all wars, occupied only a tiny portion of each soldier's military career. Most of his time while in uniform was spent in cleaning things, counting, them, and guarding them, not to mention cooking them and eating them.

In good units, a rigidly structured day

began with a bugle call at dawn, which was defined as the moment at which the sentries could see 1,000 yards. All of the soldiers lined up for inspection. Roll call was taken at an evening formation.

Every day there was a new password and countersign to be learned, and it had to be repeated whenever one passed the line of guards, or sentries, on the perimeter of the camp.

Prior to the arrival of the Baron von Steuben at Valley Forge in 1778, training was haphazard and cursory. The idea of the Continental Congress — and, indeed, many of the American officers — was that any intelligent citizen could be given a uniform and a rifle, and immediately become a proficient soldier.

The concept died hard, even after the string of American defeats on Long Island and in New York should have given the new nation's leaders something of a clue that they had miscalculated.

Living conditions were generally poor, and often downright unhealthy. When in winter camp, as at Valley Forge, the army hastily constructed cabins. A squad of ten or twelve enlisted men would live in each 16 by 14-foot cabin. The clay, mud, or shingles often leaked, and the poorly constructed fireplaces were always a threat to set the building afire.

Sanitary provisions were rudimentary, and there was some difficulty in getting men to trudge into the woods to a latrine when the call of nature came on a wintry night. As an inducement to the men to do so, one unit commander ordered his sentinels to shoot any man seen "easing himself elsewhere than at ye vaults."

Medical care could prove fatal. Cure-alls such as calomel, julep, nitre elixir, vitriol, Peruvian bark, and Virginia snake root were dispensed for everything, from smallpox to pneumonia. Women and orderlies assisted the few doctors available for the care of the wounded, which was a rough and ready process. The doctors tended to amputate first and ask questions later.

The greatest killer in the field hospitals, though, was "camp fever," which today is known as typhus. In a kind of warfare that predated mass destruction, a soldier's chances of survival on the battlefield were relatively good; but his chances of surviving once he went to the hospital were slim indeed. It has been estimated that nine out of ten fever cases died.

The sick and wounded lay on the floor, according to one account of hospital operations, about two feet apart. Some had been wearing the same clothes for four or five months without change, and their diet consisted of little more than corn meal, rice, and water.

To "purify" the fetid smell, pitch, or tar, or the powder of a cartridge was burned in the room each day.

Uniforms created several problems. First of all they were insufficient supply. Secondly, there were too many different kinds. Each state established its own, with an eye toward making its troops the most distinctive. One Pennsylvania unit's uniforms so closely resembled those of the Hessian mercenaries that the unit was fired upon by other American units on several occasions, which didn't help unit morale.

Some soldiers wore the fringed leather shirts and trousers of the frontier, which Washington approved of. "It is a dress which is justly supposed to carry no small terror to the enemy, who think every such person a complete marksman."

As the war wore on, though, uniforms wore out and the dress of most battle-tested units tended to become increasingly nondescript. "Here comes a soldier," a doctor wrote. "His bare feet are seen through his worn out shoes ... his legs (are) nearly naked from the tattered remains of his only pair of stockings. His breeches are not sufficient to cover his nakedness ... his shirt hanging in strings — his hair disheveled — his face meagre ..."

Although Congress had decreed that all recruits must be male, 16 years or older, and over 5'2", recruiting officers were often willing to bend the rules. There are stories of a few women who enlisted as men, and two members of the Pennsylvania Continentals, David Hamilton Morris and Jeremiah Levering, were 11 and 12 years old, respectively.

Morris's mother had enlisted him with the thought that his salary would be a boon to the family's finances. Levering had run away from home and signed up for a three-year hitch on his own. His military efficiency was apparently unimpressive. One of his comrades in arms complained that he hadn't even been taught "to beat the drum or blow the fife."

Another intriguing characteristic of the American citizen-soldier was that whenever the going got tough, he tended to desert in droves.

Sometimes there was justification. Soldiers who hadn't been paid for several months often simply couldn't afford to continue to serve their country.

Others felt that desertion was a necessity — for the welfare of their families. They would leave the army in the springtime to go home and plant, then return to their units until harvest time, when they would absent themselves without leave again.

While commanders tried to be understanding of the exigencies involved, the habit made long-term planning difficult.

Still and all, some Revolutionary soldiers were able to maintain a sense of humor. "If the war is continued through the winter," one enlisted man at Valley Forge wrote, "the British troops will be scared at the sight of our men. For, as they never fought with naked men (before), the novelty of it will terrify them."

The American troops took advantage of every holiday to celebrate, including the new holiday, July 4, which replaced the King's birthday, June 4. They played ball and cards, conducted target-shooting contests called "rifle frolics," and drank heavily.

And, ultimately, they won. Along the way they were admired by visiting military men from Europe, including a Baron von Closen, who wrote:

"I admire the American troops tremendously. It is incredible that an army composed of men of every age, even children of 15, of whites and blacks, almost naked, unpaid, and rather poorly fed, can ...withstand fire so steadfastly ..." ★★★

An early call to arms issued by the American Continental Army.

The British: The World's Best Had Their Problems

By David Markowitz

The British soldier came to America with the reputation of being the finest fighting man in the world. He had whipped the French only one decade earlier, and in 1815 he would again prove his ability on the fields of Waterloo against Napoleon.

Their mere presence impressed colonial observers. "They came with pomp," said one. "The grand army of Britain — the Highlanders in their kilts and plaids, the stalwart grenadiers in martial scarlet, with their burnished arms, the proud calvary, the mercenary Hessians — all marshaled by their dashing officers, the chivalry of England."

And the finest fighting force in the world came brimming with confidence to quiet the Revolution, only to fail. How? The traditional theory of history states that the American soldier, fighting for liberty, fighting for his family, fighting for his homeland, simply outfought the British soldier.

Very little could be further from the truth. The British soldier was rarely beaten on American battlefields. More plausibly, the mere impossibility of the British task, asking an army of 20,000 to 30,000 men to conquer territory ten times the size of its home island, was a more likely reason.

The British soldiers themselves were unable to understand how the war was lost, and had their own beliefs on what brought their eventual defeat. Observed Ewald Gustav Schaukirk in his diary in December 1780, "The general language . . . of the common soldiers is that the war might and would have been ended long before now, if it was not for the great men who only want to fill their purses."

It's easy to understand why the British soldier was resentful of those in power. For even though the British soldier was the best in the world, he was treated with all the respect given to a back-alley drunk.

"The treatment of enlisted men was inhuman," wrote historian Felix Reichmann. "Punishments even for minor offenses were brutal; (as to) . . . rights, there were almost none. The European soldiers (were) . . . regarded as slaves, objects, not human beings. . ."

Nor was the British soldier appreciated in his pay. "Scanty from the outset, it reached their pockets after many deductions," wrote Reichmann. "During the war, the British private received 16 cents a day, but food and supplies were deducted, if any cash was left for payday."

The provisioning of the army was not handled much better. Although it is difficult to precisely determine a soldier's rations, Curtis believed that a typical week's ration per man consisted of "seven pounds of flour, of the first quality, made from wholly kiln-dried wheat; seven pounds of beef, or in lieu thereof four pounds of pork; six ounces of butter, or in lieu thereof eight ounces of cheese; three pints of peas ; and one-half pound of oatmeal."

Rum, usually well diluted with water, was also a regular part of the soldier's ration.

But the provisions were frequently so poor in quality that they were absolutely inedible. Commissary generals continuously complained of "mouldy bread, weevily biscuit, rancid butter, sour flour, worm-eaten peas and maggoty beef." Large quantities of provisions had to be condemned.

The British man in the ranks never could understand how he lost the war — though he had his theories. A generation later he would redeem himself at Waterloo.

General Sir William Howe, on leaving Boston in March 1776, left behind as "unfit for His Majesty's troops to eat" 61 barrels of pork, 32 firkins of butter, 1,000 pounds of cheese, 12 casks of raisins, and 393 bags of bread.

The big problem was that all the food had to be brought by sea from England. Much food was damaged or destroyed by rats and other vermin through careless storage or through being packed in bags and barrels too flimsy to survive an ocean voyage.

Even the British soldier's uniform was poorly designed, being "ill adapted for comfort and speedy movement." In

When the British Army needed a few good men, the recruiting officer visited the local tavern. One happy lad who evaded the draft is shown peering around the corner at left in this British drawing.

British and Hessian soldiers

most regiments, it consisted of the famous red coat, stock tie, waistcoat, close-fitting knee breeches, gaiters reaching just above the knee, and cocked hat.

Over his left shoulder the foot soldier "wore a broad belt supporting a cartouch box, while another belt around his waist supported a bayonet and a short sword."

The infantryman also carried a knapsack containing extra clothing, a blanket, a haversack with provisions, a canteen, and a fifth of the general equipment belonging to his tent. Added to his other accoutrements, arms and 60 rounds of ammunition, it added up to a load of 60 pounds — enough to slow down any long charge.

The dragoons were armed and clad much like the foot soldier's, except they wore high boots and carried pistols, long swords, firelocks, and occasionally bayonets.

The artilleyman's uniform consisted of a blue coat, cocked hat, white waistcoat, white breeches and black spatter dashes.

One reason for the inhuman treatment the British soldier received was that many soldiers were criminals who accepted military service as an alternative to prison. Others were country boys who chose the soldier's hard life over one of poverty and starvation. The British soldier "commonly was a simple country boy overpersuaded by smooth talk and gin to volunteer."

The relatively better treatment and pay afforded the Hessian mercenaries created another source of friction. "There never was an army so well paid as the Hessians in the English service in America," noted one historian.

"The Hessian soldiers became individually rich and (were) well provided with those little comforts and conveniences that constitute the luxury of a soldier," noted another. "A kind of rivalry ensued between the two nations."

In spite of all their adversity, the British soldier often was able to find outlets from the war. Cockfights and cricket games were organized, horse races were held, and at least one foot race run in which one soldier from each battalion raced three miles in full uniform and equipment.

Religion too was an outlet for the soldiers. Jacob Coats reported that while the British occupied Philadelphia, most British soldiers attended Christ Church, where a fife was used for music when the common soldiers attended.

And on holidays, the British soldiers celebrated as if they were safe back home in England. "This is Christmas Eve," noted Quaker Elizabeth Drinker, "and the few troops that are left in this city (Philadelphia) I fear are frolicking."

But unfortunately for the British soldier, most of the time he spent in America was not spent frolicking. Under one burden or another, the finest fighting man in the world tried to quell the revolution. He felt that his own superiors' incompetence hampered him nearly as much as the enemy. It was as if he was fighting two armies.   ★ ★ ★

In the 1800s the story of Molly Hays was romanticized as "Molly Pitcher," and depicted in romantic paintings like this one painted by Dennis Carter in 1859, showing her being presented to Washington and von Steuben. According to one legend a British cannonball passed between her legs, damaging only her petticoat.

THE WOMEN

By Patricia Tice

Today the fields of Monmouth are peaceful. Winter chills the air and only a shot fired by a solitary hunter breaks the silence. The apple harvest was bountiful this year and making cider is still the order of the day. As one passes the orchards and meadows, it is difficult to envison the way those same fields looked on June 28, 1778.

A hot and humid haze covered these same fields. Cannon and musket thundered. The 100 degree heat, "almost too hot to live in," as one veteran recalled, grew hotter when artillery fire increased. Men collapsed from heat exhaustion.

A camp woman, according to the same account, "was busily engaged in carrying canteens of water to the . . . soldiers." She returned with more water to see her husband, a gunner named William Hays, fall in battle. The officer in charge at first ordered the removal of his gun — there was no one left to man it — but Molly Hays moved forward and began loading. And there she remained, "discharging the piece with as much regularity as any soldier present," sending shot after shot into the advancing British ranks.

The story of Molly Hays has come down through various 19th-century romanticizations as the story of Molly Pitcher, and has been widely retold and commemorated. (There is even a Molly Pitcher rest stop on the New Jersey Turnpike.)

What is not so widely known is that Molly Hays-Pitcher's story is only a small portion of the story of women in the Revolution.

Many women committed to American independence participated actively in the war effort. The efforts and writ-

"Even in their dresses, the females seem to bid us defiance," a British officer wrote.

ing of socially prominent women like Martha Washington, Abigail Adams and Mercy Otis Warren are matters of record. Of equal dimension were the actions of women now forgotten.

No less than 12 editors of Revolutionary newspapers happened to be women. One of them, Mary Katherine Goddard, was the first to publish copies of the Declaration of Independence. Lydia Darragh, Grace and Rachel Martin, and Emily Greiger were only four of many women to serve in an espionage capacity.

Most women, of course, served by keeping home fires burning and acting as a line of quiet resistance. One exasperated British soldier exclaimed: "Even in their dresses, the females seem to bid us defiance . . . they take care to have in their breasts . . . and even on their shoes something that resembles their flag of thirteen stripes. An officer told Cornwallis that he believed if he had destroyed all the men in North America, we should have enough to do to conquer the women."

Defiant females of Philadelphia drove 10 teams of oxen to Valley Forge through British-held territory. How they passed unchecked remains a mystery. Their wagons also contained 2,000 shirts, sewn by Philadelphia women.

A substantial number of women, apparently including Molly Hays, were made homeless by the war as they fled areas occupied by enemy troops. And as the war lengthened, impoverished wives of unpaid soldiers joined the ranks of the uprooted.

For many, the only solution was to gather the children and follow the troops, a practice that actually was common with all armies of the time. The exact number of women and children accompanying American troops varied throughout the war, and only partial counts have been found by historians. A report of "the number of women and children in the several regiments and corps stationed at and in the vicinity of West Point" for example, mentions 405 women.

The women like Molly Hays played an intricate part in keeping the Army intact. They laundered, cooked and sewed for the troops.. During battle, they swabbed hot cannons and loaded muskets. As nurses, they fought one of the most deadly battles of the Revolution: the battle against disease.

When epidemics erupted, Washington relied upon camp women to ease medical emergencies. After smallpox appeared in the ranks in May 1778, Washington requested that "commanding officers assist regimental surgeons in procuring as many women of the Army as can be prevailed upon to serve as nurses; to them will be paid the usual rate."

The expense of keeping women and children "on the ration(s)" of the Army drew criticism from the armchair generals in the Congress. An irritated Gen. Washington responded: "I was obliged to give provisions to the extra women or lose by desertion . . . some of the best soldiers in the service . . . who very probably would have followed their wives."

But although Washington understood the necessity of

tolerating the women, that didn't necessarily mean that he was pleased about it. While camped at Roxborough in August 1777, he wrote: " . . . the multitude of women, especially those who are pregnant, or have children, are a clog upon every movement."

Moreover, the women insisted upon riding in the baggage wagons, despite Washington's frequent instructions to the contrary. (Gen. Washington tactfully "recommended" rather than "ordered" in affairs relating to the camp women.)

It was to prove a continuing problem. A year after Monmouth, Washington was again complaining. "The General," he wrote, "was sorry to see thro'out the march a much greater proportion of men with the baggage than could possibly be necessary . . ."

What kind of person was the American woman of the Revolution? Generalities, as always, are difficult. But if it is impossible to draw a composite portrait, it is, at least, possible to tell something about the woman who ultimately became the best known, Molly Hays.

She could not write; she made her mark with an X. Harriet Foulke, whose father employed Molly Hays, described the heroine of Monmouth: "She was homely in appearance, not refined in manner or language, but ready to do a kind act for anyone. She was of average height, muscular, strong and heavy-set.

"She was a very busy talker. She wore a short gown, white or calico, a linsey-striped skirt, very short and full, woolen stockings, heavy brogans, and a broad white cap with flaring ruffles."

After the battle of Monmouth, Molly Hays slipped back into the routine of camp life. When William Hays received his discharge in January 1783, the couple returned to Carlisle, Pa. A barber by trade, William Hays probably opened a shop there. That same year saw the birth of their only child, John L. Hays. Evidently the couple prospered, for the tax records of 1785 list Willian Hays owning "one house and lot rented" and "one house and lot his own."

William Hays lived only another three years and in 1792 his widow married one John McCauley (or McAuley). Molly McCauley supplemented the family income by scrubbing and cleaning the Carlisle courthouse.

In 1813, she became a widow again. While her son fought in the War of 1812, she supported herself by working as a nurse and charwoman. Early in 1822, she entered the Miles household in Carlisle as a nurse.

In February, a Mr. Molon presented a petition to the Pennsylvania State Senate from "Molly McKolly, a widow of an old soldier of the Revolutionary War praying for pecuniary aid." The legislature granted her request. On Feb. 21, a bill passed, "for the relief of Molly McKolly, for her services during the Revolutionary War . . . the sum of $40 immediately and the same sum yearly during her life."

The 1830 census indicates that by that time she had moved from her home at Bedford and North Streets in Carlisle to live with her son, daughter-in-law, and their seven children.

Upon her death in 1833, the *Carlisle American Volunteer* commented: "Died Sunday last, at an advanced age, Mrs. Molly McCauley. She lived during the days of the American Revolution, sharing its hardships and witnessed many scenes of blood and carnage. To the sick and wounded, she was an efficient aid."

The galleys of the Pennsylvania Navy engage British ships of war off Fort Mifflin. One of the British ships, the Augusta, *caught fire and exploded with such force that many residents thought there had been an earthquake.*

THE NAVY

By Laura Lippstone

Most Philadelphians know of Philadelphia's long connection with the United States Navy.

For starters, it was founded here. The Continental Congress approved a fleet of 13 ships in October 1775, and only a couple of weeks later added a force of "sea soldiers" — the United States Marine Corps.

Many of the ships were outfitted here, and it was to Philadelphia that John Paul Jones came to take command of the *Alfred* — and to complain about the rattlesnake ("Don't Tread On Me") flag that was flown on American ships-of-war at first.

"I could never see how or why," Jones said, "such a venomous serpent should be the combatant emblem of a brave and honest folk, fighting to be free . . ." Perhaps in part to satisfy Jones's criticism, the Stars and Stripes was sewn here, and first flown on Navy ships.

Many of the first seamen of the Continental Navy were recruited from Philadelphia, and from here American ships debarked to attack British commerce and British fighting ships. Two Philadelphia captains, Nicholas Biddle and John Barry, steered their ships, the *Black Prince* and the *Randolph,* halfway around the world before the war's end. Barry became the first commander of the U. S. Navy.

What most Philadelphians don't know is that most of the waterborne fighting in and around Philadelphia had little or nothing to do with the Continental Navy, which became the U.S. Navy. The naval fighting in the Delaware was handled instead by the somewhat less known, and long since defunct, Pennsylvania Navy.

Most of the states had their own navies, just as they had their own militia. They also outfitted privateers, which was, in effect, legalizing piracy. The potential financial reward of serving aboard a privateer, whose crew was entitled to a cut of the proceeds from the sale of any ship and cargo they captured, made it difficult at first to recruit seamen for less lucrative service in the Continental Navy.

Service in the Pennsylvania Navy appealed to those sailors who preferred living peaceably in the port of Philadelphia to roughing it on the high seas with the Continental Navy or aboard a privateer. The Pennsylvania Assembly tried to make service in the ranks of its floating fighting arm even more attractive by offering enlistees an annual stipend consisting of "ten pounds of beef, fifty shillings per month, seven pounds of bread, sixpence worth of vegetables . . . seven half-pints of rum a week . . . free house rent . . . victuals and drink . . ."

The Assembly even offered to let its sailors moonlight. When not on duty, the Pennsylvania sailor was welcome to be with his family, "or to fill his pockets for his own amusement."

"This," the recruiting broadside noted, "is an encouragement no other service in the continent can give."

All the members of the Pennsylvania Navy had to do was patrol the Delaware in search of " . . . the King's ships, sloops, cutters, or other vessels." This they did in small, open boats called galleys, which were basically oversized rowboats, with a medium-sized 18-pound cannon mounted in the front.

What the boats lacked in size or firepower they made up for in names. They were christened with such names as *Washington*, *Franklin*, and *Bull Dog*. One of the more appropriate galley names was *Experiment*.

The galleys, which were stationed between Cape Henlopen, Del., and the Frankford Creek above Philadelphia, were supposed to work with the three Delaware River Forts, which overlooked the submerged obstacles called *chevaux de frise*, to keep the British from gaining access to Philadelphia by way of the Delaware. And, in point of fact, they were able to do this despite the strongest British efforts for several months in the late summer and fall of 1777.

Still and all, it cannot properly be said that the Pennsylvania Navy wrote its page of the history of the Revolution in glory. Its achievements were, as the expression goes, mixed.

The fleet's first encounter with the British came when its galleys rowed out to assault two British frigates that came up the Delaware Bay to fill their water casks. (The Americans mistakenly believed that the frigates intended to launch a full-scale attack on the river defenses.)

Initially the British laughed at the feeble marksmanship of the Americans in their little boats with the little cannons. They stopped laughing when they discovered that it was darned difficult for their guns to hit the little boats.

Luckily for the British, the galleys stayed too far away to do any real damage, though. Eventually the Americans ran out of ammunition, and retreated upriver.

Then the Americans got a break. The *Roebuck*, its crew possibly still a little giddy after the amusing encounter with the Americans, ran aground. The next day the Americans returned and did somewhat better, scoring a number of hits "betwixt the wind (sails) and water," according to an American prisoner on board, but didn't sink the still stuck *Roebuck*. Each side suffered one fatality.

The Pennsylvania fleet was used mainly for reconnaissance during Howe's campaign up the Delaware. It was troubled by criticism from the Philadelphia Committee of Safety, some of whose members were unimpressed with the galleys' performance in the shoot-out with the *Roebuck*. Many Philadelphians had come down to watch the fight from the river banks while munching picnic lunches. And as Howe approached, desertions became another problem. Advertisements were posted offering $4 to anyone "apprehending and delivering a deserter to the galleys."

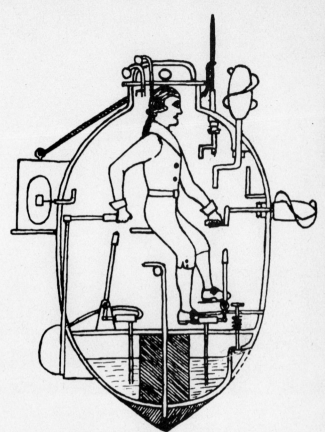

David Bushnell's submarine actually worked — but never sank anything.

After the British took Philadelphia, the little Pennsylvania Navy continued to do the best it could. Its commander, Commodore Hazelwood, graciously declined an offer of amnesty from the British, saying that he "recognized the valour and bravery of the British Navy," but would "endeavor to gain their esteem by a glorious defense."

Six of his galleys attacked the *Vigilant*, a man o' war that had been pulled upstream to shell Fort Mifflin, but their effort failed to win any kudos from the commander inside the besieged fort, who alleged that the galleys had simply "lost a few of their men, and then returned without attempting anything." Hazelwood and the commander got into a brief fist fight over the galleys' effectiveness.

After the forts fell, the navy went inactive, finally disbanding in 1782. Its last try for glory was the scheme of David Bushnell to float kegs of powder down the river to blow up the British ships off Philadelphia during the British occupation.

Bushnell was a man with authentic ingenuity and scientific vision. He had drawn up designs, for instance, for a one-man submarine. But the keg plan didn't work.

The kegs dispersed, and exploded prematurely. They did give the British something of a bad moment, though, and after the Royal sailors realized what was being done, they began firing like crazy at anything they spotted in the water, riddling all manner of floating objects, including a keg of butter that had somehow fallen in.

The only casualties were two small boys who spotted one of the kegs, and were blown up when they tried to examine it. ★ ★ ★

"The Battle of Princeton," painted by William Mercer, the deaf-mute son of General Hugh Mercer, who was bayoneted to death in the battle.

THE WAR

By Willard S. Randall

Within hours of declaring America independent of Great Britain on July 4, 1776, delegates to the Second Continental Congress turned to the somber business of prosecuting the war they were now irretrievably enmeshed in, and of providing for the defense of Philadelphia, the new nation's capital.

By unanimous resolution, Congress purchased its first piece of real estate for 600 pounds of Pennsylvania currency — a flat, 96-acre wedge of South Jersey riverfront 12 miles downriver from Philadelphia where Great Mantua Creek oozed into the Delaware. The fort site, then covered with peach orchards, was purchased from Quaker widow Margaret Paul and named Fort Billings.

Intended by the congressman who had selected it, Board of War member Benjamin Franklin, to be Philadelphia's first line of defense against the expected invasion upriver of the British fleet, the site was promptly cleared by 500 New Jersey militiamen. Then they began to lay out earthworks according to plans drawn by a recently-arrived volunteer Polish military engineer, Captain Thaddeus Kosciuszko, who also designed smaller fortifications at Red Bank and Fort Island, eight miles upstream on either side of the river, just four miles below the city.

A mood of optimism prevailed. By July 1776, the American rebels were confident they could defend any city against British attack, Indeed, the heady series encounters with the British regulars in the preceding months had been a factor encouraging the Congress to cast caution aside and openly declare for independence.

American militiamen had slaughtered Redcoats by the score at Concord and Bunker Hill, American strike forces had besieged Montreal and Quebec in a bold winter offensive that very nearly conquered Canada. These invasion forces had ultimately been defeated, but they had created the impression that the rebels were on the offensive.

To the South, rebel forces had blunted a major Loyalist rising in North Carolina by cutting down the Scots Highland regiments at the Battle of Moore's Creek Bridge. Then they had repulsed a major British invasion force at Charleston, S.C. In Virginia, the attempt by the British governor, Lord Dunmore, to arm slaves and put down the rebellion had failed miserably, serving mainly to make Virginia, the largest American colony, a hotbed of rebel militance.

Yet every realistic American expected a counter-attacking response from the mighty British Empire, and they did not have to wait long. On July 4, 1776, the same day independence was declared, the British fleet arrived silently on the American horizon, as the first sails of the mightiest armada ever seen in the New World tacked majestically off Sandy Hook. They came onward through the narrows between New York and New Jersey into New York harbor.

Inside two weeks, some 52 men-of-war

and 427 troop transports jammed with artillery, supplies and 34,000 of the world's toughest soldiers crowded the anchorages. It was the largest expeditionary force ever launched by the British.

Their mission was straightforward: to crush the American rebellion, to restore America to subjugation as a string of dutiful colonies subservient to the British Crown, and, especially, to carry out King George's command to "punish America."

As if in defiance to the red-coated British regulars and blue-coated Hessian mercenaries disembarking on Staten Island, the Sons of Liberty across the harbor in Manhattan reacted wildly to the Declaration of Independence, celebrating by throwing ropes around a metal equestrian statue of the king, hauling it down, and shipping it off to Ridgefield, Conn., to be melted down into 42,088 bullets to fire back at the invaders.

Their celebration was, however, short-lived.

In the sweltering weeks that followed, the British unleashed a stunning series of amphibious assaults and overland quick-marches that shattered the main American army on Long Island, drove it from New York City, chased it as if it were a tired and frightened fox through the hills of Westchester County, and then hounded its ragged remnants all the way across northern New Jersey.

Burning, plundering, killing, shelling towns and countryside, the British and their hired Hessian mercenaries gave no quarter. At the brutal Battle of Long Island, Hessian *jaegers* with fixed bayonets pursued the screaming Americans into the woods and skewered them to the trees with their bayonets, ignoring the Americans' supplicative attempts to surrender.

Looting Loyalist and Patriot homesteads alike, the merciless Hessians showed America what warfare was really all about, carrying on the fire and sword affair they had practiced dispassionately for one employer or another in Europe for centuries. In three months, the prosperous countrysides of New York and northern New Jersey were reduced to a smoldering wasteland.

By December 1776, it had become abundantly clear to the beleaguered American commander, General George Washington, that the British planned to take advantage of unseasonably warm autumn weather to quick-march overland to surprise and seize Philadelphia. He realized, too, that the river defenses constructed by summer-long labor of upwards of 6,000 of Philadelphia's whites and 1,000 freed blacks were rendered useless by the sudden British overland onslaught. There was every reason to believe that the war, so recently begun in

At the brutal Battle of Long Island, Hessian *jaegers* with fixed bayonets pursued the screaming Americans into the woods and skewered them to trees . . . "

earnest, was almost over.

Late in November, British General Sir William Howe had ordered the lightning British offensive, unleashing his boldest field commander, Earl Charles Cornwallis, with a handpicked force of 4,000 British grenadiers, light infantry, and Hessian grenadiers with heavy artillery, up the Raritan River Valley to cut off Washington's retreat from New York.

For a month of sleepness nights and dogged, hungry days, the rebels were pursued from town to town across New Jersey.

Washington had counted on Jerseymen to rise to his standard. But at Newark, only 30 turned out to join the Americans. On that same day, 300 New Jerseyans joined the British.

As Cornwallis dispensed grapeshot to rebels and amnesty to Loyalists, the British occupied Hackensack, Newark, New Brunswick, Perth Amboy, Princeton, Trenton, and Bordentown; their skirmishers spread out ahead of the assault and reached the east bank of the Delaware River, within 12 miles of Philadelphia.

"I tremble for Philadelphia," Washington wrote privately as he retreated across the Delaware into Bucks County with fewer than 3,000 men, all that remained of the confident 20,000-man force he had commanded only three months earlier.

In a panic, Congress issued a series of pompous resolutions declaring that it

Free Library of Philadelphia

Thaddeus Kosciuszko:
Engineered the city's defenses . . .

wasn't really fleeing the capital, but then proceeded to bundle up its records and

At the Battle of Long Island, in August 1776, the British landed with 32,000 troops — the largest invasion force up to that time — and routed the Americans.

laundry and desert Philadelphia at the critical moment.

All the signers of the Declaration of Independence were considered arch-traitors by the British, and while it would be another year before the signers made their names public, the Loyalists knew who they were. As the British moved forward they hunted the signers down.

As the British occupied Princeton, they sacked all its houses, but saved especial wrath for Morven, the home of signer Richard Stockton. They burned its library, stole all of Stockton's furniture and belongings, they hauled Stock-

ton himself to a New York prison for a special regimen of torture.

Congress fled, first west, then south 110 miles to the town of Baltimore, and turned over dictatorial powers to Washington. Washington, who preferred to allow civilian control when there was a civil government to exert itself, now had his military duties compounded with civil responsibilities.

By now, though, much of the capital was deserted. As British troops tramped toward it on December 3, Philadelphia journalist Christopher Marshall scrawled tense entries in his notebook:

"This city alarmed with the news of Howe's army ... proceeding for this place. Drums beat a martial appearance; the shops shut, and all business except preparing to disappoint our enemies has been laid aside." Nine days later, Marshall noted that every able-bodied resident had been ordered "to go this day and assist in entrenching the city."

●

The overland attack could not have come at a worse time for Philadelphia. More than 3,000 of the city's best troops had been lost in the New York campaign, with most of them having been captured at Fort Washington, a makeshift mud fort along the Hudson River in which they were bottled up. Nearly 1,500 more had contracted typhoid fever at the "flying camp," a reserve base in Perth Amboy, and had been brought back to Philadelphia to die.

Among the sick and captured were many of the city's best artisans, shipwrights, carpenters, laborers, and apprentices, as well as the sons of many of the city's leading families. More than three out of four of the prisoners would die in filthy British prison ships and jails before the winter was over. Little of the revolutionary zeal remained in Philadelphia by mid-December 1776.

"Vigor and spirit alone can save us,"

clockmaker-turned-politician David Rittenhouse told his fellow members of Pennsylvania's hard-pressed Council of Safety. "There is no time for words. Exert yourselves like freemen."

As Philadelphians loaded their wagons with bedding, furniture and food and fled west toward summer houses and relatives' farms and refugee camps as far west as Reading, Lancaster and York, Washington tried to reassure the citizenry, and stem the evacuation by sending in Major General Israel Putnam, the hero of the French and Indian Wars and, more recently, Bunker Hill, as military governor.

The corpulent "Old Put," whose sneak march out of New York City had saved

5,000 Americans from capture, declared martial law in the city, ordered the execution of anyone caught setting fires in the city (Americans had just put New York City to the torch), and rounded up all suspected Loyalists, whom he herded west along with the British prisoners in the area.

Still, in a report dated December 12, Putnam had to report ruefully to Washington upriver at Bristol: "All things in this city remain in confusion."

At his camp in Bucks County, Washington had to turn and face a threat from the rear. The Bucks County militia had turned out as ordered all right, but it turned Loyalist. Washington, still desperate for recruits, had to order it dismissed and dispersed.

The army at Lexington was a rag-tag bunch of Massachusetts militia.

The British bombarded Fort George prior to Lord Howe's capture of New York City in September 1776.

Writing to Virginia to his cousin, Lund Washington, Washington said "the game is pretty near up," but even so saying, he had begun to formulate one last bold turn of the cards.

Weeks earlier, bottled up with the survivors of his routed army on Brooklyn Heights, Washington had first detected a British flaw. Howe, he saw, had no trouble defeating him, but he did not follow up his battlefield victories. After a stunning victory, he would order his troops to stop, eat, rest, clean their weapons and polish their brass — while the enemy slipped away.

From this observation, the harried Washington stumbled onto a revolutionary new strategy. By the time it became evident the British were aiming for Philadelphia, he wrote early in December, "Should they now really risk this undertaking, then there is a great probability that they will pay dearly for it, for I shall continue to retreat before them so as to lull them into security."

After yielding all of New Jersey to the British, he would establish as formidable a line as possible along the western bank of the Delaware, and then rely on the puzzling lack of instinct for the jugular that characterized his enemy to give him more valuable time.

Washington ordered all boats and barges along the Delaware for 60 miles seized and brought to the ferries near his Bucks County encampment; then he ranged his artillery along the western river banks and forced the British to extend their line of advance posts for 30 miles along the east bank of the river. The artillery repulsed British skirmishers with brisk fire if they ventured near the water.

However, it would have been a relatively simple matter requiring scarcely another week for the British to gather wagons and haul their assault barges from the fleet in New York overland for the attack on Philadelphia. Moreover, Loyalists pointed out a large supply of cut lumber at a lumberyard adjoining the British barracks in Trenton, but it was now mid-December, and the temperatures plummeted. The British decided to go into winter quarters and rest a bit before the spring offensive to take Philadelphia.

For the Americans, it was an incredible piece of good fortune. Instead of imminent and possibly conclusive disaster, they could look ahead to several months of safety. What's more, Washington realized that despite the success the British had enjoyed in the campaign, they were now strung out along a 30-mile front — and eminently vulnerable.

In his official report to Lord George Germain, mastermind of the war effort, the British commander Howe said he had found the weather "too severe to keep the field," despite the fact that his men were far better clad, armed, and fed than the desperate Americans.

"The troops will immediately march into quarters and hold themselves in readiness to assemble on the shortest notice," Howe assured Germain.

But then he added a disquieting note, that "the chain (of outposts), I own, is too extensive."

The Winter Soldiers

Cornwallis, eager to return to his wife in England for the winter, turned over the command in New Jersey to a cocky but thoroughly mediocre field officer, General James Grant. Grant sent the British troops back toward New York, and garrisoned the outposts with Hessians.

The Hessian officer placed in command at Trenton, the British strongpoint nearest Washington's forces, was Col. Johann Gottlieb Rall. It was his troops who had slaughtered Americans as they tried to surrender on Long Island, and again on the slopes around Fort Washington.

A noisy, fastidious, hard-drinking gambler who spoke no English and scorned all Americans, Rall had trouble in Trenton from the outset. His 1,600 troops had a reputation for plunder and raping that worried even the British. Lord Howe's secretary, Ambrose Serle, had commented in his reports on their behavior during the fall offensive:

"It is impossible to express the devastations which (they) have made upon the houses & country seats of some of the rebels. All their furniture, glass, windows, and the very hangings of the rooms are demolished or defaced. This with the filth deposited in them makes them so offensive . . . that it is a penance to go into them . . . ."

In mid-December, the Hessians in the 100-house village of Trenton crowded into commandeered winter quarters, made the best of the monotony of winter garrison duty in the manner to which they were accustomed. One day an American patrol on the Pennsylvania river bank heard a group of women calling for help. Rowing over, they learned that all of the women, including a 15-year-old girl, had been raped that morning by the invaders.

Hessian brutality succeeded where all of Washington's appeals had failed. The fence-straddling Jersey farmers began to come over to the American side. Until now, they had refused to help the Americans, and had sought instead to protect their property by swearing allegiance to the King. They tacked red ribbons on their doors to mark their loyalty. Now, they angrily formed marauding milita bands that ambushed Hessian patrols and British scouting parties whenever they ventured outside the Trenton strongpoint. Not a day passed that the Hessians didn't lose a few more men.

"We have not slept one night in peace since we came to this place," a Hessian officer bemoaned to his diary on Christmas Eve. So serious had the skirmishes become that Colonel Rall saw fit to send a 100-man escort with a letter to General Grant in which he complained that his position was "too much exposed."

From his base camp at New Brunswick, Grant pooh-poohed the danger. He reassured Rall there were fewer than 300 rebels in all New Jersey and that he had little to fear from Washington's men who, according to his latest intelligence reports from Loyalists, were "almost naked, dying of cold, without blankets, and very ill-supplied with provisions."

While Washington's tired army was anything but comfortable, its condition was not so dire as he had carefully led the British commander to believe. Indeed, for weeks Washington had shrewdly used spies to cultivate the muth of his army's impotence.

One of the most effective members of Washington's fledgling secret service was a weaver named John Honeyman, who had been conscripted to serve with the British in the French and Indian Wars and who had once been a bodyguard to General James Wolfe, conqueror of Quebec. He was eager to serve against the British now, though, and he used their trust to provide vital information to

A courier rushed up to tell Washington that one unit's powder was wet. "Tell them to use the bayonet," Washington replied. "I am resolved to take Trenton."

Before embarking, the American commanders had read Thomas Paine's American Crisis *(right) to their troops.*

Washington and misleading information to the British. Posing as a cattle dealer and butcher, he lived in Griggstown, near Princeton and, whenever he had information for Washington, he arranged to be captured by the Americans.

On December 22, he walked into a woods inside the American lines, cracking his bullwhip as if chasing cattle, attracting the attention of an American patrol that took him into custody. The patrol delivered its prisoner to Washington's headquarters.

Washington excused the guards and closed the doors as Honeyman gave him detailed information on the Hessian forces and routines in Trenton. Washington then handed him a key to the guardhouse where he was to be locked up, and ordered him taken away.

To pay for his spy network, Washington had appealed to one member of Congress, Robert Morris, who had not fled Philadelphia. Washington asked him to send him 150 pounds in gold immediately on his own account and, if there was any way to raise it, $50,000 in Continental money to pay his troops a bounty to stay on past the expiration of their enlistments.

Morris knew that the only people in Philadelphia with that kind of money were the rich Quaker merchants. They would not lend money directly to the war effort, but they would loan it to Morris personally. What he did with it, of course, was up to him.

Soon canvas bags began to arrive at Washington's headquarters with the cash Washington needed to carry out his bold plan.

By now, Washington had decided to attempt what no one, British or American, believed possible: he would attack, and attack quickly, before the enlistments of his best Continental troops expired at midnight December 31. By this bold, almost foolhardy, stroke he hoped to keep his army from melting away. Perhaps he couldn't give them the pay, clothing, and equipment they needed, but he could give them what they had

come for: a chance to attack the enemy. He may even have felt he was giving them more — a small but real opportunity to win.

On the morning of December 24, Dr. Benjamin Rush of Philadelphia, another member of Congress who had remained behind, rode out to William McKonkey's handsome three-story stone house on the Delaware to visit Washington, who appeared to be "much depressed."

Rush reassured the general that Congress was behind him all the way, if at a considerable distance, and as Rush held forth, Washington kept scribbling on small pieces of paper. One fell to the floor, Rush picked it up and read, "Victory or Death."

It was the watchword for Washington's boldest gamble: an all-out, do-or-die attack on Trenton while its garrison slept off the effects of its Christmas celebration. If he won, Washington foresaw that he would inspire the lagging Patriots, cow the Loyalists, encourage enlistments and reenlistments, drive the British from the approaches to Philadelphia, and keep the Revolution alive. If he lost, Washington felt, the American cause was dead.

The tall, slope-shouldered 44-year-old officer had no illusions left. While Philadelphia's Gen. John Cadwalader had recruited 1,800 Pennsylvania militia to attack directly across the river at Trenton and Gen. James Ewing was to strike Trenton from the south to cut off retreat by the Hessians. Washington had learned from bitter experience not to rely on militia. They were, he would say later, never worth anything when it came to "the real business of fighting."

His principal reliance had to be on the main assault force, which he would lead himself. It was made up entirely of toughened American veterans — regulars from Virginia, Delaware, Maryland, and New England. And it was led by reliable officers: Henry Knox, Nathaniel Greene, James Monroe, John Sullivan, John Glover, and William Washington.

The future leaders of America's army and republic were huddled around McKonkey's Ferry that frigid afternoon of December 25, 1776, as Washington gave his marching orders.

The men had eaten uncured beef the day before and repaired their shoes with strips of the raw hides. Many wore capes made out of their blankets and kept warm only by pounding their feet and slapping themselves with their crossed arms.

Washington had decided to fortify the resolve of his soldiers by an unusual method. He was counting on a splendid piece of oratory provided at exactly the right moment by journalist Thomas Paine, who had been writing essays for weeks on a drumhead in General Greene's tent as the American Army retreated across New Jersey.

Hurrying to Philadelphia in mid-December, Paine had the first copies of *The American Crisis* printed on December 19. Now, as the troops prepared to get in the boats to be rowed across the ice-clogged river in a swirling snow squall on Christmas night, Washington ordered his commanders to read the essay to his men.

" ... The summer soldier and the sunshine patriot will, in this crisis, shrink from the service of his country," they read, "But he that stands it now, deserves the love and thanks of man and woman. Tyranny, like hell, is easily conquered; yet we have this consolation with us, that the harder the conflict, the more glorious the triumph."

"These," Paine had written, "are the times that try men's souls."

Solemnly, the men horsed the heavy artillery pieces into the nine-foot-wide, 60-foot-long Durham iron-ore barges Washington had seized the week before. Quietly they pushed the horses aboard and waded through the freezing water, huddling for warmth as Massachusetts seamen under Colonel John Glover poled

the encumbered craft carefully through the ice floes to the Jersey shore.

A 19-year-old officer, Major James Wilkinson, would never forget the scene, noting in his journal that footprints down to the river were "tinged here and there with blood from the feet of the men who wore broken shoes."

Jut-jawed Marblehead ship captain John Glover, who had managed the cool retreat of Washington's vanquished army by boat under the British guns at Long Island, ordered the first boatloads to push off from McKonkey's Ferry at two in the afternoon, into the storm. By evening a faint wintry moon overshadowed the operations, the wind was rising, and the ice floes could be heard crunching against the awkward barges. By 11 o'clock, snow and sleet slashed into the boatmen's eyes: "It was as severe a night as I ever saw," Delaware officer Thomas Rodney remembered later.

On the Jersey side, Gen. Washington, wrapped in his cape, sat grimly, quietly, on a crate, talking softly from time to time to his men. By 4 a.m., after 14 terrible hours, they were all across, and the commanders formed them into ranks. Washington personally urged them on, as they moved out down the River Road. The wind, howling by now, drove in from the northeast.

"Press on, boys, press on," Washington urged from his tall white horse. "Soldiers, keep by your officers, for God's sake, keep by your officers." Two men sat down by the roadside to rest — and froze to death.

Tramping silently past darkened farmhouses, the force divided into two columns at Birmingham. Greene's division swung off to the east to skirt the town. Sullivan's men trudged due south along the River Road straight for the main Hessian barracks on King Street.

A courier raced up to Washington, informing him that Sullivan had noticed his men's gunpowder was soaked and useless. Washington told Colonel Samuel Webb of Connecticut, "Use the bayonet. I am resolved to take Trenton."

It was a cruel 10-mile march before they reached the outskirts of Trenton, where, incredibly, word of their approach had been ignored by the Hessian commander.

As was his habit, Rall had eaten heartily and late, then adjourned for an evening of cards with a few aides and his host, a mysterious figure named Abraham Hunt, who had a way of getting along with both sides. When a uniformed servant answered the front door shortly after midnight and found a shivering Loyalist from Bucks County with a mes-

sage for Rall, the Hessian refused to be disturbed.

Before disappearing into the storm, the informer left a note telling that the American Army was marching on Trenton. The servant gave it to Rall, who, without reading it, tucked it into his waistcoat pocket, and continued playing cards.

Rall and all but a few Hessian pickets were asleep at eight a.m. when the first American units, already an hour behind schedule, double-timed toward the town.

Attack At Dawn

One mile north of the town, Washington ordered Greene to halt a few minutes to give Sullivan's column time to reach its target, the barracks. At precisely eight, Sullivan's advance guard arrived and rushed Hessian Lieutenant Andreas Widerhold's 10 pickets.

At three minutes after eight, Washington heard the firing to his right, indicating Sullivan was attacking. He ordered his advance force to storm the town. The sun had been up for half an hour.

Having difficulty making out the surging Americans through the wind-driven snow, the Hessian pickets, dropping their knapsacks, took up posts behind fences and returned the fire until they were overrun by a horde of Americans, who were now treated for the first time to the sight of Hessians turning and running for their lives.

By now the Americans were pouring into the town and driving the Hessians with their bayonets. The Americans charged into houses, clambered upstairs, and watched as the groggy Hessians awoke, threw on their coats, and attempted to form up in the streets. Then the Americans opened fire.

The mercenaries were cut down by shattering sheets of grapeshot sent slashing from both ends of the town by Henry Knox' artillery batteries, now massed at the ends of Trenton's two main streets.

The Hessians sought cover, but were driven back from house to house by General Hugh Mercer's sharpshooters, now racing in from the west.

Hessian artillerymen managed to get off 13 rounds before the deadly American crossfire silenced them. Half the Hessian cannoneers were dead, along with most of their horses.

Running from the Hunt house, Rall jumped on his horse and lashed it down an alley toward his regiment, by now formed into ranks and marching down King Street into the hail of grapeshot.

"Lord, Lord, what is it, what is it?" Rall kept shouting in German as he tried futilely to regroup his men and form them for a desperation bayonet charge.

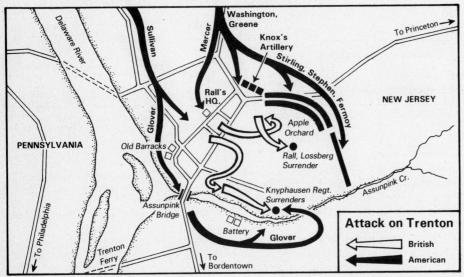

Washington (top) personally encouraged his force during the two-pronged advance on Trenton (depicted on the map), which enveloped the Hessian force.

Princeton

But Washington had little time to celebrate: a hasty council-of-war with his officers brought together the sobering fact that a fourth Hessian regiment had escaped and would now alert Count Karl von Donop's force of Hessians at Princeton. It was painfully obvious to Washington that he had to either attack Princeton swiftly, or turn around and, with 918 Hessian prisoners, slog back upriver and recross to Bucks County.

Even though they had suffered only four casualties, Washington decided his men were in no shape to take on a fresh, angry, entrenched force of Hessians. He ordered his weary men to gather the Hessian supplies, weapons, and prisoners — and head back to McKonkey's ferry.

In the fading daylight, they began the 12-hour process of crossing the river again. By now it was so cold the Hessians and Americans had to stamp their feet in time in the boats to break up the new ice that was forming, and slowing down the boats. In the bitter cold, three more men froze to death.

After 48 hours without food and 25 miles of marching, the troops collapsed into their tents as the Hessians were marched south toward Philadelphia to the tune of their marching band.

The sight of all those ranks of neatly-groomed pris0ners tramping in cadence under the guns of their ragtag, shambling guards made the Tories laugh a moment, then shudder. The procession did more for American morale than any sight in months.

Predictably, Philadelphia's own militia had not shown up for the Battle of Trenton. Cadwalader and Ewing marched as far as the river, saw the ice floes, figured Washington wouldn't risk an attack in such a storm, and pitched camp. Cadwalader's failure to cut off the Hessian retreat at Trenton was a major factor in the grim week's events that followed.

Crossing the river when the storm abated on December 27, Cadwalader sent word to Washington that he was in position with 1,500 men to join the attack — which was, of course, now over. Washington had to either recross to protect the Pennsylvania and New Jersey militia, or leave them to be slaughtered by the infuriated British and Hessians.

Stung by the Trenton attack, Cornwallis left his ship and his luggage and, with a picked force, raced across New Jersey to join von Donop's Hessians in a relatiatory attack.

Preparing to cross the river once more to meet him, Washington also had to face

---

But the Hessians broke and ran, even as the brigade band kept playing its fifes, bugles and drums.

Finally Rall was hit, shot in the side. It was only a slight wound, he said at first, but he was bleeding badly. His aides helped him off his horse and half-carried him into the sanctuary of the Queen Street Methodist Church.

Completely demoralized, many of their officers killed or wounded, and almost totally disorganized, the Hessians' best regiments, the Rall and Lossberg, surrendered. The remaining officers put their hats on their swords, the corporals lowered their flags, and the infantry men grounded their arms.

One more regiment, the Knyphausen, tried to fight its way out, even though its commander, Major von Dechow, also had been shot and, seeing the others surrender, had given the surrender order.

His officers refused, however, and led their men across the shoulder-deep Assunpink Creek.

On the far shore, however, they were surrounded, and shelled by artillery at point-blank range. An American officer offered a white flag, but was told to stop or be shot.

Then General Arthur St. Clair told a Hessian captain, "Tell your commanding officer that if you do not surrender immediately, I will blow you to pieces." The Hessians said they would —if they could keep their swords and their baggage. The two officers shook hands.

The Battle of Trenton was over.

Galloping off to find Washington, Major Wilkinson reported the capitulation. Washington gave him a rare smile, grasped his hand: "Major Wilkinson, this is a glorious day for our country!"

the possibility that his army would disappear.

While he had offered a $10 bounty — almost two years' pay for a private — Washington was having little luck in getting the soldiers of his victorious army to re-up. Almost half of Washington's 2,400 men had gone home by December 29, and no bread and meat had been brought up to feed them.

Nor was that the only crisis. The ice was too thin to march across the river, and Colonel Glover's Marblehead fishermen had gone home to resume privateering.

With one day in the enlistments of his Continental soldiers remaining, Washington announced he was going to attack again, whether the regulars were with him or not. Lining up his men, he talked to them softly. One man said later that Washington spoke "in the most affectionate manner, entreating us to stay."

When he was finished, he rode off to one side while the regimental commanders asked each man willing to reenlist to step forward. No one moved.

Wheeling his horse around, the embarrassed Washington poured out one last appeal to his embarrassed men: "You have done all I asked you to do, and more than could be reasonably expected. But your country is at stake, your wives, your homes, and all that you hold dear.

"You have worn yourselves out with fatigues and hardships, but we know not how to spare you. If you will consent to stay only one month longer, you will render that service to the cause of liberty and to your country, which you probably never can do under any other circumstance."

He closed, saying the army that day faced "the crisis which is to decide our destiny," then rode off to one side again.

At first no one moved. Then a few began looking at each other. One lone veteran stepped forward, then a few more, then others until only the very sick and the naked held back.

By the end of the day, 1,200 men had accepted the bounty and reenlisted.

Washington had taken a bolder step than most imagined: he had pledged a bounty without consent of Congress, but as he wrote its president, John Hancock, "What could be done?"

And the men wanted the money immediately. Fortunately and incredibly, Robert Morris kept the sacks of money coming from Quaker Philadelphia: 410 Spanish dollars, two English crowns, 72 French crowns, 1072 English shillings, all the hard money he could find in the city.

As the British army drew up its lines across from the Americans late on January 2, Washington saw that he had left

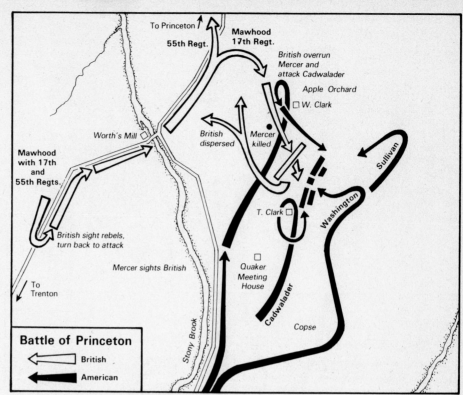

The British (moving from Princeton toward Trenton on road at left) turned to attack Mercer's column (center). Sullivan, heading the main column, turned back to join in the attack. Washington, coming up behind him, rallied the forces.

himself no chance to retreat if things went badly for him the next day. He also saw that the British were about to make their characteristic mistake — resting up before going into battle.

Washington ordered a rear guard to continue noisily digging trenches within the hearing of Cornwallis' pickets all night, and to pile firewood on the roaring campfires. But he formed the main body of troops into three columns and sent them silently marching off under cover of darkness around the British right flank to attack the British rear guard in Princeton.

Not all of the British officers had felt that it made sense to wait until the next morning to attack Washington's army; not all were content with Cornwallis' analysis that the men were not ready to fight after slogging over miles of muddy roads for two days.

Fortunately, too, Congress agreed with Washington and sent along the necessary resulutions giving him authority to take "whatever he may want for the use of the Army."

The effect of the news of the victory was now also taking hold on the populace at large. Militia began to swarm to the American standard. In addition to Cadwalader's 1,600 troops, General Thomas Mifflin rounded up 1,600 more eager Pennsylvania and New Jersey recruits.

Washington ordered them to join him in Trenton to face the British.

One more piece of good luck came Washington's way. As Col. Joseph Reed led his small detachment of Philadelphia Light Horse toward Princeton and his rendezvous with Cadwalader, he followed a little-known local route called the Quaker Road. And while on it, he stumbled upon 12 dismounted British dragoons "conquering a parcel of mince pyes." Reed took them prisoner.

Interrogated separately, they gave up the information that 6,000 Hessians and British were marching on Princeton, that Howe had dispatched another 1,000 men from New York several days before.

The message arrived almost simultaneously with word that Cornwallis had led a forced one-day, 50-mile march by 1,000 men from Perth Amboy to Princeton, and was preparing "to bag the fox (Washington) the next morning." The British quartermaster general, Sir William Erskine, argued that they should strike immediately. "If Washington is the general I take him to be," he told Cornwallis, "his army will not be found there in the morning."

Cornwallis, however, dismissed this interesting bit of prescience, again using his favorite metaphor. "We've got the old fox safe now," he assured Erskine. "We'll go over and bag him in the morning."

Morning found Cornwallis wrong. The American trenches were empty, the fires smoldering low, the roads frozen, and Washington gone. Washington had split his force, sending the main column along the little-used Quaker Road, the wheels of its cannon wrapped in blankets to deaden the sound. In its vanguard was General Hugh Mercer, a tough Virginia doctor turned soldier, with 350 veterans from Virginia, Delaware, and Maryland.

Just after dawn, the column ran into British Lieutenant Colonel Charles Mawhood's crack troops, the 17th and 55th Regiments, marching to reinforce Cornwallis at Trenton. The British were not expecting to meet the Americans. Henry Knox reported later, "I believe they were as much astonished as if an army had dropped perpendicularly upon them (out of the sky) . . ."

Mawhood, riding a pony and escorted by his pet dogs, reacted quickly, however, and sent the lead element of his troops running across Stony Brook bridge after what appeared to be a small party of Americans. At the same time, Mercer turned his men to engage them, cutting through an orchard on the William Clark farm.

At forty yards, the British opened fire. The Americans answered with their rifles and canister shot fired from two cannons hastily lugged up a hillside through foot-deep snow. Through badly outnumbered, the Americans held off the British for about 10 minutes.

But the American rifles took much longer than British muskets to load, and Mawhood, seeing this, ordered a bayonet charge. Breaking into a run, the long line of redcoated regulars charged the 40 yards and, yelling and swearing, bayoneted their way through the orchard. Mercer's horse was shot from under him.

"Surrender, you damn rebel," the British soldiers yelled, mistaking Mercer for Washington. Instead, Mercer drew his sword and slashed about him with it until a British grenadier smashed him in the head with the butt of his musket, dropping Mercer to his knees. The redcoats then bayoneted him in the stomach, legs and arms — and left him dead.

Trying to rally the Americans, Colonel John Haslet, last of the 550 proud "Delaware Blues" who had marched off to New York six months before still in service, was killed by a shot through the head.

But now American reinforcements started to stream over the hill and through the field. In addition, Sullivan, who had been marching a parallel route toward Princeton, and who had been well beyond Mercer when news reached him of Mawhood's attack, turned back. As he did so, he ran hard into the 55th British Regiment, sent to intercept him by Mawhood. The two forces deadlocked.

Cadwalader also came up with his raw militia, but as the militiamen came up beside the veterans under Sullivan, and were met by the full force of British artillery firing at close range, the citizen-soldiers ran for their lives.

●

Still, back at the Clark farm it was a handful of Philadelphia Associators, also militiamen, who prevented a rout from becoming a major American disaster.

One Philadelphia artillery officer in Mercer's column, Captain Joseph Moulder, managed to swing two guns into position on the edge of a woods near the Clark farmhouse itself. He opened fire on four British guns and a company of British light infantry as they formed for a second bayonet charge at the reconstituted American position.

Those two guns slamming grapeshot at close range stopped the British attack just long enough for Lt. Thomas Rodney to bring up a score of militiamen to support the gun emplacement, whose fire kept the British on the defense. The fire also afforded just enough time for Washington to arrive on the scene, riding up and down in the woods among the panicked militia, "Parade with us!" he shouted above the smoke and din. "There is but a handful of the enemy and we will have them directly."

Slowly the militia began to fall into line around him, joined by the remains of Mercer's men, who had fallen back in the same general direction. Soon New England troops came along, and Washington led the ad hoc task force into battle himself. Riding ahead, his hat in his hand, he waved them onward, forcing the British to shift to the left as he edged closer to their murderous fire with an ever-lengthening American line. Washington told the Americans to hold their fire, until he gave the signal.

Then he screamed his order: "Halt! . . . Fire!"

Two thundering volleys followed, one from each side, and when the acrid blue-black smoke rose, Washington's aides were amazed to see the American commander still on his horse, and still waving his troops forward.

For the first time, American troops, mostly raw recruits, were marching in rank and file against regular British troops and keeping up an incessant fire. The novel spectacle unnerved the British; they slowly gave way, then turned in panic and bolted from the field. The Americans, finally realizing what they had done, broke into a cheer and pursued them all the way into Princeton.

"It's a fine fox chase, boys," Washington shouted encouragement, overjoyed at the moment of victory.

●

Falling in with the Philadelphia Light Horse, Washington joined the chase momentarily, then ordered his men to take time to scoop up the gear the British had left in their wake.

Mawhood was able to regroup some of his regulars who were now trapped between what had originally been the Sullivan and Mercer columns. They turned and bayoneted their way through a portion of the American line, and ran away over the hills nearby.

The last episode of the Battle of Princeton was an anti-climax.

When Sullivan's men stormed into the town, the British, including some of the best troops in the British army, fled their redoubts and barricaded themselves inside Nassau Hall at the town's college.

It was the largest building in America and solidly built of stone. It should have been easily defensible. But when Captain Moulder and Lieutenant Alexander Hamilton wheeled up their guns to begin blasting away at the building, and when an angry Princetonian named James Moore (whose house had been looted by the British) led a storming of the front door, and when a cannonball crashed through the hall beheading the portrait of King George II, all at about the same time, the terrified British surrendered.

The Battle of Princeton was over. It was a smashing success for Washington and a humiliating debacle for the British. But more than that, the War of the Revolution was alive again.

Now Washington could safely march into winter camp in Morristown and train and recruit a permenent army. Now the French would stop their diplomatic flirtation with the Americans and openly send aid. When the new American emissary to the court of King Louis XVI announced the twin American victories at Trenton and Princeton, the monarch dispatched four shiploads of guns together with the best gunpowder in the world, developed by chemist Antoine Lavaisier.

The campaign of 1776, which had begun in overconfidence, which had survived defeat, despair, and bitter experience, now came to an end in jubilation. The United States of America now existed in fact as well as on paper.

It would take the British only five more years of bloody, blundering struggle to realize the changes that had taken place in the war as a result of those battles in the two small country towns of Trenton and Princeton.

A change in British strategy, though, was immediate and obvious. Howe pulled back from the outposts in New Jersey all the way to New York. Never again would the British try to hold large portions of the countryside. Their concept became to capture the coastal cities, and, from these defensible bastions, try to dominate the countryside.

The strategy was doomed to failure; yet as soon as news of the disaster in New Jersey reached England, the British government, in the zenith of its incompetence, set to work to compound its errors. By summer 1777, the beginnings of an even more colossal disaster for the British began to emanate from Lord George Germain's colonial ministry offices in Whitehall.

The plan was as old and simple as warfare: divide and conquer.

What Germain had in mind was to divide the colonies by attacking down the Hudson from Canada at the same time as striking northward up the Hudson River from New York.

The two grand armies would meet victoriously in Albany where, supposedly, America would surrender.

It was a good plan when drawn on maps in London. What Germain didn't plan was that the British forces would let a simple omission destroy it. Germain didn't bother to send off a written order in time telling Howe, in New York, to cooperate with General John Burgoyne, coming down from Canada.

While Burgoyne pushed toward his rendezvous with disaster at Saratoga, Howe in New York was blissfully unaware of his supposed role in the undertaking. Howe, in fact, was busily at work on a plan of his own to pick up where he ought not to have left off the previous winter. He decided to take Philadelphia, the rebel capital.

Only it was a year later. Washington had built an army of sorts, with three-year enlistments and French weapons and advisers and, most important, some tactical experience in how to deal with Howe on the battlefield.

There was one peculiar problem. Washington, not unlike the British high command in London, could not really be sure what Howe was up to in the summer of 1777. In July, Howe had loaded his forces aboard ship in New York harbor — and there they stayed for six weeks, roasting in their wool uniforms and getting sick.

Then in August he had his brother, the admiral of the British fleet, sail to Delaware Bay by a long seaward route, possibly to keep Washington in suspense. Then General Howe, while still aboard ship, heard from his spies that the Dela-

ware River had been heavily fortified. So he went out of the Delaware Bay, and sailed down to the Chesapeake, finally landing his army at Head of Elk, Md., where thousands of Loyalists were supposed to be eagerly waiting to flock to his arms.

But instead, there was the Old Fox, Washington, whose sentries had watched the British fleet's every move along the coast from watchtowers and lighthouses. They had flashed word of the landing to Washington in time for him to quick-march his army from the Watchung mountains in New Jersey through Philadelphia and on south. The soldiers wore sprigs of pine in their hats to symbolize their hope of keeping the British out of the city.

To be sure, Washington was unable to be there for the actual coming ashore of Howe's troops, camp followers, and the few horses that had survived the cruise.

But Washington knew his man. There was little chance that Howe would be moving north toward Philadelphia quickly. Indeed, many of Howe's men were in only slightly better condition than the dead horses, and badly needed some rest on shore.

There was also the need to steal horses — at least enough for the generals to ride — which also took time.

It was September before Howe finally began moving north with his 18,000-man force, and he was harried all the way in a dogged retreating campaign by that master of the retrograde maneuver, George Washington.

Washington concluded his retreat at Brandywine, where he intended to defeat the British as he had at Trenton and Princeton. But instead of the bold, surprising tactical sleight of hand he had practiced in the New Jersey counterattack, this time he intended to engage the British in a set-piece, textbook battle.

He was not yet good enough to do that.

Actually, the question of whether Washington hoped to win at Brandywine is open to debate. (The fact that he didn't is not.) What he may have had in mind was — delaying though probably somewhat longer than he did — the British occupation of Philadelphia. More importantly, he wanted to keep Howe from marching inland. At least half of America's iron industry and much of its agriculture were in the counties to the west of Philadelphia.

There were 250 mills along Darby and Ridley Creeks alone and scores of furnaces and forges in the rich hinterlands of Bucks, Delaware, Berks and Lancaster Counties. Ultimately,

---

In COUNCIL OF SAFETY,

PHILADELPHIA, *December* 2, 1776.

SIR,

THE army under General Howe has taken poſſeſſion of Brunſwick---General Waſhington, not having a ſufficient number of men to oppoſe the enemy, is obliged to retreat before them---Vigor and Spirit alone can ſave us---There is no time for words---Exert yourſelves NOW like FREEMEN.

By Order of the Council,

DAVID RITTENHOUSE,

VICE PRESIDENT.

To the Colonels *or* Commanding Officers *of the reſpective Battalions.*

Bulletins to the commanders of the Philadelphia militia units kept them abreast of the deteriorating situation in the late fall of 1776. They also offered encouragement.

Unsuccessful attempts to assault the British holed up in Cliveden undermined the American attack on Germantown.

when it came to a choice between defending these resources or defending Philadelphia, Washington abandoned the city.

To Howe, there was no choice involved. The main issue was getting to Philadelphia. Washington was in the way, and the problem was to simply get him out of the way. Even Howe's severest critics have to admire the speed and precision with which he carried out that mission in classic fashion.

Washington's supporters, on the other hand, have to figure out some excuse to explain how the Old Fox was victimized at Brandywine by much the same misdirection play Howe had pulled on him at Long Island a year earlier. The opposing forces at Brandywine were about even in strength.

As soon as Washington had retreated behind the strong, prepared works at Chadds Ford on the Brandywine, Howe sent General Knyphausen and his Hessians straight against the center of the American lines. The roar of the Hessians' guns fooled Washington into believing that this was the entire British force.

Meanwhile, Howe and Cornwallis led 10,000 troops up the Brandywine 15 miles, crossed well beyond the American lines, and marched around the American right flank.

In fact, Washington had warned his best general, John Sullivan of New Hampshire, who occupied the position of honor on the right flank, to watch for just such a maneuver. But it was a foggy day in those wooded hills and valleys, and even though Sullivan was also warned by the locals that the British were coming, he ignored the warning until it was too late.

One of these locals, a determined country gentleman named Squire Cheyney, after getting nowhere with the stubborn New Hampshireman, carried his warning on to Washington. Washington, however, had already received word from Sullivan that the warning was a false alarm.

By about this time, though, there was sufficient gunfire from the vicinity of Birmingham Meeting House on the right flank to confirm Cheyney's intelligence, and Washington set off to meet the main British attack.

It was too late. His stand at the Brandywine was over — almost as soon as it had begun.

Once again, though the British blew their chances of total victory by hesitating at the pivotal moment. When they were one mile from the American right, Howe and Cornwallis stopped — for lunch.

The British lunch hour gave General Nathaniel Greene a chance to escape, leading his division on an incredible four-mile double-time march through thick underbrush and fog from Chadds Ford to Birmingham Meeting House in only 45 minutes.

His advance troops were already lined up behind a stone wall at Birmingham Meeting House when the British attack came. They absorbed a terrible beating from artillery, then held their own in bayonet duels for an hour. But then the British broke through.

By this time, though, even the diversionary attack was succeeding. Knyphausen drove across the creek and attacked Gen. Anthony Wayne's forces, pushing them back. Wayne fought back marvelously with the aid of a half-mad Polish cavalryman named Count Pulaski, and they slowed down the British until Washington could rally his men after dark. The Americans then retreated 15 miles to Chester Heights, to the northwest, between Howe and the interior country.

The British took the night off.

After a week of feverish marching and countermarching, Cornwallis finally managed to get around Washington, and, in his own mind at least, win the prize by taking Philadelphia.

Massacre at Paoli

There were a few more nasty close calls for Washington in the meantime: when he sent Wayne too close to the British rear to harass its flanks, the British sent a major force out one night without flints in their muskets — just bayonets.

Occasionally brilliant, but characteristically careless, Wayne had left weak pickets, and his campfires were beacons to the attacking British. As his groggy troops came out of their tents to meet the attackers, more than 300 were bayoneted in what became known as the Paoli Massacre.

Patriot propagandists attempted to portray the brilliant commando raid as a horrible instance of British bestiality in combat. In point of fact, Wayne himself carried out a raid on the British at Stony Point in July 1779 in exactly the same manner.

And if anyone had a complaint about unorthodox tactics, it was probably the British. The American tactic of picking off officers by snipers, and the habit that some American troops had of scalping British corpses, were both violations of European war codes.

Wayne went on trial for the defeat, but was exonerated.

Plans Go Awry

If Howe had hoped that he would now be left free to dine and dance in Philadelphia while Washington and his troops made camp in the suburbs, he was in for an annoying surprise.

No sooner had Washington marched to Reading, the main American supply base, to refill his cartridge cases — 400,000 cartridges had been ruined in the rain near Warren's Tavern because of the shoddy workmanship of the cartridge boxes — than he was ready to attack again.

From his base at Pennypacker's Mill (now Schwenksville), Washington reached back more than 2,000 years in military history to borrow a page from Scipio Africanus, the Roman general who crushed the armies of Carthage, and unleashed his most complicated attack. (Visions of his complex maneuvers at Trenton and Princeton may also have danced in his head.)

He separated his army into four columms, all marching 24 miles to Germantown on different axes, to attack the main British army in Philadelphia. Washington underestimated the difficulty of timing such a march in the dark, and dense fog multiplied the control problems, but the British were so thoroughly surprised that Washington very nearly won the battle.

A few American mistakes — bad ones — turned the victory into a defeat. One American general, a Virginian named Adam Stephen, got himself drunk in a farmhouse along the way and, in the fog, his men attacked the American column on their flank, led by General Sullivan.

Later, when the Americans ran low on ammunition, they shouted the information loud enough for the retreating British to take heart and charge, in a successful counterattack.

But the classic blunder belonged to Henry Knox, whose years of reading military books in his shop in Boston apparently didn't include anything about bypassing strongpoints to keep the main attack rolling.

When the Americans encountered stiff resistance at Cliveden, the fortress-like home of Loyalist Benjamin Chew, Knox insisted on laying siege to the house with heavy artillery and prevailing on Washington to throw in wave after wave of troops to storm it.

Rows of dead and wounded Americans from these piecemeal attacks, which met withering fire from two companies of British marksmen directed by Colonel Musgrave, piled up before Washington realized that the overall attack had lost its momentum, which had been focused instead on this meaningless assault on Cliveden.

By then his men, out of ammunition and pursued by Howe's counterattack, pelted past Washington. They kept moving for 24 miles, back to Pennypacker's Mill where they had started.

Sure enough, the British gave up the chase and returned to Philadelphia, and once again the sheer boldness of the American attack worked wonders for the American cause. That Washington's troops should bounce back from defeat at Brandywine and attempt such a difficult feat so quickly drew the admiration of kings and generals abroad, and very shortly their open support.

The gay social season the British had embarked on in Philadelphia was soon blighted yet again by the grim news that Burgoyne, his forces drained and destroyed piecemeal, had surrendered after two humiliating battles at Saratoga, New York.

Assault on the River Forts

Howe had other problems. Washington had stripped the city of every scrap of food before turning it over to the British, and housewives were begging and stealing provisions by late October.

The cause of the shortage was the complicated set of defenses the Philadelphians had erected over, under and on both sides of the Delaware River over the past 15 months. The defenses prevented the British fleet from supplying the British army there.

After failing to dislodge Washington from the strong base he had chosen at Whitemarsh, where he camped before going to Valley Forge, Howe turned his army and navy loose to tear apart the string of river forts and the chains and other assorted hazards to navigation the Americans had placed in the way to make living difficult. Washington now directed a defense of the river fortifications that preoccupied the British for months.

The Americans, over the preceding year, had developed a formidable and surprisingly sophisticated set of fortifications.

Before riding north to redesign Ft. Ticonderoga and lay out the brilliant defenses that ensnared Burgoyne at Saratoga, the French-trained engineer Thaddeus Kosciuszko had spent weeks on the river defenses under the paternal guidance of Benjamin Franklin, a man who had defended Philadelphia against various attacks in earlier wars.

On the Jersey shore opposite Tinicum Island, near the present site of Paulsboro, Kosciuszko laid out Fort Billings. He created a large, squarish redoubt 180 feet on each side, with strongpoints at the corners, and parapets for riflemen. The walls were pierced to accommodate 18 heavy guns. He also designed a powder magazine, officers' and enlisted men's barracks, bakeshop, and supply rooms.

Outside, on the land side, were earthen breastworks and a deep ditch, or *fosse,* filled with felled trees. The tree branches were sharpened to foil infantry attack.

The main purpose of the fort was to protect the downstream end of the *chevaux de frise,* an ingenious underwater barricade designed to pierce the hulls of ships passing over them, and hold the ships while the fort poured cannon fire into them.

Both Franklin and Kosciuszko were smitten with the idea of the *chevaux de frise.* To the assembly area at Gloucester came 239 great hemlock timbers, 15 to 20 inches thick and extremely tough.

Pine timbers were lashed together on the bottom and sides into giant caissons, or cribs, each 60 feet long. These were floated raftlike to the river, where the damaging iron-tipped prongs, or pikes — some of them 70 feet long — were attached, and braced with iron straps and angles.

The cribs were then sunk by removing plugs from their sides and bottoms and filling each with 30 tons of rock brought down the Schuylkill on barges from the quarries of Conshohocken. Submerged six or seven feet below the waterline, the pikes spread out into a fan-shape, each covering a 60-foot-wide arc.

In all, there were 70 of them — 24 under the guns of Fort Billings and 46, in three staggered rows, eight miles upstream between Fort Mercer and Fort Mifflin.

Fort Mercer, at Red Bank above Woodbury, named after the late General Mercer, showed Kosciuszko's dual genius as engineer and artilleryman. Its guns could fire down from the 40-foot-high bluffs to cover both Fort Mifflin, across the mile-wide channel and the approaches to the *chevaux de frise*. Because of its elevation, it was also beyond the reach of the British naval guns, and was virtually impervious to amphibious assault because of its formidable landward defenses.

To the north of the redoubt, a dirt road ran due west toward Deptford and Haddonfield. The road was flanked by heavy woods on the south and swamps to the north. Cutting down orchards to provide a clear field of fire, Koscisuzko had deep trenches dug around its walls, which ran from north to south slightly more than 350 yards. Long, low breastworks ran along the river for 200 yards. A moat and breastworks filled with the standard *abatis* of sharpened trees made up the outer works.

The main body of the fort was a high earth-and-log redoubt with walls 12 feet thick and 15 feet high. The moat could be manned with sharpshooters to slow up any attack.

To this, in early October, Washington sent Colonel Christopher Greene, a tough Rhode Islander, with two companies of Rhode Island Continentals, most of them blacks who had been promised their freedom — if they survived the war.

When two French volunteers, Marquis de Lafayette and Chevalier Mauduit du Plessis, inspected the fort with an eye to correcting any flaws in Kosciuszko's planning, they found the tattered black garrison waiting grimly behind 18 heavy guns for the expected British attack.

Mauduit, a skilled engineer, recognized the fort's possibilities as the ideal place to spring a trap: inside the deep embankment between the inner and outer works on the north side, he suggested Greene build another embankment to screen an artillery battery.

The attack on the forts came soon enough. On October 11, in a combined land-sea attack, 2,000 of Cornwallis' best regulars encircled Fort Billings downriver, which was garrisoned by only 250 men and six cannon. All of the cannon

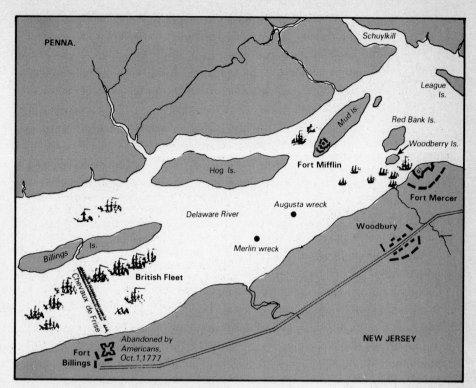

The American defenses of the Delaware River in 1777.

faced the river and were quite useless against the land attack. During the night, the New Jersey militia spiked guns so they would blow up if the British tried to use them, blew up the bakehouse, barracks and stockade, then retreated to Fort Mercer.

On Mauduit's recommendation, the Pennsylvania Navy stationed galleys with 18-pound cannon on them at the foot of the bluffs of Fort Mercer. The galleys were useless against British warships, but might deter an amphibious landing. This they did, and Howe ordered a land attack.

The assault was entrusted to the Hessian Count Karl Emil von Donop, an able, 37-year-old field commander still smarting from his defeat at Princeton. Cornwallis sent 1,000 reinforcements to the Hessian camp at Cooper's Ferry, now Camden, where they joined 2,400 Hessians and Loyalists before marching to Deptford and resting for the night.

A fleet-footed American named Jonas Cattell, whipper-in for the Gloucester Hunt Club, ran nine miles from Deptford to Fort Mercer to warn Greene, who until then had been expecting a waterborne assault. That night, the black garrison, joined by 250 Jersey militia, sweated as they hauled the big guns around to the land side — and set their trap.

After placing sharpshooters in the outer works, Greene placed two heavy guns, double-loaded with grapeshot and

canisters, inside the hidden embankment, as Mauduit had suggested. Fallen trees and brush were set in front of them.

The Hessians marched down the lane at noon the next day. Drums beating and bugles blaring, they fanned out and formed a cordon that extended from the swamp to the plain south of the fort.

Swinging down from his brown stallion, von Donop handed the reins to an aide and told him to carry this message to Greene: "The King of England orders his rebellious subjects to lay down their arms, and they are warned that if they stand the battle, no quarters whatsoever will be given."

Greene hurled back a loud reply: "We'll see King George damned first. We want no quarters and we'll give none."

Attacks were made against both the north and south walls of the fort. On the south the Hessians hacked through the *abatis* and bayoneted their way through the thin line of skirmishers in the south ditch, ignoring the heavy, well-directed musket fire from the black garrison inside.

Then the attackers charged the walls. A few made it to the top before they were riddled by point-blank fire.

On the north the American trap was being set. At the first volley, the American skirmishers fired one ragged salvo, and then dropped back.

Charging and huzzaing wildly, the

Hessians poured through the breastworks and into the outer fort, then on toward the tall north wall of the fort.

Then the trap was sprung.

Yanking away trees and brush, the hidden gun crews fired ... and fired again. The fort's cannon and the marksmen on the parapets poured in a brutal crossfire. Shot in the hip, chest and face at such close range that the cannon's wadding was pounded into his face, blinding him, von Donop staggered and fell along with scores of his troops and 15 officers.

From below, the river gunboats opened up a crossfire against Hessians now attempting to climb the west wall, on the river side. The grenadiers were mowed down.

Inside 15 minutes, the battle was over. The Hessians — the live ones, that is — ran back to the woods, jettisoned their cannon in the creek, and after pausing to make stretchers for their wounded officers, fled back to Woodbury. They left 414 dead and dying on the field, in the ditches, spawled all over the fort.

Carried to the Whitall house nearby, von Donop died slowly and painfully, telling Mauduit, architect of the trap, who nursed him for nine days: "I am content. I die in the hands of honor itself. It is finishing a noble career early, but I die the victim of my own ambition and the avarice of my sovereign."

It was, numerically, the greatest American victory of the war; only 24 rebels had been killed or wounded, 19 of them when a cannon carelessly swabbed by its crew exploded while being loaded.

The British were not amused. Furious, they tossed caution to the wind that night and tried to maneuver the 64-gun British flagship *Augusta* and its 18-gun escorting sloop *Merlin*, through the upper *chevaux de frise* to avenge the defeat. Both ran aground.

At dawn, the Americans in the two forts discovered the ships' plight, to their delight, and poured in more than 100 cannonballs, many of them heated in a special shot furnace at Fort Mifflin. Both ships caught fire. The *Augusta*, its powder magazine catching fire, exploded with a force that shattered windows 20 miles away at Washington's headquarters at Whitemarsh. The *Merlin* was scuttled.

The next night, as British bodies and bits of bodies floated past, the Americans rowed out, salvaged some cannon from the ships, and distributed them between the two forts.

The stage was set for the most vicious and pointless battle of the war, the battle for Fort Mifflin. For more than a month, the guns of Fort Mifflin had punished the proud British fleet. Now Howe decided on a classic siege, ordering the man who had originally built the fort for the British five years earlier to take on the task of reducing it.

He was Major John Montresor, a military engineer who had lived in New York for several years after retiring from the British Army, but who had been roused to re-enlist after witnessing the excesses of the Patriots in that city before the British invaded it.

It was Montresor who befriended Nathan Hale before he was hanged by the British provost Cunningham without benefit of clergy, and it was Montresor who paid Loyalists to retrieve the head of King George III's equestrian statue from the spike outside a Bronx bar where the rebels had displayed it, and it was Montresor who arranged to have the head sent back to Parliament to show the members the depth of the rebels' defiance to King and Crown.

Now Montresor proceeded to reduce the fort he knew so well with fierce cannonades from artillery batteries protected by encircling earthworks that were built steadily closer.

Before the Americans in the fort could carry out the central point of Kosciuszko's scheme of defense by breaking holes in the dikes along the river to flood the low-lying land and make the fort an island, the British stormed American positions on two marshy islands adjoining the fort, Carpenter's and Province Islands.

Then Montresor was free to set up his heavy guns, which began an intermitent barrage, firing roughly every half hour.

At the outset of the 40-day siege, the American garrison, now commanded by a Marylander, Colonel Samuel Smith, and a French artillerist-engineer, Major Andre de Fleury, was incredibly high-spirited. Even as the noose of the British gun emplacements was tightening on November 10, Fleury confidently noted in his journal:

"The 24 and 18-pound shot from the batteries Number 16 and 17 broke some of our palisades this morning, but this does not make us uneasy — they save us the trouble of cutting ... (the fort walls) to the height of a man, which we should do."

But problems were foreseen. Critical of Montresor and Kosciuszko, Fleury later complained in his journal about the useless blockhouses at the corners of the riverfront fort:

"The fire of the loopholes is in itself not very dangerous, and our loopholes in particular are so badly contrived as to leave two-thirds of the ... (earthworks invisible) ... the wall of masonry is only ten feet high, and is not out of the reach of an escalade (assault by ladder), notwithstanding the ditches, pits and stakes with which we have endeavored to surround it."

The British barrages were also becoming more troubling. Fleury closed his notation, saying, "I am interrupted by the bombs and balls, which fall thick."

When Colonel Smith was wounded, he was rowed over to Fort Mercer at night. In the course of the siege, some 1,000 men would be rotated by night between the two forts.

After Nov. 10, the cannonade became so intense the men could not sleep. If they went into the shattered barracks, they were dead within minutes from the bombs that landed there with regularity. Most could only doze minutes at a time sitting upright against the walls.

Sensing the approaching climax, Fleury made almost-hourly entries in his journal.

"(Nov.) 10 at noon: The firing increases but not the effect — our barracks alone suffer;

"At 2 o'clock: The direction of the fire is changed — our palisades suffer — a dozen of them are broke(n) down.

"Eleven at night: The enemy keep up firing every half hour. General Varnum (now at Fort Mercer) promised us fascines (baskets filled with earth) and palisades (to repair the damage) but they are not arrived and they are absolutely necessary.

"Nov. 14: Daylight discovers (for) us a floating battery of the enemy, placed a little above their grand battery and near the shore ... "

But the defiance continued. In the same entry Fleury added: "The fire of the enemy will never take the fort; it may kill us men but this is the fortune of war, and all their bullets will never render them masters of this island ... We must have men to defend the ruins of the fort. Our ruins will serve us as breastworks. We will defend the ground inch by inch, and the enemy shall pay dearly for every step ... "

The next day, Nov. 15, the fate of the fort was sealed, however, as the British plan went into its final phase. This was triggered in part because, on Nov. 14, Lt. Samuel Lyons of the Pennsylvania Navy had deserted to the British. He, in Fleury's words, gave "sufficient intimation of our weakness."

The British now hauled the *Vigilant* off a mud bank downriver, cut off its masts to raise it in the shallow water, fitted it with four big 24-pounders, and towed it within 40 yards of the fort, slipping it over a sandbar at Hog Island in the process.

With the light sloop *Fury*, with six 18-pounders and its rigging crowded with Royal Marine sharpshooters, the Vigilant began pouring murderous fire into the fort from its weak side at point-blank range.

At the same time, the British fleet sailed up to the *chevaux de frise*. The 64-gun *Somerset*, along with the *Isis*, *Roebuck*, *Pearl*, and *Liverpool*, commenced uninterrupted barrages all day and night into the now flattened quagmire that had been Fort Mifflin.

Americans who raised their heads above the parapets or attempted to return the fire were slaughtered by volleys from the marines and grenadiers, who continually hurled their grenades from vantage points an easy toss from the fort.

After four broadsides from the *Vigilant*, not only were the parapets and gun carriages smashed, but even the iron of the guns was broken to bits. The gun platforms were destroyed.

The *Vigilant* now moved to 20 yards, belching shot and canister, blasting big pieces of debris into smaller pieces of debris. Every 20 minutes, another 1,000 shots smashed into the ruins in one of the heaviest bombardments in history.

When the officers in the fort ordered the Stars and Stripes lowered so a blue flag of distress could be hoisted, the British cheered loudly.

This wasn't a surrender; it was meant as a signal to the other American forces in the area. But the Stars and Stripes remained lowered. When a sergeant ran out to try to put the new American symbol back up, he was shot to death.

Out of ammunition, its gun useless, with exploded splinters in its blockhouses and palisades impaling the survivors, the fort was a death trap. That night, the officers ordered it evacuated when the British paused in their bombardment, apparently to figure out if there was anything left to shoot at.

A message brought boats from Fort Mercer and 250 wounded men were taken off while the other 200 set fire to the wreckage of the barracks.

The next morning the British grenadiers stormed the fort. A herd of sheep and some oxen were the only living things they found standing. Dead animals and men were piled around the fort.

One man was found lying down drunk in the barracks. He maintained that he was a Loyalist and a prisoner, and was enlisted in the British Army. For that, he received a bounty and a new uniform. But he had apparently not told the British the truth, for later that winter he deserted and rejoined the Americans at Valley Forge.

Two weeks later, Fort Mercer, too,

was evacuated as Washington began the long march along the Schuylkill to Valley Forge.

The battles for Philadelphia had, on paper, gone badly for the Americans: one win, three losses, two draws. But coupled with the news of Burgoyne's defeat and Howe's incredibly poor generalship, they encouraged the French a few months later to take the ultimate step and officially declare war on England.

Now the American Revolution was a world war in which Britain was outnumbered, and if American could only keep an army in the field long enough, it could not lose.

The news of France's intervention came to Washington in the midst of the cold, sick depression of winter at Valley Forge. Characteristically, he could not react spontaneously to good news. Instead, he wrote out an elaborate order for the celebration. On May 7, six days after receiving the news, Washington issued this proclamation:

"It having pleased the Almighty Ruler of the universe to defend the cause of the United American States, and finally raise us up a powerful friend among the princes of the earth, to establish our liberty and independence upon a lasting foundation, it becomes us to set apart a day for gratefully acknowledging the divine goodness and celebrating the important event ... "

There followed hundreds of words od detailed orders for the joyful outburst, ending with, "Long live the friendly European Powers! The last discharge of 13 pieces of artillery will be given, followed by a general running fire, and huzza (for) ... The American States!"

The pain and suffering that Washington's troops suffered that winter at Valley Forge have become almost a cliche in American history. The trials that that the Army faced were, indeed, horrible enough. Three thousand men, it has been estimated, died in the American hospitals of typhoid and smallpox, which many of them contracted after coming to the hospital with wounds or other ailments. The lack of food and clothing was acute.

But there are a couple of facts that should be added to the story of Valley Forge, even if they interfere somewhat with the romance and legend that now surrounds the winter encampment of 1777-78. It was for example, not an un-

usually cold winter. In fact, it was one of the warmest in memory.

Second, the privations suffered by the army did not reflect any shortage in the land. Instead, they reflected the inefficiency of the Congress in arranging for adequate logistical support for its army. It also reflected the reluctance of farmers in the area to accept the atrociously inflated Continental currency.

Washington, as a result, was forced to resort to somewhat unsavory methods that winter to provide food for his troops. General Wayne and about 300 of his men were detailed to cattle rustling, stealing herds from Loyalist farmers in New Jersey.

From the standpoint of the military history of the war, the single most important fact about the winter at Valley Forge was not that the army suffered — but that it survived.

And not only survived, but, incredibly enough, emerged as a much more effective fighting force that it had been when the encampment began. This was largely attributable to the efforts of one man, a Prussian drillmaster and former aide-de-camp to Frederick the Great. His name was Friedrich Wilhelm Ludolf Gerhard Augustin, Baron von Steuben.

Von Steuben, spouting profanity in several languages, imposed a sense of military discipline, a new method of organizing the army, and a rigorous program of military training. The new organizational plan included the designation of light infantry companies that could fulfill the specialized need for skirmishers that warfare in the wilderness presented.

It would be wrong to say, however, that he "Prussianized" the army. His genius was in being able to distill the essential portions of the military tradition he knew.

The British decision to evacuate Philadelphia and consolidate at New York, however, caught Washington by surprise. The evacuation, which began on June 16, 1778, was brilliantly executed by the new British commander, General Sir Henry Clinton. Incredibly, it was two full days before Washington caught on to what the British were up to. When he did, the chase was on.

Washington now had the superior force, with 13,000 well-trained regulars. And Clinton had another big worry —

possible interception by the French fleet, a major factor in causing the choice of an overland route.

Clinton, for a variety of strategic considerations, chief among them the possibility of losing, wasn't seeking a showdown battle with Washington at this time, and Washington had to chase him hard for seven days in a terrible early summer heat wave. Clinton was slowed by the fact that his entourage included a huge, 1,500-wagon baggage caravan, 3,000 Loyalist refugees, and a goodly number of camp followers. The heat also may have had more effect on his troops, who were wearing their heavy red-winter uniforms in the 100-degree heat.

Washington finally caught Clinton's rear guard at a place called Monmouth Courthouse. Here, not far from places where his army had narrowly escaped annihilation at the hands of Cornwallis' quick-marching columns in 1776, Washington was to get a chance do exactly that same thing to the main British army in America.

And if it hadn't been for a loudmouthed American general named Charles Lee, he might have done it. Lee, who had been captured in 1776, had recently been repatriated in an exchange of prisoners. By and large it would have been a far, far better thing if he had remained in enemy hands.

Lee had once been Washington's rival for the position of commander-in-chief. He was a cynical, self-serving solider of fortune who had been an officer in the British Army. He had resigned after quarreling with some of his fellow officers, and had spent his time after that floating from one military adventure to another in Europe.

He had come to Virginia in 1774 with a half-pay pension from the British Army, and settled on a large estate.

When the Continental Army was formed, Lee had ideas of being named its commander-in-chief. But Congress chose Washington, and, adding insult to the injury Lee already felt, made General Artemas Ward of Massachusetts second-in-command. Lee wound up with the third spot.

Washington, though, had been on Lee's side, and had urged that he be given the number-two spot. When Ward unexpectedly resigned, Washington promptly promoted Lee to fill it. Washington was willing to put up with Lee's eccentricities, which included a vile, sarcastic way of expressing himself, both in conversation and reports, because he felt that he needed Lee's grasp of military drill, maneuvers, and planning.

It was not until the years after the Revolution that documents were found establishing that during the time that he had been in British custody, Lee had turned traitor. He had drawn up a plan for the military conquest of the colonies, and submitted it to Howe, who, perhaps fortunately for American history, chose not to act on it.

But at the time Washington knew nothing of this. To be sure, he had heard, somewhat to his dismay, Lee's vitriolic discourses on the quality of the American soldier, who, Lee maintained in this monologues, could not stand up to British bayonets. But that was the man's style.

Because Lee was the second-highest ranking officer, he had to be placed in command of the American right wing in the American attack against the British rear guard at Monmouth. Washington gave him the order on June 27 for Lee to attack in the morning, but left the details of the maneuver up to Lee.

•

The next morning, the British rolled out of Monmouth for New York, with Knyphausen in the lead, the wagons in the middle, and Cornwallis and Clinton, together with the main British force, guarding the rear. By 10 a.m., large bodies of American troops had come up on all sides of the British rear guard.

Quickly, Clinton, a fine field officer, gave Cornwallis orders to attack, even though the British were outnumbered. Clinton hoped his bold move would delay or drive off the Americans.

Clinton was surprised to see the Americans, after a few feeble efforts, begin to retreat. Quick to seize an advantage, Clinton promptly gave orders to pursue and destroy the enemy.

The problem, of course, was not with the high-spirited American troops, but with Lee, who had issued a few halfhearted orders, then contradicted them. As these senseless orders passed down the chain of command, units found themselves advancing while the adjacent units on their flank were retreating.

The general confusion quite pleased General Lee. If treachery was his goal, he was succeeding marvelously; if he was looking for evidence that Americans still couldn't fight head to head with Englishmen, it was all about him.

The whole business was also pleasing, if somewhat perplexing, to Clinton. But Clinton was also the first to notice an odd fact: the Americans, while clearly in a confused state, were not running in panic. There was no litter of packs and weapons in their wake. Unfortunately for him, he was unable to make use of this perception in time.

Suddenly, just after the British forded Middle Ravine, the Americans turned around smartly and fired a volley. The volley had a discouraging effect on the thentofore pell-mell British bayonet charge. The abrupt about-face was due the none-to-soon arrival of a very angry General Washington.

In a towering rage, Washington ordered Lee to the rear, and continued cursing and swearing for the first time anyone could remember since the rout at New York.

Lee was placed under arrest, and ultimately court-martialed and convicted. His sentence was to be suspended from the Army for 12 months. Before the year was out, however, Lee had resigned.

Washington now put "Mad Anthony" Wayne in charge of the thin American vanguard, which hung on grimly against the swarming British attack; but still slowly giving way, foot by foot, Wayne halted them in front of Washington's hastily formed main army.

Clinton decided that he could not halt the assault, or it would look like a defeat; the prestige of the flower of the British Army was on the line. And there was wisdom as well as pride in his tactics. Certainly his chances of making good his escape were improving with each minute that he could keep Washington on the defensive. and he saw an opportunity — the American left was still not organized. He struck it.

But here von Steuben's training paid off. The troops in the center swung to intercept the British charge and fought it out, hand-to-hand, for more than an hour. Then the Americans mounted an attack that rolled the British back. If Lee had seen it, he would have been amazed.

Clinton, however, wasn't through yet. He ordered an attack against the other end of the American line. He failed, probably, to anticipate that this would put his troops into a brutal artillery crossfire. Next the American infantry tightened ranks and sent volley after volley crashing into the attackers — just as von Steuben had taught them. Even the invincible British Guards could not keep up such an attack.

Still, Clinton demanded one more effort. Taking an hour to reorganize his troops, he hurled them at Wayne's men, the front and center of the American line.

Clinton's audacity almost succeeded. The roaring British were too numerous for Wayne to stop, and he had to fall back, but only until he was joined by the main American force again. The British, exhausted, stopped the attack.

Reasoning that he had protected his wagons and given a good accounting, Clinton called off the fight at dark. The next day he was gone, leaving Washing-

American artist John Trumbull spent 11 years preparing this depiction of the British surrender at Yorktown, during which he traveled to France to sketch the French officers who were present. The painting shows American General Benjamin Lincoln leading the British officers through the lines of American and French officers.

ton the battlefield, which is considered one sign of a victory. The British could, however, claim the same sort of success that the Americans used to take heart in. They had gotten out of a potential disaster alive.

Both sides had suffered exactly the same casualties: 350 killed, wounded and missing. The British suffered 59 dead of sunstroke, the Americans 37. The day had been another scorcher.

The effect, of course, was that the British were now right back in New York, where they had started two years before. The big difference was that now they were the besieged, and Washington had a formidable army of veterans, and powerful allies with a fleet equal to Great Britain's.

Victory at Yorktown

The war in the North now became a stalemate. The British tried a fresh attack, this time to the South, supposed even more Loyalist.

Clinton began, with his able lieuten-ant Cornwallis, a three-year campaign to tear away the South from the United States. They proceeded by classic sieges that were usually successful. Clinton took Charleston eventually, as well as Mobile and Savannah.

But he could not hold them.

Cornwallis force-marched all over the South, pursued and pursuing the tough guerrilla bands of Francis Marion and Thomas Pickens and a dozen more wily partisans through swamps and mountains and forests.

But he only managed to bleed away his strength slowly until Washington, joined by a French army even larger than his own, was ready to spring the trap at Yorktown, while Clinton sat ineffectually and stubbornly at New York.

Cornwallis had gone to Yorktown, located at the end of one of the Virginia capes, hoping to rendezvous with the British fleet. It didn't occur to him right away that if the fleet could not get through to him — and the French fleet prevented that — he could be trapped there.

The Americans and French used siege tactics to reduce Cornwallis' position to a status reminiscent of Fort Mifflin at the end of its career as an American fortification.

Cornwallis surrendered. The band, as every schoolchild knows, played "The World Turned Upside Down." The best British army, and the best British general, were now out of the American war, which was, for all intents and purposes, over.

The state of war was now world-wide, however, and continued, in a technical sense, until Great Britain was able to rack up enough victories in other theaters to risk going to the peace table for a negotiated settlement. That took two years.

Ultimately, the British were able to take the position at the peace talks, and later, that the American Revolution had been a nasty annoying little skirmish that they had unfortunately, and somewhat unaccountably, lost.

For Americans, it would mean much more. ★ ★ ★

British soldier guards American prisoners aboard the prison ship Jersey.

THE PRISONS

By Jeffrey St. John

No single aspect of the long War for Independence produced so much bitterness and so threatened to plunge the conflict into a brutal civil bloodbath as the treatment of prisoners.

Prior to Howe's capture of Philadelphia, Franklin grimly warned the British ambassador in Paris, Lord Stormont, on the prisoner issue. "If your conduct toward us is not altered," he wrote on April 2, 1777, "it is not unlikely that severe reprisals might be thought justifia-

ble, from the necessity of putting some check to such abominable practices."

Stormont's short and stony reply reflected the official British view; captured rebels embarked on illegal insurrection against their sovereign did not deserve treatment as prisoners of war. "The King's Ambassador receives no applications from rebels." he wrote, "unless they come to implore His Majesty's mercy."

British prisons and prison ships in New York, Boston and Philadelphia killed more Americans than did British soldiers on the battle-

field; estimates of the number of prisoners who died range from as low as 8,000 to as high as 11,500.

Official incompetence and individual brutality account for the high mortality; both sides throughout the war lacked the facilities for handling large numbers of captured prisoners. Local jails were soon filled to capacity, making necessary the use of warehouses, churches and even ships.

Prison ships actually took the highest toll of lives, although initially they were thought to be the most secure and sanitary. They soon turned into what survivor Jon-

Hunger aboard the British prison ships, Stone recalled, reached such a state that "old shoes were bought and eaten with as much relish as turkey."

athan Gillett later termed "a floating hell."

Thomas Stone, who was imprisoned with Gillett aboard the same stripped-down ship, the *Jersey*, anchored off New York's Manhattan Island, recounted a tale of guard brutality, overcrowding, and disease. Hunger, he recounted, reached such a state that "old shoes were bought and eaten with as much relish as turkey." In the winter weather the cruel winds along the Hudson swept over the *Jersey* producing among the American prisoners "frozen feet that began to mortify" and, Stone continued, "death stared the living in the face."

Two sons of a New Jersey signer of the Declaration of Independence, Abraham Clark, became prisoners on the *Jersey*. They were promised better treatment by the British if their father would denounce the Declaration and renounce his signature.

He refused.

The British had better luck with Richard Stockton, a second New Jersey signer. He himself was captured and confined in a New York land prison, where the subsequent brutality and privation broke his body and spirit. Stockton, who had made heavy financial contributions to the Revolution, renounced his signature, signed a British amnesty proclamation, and urged his fellow patriots to do the same. He later died as a direct result of his prison experience, alone and shunned by his former friends.

Stockton's defection is perhaps more understandable when one knows more about the individual most responsible for the appalling number of deaths in New York prisons — the British provost marshal of New York, Captain William Cunningham.

Cunningham, an erstwhile horse-breaker, was subsequently convicted of passing bad checks in England. His remarkably complete confession included a section on his activities in New York. It was published in London shortly before Cunningham went to the gallows in 1791. (Bouncing checks was a capital offense at the time). It read, in part: "I shudder to think of murders I have been accessory to both with or without orders from government, especially while in New York, during which time there were more than two thousand prisoners starved in different churches by stopping their rations, which I sold."

The three-year captivity of patriot Ethan Allen, first in Canada and later in London, provides a sharp contrast to the conduct of Stockton. It is a record of pugnacious defiance, in which he mixed bursts of humor and cheerfulness with crude invective to taunt his jailers.

For example, while held in close confinement in London's Pendennis Castle, Allen would be taken out on the green of the fortress and tied to a stake with a chain for the curious to come stare at.

It became a pastime of sorts for onlookers to wager on how long it would be before Allen would enjoy the King's justice at the end of the rope.

"I often entertained such audiences," he later wrote in his colorful account of his captivity, "with harangues on the impractibility of Great Britain conquering the colonies of America."

Later in the war the infamous Tower of London would hold one of the British Crown's prize prisoners, Henry Laurens, the former president of the Continental Congress. He would suffer 15 months in the Tower charged with "high treason" after his capture at sea while on his way to a diplomatic assignment in Holland.

His captors twice offered him a pardon if he would turn on his own cause, but he refused, despite crippling ill health caused by a combination of physical privation and mental torture. "There is in this country," the wealthy South Carolina planter wrote of his time in the Tower, "a facility for murdering a man by inches; I have experienced it in a degree not to be parallel in modern British history."

Later Laurens would be exchanged for Lord Cornwallis after Cornwallis' surrender at Yorktown, and it was at this time that the issue of treatment of prisoners came to a crisis.

During the long conflict Washington and Congress had warned the British that their brutal policy toward prisoners would invite stern countermeasures.

When Loyalists captured and hung American patriot Joshua Huddy, at about the time of Cornwallis' defeats, Washington responded by threatening to hang a young British officer of aristocratic birth, Capt. Charles Asgill, who had been captured at Yorktown.

The "Asgill Affair" caused consternation on both sides of the Atlantic. Some feared that hanging the only son of the former mayor of London would place in peril diplomatic recognition of the new American government, and make any real peace with Britain impossible. Only after Asgill's mother made a direct and emotional appeal to France's Louis XVI did Washington, with a sigh of relief, agree not to make good his threat as a favor to America's most potent ally.

If American treatment of British prisoners was generally less brutal, it probably reflected the fact that the Americans, who were usually on the run, lacked the time, manpower, and facilities for carrying out inhumane treatment in a truly practical manner.

Escapes from crude American prison camps were numerous. In fact man captured British Hessians, rather than return to their regiments, escaped to become farmers. It is impossible to know how many current residents of Pennsylvania and southern New Jersey might be able to trace their family tree back to those Hessian prisoners who became farmers rather than fight.

Still the Americans did the best they could with what they had to emulate British brutality.

In Kingston, N.Y., Loyalists were confined in the basement of the local courthouse. The crowding and neglect reached such a state that the stench from the basement dungeon seeped up through the floorboards to the main room, where the patriot Provincial Convention held its meetings.

Gouverneur Morris found the smell so putrid that he offered and had passed a resolution that members of the body be allowed to smoke as a way of stifling the stench from below and preserving the members' health.   ★ ★ ★

The British prison ship Jersey *was described by one inmate as "a floating hell."*